THE CREATIVE DESTRUCTION OF MANHATTAN, 1900–1940

THE CREATIVE DESTRUCTION

 HISTORICAL STUDIES OF URBAN AMERICA • *Edited by James R. Grossman and Kathleen N. Conzen*

Also in the series:

OF MANHATTAN, 1900–1940

MAX
PAGE

THE UNIVERSITY OF CHICAGO PRESS • CHICAGO AND LONDON

MAX PAGE teaches American
history at Yale University. From
1996 to 1999 he was assistant
professor of history and director
of the Heritage Preservation Program at Georgia State University
in Atlanta.

The author wishes to gratefully acknowledge Furthermore, the publication program of
the J.M. Kaplan Fund, for its generous grant.

A previous version of chapter 6 was published in the journal *American Studies* 40, no. 1
(Spring 1999). Reprinted by permission of the Mid-America American Studies Association. Copyright © 1999 by Mid-America American Studies Association.

The University of Chicago Press, Chicago 60637
The University of Chicago Press, Ltd., London
© 1999 by The University of Chicago
All rights reserved. Published 1999
Printed in the United States of America
08 07 06 05 04 03 02 01 00 99   1 2 3 4 5

Library of Congress Cataloging-in-Publication Data
Page, Max.
The creative destruction of Manhattan, 1900–1940 / Max Page.
    p.   cm. --(Historical studies of urban America)
Includes bibliographical references and index.
ISBN 0-226-64468-5 (cloth : alk. paper)
1. City planning--New York (State)--New York--History--20th
century. 2. New York (N.Y.)--Social conditions. 3. New York
(N.Y.)--Economic conditions. I. Title. II. Series.
HT168.N5P34   1999
307.1´216´09747109041—dc21   98-22544
                                        CIP

For my Eve,

‏. . . כִּי־קָרוֹב אֵלֶיךָ הַדָּבָר מְאֹד בְּפִיךָ וּבִלְבָבְךָ‎
‏לַעֲשֹׂתוֹ . . .‎

DEUTERONOMY 30:14

CONTENTS

ILLUSTRATIONS

ACKNOWLEDGMENTS

This book is at its heart about the idea of place, and about how places of the mind are invented and transposed into forces that shape the city. Not surprisingly, my life has been powerfully shaped by the places I have lived, and by the people who have turned towns and cities into homes.

Amherst, Massachusetts, has been the starting point for my explorations of place. My parents, Alex and Anita Page, created a home at 84 McClellan Street that nurtured us all, and when it was time, showed me how to create my own. Though they know little about the research for this book, my oldest and closest friends—David Silver, Paul Johansen, and Jonathan Stein—have walked with me through it all for more than a quarter century.

At Yale, I found inspiration in the teaching of Vincent Scully and Bill Cronon, who shaped my twin interests in American history and American architecture and urbanism. There I also made a group—one might even say a ranch—of friends who have challenged me in work and life: You Mon Tsang, Anthony Bregman, Mike Berman, Dan Schrag, and David Bradley.

A recent visit to Philadelphia reminded me of the remarkable community of people with whom I journeyed through graduate school at the University of Pennsylvania. Susan Schulten, Alison Isenberg, Liam Riordan, David Goldston, Paul Howard, Beth Clement, Bertie Bregman, and Tracy Nathan all turned what was supposed to be a five-year marathon (a good metaphor, Walter!) into a pleasant and mind-opening ride. Steven Conn especially has offered me his own jazz riffs on the place of cities in our past and, more importantly, his invigorating friendship.

Michael Katz was all that I could ask of in an adviser: brilliant, challenging, and endlessly supportive of my work. I was unflinchingly sustained in my effort to bridge the worlds of American social and cultural history and architectural history by Bruce

Kuklick, Anne Whiston Spirn, and David De Long. Along the way, from dissertation to book, I was the beneficiary of wise advice from Gary Gerstle, Tim Gilfoyle, David Schuyler, Jim Grossman, Gwendolyn Wright, Michael Wallace, Peter Hales, and Robert Brueggeman.

It is not too much of an exaggeration to say I chose the topic of this book in order to be able to spend two years living in New York City. In the great metropolis I found myself welcomed into the dissertation seminar of Ken Jackson, the office of Elizabeth Blackmar, the home of Richard Rabinowitz, the Lower East Side of Big Onion Walking Tours (run by Seth Kamil and Ed O'Donnell), the creative mind of Helen Kaplan, and the collegial friendship of Randy Mason. I also found myself sitting day after day in the New York Public Library Reading Room, marveling at that tangible embodiment of the democratic ideal. While I cherished my time in Room 315, as it was called before its restoration, I also benefited enormously from a host of other institutions in New York: the New-York Historical Society, the Museum of the City of New York, Avery Architectural Library at Columbia University, the Grolier Club, the New York City Department of Parks (and its historian, Jonathan Kuhn), and New York's Municipal Archives (expertly run by Ken Cobb).

In an era of the downsized, part-time university, I was fortunate enough to begin my academic career at a dynamic state university with a blossoming history department. My colleagues at Georgia State University, especially Chuck Steffen, Hugh Hudson, Seth Fein, Ian Fletcher, Nancy Floyd, and Charles Rutheiser, all had their eye on the appropriate prize: the delicate nurturing of a true intellectual community.

This book would not have been possible without the support of numerous grants: an Andrew Mellon dissertation grant at the University of Pennsylvania, a Research Initiation Grant and Office of Research publication subvention grant at Georgia State University, a Furthermore publication grant of the J.M. Kaplan Fund, and a Leverhulme Fellowship at the University of Nottingham. I would also like to thank the journal *American Studies*. Chapter 6 appeared, in a different form, in their spring 1999 issue.

When it came time to find a publisher, I was lucky enough to be steered in the direction of the University of Chicago Press. Doug Mitchell is a publishing mensch in a business that has a dwindling supply of them. Matt Howard, my editor, has with unfailing good humor guided this book (and its nervous author) through every step of a decidedly drawn-out process.

And then there is Eve. She has been all things to me since I met her just three years ago: my best friend and most enjoyable travel companion, my shrewdest critic and greatest inspiration, the mother of our little reluctant prophet, Jonah, and my one true love in this life.

THE CREATIVE DESTRUCTION OF MANHATTAN, 1900–1940

1 THE PROVISIONAL CITY

> I could tell you how many steps make up the streets rising like stairways, and the degree of the arcade's curves . . . but I already know this would be the same as telling you nothing. The city does not consist of this, but of relationships between the measurements of its space and the *events* of its past. . . . As this wave from memories flows in, the city soaks it up like a sponge and expands. . . . The city, however, does not tell its past, but contains it like the lines of a hand, written in the corners of the streets, the gratings of the windows, the banisters of the steps, the antennae of the lightning rods, the poles of the flags, every segment marked in turn with scratches, indentations, scrolls.
>
> —Italo Calvino, *Invisible Cities*

> In our town memories like rats are chased away by the ever-rising flood of progress. There is no room for ghosts or landmarks in New York.
>
> —James Huneker, *The Pathos of Distance*

During his brief return in 1904 from self-imposed exile in Europe, Henry James played an eloquent variation on a powerful theme about New York: The city is "crowned not only with no history, but with no credible possibility of time for history." New York is, always has been, and always will be, wrote James, a "provisional city," defined by a "dreadful chill of change."[1] From the time of nineteenth-century New York's great diarist, Philip Hone, who first declared New York's favorite maxim to be "overturn, overturn, overturn!" to today's Luc Sante and his biting critique that in New York the "past has no truck," New York has lived up to its cliché.[2] It is a city where the physical remnants of early generations are repeatedly and apparently inevitably visited by the wrecking ball (see figure 1.1).

The trope of the "provisional city" has been a persistent metaphor for New York City. Scholars and teachers, novelists and critics, artists and poets have dipped into the waters of this metaphorical well to explain New York to itself and to the nation. Although historians have quoted the poignant voices of city dwellers to emphasize this quality of urban experience, they have never placed it at the center of the study of the process of city building and the experience of the modern city. Indeed, New York's casual as well as scholarly observers have dipped far more regularly into a different well. They have preferred to perpetuate a view of New York—and by extension all cities—as growing rapidly but steadily, upward and outward. Terms such as "expansive" and "burgeoning" have attached themselves to descriptions of New York's growth at the turn of the century.[3] The classic portrayal of the transformation of cities has been through a series of time-lapse photographs, the "then and now" comparisons, showing the city as something akin to a flowering plant. Each time this natural metaphor of city growth is repeated, it further obscures a crucial dynamic of urban life: the intentional destruction and rebuilding of the city.

By examining debates surrounding city building in Manhattan in the first four decades of the twentieth century, this book describes an urban development process whose central dynamic was not defined by simple expansion and growth but rather by a vibrant and often chaotic process of destruction and rebuilding. The upheavals of Manhattan were not the result of dramatic, isolated natural disasters or government-sponsored urban renewal projects but rather were necessary episodes in the process of capitalist urbanization.[4] In 1942, economist Joseph Schumpeter captured the essential process of capitalism—the never-ending cycle of destroying and inventing new products and methods of production—with his term "creative destruction": "Capitalism is by nature a form or method of economic change and not only never is but never can be stationary. This process of Creative Destruction is the essential fact about capitalism. . . . To ignore this central fact is like *Hamlet* without the Danish prince."[5] Nearly one hundred years earlier, Karl Marx had anticipated Schumpeter. "All that is solid melts into air," Marx wrote in the *Communist Manifesto*, expressing the deeply paradoxical nature of the modern experience. The most concrete objects of capitalist society, the sociologist Marshall Berman has written in a modern interpretation, "are made to be broken tomorrow, smashed or shredded or pulverized or dissolved, so they can be recycled or replaced next week, and the whole process can go on again and again, hopefully forever, in ever more profitable forms."[6]

By applying Schumpeter's concept of economic creative destruction to the literal, physical destruction and creation of buildings and natural landscapes in Manhattan, this book shows how capitalism inscribed its economic and social processes into the physical landscape of the city, and then into the minds of city people.[7] Marx's pungent phrase "all that is solid melts into air" applies to both the transitory physical landscape of New York and the social and cultural dynamism that came to characterize

Fig. 1.1 (film stills appearing at the bottom of pages in this chapter). The Star Theatre being demolished, 1902. American Mutoscope and Biograph Company. Courtesy of the Library of Congress.

the city. Schumpeter's words—but not his celebration of capitalist innovation—suggest how the creative destruction of the physical landscape posed for New Yorkers the fundamental tension between creative possibilities and destructive effects of the modern city.

The broadest methodological goal of the following pages is to suggest that we place the process of creative destruction at the heart of the story of urban development. It is not a revisionist rejection of urban growth, an analysis that tries to describe the modern city as merely "destructive." The aim is rather to highlight the fundamental tensions—both physical and cultural—at the heart of the urban experience. The literature on cities has either listed toward nostalgia for a better, lost time or veered sharply toward an embrace of "improvement" and "modernization." In fact, the most accurate and revealing path is at the intersection of these conflicting beliefs. The "creative destruction" oxymoron suggests the tensions at the heart of urban life: between stability and change; between the notion of "place" versus undifferentiated, developable "space"; between market forces and planning controls; between economic and cultural value, and between what is considered "natural" and "unnatural" in the growth of the city. While some observers celebrate planning by destruction, or marvel at the rapid domestication of the natural environment, others decry the devastation of their homes and lament the passing of the architectural heritage of the city. Celebrated and condemned, encouraged and resisted, this process defines the experience of the city. It also poses in the most jarring manner the dilemmas of modernity.

One of these central dilemmas has been the role the past would play in the modern world. "The most intractable of our experiences," Aldous Huxley has written, "is the experience of Time—the intuition of duration, combined with the thought of perpetual perishing." [8] This book explores the links between the transformation of the urban landscape and the shape of modern memory in early-twentieth-century Manhattan. The quest to be "modern," in its often defiant rhetorical attempts to break cleanly with tradition, was in fact deeply enmeshed in the insistent demands of history. [9] One of the roles the landscapes of cities have played is to offer physical remnants of past times to present generations. "In the city," wrote Lewis Mumford, the great architectural historian and cultural critic, "time becomes visible." [10] What New Yorkers living in the first third of this century confronted so openly was a city

of their own making, in which they feared that in fact the opposite was true: time had become invisible. [11]

New York's landscape, a place swept by James's "dreadful chill of change," rarely offered the opportunity to look forward and backward. This did not mean, however, that New Yorkers abandoned the past. Contrary to the popular sense of New York as an ahistorical city, the past—as recalled, invented, and manipulated by powerful New Yorkers—was, in fact, at the heart of defining how the city would henceforth be built. Indeed, all of the diverse city-building efforts New Yorkers took part in and witnessed were shaped by the use and invention of collective memories.[12] Collective memories were fashioned and used with abandon by the city's builders, in complex and some-times contradictory ways: by real estate developers hoping to enhance the prestige of Fifth Avenue; by historic preservation advocates seeking moral inspiration and assim-ilationist lessons through the preservation of historic landmarks; by tenement re-formers eager to expunge deplorable memories of slums; and by street tree advocates who saw in nature a link to a more stable pace of change that would serve as a pal-liative for the ills of the modern city. In the ultimate capitalist city, where a square foot of earth in 1900 could command upwards of a thousand dollars, and where time itself no longer seemed a dependable substance, collective memories anchored in sub-stances more tangible than words were a rare and powerful commodity. For those who had the capital to impose their economic and political programs on a wider public, collective memories became valuable tools in the development of space.

While New Yorkers exploited the past and rarely provided a satisfying answer about how tradition would be woven into the pattern of modern life, a consistent message endured for city builders of later years. Across the range of city-building endeavors—real estate development, slum clearance, historic preservation, street tree planting, historical interpretation—New Yorkers codified the idea that New York (and, by intimation, all cities) would be built through this vibrant but divi-sive, electrifying but inequitable, process. Despite potent attempts to arrest the "dreadful chill of change" in New York—through zoning and building restrictions along Fifth Avenue, or efforts to preserve historic landmarks—in the end even those most committed to slowing the pace of change and holding on to physical rem-nants of the past did their part to enshrine the trope of the "provisional city." Through observations of city building, by viewing the detritus of creative destruc-

tion in museums, by glorifying depictions of change in paintings and photographs, and through the manipulation of traditions by private developers and equally savvy reformers, New Yorkers learned to see the cycle of destruction and rebuilding as "second nature"—self-evident, unquestionable, and inevitable.[13]

Manhattan in the first four decades of the twentieth century, from the Consolidation in 1898 to the World's Fair in 1939, is the logical place to study the tensions inherent in the city of creative destruction. Although the city's development in this era has been studied extensively, it merits a new look. Viewing the process of urban transformation through the lens of creative destruction means perceiving the dynamic upheaval of the urban landscape to be as much a defining characteristic of Manhattan in this era as the temporary products of the process—skyscrapers, tenements, bridges. This lens brings familiar subjects into new focus.[14]

Manhattan has promoted and experienced the process of creative destruction like no other city. Although the areas that became boroughs of Greater New York with the Consolidation in 1898 would be dramatically remade in ensuing years, city building was at its most vibrant on Manhattan Island. In the process of developing the land of the city to accommodate the five million people who would flow into Manhattan over the course of the first half of the century—laying sewers and subways, demolishing slums, removing smaller buildings for taller ones—New Yorkers created and confronted a city dominated by a destructive logic.[15] At the end of the nineteenth and in the early twentieth centuries, Manhattan experienced its greatest eras of transformation. In a generation, developers largely wiped away the city of brownstones and church spires and replaced it with the modern, skyscraper metropolis we recognize today. "New York is never satisfied with itself," wrote the editors of *Architecture* in 1927. "Its new buildings are scarcely occupied before they are torn down to make way for better ones. The great steel frames of its structures will never disintegrate from rust—they are scrapped before rust can start."[16] O. Henry may have captured New York's essence most succinctly: "It'll be a great place if they ever finish it."

The list of what was destroyed, and what was built and destroyed again in this era, is stunning. Individual monuments of American architecture and engineering fell regularly, often only a few years after being built: Madison Square Garden (figure 1.2), Temple Emanu-El, the Fifth Avenue Hotel, and the Waldorf-Astoria, to name just a

Fig. 1.2. William C. McNulty, *De-molishing Madison Square Garden,* 1925. Etching. Museum of the City of New York. Gift of Richard M. Lederer.

few.[17] Mansions of the wealthiest and most powerful Americans came down like dominoes in the 1920s, replaced by apartment towers and museums. But as stunning as the disappearance of important landmarks was the removal of the anonymous buildings that were the very fabric of the city. Rows of brownstones and acres of tenements were demolished to make way for widened thoroughfares, skyscrapers, bridges, and tunnels (see figures 1.3 and 1.4).

Equally important, this era was a time of unprecedented cultural interpretation of the convulsions of urbanization. Artists, writers, city leaders, and intellectuals all confronted with a striking intensity the problems and opportunities posed by a city undergoing "cycles of demolition and construction" (see figure 1.5).[18] For many, New York was the creative city *par excellence*, a place where new political ideals, as much as new artistic forms and architectural designs, could be pioneered. Avant-garde writers and artists now began to describe New York's particular "sense of place" as precisely this sensation of vertigo amid the dynamism of a bustling commercial center packed with an overwhelming diversity of peoples. The physical transformation of the city was glorious because it gave visual form to the consciousness of its inhabitants. "The physical and architectural upheaval of the city," notes cultural historian Ann Douglas, "was a symbol of its inner spirit . . . its protean ability to assume new shapes and discard old ones; the city changes before your eyes."[19] Indeed, John Dos Passos, Dorothy

Fig. 1.3. Delancey Street, from Orchard to Allen Streets, June 11, 1904. The Williamsburg Bridge required the demolition of hundreds of buildings to make way for the bridge approach. In the distance are the tenements of Allen Street, which would be demolished to allow for the widened road and the elevated train line. © Collection of The New-York Historical Society.

Fig. 1.4. George P. Hall, *Construction of a Building.* George P. Hall collection, 1902–1906. Museum of the City of New York.

Fig. 1.5. George Bellows, *Excavation at Night,* 1908. Oil on canvas, 34 x 44 inches. Signed (lower right): Geo Bellows. Photograph courtesy Berry Hill Galleries, Inc., New York.

Parker, and others gloried in what might be called a landscape of amnesia, where the past would hold no authority and would offer no restrictions.

As E. B. White put it, the New Yorkers who came to build and define the image of the city, in stone and in words, were "born somewhere else and came to New York in quest of something."[20] A majority of New Yorkers by the 1920s had come from elsewhere, with immigrants from small American towns and farms adding to the 40 percent who were foreign born, from places like Slovakia or Sicily.[21] In 1890 William Dean Howells had fictionalized his own move from Boston to New York in *A Hazard of New Fortunes*. He was but one of an overflowing ferry of native-born Americans who were drawn to New York in this period—Hurston, Ellington, Fitzgerald, Wilson, O'Neill, Kern, Lippman—and would transform American culture in their new home. New York was the "city of final destination," the ultimate city of migrants

in a nation of immigrants.²² Many recent migrants reveled in the "gift of privacy" offered by a place with little social policing.²³

Even for those who felt that Manhattan was the people more than the place, it was the skyscrapers and subways, the tenements of the Lower East Side, the mansions of Fifth Avenue, and the lights of Times Square that served as the essential stage set for the human drama of New York.²⁴ The landscape of Manhattan came to symbolize not only the city but the idea of "city." That is why it is not surprising that controversies over the fate of specific places in Manhattan were suffused with contemporary battles over the most fundamental issues of the day: efforts to control and assimilate immigrants, to develop a democratic commercial culture, and to pose competing visions for government activity. Indeed, to a remarkable degree these social and cultural issues were played out on the stage of the urban landscape. What kind of "place" Manhattan would be—and hence, what kind of place the modern city would be—was intimately bound up with what kind of buildings were built and how the city changed over time. From the shape of the landscape and the nature of its transformation from past into future, New Yorkers gleaned insights about the shape of modern America. Thus, the "politics of place"—so central in urban development debates—was defined in this era by city builders setting the tools of memory to the substance of the urban landscape, in order to transform the metropolis.

Manhattan was, we can safely say, the proving ground for the American penchant for destroying the old. In the "landscape of American democracy," Daniel Boorstin has written, "mental ties to the past are precious few."²⁵ But New York has produced the inevitable antithesis to this national characteristic: the lament for a past that never was. Many New Yorkers, especially those who called themselves "old New Yorkers," saw in the foreign and domestic immigrants, new forms of art and literature, and political ideas and social organizations trends that would be corrosive and destructive of "American" traditions. "To old New Yorkers," observed *Vanity Fair* in 1925, "the real melancholy comes, not from the fact that the houses are soon to crumble into dust, but that the old and well ordered social fabric . . . has itself crumbled and vanished utterly from view."²⁶ For these people, many progressives among them, nostalgia and a longing for a past city that was largely invented anchored their efforts to secure a sense of place. Gutzon Borglum, the sculptor of Mount Rushmore, noted that the "cruel thought" about New York "is the transient character of her life. . . . Her greatest build-

ings are ephemeral." How, he asked, "can a people so transient develop municipal spirit?"[27] For many of these city builders and reformers, the destructive aspects of the city's social and cultural life were reflected and perpetuated—but also could be solved—in the creation of new physical forms and in the protection of older landscapes.

To fully grasp the politics of place we must focus on specific sites and their development (see figure 1.6).[28] This book does not offer a comprehensive history of Manhattan in the early twentieth century, or even a complete history of city planning, tenement reform, or historic preservation.[29] Rather its goal is to link the histories of various city-building efforts—usually told separately—by showing how the politics of place pervaded and shaped these efforts. I locate the tensions inherent in the creatively destructive city in the battles over the planning controls for Fifth Avenue, efforts to return nature—in the form of street trees—into the heart of Manhattan, government-initiated programs for ridding the city of slums in the Lower East Side, and efforts to preserve "indoor" and "outdoor" physical landmarks of the city's past. In these various battles lay the fundamental tension between a celebration of the metropolis—its dynamism and diversity—and a profound nostalgia born of a fear for what the modern city portended.

Chapter 2 describes the convulsive process of real estate development that reached its consummate expression on Fifth Avenue. I trace the reaction to creative destruction in one of its rawest forms: its role in shaping new attitudes toward city building and new efforts to manipulate the chaotic market in urban space. Even as Fifth Avenue symbolized in physical form capitalism's most tremendous accomplishments, New York City also pioneered the most significant controls on urban space the nation had yet seen. Fifth Avenue's history highlights the tension between the market forces at the heart of the celebrated dynamism of the city and planning controls that sought to shield particular places from change. History—in this case, the narratives invented and deployed by Fifth Avenue boosters—was a crucial tool for "preserving" the Avenue in its most profitable form. The resulting struggles over land and ideas provide an excellent window into the politics of place in Manhattan.

Shifting from the overdevelopment along the "spine of Gotham," chapter 3 examines the problem of "underdevelopment" in Mulberry Bend in the Lower East

Side. The failure of the private real estate market to rid the city of its "foul core" inspired the city's—and the nation's—first wave of slum clearance efforts. While slum clearance has often been seen as the inevitable, "natural" solution to the tenement problem, the story of the creative destruction of tenements is, in fact, far more complex. Battles over slum clearance reveal fault lines in the beliefs of elite New Yorkers, the awkward adolescence of city government itself, and powerful cultural dilemmas concerning the assimilation of immigrants—all centering around these vilified buildings. Over the course of three decades, reformers and officials successfully promoted the physical elimination of tenements as the natural solution to the housing problem. It was a solution for which New York and its residents would pay an enormous price.

Chapter 4 focuses on the fight to preserve City Hall in order to explore issues surrounding the destruction of historic buildings and the rise in an ethos of historic preservation. Just a few blocks from the government-sponsored demolition of tenements, preservationists launched their first major battle to protect a historic landscape. City Hall was also at the heart of visions of the modern, redesigned "City Beautiful," and thus highlights the tensions between planning and preservation, between protecting the past amid an overheated real estate market and creating new public buildings and spaces for the modern city. At the start of the century, preservationists articulated far-reaching ideas about how the past might coexist in the metropolis. By 1940, however, a narrowly focused preservation movement had become a partner in the speculative destruction of the city's historic fabric.

Chapter 5 describes the "indoor" preservation movement that paralleled the "outdoor" preservation efforts of chapter 4. Bringing preservation indoors meant creating museum space and exhibits to preserve the city's past. I study the founding and early years of the Museum of the City of New York, which pioneered period rooms and the use of visual materials to document the physical transformation of the city. The museum exemplified a booming "indoor" preservation movement that took hold, not coincidentally, just as the "outdoor" preservation efforts failed to make an appreciable change in the city's landscape. In its work of collecting and displaying pieces of New York's physical past, the museum enshrined a particular version of the city's history, which emphasized physical change and celebrated the city's growth, even as the museum lamented the passing of so much of New York's nineteenth-century fabric.

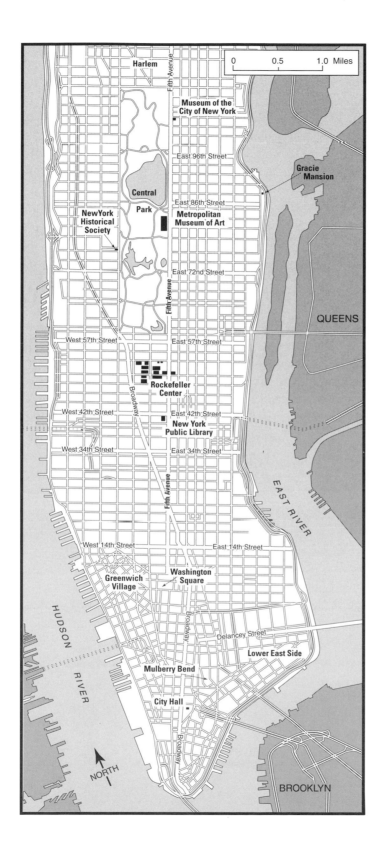

Fig. 1.6. Map of Manhattan. University of Wisconsin Cartographic Laboratory.

In the end, indoor preservation efforts served to rationalize the rapid destruction of the city's buildings and monuments.

Chapter 6 considers an unlikely topic—street trees. The tensions highlighted in the first five chapters—between market prerogatives and planning controls, between preserving the past for the purposes of education and assimilation and envisioning a new city, between creation and destruction—are highlighted in the most personal way in the problem of nature in the city. Chapter 6 describes the transformation of Manhattan's natural environment into a setting for real estate transactions and commercial enterprise, and a vocal group of social reformers' efforts to resist this transformation. I focus on the elimination of street trees, in order to approach the larger question of the contested place of nature in the early-twentieth-century city. At the cusp between private and public extramarket entities planted within the heart of commercial Manhattan, the fight over street trees reveals the tug-of-war between real estate developers, a growing government apparatus, and individual land- and home owners. Furthermore, the fragile existence of trees on the streets of Manhattan contributed to a widespread acceptance of a new truism for the city: constant, rapid change in its physical and social spheres was inevitable.

Finally, in chapter 7, I focus on the life of one individual. The figure of Isaac Newton Phelps Stokes—banker, architect, housing reformer and slum clearance advocate, historic preservationist, collector of prints and photographs of Manhattan, and author of a six-volume visual guide to Manhattan's physical development—brings together the variety of city-building projects explored in this book through one individual's experience. In his *Iconography*, a massive timeline and compendium of images of Manhattan from 1626 to 1909 (written between 1909 and 1928), Stokes in essence sought to assemble a "complete" record of a place. But even as he researched and wrote the book, the city underwent some of its most rapid and fundamental changes. Stokes's personal efforts to shape and comprehend Manhattan's physical landscapes of the present and past illustrate the tension between creation and destruction in the twentieth-century city.

In 1935, a long-awaited visitor came from Europe to inspect Manhattan. Like Henry James, who had journeyed back to his hometown thirty years previously, the Swiss architect Le Corbusier came to see how well the most modern of cities

measured up. In Manhattan he found a perfect soapbox for pontificating about his vision of the modern city, a "radiant city" of mile-high towers, submerged highways, and wide-open park space. Accompanied by reporters and architects, Le Corbusier toured New York, walking the narrow streets of Lower Manhattan and gliding to the top of the Empire State Building.[30] Summarizing the essence of the island, he echoed James, declaring ephemerality to be the city's most defining feature: "New York is nothing more than a provisional city. A city that will be replaced by another city."[31]

Though they used the same words, there was little similarity between these two men. For Henry James the "restless renewals" of Manhattan were a nightmare. The

Fig. 1.7. View northward from the Woolworth Building. Photograph courtesy of Iguana Photo.

Fig. 1.8. Democracity Exhibition in the Perisphere at the New York World's Fair, 1939. The Norman Bel Geddes Collection, The Theatre Arts Collection, Harry Ransom Humanities Research Center, The University of Texas at Austin. By permission of Edith Lutyens Bel Geddes, Executrix.

Fig. 1.9. Destruction of the Trylon and Perisphere at the New
York World's Fair, 1939. Collections of the Municipal Archives of
the City of New York.

city's mad, money-hungry speculation had brought down his boyhood home and replaced it with a factory, and his genteel Fifth Avenue was transformed by garish mansions of the nouveau riche. But what Henry James had considered an indictment, Le
Corbusier now offered as high praise. New York was "a city in the process of becoming." He celebrated the city for being "overwhelming, amazing, exciting, violently alive—a wilderness of stupendous experiment toward the new order that is to
replace the current tumult." [32]

Fig. 1.10. A model home adapted from styles of the New England past for the postwar period, exhibited at the New York World's Fair, 1939. Collections of the Municipal Archives of the City of New York.

Indeed, New York was only a suggestion of what the truly modern city should be. In so many ways, according to Le Corbusier, New York had not gone far enough. The skyscrapers, though the tallest in the world, were "too small" and too appallingly disorganized. Far too much of the nineteenth-century fabric was left still standing. While Le Corbusier found the contrast between old and new, historical and modern, intriguing—he called the setting of the early-nineteenth-century subtreasury building on Wall Street, a charming, "accidental composition"—in general he believed that historic buildings had to go. "Older architecture," Le Corbusier argued on his visit and throughout his writings, "is incompetent to solve" the modern problems of city life.

Le Corbusier journeyed to the top of the Empire State Building for a view of the city and to proclaim the future of Manhattan (figure 1.7). From his aerial perspective, which would be shared by so many planners in the postwar era, Le Corbusier

declared his faith in future processes of change: "The old city dies and the new city rises on its ruins—not gradually, but in a burst, suddenly—as the butterfly emerges from the cocoon of the caterpillar." The World's Fair, which opened four years after Le Corbusier's visit, presented to New Yorkers Le Corbusier's vision for the future. In the Perisphere—the white orb that, along with the Trylon, was the symbolic and physical heart of the fair—was General Motors's Democracity exhibit (figure 1.8). From an aerial perspective, New Yorkers saw a city of sleek towers and wide highways that would replace the nineteenth-century city. Outside, in the temporary city that was the fair, they could visit model homes of the past and future. Afterwards, they would drive home on the highways that had already started to create that vision of the future (figures 1.9, 1.10, and 1.11).

A remarkable transformation had taken place in thirty years. Not only Le Corbusier but also New York's city builders and imaginers, its developers and preservationists, had come to believe that the remaking of the city was not only desirable but possible—and perhaps inevitable.

Fig. 1.11. New York World's Fair parking lot, October 13, 1940. Collections of the Municipal Archives of the City of New York.

2

FIFTH AVENUE'S "RESTLESS RENEWALS"

Real Estate Development along the "Spine of Gotham"

It is a remarkable evidence of national prosperity. . . . It shows that the jubilant wealth of the country is manifested not only in the stock exchange, in
capitalistic combinations and the purchase of foreign steamship lines. There
are pessimists, of course, who declare that all these things are only signs of
delirious extravagance; that the end will come, the bubble burst and our
money-madness subside into peaceful sanity. If the baseless fabric is to be
dissolved, the splendid pageant created along Fifth Avenue will make a most
phenomenal ruin—a wondrous reminder to coming generations of the
great American age of gold.

—Burton J. Hendrick, "The New Fifth Avenue"

Thus it goes in this great town—sections changing so rapidly that the New
York of one generation remains little more than a memory to the next. And
of all the changes none have been so impressive as those which have come
to Fifth Avenue—New York's street of streets, its wonderful thoroughfare
known the world over.

—*Real Estate Record and Builder's Guide* (1924)

In 1904, Henry James left his self-imposed exile in Europe and returned to the United
States. The journey was partly nostalgic, giving him an opportunity to search out his
old haunts and homes in New York and Boston. But like most attempts to relive the
past, this visit was a disappointment, if not a disaster. Expecting to return to the city
of his youth, James instead found a radically changed city, where vulgar pursuit of
profit manifested itself in gaudy, ostentatious buildings. Returning from Europe, a
continent of ancient cities stretching back several millennia, James found in New York
only a "provisional city" (see figure 2.2).[1]

On Fifth Avenue, James found the soul and source of the destructive spirit he sensed
throughout his travels. For Fifth Avenue spun through cycles of construction and destruction at a rate unmatched in the city. The Avenue, and the city as a whole, had become a "monster of the mere market."[2] In the course of only a hundred years, the Avenue had been transformed from an empty country road into a "millionaire's mile" of

Fig. 2.1. Alfred Stieglitz, *Old and
New New York,* 1910. Alfred
Stieglitz Collection, National
Gallery of Art, Washington, D.C.

Fig. 2.2. Berenice Abbott, *Numbers 4, 6, and 8 Fifth Avenue*. March 6, 1936. A few of the remaining brownstones at the beginning of the Avenue, not far from the boyhood home of Henry James, are captured by Berenice Abbott, the finest chronicler of New York City in the 1930s. Her *Changing New York* was completed under the aegis of the Works Progress Administration. Museum of the City of New York.

estates and then into a densely inhabited line of wealthy apartments, stores, and manu-facturing lofts. If we are to locate and understand the essence of the creatively destruc-tive logic of private real estate development—the primary engine of Manhattan's con-tinuous transformation—it is to Fifth Avenue, the "spine of Gotham," we must look.[3] This chapter describes the process of real estate development that reached its consum-mate expression on Fifth Avenue, and then traces how the reaction to this process in one of its rawest forms inspired new attitudes toward city building and regulation.

The histories of Fifth Avenue's rapid development and the efforts to control it have been told before.[4] But these events are usually described as virtually inevitable outcomes of what is commonly referred to as the "march uptown" and as expected responses to normal problems of urban growth. What is usually ignored is the creation of the identity of Fifth Avenue as valuable, a place worth "saving." For at the heart of Fifth Avenue's growth, and the efforts to preserve it, lay the "illogic" of its cultural values and the social meaning attached to the place.[5] What makes Fifth Avenue so fascinating is its hold over the imaginations of New Yorkers and Americans more generally. It has been called the "Via Maxima of the Metropolis," the equivalent of Paris's Rue De la Paix and London's Bond Street. One guidebook perhaps encompassed what so many have said: "There is but one Fifth Avenue. New York is understood."[6] Although the allure of Fifth Avenue has receded from its height in the first years of the twentieth century, it remains an indelible part of our vocabulary, an adjective that lends exclusivity to any noun to which it is attached. An apartment with a Fifth Avenue address, a parade whose route runs along it, or a store with the Avenue in its title—Saks Fifth Avenue—immediately jumps in value.[7] In the first decades of the century, as the entire island was a churning landscape of development, redevelopment, destruction, and construction, few places received the attention Fifth Avenue did. Virtually every demolition, every construction project, and every increase and decrease in property values was recorded and reported.

Fifth Avenue captivated writers and citizens of the time because it represented like no other street in New York the forces of capitalist industrialization remaking America. The "spine of Gotham" was, in many ways, the symbol and reality of capitalist America, with its gleaming wealth, aspirations to outdo European civilizations, and chaotic, greedy manipulation of the landscape for profit. What happened on Fifth Avenue—what was designed on it, who lived there, what was sold, and, equally important, the process by which Fifth Avenue was built and rebuilt—informed people around the nation about the growth of cities.

The history of Fifth Avenue lies in the interaction between Fifth Avenue as a place of intense economic processes and a complex cultural symbol, a locus of invented traditions. For Fifth Avenue was, in one sense, nothing more than an idea, an image that lent great prestige not only to those who lived there but also to those who traded in the land represented by its name. Fifth Avenue thus exemplified the apparent detachment of real estate transactions from the actual creation of homes and businesses. The process of disassociating property from its physical dimension has, of course, a long history, bound up with the rise of capitalism and its commodifying logic.[8] In the Progressive Era, legal rulings codified the intangibility of property, translating the definition to focus primarily on the market value of all varieties of property. Land was now defined not as a physical place but as a commodity like any other.[9] But if the ability of capitalism to sever the connections between product and production—or between a product and its source—was ever to be seen, it was in the translation of the solid rock of Manhattan into numbers on a page. Marx's description of capitalist logic where "all that is solid melts into air" was most jarringly apparent in the trading of land and buildings as if they weighed little more than the paper on which they were exchanged.

And yet, Fifth Avenue was most assuredly a "place." In fact, the extent to which Fifth Avenue was sketched, painted, photographed, analyzed, and interpreted made it one of the most visually "imageable" of all New York City neighborhoods.[10] It was at once a string of homes sheltering familial and personal attachments, a prestigious business neighborhood providing luxury goods to the wealthy, and a work site for thousands of immigrant textile laborers. Those who lived, worked, sold, and purchased there had stakes—often, as we shall see, competing and clashing—not only in the idea of Fifth Avenue, but in the physical place itself.

This accounts for the peculiar paradox of Fifth Avenue: even as it displayed the "pure" market forces that drove the creative destruction of New York, Fifth Avenue became, in the early years of the twentieth century, the center of intense efforts to resist that market's destructive dynamic and to preserve a particular, tangible sense of place. Indeed, Fifth Avenue, the ultimate market in private property, was also one of the most regulated pieces of land in the nation. The modern methods of controlling urban land values, uses, and aesthetics all found some of their first trials on Fifth Avenue. Fifth Avenue was the site of one of the earliest business districts and business district associations; it was influential in the passing of America's first comprehensive zoning law (the 1916 Zoning Resolution), and it was subject to informal as well as legal restrictions on architectural form. Simply put, even as it was seen as a symbol for nothing less than America's wealth generated by "free" capitalistic entrepreneurship, Fifth Avenue was the birthplace of modern city planning and some of the most far-reaching efforts at controlling the capitalist market in space.[11]

THE "VIA APPIA OF OPULENCE": SOURCES OF FIFTH AVENUE'S DEVELOPMENT

Fifth Avenue's transformation is, indeed, stunning. Looking back from 1907, A. C. David reported simply that "there is nothing precisely similar to this range of real estate values anywhere else in the world. There is certainly nothing approaching it anywhere in this country."[12] In the previous six years, David reports, the Avenue had seen

Fig. 2.3. Fifth Avenue and Forty-second Street, circa 1920. The Fifth Avenue Association sought to reform many of the "nuisances" of doing business along the Avenue, as seen here: traffic, "gaudy" advertising, and crowds. Temple Emanuel, with its two towers on the east side of the street (left), would be demolished in 1926 to make way for an office building. The large brownstone at the northeast corner of Forty-second and Fifth would remain until the early 1990s, a bizarre holdout at one of the most prized locations in New York. Collections of the Municipal Archives of the City of New York.

an average 250 percent increase in property values. The typical Manhattan 100-by-25-foot lot along Fifth Avenue had cost $125,000 in 1901; $300,000 in 1906; and $350,000 to $400,000 in 1907.[13]

But it was not simply the rise of real estate values that encapsulated the intensity of the trade in urban space. Rather, the power of real estate was made manifest in the speed with which old buildings—often actually quite young—were torn down. An indication of the speed of Fifth Avenue's transformation comes from a measure of the disappearance of single homes. In 1902, there were some fifty-eight brownstone houses along the Avenue between Thirty-fourth and Forty-second Streets. By 1910 there were half that number. Furthermore, most of the remaining brownstones were already headed for demolition; they had been converted into hair salons and clothing and jewelry stores. By 1930, virtually all of these properties had been demolished for large lots upon which department stores such as B. Altman, Bonwit Teller, and Lord and Taylor could be built (figure 2.3). The land along Central Park north of Fifty-ninth Street, which had long been the last escape for elite New Yorkers seeking to build private homes in Manhattan, was already disappearing by the turn of the century.[14] The only way to build on the Avenue, which continued to be the "nexus of fashion," was to replace the old with the new. "It is natural," wrote the *Real Estate Record and Builders' Guide* (hereafter, *RERBG*) in 1901, "now that this process [of building along Fifth Avenue] is tending to completion, that there should be a tendency for values in this part of the Avenue to increase still further, and as they increase, the inducement will be the greater to tear down the old remodeled buildings that now dominate the Avenue. . . . at the present rate of progress, there will remain five or six years from now few traces of the . . . brownstone period."[15]

Fifth Avenue exemplified more than any other place on the island the nature of what Henry James called the "provisional city." Homes—often substantial brownstones or even marble mansions—fell regularly, sometimes within a decade of having been built. Even mansions built on the "Millionaire's Mile" along Central Park rarely had a life span exceeding forty years. And even when buildings remained for a few years, they changed hands with incredible rapidity. "The history of the various deals and changes in ownership of this mile and a half," Louise Reynolds wrote in 1916, "would fill a volume and it is like the shuffling of a pack of cards."[16] Finally, the rapidity with which farmland and small communities of Upper Manhattan were leveled and settled with grandiose mansions became one of the most powerful images of private real estate's power (see figure 2.4).

Fifth Avenue developed in reaction to the cycle of building and rebuilding in Lower Manhattan. The Commissioners Plan of 1811, which laid down New York's grid of streets, had included Fifth Avenue, but it was not until 1824 that the street was laid out; it remained undeveloped above Fourteenth Street until the 1850s. After the Panic of 1837, Manhattan resumed its heady growth—especially after 1845, when the Croton Aqueduct was completed. In the following decade, the population of the city doubled, leading to the fabled "march uptown" by the wealthier classes.[17] The expansion of the commercial and industrial activity swallowed up the serenity of elite

Fig. 2.4. Cover of Henry Collins Brown, *Fifth Avenue, Old and New, 1824–1924* (Fifth Avenue Association, 1924). Boosters who celebrated the hundredth anniversary of the FAA would repeatedly tell the tale of the small country road (inset, top left) that became the "spine of Gotham" (inset, below right). United States History, Local History & Genealogy Division, The New York Public Library, Astor, Lenox and Tilden Foundations.

residential areas such as Washington Square, sending those families looking for escapes from the noise and crowds of business. At the same time, civic leaders became more alarmed by the crowding of Lower Manhattan, convinced that this had caused the 1832 and 1849 cholera epidemics. The belief that public parks could serve as "lungs" for cities, not to mention provide desperately needed recreational space, had a strong following. Rural cemeteries, such as Mount Auburn in Boston and Greenwood in Brooklyn, were ample evidence of the value of bringing "rural sights and sounds in[to] the midst of the city itself."[18]

Thus, the transformation of the land beyond Fourteenth Street, and then beyond Twenty-third, Thirty-fourth, and Forty-second Streets, was motivated by a desire to escape the rapid development of Lower Manhattan. The elite settlers of Fifth Avenue in the second half of the nineteenth century played a desperate game of catch-up as the "virtually insatiable demands for office and retail space" pushed their search for quiet, exclusively residential areas ever northward and away from the river edges where industrial development was greatest.[19] It was to Fifth Avenue that the wealthiest families in America gravitated, to embody their far-flung wealth—in western mining companies, railroad lines, steel plants—in bricks, mortar, and, more typically, marble. "This zone at once became the Mecca of American millionaires," wrote one critic. "The possessors of suddenly acquired fortunes, it would seem, could hardly wait to ensconce themselves within its sacred confine."[20]

The development of Fifth Avenue as a residential and elite shopping street had slowed by the end of the century. The market itself had overheated, creating a lack of lots for building and land prices so high that few could afford to build private mansions along the Avenue. Furthermore, the Depression of 1893 stalled virtually all building projects until the beginning of the new century. The numbers of new private homes along Fifth Avenue (and in Manhattan as a whole) declined precipitously.[21] This, however, did not signal a corresponding decline in Fifth Avenue development. With few individuals willing or able to build private homes, manufacturers—eager to join the elite cadre of Fifth Avenue businesses and be close to the rail and transport centers of the East and West Sides—began to take over space along the Avenue. The image of an elite residential neighborhood was now appropriated by manufacturing and retail firms. Above Fifty-ninth Street, the Avenue remained one of the most elite residential areas in the city, a solid wall of wealth across from the park. But the continued pressures on land values, and the push to squeeze profits out of a finite amount of land, spurred a new wave of destruction and rebuilding. Just as the wave of mansion building crested in the late 1890s, the first luxury apartment buildings were erected on the lots of recently demolished mansions.

The transformation of the Avenue was accelerated by the passage (on 25 July 1916) of the 1916 Zoning Resolution. The ordinance, the culmination of a long fight that I will discuss in a following section, subjected all land in Greater New York City to controls on use and development. First, the city was divided into zones, where different types of uses—unrestricted, residential, and business—would be allowed. Second, in order to prevent such notorious structures as George Post's Equitable Building (a sheer cube of offices covering an entire block on Lower Broadway near the City Hall, which had become a touchstone for critics of skyscrapers), the law restricted the amount of a site that could be built upon. Finally, and most importantly for the Fifth Avenue Association, the law limited heights, using an elaborate formula based on the width of the street, in order to allow more light and air into the city's streets. On most major avenues in Manhattan, the ordinance permitted buildings to rise twice the width of the street—150 feet on a 75-foot-wide street—before "stepping back" a foot for every two-foot elevation thereafter.[22] The resulting ziggurat-like form of Manhattan's skyscrapers in the 1920s and 1930s—though not intended by the authors of the 1916 ordinance—was in part a response to efforts by architects to literally design buildings within this setback constraint.

Although World War I delayed the transformation of Fifth Avenue, in the 1920s it was the 1916 Zoning Resolution that provided the legislative framework for a rapid development of tall commercial and residential towers along the Avenue, and the elimination of the nineteenth-century brownstones. As I will discuss, although the Zoning Resolution inhibited the extreme development of a lot of land—a sheer tower three hundred feet tall on a narrow lot was impossible under the ordinance—it ultimately speeded development by preventing uses and forms that might have destroyed the allure of Fifth Avenue.

Thus, beginning in the late nineteenth century but exploding after World War I, Fifth Avenue was remade into a line of skyscraping apartment houses for the wealthy. The last inhabitants of the mansions lining the Avenue and the new wealthy class fled for the suburbs or took refuge in the apartment towers. Their former homes were promptly demolished to make way for high-rise apartments or were saved as part of some of the first preservation efforts conducted by organizations such as the Municipal Art Society and the American Scenic and Historic Preservation Societies. Other mansions were converted into museums, beginning the process whereby "Millionaire's Row" became "Museum Mile." In 1940, when the *WPA Guide to New York* was published, Fifth Avenue was much transformed. Genteel houses along Lower Fifth Avenue—from Washington Square to Thirty-fourth Street—had been removed for factories and office towers. But once above Thirty-fourth Street, the *Guide* noted,

Fifth Avenue "abruptly emerges from a street of buildings housing wholesale clothing, textile, and bric-a-brac concerns to become the aristocrat of shopping thoroughfares."[23] It was still the most financially and culturally valuable commercial and
residential land on the island. For those who argued that Fifth Avenue should remain
residential, the Avenue still was home to the elite of New York even if they were now
lifted a hundred feet in the air, perched over Central Park. If the "encroachments of
commerce"[24] had effectively amputated Fifth Avenue in the middle, at least its upper
reaches retained the key elements of what made the Avenue unique.

"A COMPELLING FORCE": THE SPECULATIVE
MARKET IN SPACE

In February 1920, New York was hit with a debilitating snowstorm. Although nothing like the Great Blizzard of 1888, the storm nonetheless knocked down telephone
wires, stalled traffic for days, and slowed business to a halt. But in the *RERBG*, the
storm barely deserved mention. Facing full-page public notices by New York Telephone (urging New Yorkers to avoid using the few remaining lines open in the city
except for emergencies) were statistics showing that 1919 had turned into a banner
year for the real estate world. The *RERBG* noted a record for one day's trading—
over $10 million contracted by Frederick Brown—and estimated that 1919 valuations
for property were increasing over the previous year on the order of 30 to 40 percent.[25]
The trade and development of Manhattan's most tangible, material product had become, paradoxically, invisible and weightless.

The inability of Nature's weapons to injure or even appreciably slow the postwar
real estate boom attests to the power of the real estate market in New York. As David
Scobey has argued, the New York real estate industry did not explode in the
post–Civil War era to serve and facilitate the growth of New York's manufacturing
and finance might. The trade in space was, in and of itself, a powerful generator of
New York's wealth. The most influential and wealthy families in New York—the Astors, the Belmonts, the Vanderbilts—acquired much of their profits from holding and
trading land on Manhattan Island.[26]

And yet, the paper transactions—the conveyances that increasingly filled the heavy
ledger books in the new Hall of Records on Chambers Street and expanded the pages
of the *RERBG* with ever-smaller type—did create architectural forms on the land.
The translation of paper into substance was never smooth; the physical form of the
city was never a mirror, simply and accurately reflecting the trade in space. Indeed, it
was this conversion of commerce into tangible buildings that New Yorkers interpreted

with increasing wonder and confusion. A writer for the *RERBG*, explaining the transformation of Fifth Avenue, noted that "the compelling force is the same which about the year 1845 cleared away the shanties from the ragged edges of the common, smoothed over the potter's field, and built these old dwellings and stores, whose turn it is now to go."[27]

Observers of Manhattan's transformation spoke inaccurately of some vague, invisible force that was responsible for the "march uptown," and the waves of development that continued to sweep away old buildings, good and bad. The spectacular and, to some, catastrophic transformation of Manhattan was attributed to an inexplicable force. In his 1932 essay about 1920s New York, "My Lost City," F. Scott Fitzgerald noted that many of the iconographic sites in Manhattan "had somehow disappeared."[28] The sense of mystery in real estate development had become one of the central elements of Manhattan's folklore of growth. In fact, few accurately understood the process of land development in New York any better than the writer for the *RERBG*; for most it was a strange and awe-inspiring process. Observers who charted the rise in real estate values and watched old brownstones fall, marble mansions spring up and fall again, and office towers and apartment buildings take over could do little better than attribute the creative destruction along Fifth Avenue to a "compelling force"—a force attractive but also elusive and incomprehensible, and, some would suggest, uncontrollable.

Fifth Avenue's "restless renewals" must be understood within the larger context of New York's rise as the "capital of capitalism."[29] The tremendous demands for space were not simply due to New York's position as the greatest center for manufacturing in America; it had also become the "front office" for America's industrial giants and the country's biggest market for many goods. New York was thus unique in its leadership in industrial management, production, and consumption. It was this role, as the "principal command post of industrial capitalism in the United States," that urged on the cycles of private destruction and rebuilding.[30]

This combination of economic factors made for an incredibly diverse range of land uses. Elite residence areas bordered on the dense acres of the laboring classes, while manufacturing lofts spread quickly through Lower Manhattan, filling increasingly larger and taller buildings. The "compelling force" behind the rapid and continuous rebuilding of the island came from factors in part unique to New York. First, the growth rate of New York's population was unmatched anywhere in the nation. Ellis Island was admitting up to one million people a year, one-third of whom chose to stay, at least for a time, in New York. Thus, the city grew steadily denser, especially in Lower Manhattan residential areas, such as the Lower East Side, that were within walking distance of workplaces.[31] In 1910 Manhattan had an average density of 166

people per acre, but the Lower East Side averaged 727.9 people per acre —with some
areas exceeding 1,000 people per acre.[32]

Second, the unique configuration of New York's economy—as the center of fashion and consumption—made New York fertile economic soil not for large-scale manufacturing enterprises but rather for an incredible diversity of small manufacturing
enterprises.[33] New York's was a relatively unstable marketplace, with businesses opening and closing, rapidly expanding and contracting; few industries with apparent permanence demanded homes like Ford had created at his River Rouge plant. To meet
the proliferating desires of shoppers, New York manufacturers developed endless small
factories and satellite sweatshops that could change styles with ease. This is what drove
the explosion of lofts, the small factory enterprises located in Lower Manhattan and
increasingly in midtown. Lofts had first expanded in the waterfront areas and up along
the center of the island beginning in the 1850s—in part because of the invention of
cast iron, which allowed for multistory buildings with large interior open spaces.[34] A
series of factors pushed lofts onto Fifth Avenue and further northward. First, the garment industry followed the garment fashion center. Where the stores went, the garment factories followed. But while these exclusive stores needed the relatively close
presence of the garment manufacturers—for designs and alterations—they also
wanted to be distant from them. A game of leapfrog took place between department
stores and their wholesalers and manufacturers.[35] Lofts dominated the development
of manufacturing space in Lower Manhattan and became the archenemy, as we shall
see, of Fifth Avenue inhabitants and some commercial owners. A post–World War I
boom generated fifty to sixty million square feet in industrial loft space in the 1920s.
Furthermore, rather than expanding outward across relatively undeveloped land (as
was happening in Brooklyn), industrial buildings grew taller and wider, necessitating
the demolition of previous loft structures. Thus on the West Side, where once hundreds of small merchants and factories crowded near the Hudson River, now a few
large printing firms were housed in taller and larger buildings. Industrial lofts were
soon eclipsed in importance by the growth of corporate headquarters, housed in skyscrapers that would come to dominate the image of New York.[36]

The growth of manufacturing and commerce drove a segregation within Manhattan, whereby downtown and, increasingly, midtown Manhattan was becoming
dominated by business. A notice in the *RERBG*, advertising the sale of the Astor
midtown properties, declared that "New York, compared to other cities, is like a boy
of 18. The characteristics and features of its manhood are now discernible. The
Heart of This Great City Is Now Settled for All Time. It is the district from 34th to
59th Sts., 3rd to 10th Avenues."[37] Although this process had begun much earlier in

the nineteenth century, the combination of manufacturing and commerce expanded dramatically at the end of the century. Culminating in the 1916 Zoning Resolution, private developers and city government worked in tandem to segregate Manhattan by functions. This process—well-known to urban historians—accelerated the settlement of Upper Manhattan and then its redevelopment with ever-denser housing, and the destruction and rebuilding of Lower Manhattan's residential areas to make way for lofts and, later, office skyscrapers. While the Lower East Side, near the heart of Manhattan's industrial center, remained a primary residence for the poorest of workers, its popularity steadily declined, from 540,000 in 1910 to under 250,000 in 1920.[38] Those who could soon began to flee up the avenues to the Upper West and East Sides, and out to the boroughs of the Bronx, Queens, and Brooklyn. Real estate developers made the building of housing a primary activity: erecting rows of brownstones and apartments on the Upper East and West Sides, and large tracts of housing in the outer boroughs for those workers who could afford to commute on the new subways to work.

The result was a market for land that was incredibly destructive, and profitable in that destruction. Indeed, New York's private real estate industry was built and depended on the cyclical rebuilding of the city's physical fabric, making it increasingly dense and centered around business. Manhattan was in a constant state of "improvement"—as the *RERBG* liked to call all new building activities. Property values increased so much because private developers never stopped remaking the landscape of the city. With people and wealth flowing into the city, developers found clients for repeated demolition and construction of newer, taller lofts, offices, and, especially after 1920, apartment houses. There seemed to be no end to the need for greater density, both for homes and businesses.

The story told in this way makes almost too much sense out of an extremely chaotic process of city development. We risk buying into the boosters' ploys when we speak of the "inevitable" growth of Manhattan, the "waves" of development, and so forth.[39] This simple narrative of growth excludes important elements. As David Scobey notes about an earlier, but equally robust, period of Manhattan's growth, the city's development was anything but orderly.[40] More important, the chaos of that growth, its booms and busts and simultaneous over- and underdevelopment, was not youthful disruption but essential to the process of capitalist urbanization. Recognizing the chaotic nature of real estate development is crucial to understanding the creative destruction along Fifth Avenue and the efforts to shape and resist its transformation.

First, while it is generally fair to speak of Manhattan's incredible growth in real estate values and land development, the city's real estate economy was highly sensitive to economic booms and busts. Thus as the century opened, the *RERBG* painted a bleak picture of real estate in New York City, reporting that the market was dead—with transactions half the number of a year before.[41] But by the end of the decade, building construction and transactions had exploded, making 1909 the best year in the history of the city. The number of planned buildings had expanded from 659, amounting to $85 million in investments, in 1908 to 995, costing more than $131 million.[42] The market took a dramatic dive during World War I but immediately rebounded at the war's conclusion. The 1920s brought another boom—especially in the building of apartment houses and skyscrapers to handle the pent-up demand from the war. But even as one area was booming, others could stall in a state of "underdevelopment." The Upper West Side, long championed by the *RERBG*, only expanded rapidly in the second decade of the twentieth century as the Broadway line was built and restrictive covenants (discussed in greater detail later) ended.[43]

Just as rapidly as property values could increase— doubling every year in some places—so too could they drop like stones. John Flavel Mines, while repeating the usual awestruck tropes about Manhattan's miraculous growth, also noted the catastrophic speculative crashes that occurred in Harlem and elsewhere. In their excitement over the arrival of the Harlem train line, realtors paid up to $1,000 per lot, only to find them worth only $9 per lot two years later.[44] Although the *RERBG* constantly warned its readers about the dangers of overdevelopment—for example, during the loft construction craze of the 1910—few heeded this advice.[45]

Beyond the chaos of the market, its propensity toward underdevelopment and overproduction, were inexplicable developments that confounded the simplistic descriptions of New York's miraculous, "inevitable" growth. Edward Pratt, an important advocate for city planning and especially the removal of manufacturing from Manhattan, wondered how manufacturers were "able to thrive in the centre of New York City, where land values are so excessive, and where rentals and insurance charges are proportionately high."[46] To Pratt their success remained a mystery, even after he interviewed hundreds of manufacturers in the city.

Their "mysterious" success was due to the same "compelling force" that confounded other observers—even the experts of the *RERBG*. The agglomeration economies—what economists call those benefits that come from being in close communication with others in the same industry, including suppliers, consumers, inventors—offers only a partial explanation. Equally important was the "almost indefinable and sometimes even fanciful advantage, the proximity of the New York market."[47] What Pratt only barely alluded to but remained at the heart of New York's allure was the prestige and social esteem that came with having a store or office in Manhattan. The sources of a place's allure are as much in "illogic" as in rational economic calculation. As Elizabeth Blackmar has written, "Real estate investment is an enterprise that builds on omens and prophecy," a social and cultural phenomenon as much as an economic one.[48] And if there was an area that was most beset by the intangible cultural valuations of space that were so important to the creative destruction of New York City, it was Fifth Avenue. For even as Fifth Avenue represented the extremes of the processes affecting Manhattan more generally—the rise of manufacturing and offices below Fifty-ninth Street, the gradual segmentation of the island, the fitful development of land—it also exemplified how fashion and cultural valuing could dictate the focus, rate, and form of creative destruction.

It was the effects of the mysterious, "compelling force" of real estate development that elites of Fifth Avenue in the first decades of the twentieth century tried to understand and control. This force had produced untold wealth and beautiful buildings, and spurred the development of Manhattan Island. And yet this same force had also destroyed historic homes and the fabric of a residential neighborhood and its tightly connected society. John Flavel Mines, who combined his boosterism with a powerful nostalgia for "old New York," approvingly noted in 1890 the views of a farmer who refused to sell his land in Upper Manhattan because of his faith in its stability:

> I like the land. It's always there. It's been there these eighty-seven years, right before my eyes, while the money comes and goes, and I don't know where it is. The land can't run away. . . .[49]

In fact, in Manhattan, and along Fifth Avenue, this was no longer true. The "bit of earth" had become a commodity, as smoothly bought and sold as any other commodity. Its apparent solidity—people spoke of acquiring "a piece of the rock"—had melted into thin air. It was against this notion that land, buildings, and neighborhoods were merely assemblages of rentable, speculative space—no more meaningful than bushels of wheat or heads of cattle—that the residents and businesspeople of Fifth Avenue organized. The stories they told themselves about change along Fifth Avenue shaped their program for "conserving" the Avenue.

But first they would have to make sense of the forces behind the Avenue's "restless renewals."

REAL ESTATE STORIES

The relentless trade in the market for space prompted a giddy euphoria among observers of the city's growth. Recalling, measuring, and evaluating the phenomenon of real estate development became a cottage industry in its own right. Not unlike Holland's infamous tulip mania in the seventeenth century, New Yorkers were gripped by a real estate speculative fever and observers watched in amazement. Writers of guide-books and histories, and commentators in the *RERBG*, all sifted tirelessly through the data on the miraculous developments along Fifth Avenue. No one, including readers, seemed to tire of the game. Articles with titles such as "The Bixby Fortune: A Romance of Land Values in New York City" were regular features of daily newspapers and trade magazines, in part because the events they described were so common.[50]

In telling the stories of real estate development in New York, civic boosters—especially in the architectural and real estate press—became historians of a sort: they applied their visions of future development onto the past, building an invented history for Manhattan's rapid but steady, prosperous, and profitable growth. John Flavel Mines offered a rousing celebration of the work of real estate developers in 1890, finding in the statistics of real estate values evidence of their heroic work and the potential dangers they faced:

> There are those who object to dry statistics, and say there is no poetry in figures. I maintain that the man who says there is no romance in the vagaries of arithmetic does not know what he is talking about. Is there no poetry in the statistics of Thermopylae, whose three hundred men kept three hundred thousand at bay until the homes of Sparta were safe? Is there no romance in the record of the three score minute-men of Lexington who, in defiance of the rules of arithmetic, stood up against twelve times their number? . . . So, running through the dry statistics of annual assessments just quoted, there is a suggestion to gray-haired men of business who are still among us of a wild speculation in Harlem real estate which created millionaires of a day to make them paupers on the morrow.[51]

The reference point for city builders' achievements remained, as it had since New York's boom had begun a half century earlier, the original real estate transaction, and first real estate jackpot, on Manhattan Island: the sale of the island to Peter Minuit by a group of Delaware Indians in 1626 for twenty-four dollars in trinkets.[52] This event grew in mythical importance in the minds of New Yorkers as they yearly amplified the ludicrousness of the deal. With the 1626 "trade" as the birth date of New York City, the ever-increasing value of land, which by the end of the century and beginning of the new was approaching unimaginable sums, seemed to redeem that history. As Mines enthused, "It would have surpassed the wildest imagination of those worthy men if they could have looked forward to our times and have seen the assessed valuation of the real estate on this island of eleven thousand Dutch *morgens*. . . ."[53] Estimating the value of the land of Manhattan Island became something of a public parlor game. For example, Edward Ewing Pratt, who studied the "causes of congestion" in New York with a sense of awe and frustration, noted in 1910 that "Manhattan has become the most valuable piece of the world's surface. Its value is reckoned at $3,123,925,788."[54] Developers and New York boosters relished the inflation of property values, using that "first," most stupendous real estate deal as the justification for and the barometer of New York's real estate market.

As the exemplar of New York's growth, Fifth Avenue attracted hyperbolic commentary as rapidly as the city attracted wealth and population. Louise Frances Reynolds, in a history and guidebook to the Avenue published in 1916, declared that Fifth Avenue was simply the "most magnificent street in the world . . . the Via Appia of Opulence."[55] On the hundredth anniversary of the Avenue in 1924, William Pedrick stated simply: "Building activity in the Fifth Avenue section is one of the seven wonders of twentieth century commerce."[56]

If the story of Fifth Avenue's development can be distilled to two or three paragraphs, it is not because there was a dearth of narrative variations on the theme. Fifth Avenue's stunning development occupied the rhetorical gifts of numerous writers, from novelists to popular magazine editors and real estate analysts. Although perhaps the most famous and eloquent of tour guides, Henry James was but one of many to offer comments on architecture, morality, New York's stature, and America's destiny based on a walk up Fifth Avenue. As the backbone of New York, the largest and most powerful city in the country, as the home to America's wealthiest families, and as the setting for the most expensive stores in a burgeoning consumer culture, Fifth Avenue was for many observers a barometer of American progress. Fifth Avenue was known, and in some ways belonged, to the whole nation.

Each "tour" offers a different interpretation of the same set of buildings and the same process of city building. These tours are history stories and sources: they give us hints about the process of capitalist real estate development, and, at the same time, offer insight into the cultural symbolism of Fifth Avenue. If we look closely at how writers in tourist guidebooks, architectural journals, newspapers, and novels interpreted what they saw on Fifth Avenue over the course of the last decade of the nineteenth and first several decades of the twentieth centuries, we will gain an impression of the variety of stories people told themselves about urban transformation.

J. F. L. Collins published a guide for tourists taking a popular bus tour up the Avenue. Similar to the maps of Hollywood today that guide tourists to the homes of celebrities, Collins's guide highlights the great mansions, clubs, and hotels of the wealthy that had ensconced themselves on the Avenue. At ten cents per seat, the bus tour was aimed not at the readers of *Harper's*, where Henry James's rarefied critique of New York was serialized, but to more middling visitors to the city. Collins's

Fig. 2.5. From J. F. L. Collins, *Both Sides of Fifth Avenue* (New York: J. F. L. Collins, 1910). In Collins's tourist guide of the Avenue—not unlike Hollywood's celebrity driving tours of today—the photographs are at odds with the text. The photographs reveal the uneven development of the Avenue, the socially uncomfortable mixing of lofts and brownstones, mansions and apartment towers. © Collection of The New-York Historical Society.

tour—with accompanying photographs of the important homes and institutions—appealed to and perpetuated the mythology of Fifth Avenue that brought visitors to Fifth Avenue in the first place (figure 2.5). "You need only say, 'Fifth Avenue,'" declared Collins:

> New York is understood, and this is true whether you say it to the miner in Alaska, the alfalfa grower in the Great Southwest, or the farmer in Pennsylvania. There are many cities having streets called Fifth Avenue. There is but one Fifth Avenue. Fifth Avenue with its millionaire's row; Fifth Avenue with its multi-million-dollar residences; Fifth Avenue with its magnificent clubs; Fifth Avenue with its luxurious shops; the most luxurious in the new world, perhaps in all the world.[57]

For Collins, the rapidity of the change—with new wealth replacing old wealth, marble mansions replacing brownstones—was to be viewed with proud awe, as evidence of not only New York's but the nation's prosperity.

But even as Collins's guide celebrated the Avenue, the photographs reveal something else. Tourists who boarded the Fifth Avenue bus at Washington Square might immediately have been struck by the sad condition of many of the old redbrick townhouses leading to Fourteenth Street, largely overshadowed by nearby loft buildings—such as the Asch Building, which housed, in its top three floors, the Triangle Shirtwaist Company. Though Collins noted that the square had for years "served the purpose of separating the abodes of fashion and the prosperity from the slums to the southward," the visitor could not help but notice that the Italian and Jewish immigrants who had once lived "southward" now filled the streets during their lunch breaks from the nearby manufacturing lofts around the square and along the Avenue. Collins's guide was silent as the bus drove between Fourteenth and Twenty-third streets, home to the greatest concentration of these loft buildings. The photographs he offered were tightly cropped to show only the Union Club, or the home of Henry Frick. But solid brownstone homes were being superseded by twelve-story

office buildings, and vacant lots pockmarked the Avenue even in the most prestigious blocks, which Collins called "one of the costliest portions of the earth's
crust."[58] These question marks in the landscape were brushed over by Collins; they
did not match the narrative related in the text of his guidebook. The story remained
one of miraculous, steady growth, a model of what capitalist urban development
could create:

> Possibly no street in any city of the world has been so expensively built as this Avenue
> between Fourteenth and Fifty-ninth Streets, which in the lifetime of a single genera-
> tion has been an unimproved waste, a street of stately homes, and finally a centre of
> luxurious trade.[59]

Collins's contradictory accounts of Fifth Avenue suggest the complexity of private
real estate development in New York and the range of responses it inspired. On the
one hand, the mansions and glittering stores of Fifth Avenue expressed the rising cultivation of American arts, as well as the proof of a truly "American" architecture. On
the other hand, the history of Fifth Avenue might have suggested a different lesson:
that bad development patterns and unsightly buildings had to be combated aggressively with the aid of government regulation in order to protect and preserve the glo-
ries of Fifth Avenue.

In Collins's tour, and in so many others, Fifth Avenue was an apparent contradiction of miraculous creativity and terrible destruction. Some saw the process of destruction and rebuilding along the Avenue as the most robust and optimistic example
of America's miraculous modernization. The thundering steel mills of Carnegie and
the endless miles of Vanderbilt's railroad tracks found a symbolic residence on Fifth
Avenue, in the mansions of the monumentally wealthy and the stores where America's wealth was consumed. Celebrants of Fifth Avenue looked on the brownstones,
so loved today, as drab reminders of an old, stodgy wealth, "hopelessly pedestrian and
dull"; their replacement by the mansions of the new industrialists was heralded as the
culmination of American economic enterprise.

Moses King, for example, in his widely read 1893 two-volume guidebook of New
York, celebrated Fifth Avenue's stature as "one of the most magnificent thoroughfares
of the world."[60] He presented a quick tour of the Avenue, citing in rapid succession
the mansions of the "Old New-York families" below Fourteenth Street, the new businesses along the Avenue between Twenty-third and Forty-second Streets, and the
"palaces of some of New York's millionaires" above Forty-second Street. King called
the Vanderbilt houses, located just below Central Park, the "finest examples of domestic architecture in the United States."[61] Boosters saw American prosperity repre-

sented in Fifth Avenue, which, according to Burton Hendrick, had "lost its old New York character":

> It has been said that Wall Street is the pulse of the national life. Not more so than Fifth Avenue. To its upbuilding the whole nation has made tribute. . . . its importance has broadened, and its national character increased. . . . The avenue has thus become cosmopolitan; has, to a considerable extent, lost its old New York character, has dedicated itself not to a single city or a single state, but to the country at large.[62]

For many of the period, Fifth Avenue was an unblemished record of American economic and social progress, an indication of the heights of cultivation and wealth Americans could attain.

However, others, such as Henry James, saw in the marble mansions and baroque ornamentation only crass materialism and in the rapid changes only the "restless renewals" of a morally defunct society. Fifth Avenue was, for James, a dramatic warning about the excesses of modern society in the "age of gold," where the past was sacrificed for a more profitable but equally transitory present. The Avenue, and the city as a whole, had become, according to James, a "monster of the mere market."[63] In his tour up Fifth Avenue, after an angry visit to his now-demolished childhood home, James had few kind words for the wealth displayed in stone along the Avenue. His tour had a didactic purpose: to offer evidence in brick and mortar of the moral decay of New York and of American society more generally. What truly infuriated him about Fifth Avenue was the orgy of change that gripped the nouveau riche of Fifth Avenue. James considered the process by which the houses of his youth were ripped down in favor of mansions for the wealthy to be the ultimate symbol of a destructive spirit at the heart of America. The endless building up and tearing down left nothing but raw symbols of greed in their wake, gargantuan estates covered in gold "inches thick" but impermanent and transient as the rest of the "monstrous" buildings of the city.[64] Where once he saw in the architecture of New York a possibility of a sense of permanence, in 1904 he felt only the "dreadful chill of change."[65]

Representatives of the real estate and architectural industries struck an ambivalent tone in their repeated surveys of "new Fifth Avenue," which they narrated in the pages of the *RERBG*, the *Architectural Record,* and other journals. For these writers as well, Fifth Avenue was a barometer of the state of real estate in the city and the condition of architecture in the nation as a whole. They expressed their incredulity about the stunning growth in real estate values and the lightning speed with which property changed hands and buildings were torn down and built up. But they also praised the outdoor museum of architecture that Fifth Avenue had become, a virtual exhibition hall for America's most influential architects—Carrere and Hastings; McKim, Mead and White; Ralph Adams Cram. They applauded the removal of the "dull, monotonous, high-stoop brownstone houses" and welcomed the possibility of a truly American architecture.[66]

But unlike King and other boosters, the architectural and real estate professions were less sanguine about the changes they saw. These critics proffered a strong dose of skepticism about what the dramatic destruction and rebuilding had brought. A. C. David considered the intense creation and destruction along the Avenue to be dangerously chaotic, "somewhat barbaric and decidedly miscellaneous."[67] However, he noted that a few buildings rose above the base speculative cacophony—the Altman Building, the Knickerbocker Trust Company, McKim's Gorham Building—to "linger in the minds of visitors to New York," creating a "glorified vision of the thoroughfare, as the most remarkable and interesting business street in this country."[68] Louise Frances Reynolds, in her 1916 *History of a Great Thoroughfare*, offered readers an interpretation of Fifth Avenue as a symbol of the "rapidity of American growth and the national spirit of progress." But, just like Collins's bus tour of the Avenue, Reynolds revealed cracks in the armor of a purely glorious Fifth Avenue. She noted the "nightmare" of Lower (below Fourteenth Street) Fifth Avenue—where old mansions were unpleasingly surrounded by manufacturing buildings—and the effects of the "business invasion."[69]

Burton Hendrick, writing about the "New Fifth Avenue" for *Metropolitan Magazine* in 1905, also found a middle ground between the condemnation of Henry James and the celebrations of King and David. Hendrick marveled at the development along the Avenue: "It is a remarkable evidence of national prosperity. It shows that the jubilant wealth of the country is manifested not only in the stock exchange, in capitalistic combinations and the purchase of foreign steamship lines." Andrew Carnegie's mansion, built far up Fifth Avenue, encompassed what Hendrick thought best on Fifth Avenue. Carnegie's choice

> is symbolic of the present industrial era. It typifies the phenomenal period of commercial success through which the nation is now passing. It is as much a symbol of American commercialism as was the mediaeval palace of the feudal time; or the Greek temple of the age of Athenian beauty and culture. Not the success of race, but the native wit to fight one's way, to grapple with the material problems of this stirring competitive age and to bear away the palm. And this, I take it, is what is expressed in the leading residential street of America.

In essence, Fifth Avenue, when viewed in a positive light, was a symbol not only of great private wealth but of a pioneering spirit. Carnegie's colonizing venture in the wilds of northern Manhattan was a conquering of the West writ small, a step in the domestication of a distant, "wild" land.

But Hendrick and other critics who seemed to celebrate Fifth Avenue were also skeptical of its future. Hendrick, and New Yorkers more generally, had come to accept that regardless of its beauty or wealth, every building in New York had a limited life expectancy: "All over the Fifth Avenue section in the last seven years, the spirit of destruction has been abroad. The new generation had little respect for the landmarks of the old. As the larger part of the section was already built up, it was necessary to demolish large areas and build anew."[70]

The sentiment of regret for the physical remnants of the city's past permeated the writings of those who chronicled Fifth Avenue's development. Even if the tone and purpose of these observers differed radically, all at least paused to consider what was being lost as the market employed the wrecking ball. The most exultant real estate booster and the sharpest critic of change in the city were united at least momentarily in their lament before the creatively destructive transformation of their city. James's regret for his demolished homes in New York and Boston are at the heart of his *American Scene*. They mark the moments of his deepest fury at America's materialism and disregard for tradition. On the other end of the spectrum, in the *RERBG*, notices of the passing of old homes to make way for highly profitable lofts and office buildings gave the magazine editors pause. Very few offered as unequivocal a celebration of the transformation of the Avenue as J. F. L. Collins. Some decried the effects of the very same process with equal vigor. Helen Henderson, a twentieth-century flaneur in New York, London, and Paris, perhaps best encompassed the sentimental attitude as she walked through the city and noted the few remaining homes and institutions. When she came across the decrepit boyhood home of Theodore Roosevelt, a few blocks from Fifth Avenue near Gramercy Park, she launched into a diatribe about the city's care for its landmarks:

> If Henry James felt the melancholy check and snub to the felicities of his backward reach "in the presence, so to speak, of the rudely, the ruthlessly suppressed birth house" in Washington Square, what are we to suppose must be Mr. Theodore Roosevelt's emotions when he regards that terrible travesty in Twentieth Street, its entire face opened to the vulgar gaze, its discreet brownstone features annihilated by the flagrant burst of plate glass from loft to basement, across which reads the lurid inscription— "Theodore Roosevelt was born in this house."[71]

What united these writers then was a concern not necessarily for specific buildings but for some sort of permanence and stability amid the change of the city. If Fifth

Avenue inspired a cacophony of voices prophesizing many different futures for the city and nation, it also could speak one clear message: the city was heading forward with astounding and daunting rapidity. It was out of this shock that a number of investors and residents of the Avenue began to develop organized methods of slowing the pace of change and directing it in ways both more aesthetically pleasing and more profitable.

PROTECTING PROPERTY

The inhabitants of Fifth Avenue—some of the wealthiest families in America, and certainly some of the most powerful actors in city government and business—responded rapidly in the first two decades of the twentieth century to the spin of destruction and rebuilding that threatened their homes and businesses. The story of Fifth Avenue residents' and business owners' efforts to freeze Fifth Avenue in a certain incarnation—that of an elite residential area and exclusive shopping district—is a study in the rise of intervention in the marketplace of space. In essence, Fifth Avenue inhabitants and investors utilized the most modern methods of city development in order to achieve conservative results. For we find not only one of the first and certainly the most influential example of government zoning but a whole range of tools used to mold, manipulate, and control space. On one end were the private cajoling, the backroom discussions held at the Century and Metropolitan Clubs or at the Fifth Avenue Hotel. At the other end were the government measures of street widening, zoning, and policing. In between were semipublic efforts of the Fifth Avenue Association, the pressure applied by banks and insurance companies, the aesthetic arguments of the press, and private legal measures to restrict the uses of land. The approaches to managing the market for space encompass the variety of Progressive urban reform efforts, from individual moral control to the large-scale planning of the "technocrats."[72] Beginning well before the turn of the century and ranging from the most personal, informal actions to the most public and radical, inhabitants and businesspeople of Fifth Avenue took concerted steps to intervene in the market and to control the development of Fifth Avenue.

While the story is often told of the shift from private efforts to regulate space to state-sponsored means in the early twentieth century, Fifth Avenue's preservation was hardly so simple. Certainly, residents who failed to stop or shape development they thought deleterious to their investments and social life embraced new methods, including ultimately comprehensive zoning ordinances. But the older methods persisted well into the twentieth century, and were used interchangeably with these more formal and legal instruments. Protectors of Fifth Avenue employed a patchwork of methods for shaping physical transformation.

The most basic response of wealthy residents to New York's industrial development was simply to flee from it. The story of Fifth Avenue is to a large degree the story of migration, up the Avenue and then beyond the city. When Andrew Carnegie built his mansion on Fifth Avenue at Ninetieth Street, members of the press scoffed at the inaccessibility of his almost rural site. Burton Hendrick, writing for *Metropolitan Magazine* in 1905, seemed to mock Carnegie for building such a glorious home "only one remove from goatville."

> For the most part it was a dreary waste of tenements and the cheapest kind of dwellings. It was the ragged edge of Harlem, and the old-time Harlem shanty had not entirely disappeared. . . . his nearest neighbors were the inhabitants of the small shanties on the opposite side of Ninetieth Street, who persistently clung to their native soil splendidly oblivious of their distinguished surroundings.

He suggested that Carnegie was trying to re-create the Scottish Highlands of his youth, with the city's water reservoir serving as a "a faithful substitute, perhaps, for a Scottish loch."[73]

Carnegie was not alone in leaping far uptown. Mary Mason Jones, Edith Wharton's aunt, had long preceded him with a startling move to Fifth Avenue and Fifty-seventh Street in 1869, where she built her Marble Row of attached mansions. Edith Wharton memorialized her aunt's audacity in the character of Mrs. Manson Mingott in *The Age of Innocence*:

> She was sure that presently the hoardings, the quarries, the one-story saloons, the wooden greenhouses in ragged gardens, and the rocks from which goats surveyed the scene, would vanish before the advance of residences as stately as her own—perhaps (for she was an impartial woman) even statelier; and that the cobblestones over which the old clattering omnibuses bumped would be replaced by smooth asphalt, such as people reported having seen in Paris.[74]

These "pioneers" of upper Fifth Avenue were farsighted, for within just a few years most of the lots along Fifth Avenue were purchased for new mansions and even the first apartment buildings. The buyers of these lots in "goatville" were soon joined by their hesitant or stubborn friends downtown.

Those who did not see the future as clearly were faced with regular upheavals as they moved in the face of expanding business development. For example, August Belmont, son of an early park commissioner and the developer of New York's subway system, sold his house near Union Square and moved to midtown, only to flee up to Eighty-first Street a few years later. In 1910, after only sixteen years, Belmont sold this house too, and it was promptly demolished to make way for an apartment building. The Astors, long one of the most land-wealthy families in New York, also skipped their way up the Avenue, from Washington Square to Thirty-fourth Street to Sixty-fifth and Fifth. Indeed, it was Mrs. William Astor's move to the heart of the "upper" Avenue that started a mass exodus from the lower Avenue.[75] Stories like those of the Astors and Belmont abounded as elites came to recognize that their wealth was an inadequate barrier against the pressures of development.

Nonetheless, in the period from 1880 (when industrial development began to encroach upon Washington Square and lower Fifth Avenue and the first great mansions of upper Fifth Avenue were built) to the late 1920s (when the mansions were rapidly replaced with apartment buildings), elite families engaged in a spirited struggle to secure, once and for all, their exclusive residential area. As the wealthy leaped or crawled up the Avenue, establishing homes at the vanguard of development—to safer residential ground—they began concerted efforts to secure the character of their neighborhood. It was in the context of rapid development below and potential development in Upper Manhattan that elite families made a commitment to stabilize the neighborhood, if only to protect their investments in their grand mansions.

For those who refused to continue moving up Fifth Avenue in the face of "inevitable" development, the first challenge they offered was to simply not sell. Stories of those who have refused to participate in the market, and who have refused to follow the assumption that "everything has a price," are legion in New York lore.[76] For instance, Hurley's steak house refused to succumb to the offers of the Rockefellers; the three-story restaurant remains nestled beside Rockefeller Center. Perhaps the best-known holdout is the store on Herald Square that resisted Macy's bribes, forcing the largest store in the world to build around it.[77] Newspapers in the early years of the century were filled with the stories of old families—often widows living in brownstones—who refused to sell out to department stores and manufacturing firms eager to assemble plots to build their stores and factories. On lower Fifth Avenue and along Washington Square North, a number of older families who managed to hold onto their brownstones—even their redbrick homes of the first half of the century— were treated with bemused respect and humor.

More shocking, especially to the real estate press, was the resistance of established families within the heart of the business district. The Wendells, who lived in a brownstone on the northwest corner of Fifth Avenue at Thirty-ninth Street (just above B. Altman and just below the New York Public Library), held onto their home long past the time when the rest of their neighbors had fled. "The Wendells never sell," Louise Reynolds reported in her 1916 Avenue guide. "In the rear is a yard worth a million

Fig. 2.6. A classic "holdout" on Fifth Avenue, circa 1920. Wendell House, at the northwest corner of Thirty-ninth Street and Fifth Avenue, left, remained a single-family home, even as neighboring brownstones to the north were converted into stores and workshops. Note the advertisement for Knox Hats on the side of the tall building to the right. © Collection of The New-York Historical Society.

dollars which was kept it is said to give exercise room for a pet dog."[78] When the family finally did leave, they willed the property to a seminary in New Jersey (figures 2.6 and 2.7).[79] Just a few blocks south, B. Altman slowly assembled lots for his palatial department store, but one family resisted selling. Altman designed the building in a series of modular pieces so that once the family finally sold out, his department store could be completed with hardly a seam to reveal the struggle for space.[80]

Real estate developers in the 1920s and 1930s, determined to assemble large lots to create ever-taller and more massive commercial and office buildings, found them-

Fig. 2.7. The garden of Wendell House, at Fifth Avenue and Thirty-ninth Street, circa 1900. © Collection of The New-York Historical Society.

selves increasingly confounded by holdouts. In 1930, developer Irwin S. Chanin proposed that legislation be passed to prevent the "heartbreaking" collapse of building efforts when "one person . . . makes impossible an operation which would be a vast improvement economically."[81] Though New York had embraced zoning in 1916 and a range of new building codes in the 1920s, the "condemnation of property or private improvement" was indeed, as Chanin feared, seen as a "blow to our long-established conception of the sacredness of private property."[82]

Eventually most did yield to the pressures of encroachments and the enticements of increased property values. The *New York Times* reported in 1920, on the front page no less, that the Burton family had finally convinced a Miss Switzer to sell her home on Fifth Avenue between Thirty-eighth and Thirty-ninth—for nearly one million dollars. This sale gave the Burtons almost the entire lot, save for the Wendell House on the corner of Thirty-ninth. Switzer, a widow, had not been "in a selling mood." Perhaps influenced by her neighbors the Wendells, or perhaps wisely waiting for property values to jump even further, she held out until 1920.[83]

Some residents of Fifth Avenue were far more organized in their efforts, combining extensive land purchases with restrictive covenants to secure their neighborhood as an elite residential area. The Vanderbilts, for example, expended enormous amounts of money to retain the land around their several mansions between Fifty-first and Fifty-ninth Streets. The most dramatic example of their commitment to fighting the trend of business development along the Avenue occurred in 1902, when the Catholic Orphan Asylum, occupying the land from Fifty-first to Fifty-second Streets, was sold. After building had begun on an eighteen-story hotel planned for the site, William Kissam Vanderbilt bought the land and built instead what became known as the Marble Twins. Similarly, when the Langham Hotel came on the market, the Vanderbilts purchased it for $1.325 million and tore it down in order to sell the lot for private residences. Morton Plant was one resident whom the Vanderbilts were able to lure to the Avenue at a relatively late date, in 1902. Plant built a fine home, designed by Richard Morris Hunt, at Fifty-second Street. But from the start, Plant was skeptical: he insisted that the restrictive covenant on the property be limited to twenty-five years. In fact, he barely lasted fifteen years before, in 1916, he sold the property back to the Vanderbilts. In a clear admission of defeat, they leased it to Cartier, the jewelry concern in whose hands it remains today.[84]

The restrictive covenant was applied widely by Fifth Avenue magnates who sought to ensure that their land would remain residential indefinitely. Restrictive covenants, or deed restrictions, were one of the most common legal tools for controlling the use of property, utilized primarily by middle- and upper-class landowners to protect their property and to develop stable residential enclaves.[85] Because covenants usually stayed with the land—the restriction, for example, on building size bound future owners, not just the first to sign the deed—they had a wide appeal.[86] Their popularity throughout the country in the nineteenth and twentieth centuries came from their flexibility: restrictive covenants served the needs of builders of new towns (who used covenants as a form of zoning), small subdivision investors trying to attract wealthy clientele to a new development, and individual owners hoping to limit development around their homes. Indeed, the form of American cities, at least their outlying areas, is largely the product of sophisticated uses of restrictive covenants.[87] In New York, wealthy landowners and developers had long relied on covenants to control the use of their vast holdings on the island; and residential neighborhood developers utilized them to meet the demand for elite, secure neighborhoods in Lower Manhattan, such as St. John's Park (below Canal Street) and Gramercy Park.[88]

In the twentieth century restrictive covenants continued to be used liberally: well into the second decade of the twentieth century, most of upper Fifth Avenue was covered by restrictions. Aymar Embury, writing in the *Brickbuilder*, suggested that "a large part of it was restricted property, and the balance, because of the restrictions, appeared unlikely to become anything else but residential property."[89] Indeed, so rare were unencumbered plots of land—especially in the most desirable area between Forty-second and Fifty-ninth Streets—that the *New York Times* took note in 1908 of a sign at the corner of Fifty-third and Fifth: "For Sale, Without Restrictions."[90] It was the Vanderbilts, whose homes between Fifty-first and Fifty-ninth Streets demarcated the most fashionable section of Fifth Avenue from the end of the 1800s through the 1910s, who exploited the restrictive covenants to their hilt. William Kissam Vanderbilt, for instance, sold several plots of land he owned around his mansion—Plant's was one of these—with the stipulation that they remain residential for twenty-five years.[91] The real estate and architectural press regularly commented on the Vanderbilts' efforts to stem the tide of development. "That members of the Vanderbilt family have been able to preserve the neighborhood as a residence section," one writer commented, "is the most interesting part of the story."[92]

Rather than creating a cohesive residential neighborhood, however, the restrictive covenants more often than not simply stalled development. For despite their influence, the Vanderbilts were unable to sell their holdings to exclusively residential buyers. With families unwilling to challenge what they saw as the inevitable progression of business concerns along the Avenue, some vacant lots on the most exclusive Avenue in the world found no buyers. For example, A. T. Stewart's mansion at Thirty-fourth and Fifth, and the Paran Stevens plot at Thirty-seventh (later Tiffany's), sat on the market for several years as investors hesitantly counted the speculative possibilities.[93] As J. F. L. Collins guided his readers by the palaces of the wealthy in 1910, he skirted over the fact that even in the most desirable residential areas—at Seventy-second, Seventy-third, Seventy-seventh, and Eighty-first Streets—vacant lots dotted the Avenue.[94] Similarly, the Langham Hotel site lay vacant from 1902 until World War I, when it was sold and an eight-story loft building occupied by a dress factory concern was built, across from Plant's house.[95] The combination of a jewelry store and, even worse, a dress factory must have signaled the death knell for the Vanderbilts' efforts.

The postwar boom was launched in March 1920, when the Astor estate sold 141 parcels of land in Manhattan for over $5 million, in one of the most successful auctions in the history of the city. The usually sober *RERBG* allowed itself to be caught up in sentimental observance of the passing of an age. The income tax, economic conditions of wartime, and the postwar economic opportunity for development had "brought about the sale of many pieces of land and numerous buildings to the amazement of old New Yorkers, who would have taken an oath that certain well-known estates would remain intact until the end of time."[96] And indeed, there were other signs that the battle had been relinquished. Even before Cartier's arrival, the end of the Vanderbilt stronghold had been foreseen. The *RERBG* reported that the Vanderbilts' agreement to rescind their restrictive covenant on a site at Fifty-second and Fifth Avenue "must mean that they have agreed to abandon their opposition to the transformation of the district."[97] Although the Vanderbilts remained on the Avenue for more than a decade, the symbolic end of the old society arrived in 1924 when the grand mansion at Fifty-eighth and Fifth was torn down.

Few Fifth Avenue families had simply watched as their neighborhood changed. Their answer to the pressure of development was, finally, to join the real estate boom. In recognition of their impotence before real estate development and retail expansion, the families along the Avenue dove wholeheartedly into the development of upper Fifth Avenue, demolishing, selling, auctioning, and developing their plots, all to the awestruck observation of the press. Led by architect James Edwin Ruthven Carpenter, some of the most strident defenders of the mansion neighborhood now saw great profit in apartment buildings along Central Park and brought a lawsuit to overturn legislation restricting building heights there (fixing a weakness of the 1916 Zoning Resolution that had effectively allowed for the tallest of all buildings to be built opposite open space).[98] The legislation was overturned in 1924, fueling an almost instantaneous demolition spree, which brought down no less than twenty-six mansions above Fifty-ninth Street, most of which were replaced by apartment buildings.[99] For all the incredulity, New York's developers and architects were poised to take advantage of a new real estate boom and legal rulings—as well as a cultural acceptance of apartment living. As Elizabeth Hawes has argued, apartments became more attractive as the costs of maintaining a private house and the required servants escalated, country houses fulfilled the desire for private open space, and growing public forms of entertainment replaced the need for private ballrooms and massive dining rooms.[100]

The 1920s were simply a continuation of the building boom that had begun in the prewar years. In 1925 alone, fifty-three new buildings were completed on the Upper East Side and fifty-four were in progress. Architects like Carpenter, and McKim, Mead and White; real estate brokers like Douglas Elliman; and new developers like the upstart Benjamin Winter were ready and eager to exploit the possibilities of Fifth Avenue and the neighboring, and up-and-coming, Park Avenue.[101] In 1916, Carpenter himself had given a running start to the transformation of upper Fifth Avenue with his apartment building at 906 Fifth Avenue, which marked the first time a mansion was replaced by an apartment block. The lamentations for the noble past of Fifth Avenue on the editorial page of the *RERBG* were matched by reports of developers and architects eager to transform the Avenue.

The story of Fifth Avenue is clearly not simply one of a "march uptown" of the wealthy, of the laying out of permanent neighborhoods where tourists would come to gaze at America's wealth. Rather, incredibly destabilizing changes took place that even the wealthiest and most powerful families in America could not slow. The Vanderbilts, whose railroad lines had laid the foundations for western expansion, were virtually impotent before the attraction of profit in space that the land along Fifth Avenue offered. In the end, even the Vanderbilts could not hide from, nor could they prevent, the pressure of commercial expansion. Retail stores as well as hotels and offices crowded up the Avenue, taking over older homes and replacing them quickly with denser developments. While restrictive covenants could serve as the first of the modern tools of city planning, for the wealthy of Fifth Avenue they were a conservative strategy when only radical measures could succeed. Restrictive covenants were no longer powerful enough for the Vanderbilts, Astors, and Belmonts to achieve the spatial security they once enjoyed. In the end, the victor was the marketplace itself, the "compelling force" that few could accurately explain and fewer could control.

Nevertheless, if individual residents along Fifth Avenue could do little to stop development, a union of politically influential commercial investors and retailers could challenge the "compelling force." The robust real estate market, which threatened to coerce a retreat of all the elite homes and businesses, was finally shaped and stemmed by concerted political organization and advocacy. The lawsuits challenging height limitations had already indicated that, at least by the 1920s, some of Fifth Avenue's old families had learned more modern techniques of land control. But it was the retailers of Fifth Avenue who led the movement for shaping development along Fifth Avenue in a new direction—away from flight, restrictive covenants, and land acquisition and toward the new field of city planning. Just like the older residents, their goal was preservation of the unique characteristics of the Avenue. But they now defined those characteristics differently: they saw Fifth Avenue not as "Millionaire's Mile" but as America's Bond Street, the country's finest shopping boulevard.

What led to this new attitude toward the Avenue? What ideas animated the move toward insisting on uniform regulation of use and form along an avenue that had long been considered the forefront of Manhattan's celebrated private growth, a symbol of the force and prosperity inherent in unimpeded capitalist enterprise? Central to the effort was the creation of a new image of the Avenue, which portrayed it as an essential element in the economic health of the city. The link was explicitly made by Fifth Avenue's boosters between its physical appearance and desirability and its value to New York City's economy.

It was out of this extensive public discussion and image-making that the Fifth Avenue Association (FAA) articulated its message for "preserving" the Avenue and developed new methods for regulating space. The FAA translated the varied responses to Fifth Avenue's rapid transformation into public and private real estate intervention to mold and resist the changes along the Avenue. But a crucial shift was necessary: defenders of Fifth Avenue needed to persuade the city that Fifth Avenue required public intervention. They did so by constructing a new narrative of the Avenue's past and projected future that contributed to its prestige and economic value.

COMMERCE WITHOUT COMMERCIALISM: THE FIFTH AVENUE ASSOCIATION AND THE "CONSERVATION" OF THE AVENUE

William J. Pedrick of the FAA concluded his 1927 evaluation of "Fifth Avenue Today" by declaring the "sober truth" that "all things are in flux."[102] His dedication to the wisdom of the Greek philosopher Heraclitus notwithstanding, the opposite was in fact true. It had been the goal of the FAA since its founding in 1907 to ensure that all things, at least on Fifth Avenue, not be in flux. To do so, the association undertook an enormous range of activities, including legislative advocacy, policing the streets, awarding architectural honors, and placing traffic lights. It was instrumental in passing the 1916 Zoning Resolution, the first comprehensive zoning ordinance in America. The work of the FAA was aimed at solidifying Fifth Avenue in its present form as an elite residential and commercial area.

The Fifth Avenue Association was founded in April 1907 by a small group of property owners, residents, and retailers with the motto "to conserve at all times the highest and best interests of the Fifth Avenue section."[103] Always a voluntary organization, the FAA grew from a founding membership of 37 to 500 just three years later (in 1910) and reached membership as high as 1,000 in the 1950s.[104] While seemingly a simple property owners association organized to preserve the value of real estate investments, in fact a surprising number of the FAA members did not own property on Fifth Avenue.[105] In addition to real estate magnates Douglas and Lawrence Elliman,

FAA founding members included Rolan Knoedler, an art dealer; William Knabe, a maker of pianos; Simon Brentano, the publisher; and William Mitchell Kendall of the McKim, Mead and White architecture firm.[106] The actions of the FAA were motivated as much by enhancing the allure of the street for shoppers and retailers as to boosting property values for speculative investors.

The central idea behind the FAA's advocacy was to retain an exclusive retail and residential area, where immigrants would be scarce and beggars absent, where the more flamboyant popular culture growing on Broadway would be held in check, and where a genteel, controlled commercial culture would hold sway. Assimilation might have been the goal of some Progressives, and New York might have been known within the general culture increasingly as the place where cultures and peoples melded, but on Fifth Avenue the goal was always segregation and exclusion.

What made Fifth Avenue special—and eminently necessary to "conserve"—was that it remained somehow "uncommercial" even as it represented the pinnacle of the commercial culture. It represented a different idea of commerce, one that catered to a limited and exclusive clientele—as opposed to the bustling and diverse commerce of neighboring Broadway, where gaudy signs and lures of all types drew a heterogeneous mix of classes. Broadway and its entertainment arena at Times Square was based on a high quantity of business, but Fifth Avenue's elites preferred to seek out "quality." While Broadway and other commercial streets had become besieged with advertising, traffic, and the chaotic bustle of volume business, Fifth Avenue remained relatively serene. The Fifth Avenue Commission in 1912 stated the case clearly:

> If, however, our indifference to its appearance continues, we may expect that Fifth Avenue will cease to retain even its present commercial prominence but will become another and cheaper Broadway, with a garish electric sign display and other undesirable accompaniments.[107]

So, even as Fifth Avenue became the resting place of the most revered and expensive of the commercial culture's product, it somehow stood above it, thus adding to its allure. It was this delicate image that was threatened at the turn of the century, thus spurring the FAA reforms.

The FAA would not be the agent of some foreign, radical new future, but instead a logical instrument to strengthen and enhance the existing structure of the Avenue. Although the FAA would author some of the most far-reaching and momentous changes in urban land use controls, it never advertised its work in that way. Its goal, exemplified by its own historical narrative, was to freeze Fifth Avenue in a particular moment of economic organization. Ironically, then, Fifth Avenue would lead the economic prosperity of the city by moving in the opposite direction, away from unregulated loft and office development. Fifth Avenue's property values would be maintained now by regulating what was built and sold there.

The FAA succeeded where so many powerful individuals had failed. It managed to prevent the influx of manufacturing firms and stabilized the Avenue from Forty-second to Ninetieth Streets as the most valuable residential and commercial property in the city. To this day, Fifth Avenue in this stretch is the most expensive retail land in the world.[108] While remaining a private organization, the FAA was the primary motivating force behind some of the most important changes in civic land use and planning in the twentieth century: zoning to separate economic activities and land-use controls to shape the physical appearance of the city. While the 1916 Zoning Resolution remains the FAA's single most important accomplishment, its other semipublic activities at regulating the land along Fifth Avenue have equal relevance to cities today. As one of the first modern business improvement districts, it anticipated what has become a national trend: the private development and regulation of neighborhoods and even whole towns. Today, business improvement districts (BIDs) and private towns with elaborate aesthetic and land-use controls are increasingly the dominant forces in shaping manufactured and even natural landscapes.[109]

How was a private, voluntary organization able to gain such influence over the design and regulation of a district's development? First, the FAA built on the long-standing efforts of local owners and retailers to stem the change along the Avenue. But it did so in the only way possible—through concerted, unified action. The private efforts of the Vanderbilts, as we have seen, could only have limited effects, despite huge financial investments. Second, the FAA's unified effort was effective because it involved the city in regulating the Avenue's appearance and activities. Although it perpetuated an image of Fifth Avenue as the "natural" product of capitalist enterprise, the FAA skillfully utilized—and indeed supported—the expansion of municipal authority over the landscape. City intervention—through street widening, zoning laws, and policing—was essential to the successful "preservation" of Fifth Avenue as an elite neighborhood. Finally, the FAA managed to shape the understanding of Fifth Avenue's past development and thus powerfully influenced its future growth. The FAA was the most important recaller and inventor of Fifth Avenue's history, and hence did the most to secure Fifth Avenue's reputation as the premier address in the city and, perhaps, the world. In a process of capitalist urbanization where value of space was as much the product of cultural image as locational advantage, the FAA wrote the self-fulfilling prophecies of profit.

The FAA most powerfully shaped the narrative that would be used to justify new forms of regulation of urban space. For so many, telling the stories of Fifth Avenue—its rise, its morality, the social life of its inhabitants, its transformation—served important purposes, from evaluating the state of the city and nation to spurring investment and elevating property values. City builders of all types—city officials, real estate moguls, department store magnates—could all benefit from the touch of Fifth Avenue's magic.

Nevertheless, while a range of actors found reasons to relate the glorious history of Fifth Avenue, it was the Fifth Avenue Association that did the most to enshrine a particular tale of the Avenue's past: a rural street that grew rapidly and steadily—though certainly not chaotically—developing into the wealthiest residential neighborhood, and then gradually into an elite shopping area. Fifth Avenue was the inevitable product of America's and New York City's social progress and economic development. It was this story that was repeated in five-cent guidebooks, architectural journals, the *RERBG,* and city histories. Collective memory offered a tool to aid the "protectors" of Fifth Avenue in their quest to stop or slow the cycle of creative destruction along the Avenue. The FAA version of history prevailed because it was useful to a number of powerful interests. For real estate developers, businesspeople, and residents of Fifth Avenue, the FAA narrative perpetuated the image of the Avenue as the most desirable and valuable property on the island. The past invented and elaborated by the FAA was only a prologue to its present greatness. Memories of the genteel country road, or even of the brownstones and marble mansions gone by the 1920s, were primarily useful because they served as foils to the present, as a measuring stick for all that had been and would continue to be accomplished. Collective memories of the Avenue were written and retold to "remind" New Yorkers of the glory of their city's growth and to demonstrate their responsibility in preserving its prosperity. The FAA in essence "codified" New York's memory of Fifth Avenue through its annual reports, anniversary books (especially those in 1924 and 1927, and later in 1957), pageants, and essay contests for schoolchildren. Ironically, then, in the hands of the FAA and others, collective memories served as instruments for slowing or stopping history, freezing Fifth Avenue in a particularly profitable form (figure 2.8).

Perhaps the most important part of this narrative is its ending: in order to "preserve" the Avenue at its height, the FAA needed to make its own increasingly interventionist work part of the story. In a form not unlike Puritan jeremiads, the FAA articulated a crisis narrative in which they portrayed themselves as the saviors of a Fifth Avenue threatened with physical and social destruction. The danger was the future: ominous trends—especially the "invasion" of manufacturing lofts and their immigrant workers, increased traffic, beggars and peddlers—portended a downward spiral in the prestige and allure of Fifth Avenue.

The FAA, it should be clear, was not a bastion of antiquarianism, urging—like some preservation advocates—that New York simply hold onto the past. The problem, as it would be for slum clearance advocates and historic preservationists, lay primarily in "managing" creative destruction. The FAA ardently sought to prevent certain types of destruction while encouraging others. Thus, height rules were meant to preserve upper Fifth Avenue (above Fifty-ninth Street, along Central Park) as an elite row of mansions and low apartment buildings. At the same time, the FAA long advocated street widening, which required extensive destruction of stoops and front yards and walls. The association was happy for taller buildings (except lofts) to replace rows of dull brownstones. Thus, even as the FAA "resisted" the course of creative destruction, it learned how to manipulate it to achieve its own ends.

The work of the FAA was thus as oriented toward luring and keeping the elite shopping clientele as it was in raising property values. The association began its work with rather limited campaigns to enhance the appearance and experience of Fifth Avenue. At its first meeting in April 1907, the FAA declared its goals to be the "betterment of trade and traffic conditions on the Avenue by taking up for instance questions relating to heavy trucking, garbage disposal, public nuisances, the proposed widening of the Avenue etc. etc."[110] While ultimately the FAA was best known for its virtual authorship of the 1916 Zoning Resolution, what has been lost in the focus on zoning is another aspect of the FAA's work, an aspect that in present-day New York and other cities may be more relevant. Most of the FAA's energy, even after the passage of the Zoning Act, was occupied with an extensive array of landscape-policing functions that quietly but powerfully shaped the form and activities of Fifth Avenue. Just as the Charity Organization Society's Tenement House Committee served for years as a semi-official city housing agency, the Fifth Avenue Association was, for the "Fifth Avenue section" (comprising Fifth to Madison Avenues and all cross streets), the police and traffic departments, the public art commission, and the city-planning commission. Through its office, which served as a members' clearinghouse for information and assistance, and aided by a variety of ordinances passed on its behalf, the FAA restricted the types of traffic on the Avenue, forcibly removed beggars and peddlers, eliminated certain types of signs, and influenced the architectural design of new buildings.[111]

First and foremost was the regulation of traffic, human and vehicular. The attempts

Fig. 2.8. Advertisement for the Fifth Avenue Coach Company from Henry Collins Brown, *Fifth Avenue, Old and New, 1824–1924* (Fifth Avenue Association, 1924). Physical destruction and rebuilding is naturalized in this striking image of Father Time gently substituting tall office buildings for the nineteenth-century brownstones that had dominated Fifth Avenue. United States History, Local History & Genealogy Division, The New York Public Library, Astor, Lenox and Tilden Foundations.

to address the continued problem of traffic congestion in the city had been unsuccessful.[112] As the new century began, the city launched a more interventionist program of street widening along Fifth Avenue. The FAA wholeheartedly supported the
effort and continually urged that the city proceed further up the Avenue.[113] The
widening—which gave the Avenue thirty extra pedestrian and vehicular feet—helped
in the short run, but as business increased on the Avenue, the problems persisted (see
figure 2.3). In its first two decades, the FAA advocated a number of restrictions on
vehicular traffic—for example, restricting the number of cabs and delivery trucks and
the times of use for those vehicles. In 1922, in a much heralded action, the FAA placed
elaborate traffic towers at key intersections to relieve the worsening congestion.[114] Although progressive in their engineering, the traffic towers suggested the more reac-
tionary goals of the FAA: to preserve a slower-paced retail and residential corridor.

The FAA was equally concerned with the quality of traffic. It was far more forgiv-
ing of private cars than of delivery trucks heading downtown. And it was, of course,
far more receptive to crowds of wealthy women shoppers than the peddlers and beggars who gravitated to the Avenue for sales and donations. Lamenting the "growing in-
convenience caused by the great numbers of pedlers [*sic*] and beggars now infesting
Fifth Avenue at all hours of the day and night," the FAA suggested that "further active
steps be taken to rid the Avenue of this growing nuisance."[115] Parades represented a different but equally noxious type of traffic. Though the Fifth Avenue parade would come
to be an important Avenue and New York tradition, the FAA complained in the first
decades of the century about "indiscriminate use of Fifth Avenue for street parades"
that result in "a very serious loss of business to merchants along that thoroughfare,
without any real compensating gain to the public." In a letter to Mayor William Gaynor
in 1912, the FAA wrote that it was "absolutely opposed to the indiscriminate use of
Fifth Avenue, between Twenty-third and Fifty-ninth Streets for parading purposes":

> We object to all parades except patriotic and civic parades and parades in general on
> holidays or at night and the disastrous affect on business at other times makes it imper-
> ative that this protest be made. The loss to merchants during the year is enormous, ac-
> counting to millions of dollars, and we respectfully request that all other than patriotic
> and civic parades except on holidays or at night be directed to other thoroughfares.[116]

Thus, even as the painter Childe Hassam was memorializing the Fifth Avenue parade
as an icon in American life, the FAA was fighting to eliminate parades in general.

Similarly conservative goals were established for the architectural form of the Avenue. From its founding the FAA was obsessed with regulating the visual landscape of
Fifth Avenue. It was the appearance of Fifth Avenue as much as the actual activities that

took place behind the walls of brownstone (and increasingly steel) that gave it its character, its sheen of wealth and exclusivity. As a virtual outdoor museum of residential, institutional, and commercial architecture created by the day's finest architects, Fifth Avenue represented to elite New Yorkers the last and best hope for securing a grand Beaux Arts avenue, worthy of New York's prominent place in the pantheon of world cities.

Despite the praise heaped on Fifth Avenue for its magnificent growth and its stunning private residences, however, there was a nagging sense of dissatisfaction among city builders. By the second decade of the twentieth century, it seemed clear to city builders that New Yorkers were unwilling or unable to redesign the street structure of Manhattan—as had been done in Paris, and had been proposed by Daniel Burnham for Chicago and San Francisco. The Municipal Art Society's (MAS's) plans for a Beaux Arts planned city inspired by Paris had come to nothing. The 1904 City Improvement Commission report, which the MAS had inspired, followed by a 1907 plan, produced little in the way of monuments and boulevards that would transform New York's regimented grid into an efficient and elegant metropolis. The FAA, along with the MAS and other civic organizations dedicated to beautifying the city, turned its attention to shaping the basic design of private buildings along the Avenue.[117] In just its third year, the FAA made clear that its primary architectural goal for the Avenue was

> the beauty of the Avenue as a whole, rather than the beauty of each particular building, important though the latter be. The development of Fifth Avenue along the lines of beauty is largely a matter of the willingness of architect and owner to sacrifice their own interest for the benefit of the whole—in other words to erect buildings which will contribute to the beauty of the Avenue in its ensemble, and not with the purpose solely of making conspicuous their own establishment . . . there must be a certain amount of self sacrifice to bring about a generally satisfactory effect.[118]

The FAA hoped to avoid on the upper half of the Avenue the "jumble of buildings of greatly varying height and greatly varying color, without really any consideration of neighboring construction."[119] The Fifth Avenue Commission lamented the fact that "a noble approach to our finest Park and a real parkway has been permitted so to degenerate that we must abandon for the time being at least, all thought of making it the counterpart of any of the splendid avenues of Paris or other great cities abroad. Yet while the time has gone by for such a hope, we may nevertheless . . . still make of Fifth Avenue a dignified street . . . it need not be without impressive features."[120] The FAA was never able to legally enforce design restrictions, but its architectural committee regularly evaluated new building plans and planned changes to the Avenue's buildings.[121]

Because the FAA believed that one way to make existing and future buildings and stores more "dignified" was to prevent the proliferation of signs, it was vigilant in regulating and even outlawing certain types of signage. It fought against signs oriented perpendicular to the street, against lighted signs, and, most of all, "for sale" signs.[122] As early as 1910, it passed a resolution protesting the use of "unsightly" electric signs on Fifth Avenue as against the "best interests of the public. . . . [T]his Association disapproves of the construction and maintenance of unsightly electric, gas, advertising signs, or signs of any other character, on the roofs, or against the walls, or affixed to any part of the premises of buildings on Fifth Avenue. . . . That such signs, because of their appearance, use or operation, are inartistic and unsuitable, and are inimical to the best interests of the public, and to the property owners, as well as to the merchants, residents, and to others who make use of said Avenue."[123] The FAA was not utterly opposed to the new technologies of advertising. The month after declaring its commitment to the "abatement and abolishment of such sign displays" in 1910, the association initiated a series of tests of new methods of shop-window lighting; the following month, the FAA invited a lighting expert to talk about it.[124] For the FAA, these parallel pursuits were not contradictory: there was a fundamental difference between the tasteful illumination of a respectable store's wares for passing pedestrians, and the garish, large-scale lighting displays designed simply to lure shoppers. So, just as Broadway was gaining its fame as the "Great White Way" from its thousands of lights from theaters and advertisements, Fifth Avenue was succeeding in eliminating such displays.

For the first fourteen years of its existence, the FAA operated by means of informal pressure to ensure that sign styles met its approval. But under its urging, in December 1921, the mayor approved a new sign ordinance designed to eliminate virtually all illuminated signs on the Avenue. While a number of merchants protested and even legally challenged the ordinance, it ultimately prevailed. The FAA insisted that even the objectors ended up supporting the ordinance: "The removal of their own signs convinced them no harm to their business followed and that the value of the property was actually enhanced." After writing the ordinance, the FAA then took it upon itself to serve as regulatory agency, undertaking "continual and regular inspections" to ferret out "all unsightly and illegal signs." Using the political and economic prestige of its membership, the FAA sought to eliminate "obnoxious" signs from the sides and roofs of Fifth Avenue buildings. For example, a building at Fifth Avenue and Forty-second Street that sold roof space for advertisers was a particular annoyance for the FAA. Approaching the advertisers as opposed to the owner, the FAA sought and received "voluntary" commitments to "cancel their contracts upon the expiration of their leases." [125]

The FAA found early on in its life that efforts at cajoling and admonishing property owners and retailers to maintain the look and dignity of Fifth Avenue would be
ineffective against the far larger forces shaping the Avenue. The fast and radical
changes of Fifth Avenue did not go unnoticed. The FAA secretary noted in the minutes to only the third meeting that the FAA would be meeting at the Holland Hotel
(at Fifth Avenue and Thirtieth Street) because its previous meeting place, the infamous Fifth Avenue Hotel (at Fifth and Twenty-third) had been demolished.[126]
Though the FAA would never give up its more genteel efforts to shape the Avenue,
the leaders of the organization quickly realized that the forces of creative destruction
would require stronger interventionist efforts.

ZONING THE AVENUE, ZONING NEW YORK

Only a few years after it was formed, the FAA recognized that it had to be more than a
beautification agency if it wished to accomplish its goals of protecting the Avenue as an
elite retail and residential area. If the FAA began as a nineteenth-century "beautification" organization, it soon became something far more radical and far-reaching. The association's concerted lobbying bore fruit in 1916, when the first comprehensive zoning
law was passed.[127] This single law forever changed how cities would be built; governmental regulation of development now became a dominant force in shaping the form
of the city. The FAA, however, was the key force in bringing the zoning movement to
fruition in 1916. Without overstating the case, it should be clear that a private organization, advocating primarily the interests of a very particular section of the city, is behind the national movement for citywide zoning. In the name of "preserving" a place
with a particular meaning, a perceived social significance, and a distinct, measurable economic value, the FAA proposed to transform city policy concerning urban space.

The 1916 Zoning Resolution was surely "overdetermined": for years, a wide
range of citizen groups and politicians had been urging the city to intervene more
significantly to address the problems of light and air, traffic, and aesthetic monstrosi-
ties. Although historical accounts traditionally begin with the conflict over the Equitable Building in Lower Manhattan, it was a series of developments that provided the
political and intellectual setting for zoning. Though it would take years for city and
regional planning to take hold—many would say it never did—a number of factors
set the stage early in the century for zoning: the writings of key figures in city planning (George Ford, Edward Bassett, Nelson Lewis, Benjamin Marsh) that placed comprehensive city planning on the forefront of policy discussions; a strong borough president (George McAneny, 1910–13),[128] a firm and active believer in the ideas of the

nascent planning movement; a number of massive public works projects (bridges, subways, street widenings) that suggested the need and possibility of citywide planning; the 1912 excess law (to be discussed further in chapter 3) that allowed for larger government building projects; and, finally, a series of precedents in other cities that inspired zoning and height limitations in New York.[129]

Nevertheless, the efforts of the FAA—which had begun long before the Equitable Building went up and down—were decisive in passing the 1916 Zoning Resolution. Though adherents to the nascent city-planning movement had for years before the zoning ordinance been agitating for land-use controls—including height limitations and use-segregation—it was only when the FAA pushed for the creation of a quasi-governmental Fifth Avenue Commission that these ideas were brought to the forefront of public debate. The FAA viewed the rapid rebuilding along the Avenue as both a grave threat and a rare opportunity to firmly establish Fifth Avenue; failure to act would mean disaster. "There is probably no street or avenue in this great city to which the question of height limitation is of as much importance as Fifth Avenue," the FAA declared,

> no district whose interests and character are as much affected by it as the Fifth Avenue district. It is now, and for some years to come will be, in a constant, seething turmoil of tearing down and rebuilding, and it is safe to say that a few years from now, with perhaps a few exceptional houses, the busy section of Fifth Avenue will be composed entirely of new buildings.[130]

In their aggressive campaign for height limitations and ultimately citywide zoning, various members of the FAA appealed to the Commission on Building Heights with dramatic statements of the future of Fifth Avenue. Robert Grier Cooke, the founder and long-time president of the FAA, stated simply that without height limitations, "It is not too much to say that the very existence of the Avenue, as New York residents have known it for many years, is threatened."[131] Frank Veiller, a member of the FAA, declared that without legislation halting the increase of loft buildings on the Avenue, "Fifth Avenue, as now known, will be lost to this city forever."[132]

The FAA had begun its efforts to involve city government with its campaigns for street widening and signage regulations. But it took its advocacy for the Avenue further when it successfully lobbied McAneny to establish a Fifth Avenue Commission expressly to deal with the problems faced by Fifth Avenue residents and retailers. The commission, meeting in 1912 and 1913, produced an ordinance proposal on limiting heights, but the Board of Aldermen ultimately rejected it. However, the ideas put forth in the Fifth Avenue Commission were elaborated on a citywide basis in the new

Heights of Buildings Commission, formed in 1913. This commission was accompanied by the Commission on Building Districts and Restrictions, and in 1914 the standing Committee on the City Plan. It was the Commission on Building Districts and Restrictions that ultimately, in 1916, produced its report advocating comprehensive use and building height and mass limitations for New York City.

The focus of the work of these commissions, and of the 1916 Zoning Resolution, was strongly shaped by the vision of the FAA for the Avenue and its surrounding elite district. In specific instances, the Avenue was given special treatment by the commissioners. For example, virtually all of Manhattan below Central Park was divided into zones in which buildings could rise to one and one-half or two times the width of a street—except for Fifth Avenue between Thirty-fourth and Fifty-ninth Streets, where the FAA managed to procure the lowest of all ratios: buildings could rise no more than one and one-quarter times the width of the street.[133] Many in the FAA leadership had sought even lower height limitations but were satisfied to have at least secured this victory. But in far more fundamental ways, the whole focus of the commissions—on segregating residential and industrial areas, on limiting heights, on creating a stable real estate market—was shaped by the FAA's own interests.

While the FAA's program of activities was broad and wide—ranging from street tree planting to fighting the proliferation of signs—the association's most far-reaching goal was to stop the construction of loft manufacturing buildings on the Avenue. These lofts had already been built up in the lower part of the Avenue—between Fourteenth and Twenty-third Streets and even around Washington Square. Indeed, the Triangle Shirtwaist Factory, whose devastating fire of 1911 inspired labor reforms and transformed New York City politics, was a classic loft building, located almost on the site where Henry James grew up. The FAA used the fire as a springboard for its campaign to regulate and ultimately eliminate loft buildings from the Avenue.[134]

The FAA's greatest impact on New York (and on other cities) came from its advocacy of height limitations and segregation of uses, which grew from its disgust with the loft structures. In a long statement to the Fifth Avenue Commission in 1913, the FAA's lawyer, Bruce Falconer, argues that lofts "have practically ruined that part of the Avenue" between Fourteenth and Twenty-third Streets. They "have utterly changed its former high-class character, and have had a derogatory effect upon the entire neighborhood":

> These buildings are crowded with their hundreds and thousands of garment workers and operators who swarm down upon the Avenue for the lunch hour between twelve and one o'clock. They stand upon or move slowly along the sidewalks and choke them up. Pedestrians thread their way through the crowds as best they may.

The influx of immigrant workers, claims Falconer, had frightened away women shop-pers, depressed property values, and encouraged an exodus of "high-class shops and stores."[135] As always, the FAA saw its work in terms of preservation: steps had to be taken to protect Fifth Avenue "from the loft building and factory employee menace."[136]

The primary reason the FAA fought so fiercely against the expansion of loft build-ings on the Avenue was the immigrant domination of the factory workforce. Like its campaign against beggars, the FAA was concerned about maintaining the "quality" of people inhabiting and using the Avenue. At first the FAA used the tactics it had used with beggars—forcibly removing them. With the encouragement of the FAA, police arrested lunching garment workers for loitering on the Avenue. When that provoked outrage from the mayor, the FAA resorted to an education campaign: plac-ards in several languages explained to the workers the detriment to all of loitering and spitting tobacco juice.[137]

The FAA held numerous meetings to seek a private solution to the problem of immigrant workers crowding the Avenue. In February 1911, for example, the FAA's "Loitering Committee" met with the Cloak and Suit Workers Union in order to ne-gotiate "the problem of control of the crowds" and discuss the possibility of "roping off sections" of side streets for the workers.[138] At the same time, it met repeatedly with the owners' Cloak and Suit Manufacturers Association to discuss how to control the workers.[139] Thus, even amid the effort to seek the intervention of the city in re-stricting building heights and uses, the FAA was equally persistent in applying its eco-nomic and social influence to protect the Avenue.

If the fear of immigrant "hordes" ruining the high-class atmosphere of Fifth Av-enue was foremost in the minds of the FAA, this concern pointed to other, even larger dangers. The FAA saw in the orgy of loft construction a debilitating set of changes taking place in the social and physical appearance of the Avenue. Loft construction was particularly volatile: the buildings were often cheap, built rapidly, and financially inse-cure because of the unstable nature of the garment industry. When they were vacated, often within a few years of construction, the loft buildings could not be easily con-verted to other uses. Narrow and tall with long, dark interiors, usually built upon one or two twenty-five-foot lots previously occupied by brownstones, the buildings were appropriate only for factories or cheap business ventures. The presence of single, ten-story towers on narrow lots was an ironic product of Fifth Avenue's tradition as the brownstone and marble mansion home to New York's elite families. With city taxes calculated to the full market value of the site, a brownstone lot was "worth" a phe-nomenal sum if, as tax policy assumed, the owner could develop his or her land to its fullest extent.[140] But because Fifth Avenue's property was largely held in small parcels by individual landowners—many of whom were willing to "hold out" for years—developers could rarely assemble large lots. Thus, as individual families sold off their brownstones, developers quickly put up individual loft buildings to accommodate burgeoning garment-related industries. Whether by individual homeowners or by the FAA, "preservation" of Fifth Avenue as it was defied the logic of creative destruction.

The 1916 Zoning Resolution was not, in the end, a radical measure; it was only revolutionary through its influence on other cities and as the precedent for future city-planning efforts. The ordinance accelerated the demolition of Fifth Avenue's nineteenth-century past by creating an ordered framework in which developers and architects could develop and redevelop the Avenue. Had a more laissez-faire system of real estate prevailed, Fifth Avenue might have become a permanent center for the garment manufacturers and other small businesses, up to and even beyond Central Park. The problems that can be seen in J. F. L. Collins's photos, if not in his text, were the result of an unregulated market for land along the Avenue.

But not all of this can be attributed to the 1916 Zoning Resolution. The ordinance, we must remember, was not retroactive. The loft buildings and empty lots, the garish signs and "dull" brownstones, would not rapidly be removed like the massive urban renewal efforts later in the century. The grand schemes of the FAA had never worked: plans of bridges over Forty-second Street and a diagonal avenue connecting Pennsylvania Station and the public library at Forty-second Street were quickly removed from the table. The 1916 Zoning Resolution shifted the trajectory of private development along the Avenue, but almost immediately after it was passed, the FAA and its supporters recognized that its first strategies—of private pressure of landowners and businesses—would be even more important in the future. Even as the Zoning Resolution was being debated in 1916, the FAA and other groups—including the City Club—launched the "Save New York" campaign designed to force existing garment manufacturers off Fifth Avenue. The "removal of the menace" would occupy these groups well into the 1920s, when—backed by the limited new powers of state regulation and the less limited powers of capital—the Save New York campaign successfully managed to relocate the garment industry to Seventh Avenue, where much of it remains today.[141]

CONCLUSION: THE PROGRESS OF PRESERVATION

Helen Henderson's *Loiterer in the City* (1917) opens with a photograph of the Plaza Hotel at the southwest corner of Central Park. In the background is Cornelius Vanderbilt's mansion; in the foreground is the Pulitzer Fountain, which Henderson calls the "Fountain of Abundance." It is a revealing name. For many this was a suitable metaphor: Fifth Avenue was a physical manifestation of the American economic abundance. The wealth of the nation had not gushed forth randomly, but instead had been channeled almost naturally to the "spine of Gotham," where it was transformed into the grandest buildings America had yet seen, of which the Plaza and Vanderbilt's colossal mansion were two of the greatest.

Fifth Avenue's development, however, was hardly fluid. Fifth Avenue was indeed a symbol of the process of private city-building efforts; it was also a model of private and public intervention in shaping the urban landscape. But it did not grow easily, steadily, and by some natural physical laws. Rather, Fifth Avenue mimicked the fitful and chaotic creation and destruction that characterized the city as a whole, and it proved that government involvement would be necessary to manage the abundant flow.

It was the FAA that most powerfully shaped at least part of the Avenue's future. It did this by pioneering far-reaching reforms all in the name of "conserving" Fifth Avenue's economic and cultural achievements. The choice of this term—repeated on the front page of each annual report of the organization—is not simply linguistic irony. The FAA certainly was not primarily interested in historic preservation. Indeed, it encouraged height limitations in part to prevent skyscrapers and pushed for the rapid removal of "antiquated structures" that marred the "new Fifth Avenue."[142] Nevertheless, debate over Fifth Avenue's future centered around the issue of preservation, although the meaning of that term constantly shifted. The FAA primarily sought to bolster property values by preserving the physical appearance and economic uses of the Avenue. However, it often embraced the destruction of older buildings in order to literally pave the way for more efficient traffic conditions and expand the area of development. Others, such as the "loitering" Helen Henderson, expressed a sentimental attachment to a past that was quickly receding from view. "Assuredly," Henderson remarked about the sight of the decrepit homes of Theodore Roosevelt, William Cullen Bryant, and the Metropolitan Museum, "oblivion is better than this."[143] For her, the preservation of the old homes would mean the preservation of the values that once held sway along the Avenue.

The recurrent question of Fifth Avenue's future development in the first decades of the twentieth century forces a reconsideration of what was meant by preservation and modernization, development and destruction. For Fifth Avenue had few historic buildings to preserve. Only below Fourteenth Street were there old homes that could be considered "historic." Indeed, as Reynolds wrote in 1916, Fifth Avenue "represents construction more than reconstruction and as yet it has not many memories."[144] And yet, the Fifth Avenue of this era is, ironically, a preservation story. Like historic preservationists who sought to protect historic buildings, the FAA and others desperately sought to "preserve" Fifth Avenue, and they couched their struggle in those terms.

One of the tropes that powerfully describes New York to its own citizens and defines it for the rest of the world, even to this day, is the "city of extremes." While writers and guidebooks falsely elaborated an overly stark social polarization of New York life between "sunshine and shadow," their metaphor was accurate in its suggestion that Fifth Avenue and the slums of the Lower East Side were part of the same economic process, as inextricably linked as the sun and its shadow. For just as the Lower East Side and its "foul core" of slums had been created by the workings of speculative markets, so too was Fifth Avenue the product of real estate trading, building, demolishing, and rebuilding. But Fifth Avenue revealed the problems of overdevelopment and excessively rapid change, while the slums of the Lower East Side exposed the opposite dilemma of underdevelopment and sluggish rates of destruction and rebuilding. It was a remarkable irony that in the land of shadows, where life seemed to be dangling by a thin thread, the actual persistence of buildings was greater than in the august reaches of Fifth Avenue. The infuriating endurance of Mulberry's slums inspired reformers and city officials to intervene in the real estate market and accelerate the process of creative destruction.

3

THE "FOUL CORE" OF NEW YORK

The Rise of Slum Clearance as Housing Reform

> Where Mulberry Street crooks like an elbow . . . is "the Bend," the foul core of New York's slums.
>
> —Jacob A. Riis, *How the Other Half Lives: Studies Among the Tenements of New York*

> . . . when you operate in an overbuilt metropolis, you have to hack your way with a meat ax.
>
> —Robert Moses, *Public Works: A Dangerous Trade*

Joseph Mitchell, the *New Yorker*'s inveterate observer of the city's characters and cultures for half a century, explored the endless subworlds of New York. In the early 1950s, as he describes in *The Bottom of the Harbor,* Mitchell encountered lobster fishermen and oyster hunters, the few remaining citizens who could recall a time when New York was built on the work of its harbor industries. Mitchell's story is tinged with regret for this passing world, of marshes filled in for sports fields or for airports, of docks and piers removed for highways.

Then there were the tenements of the "Lung Block" (so called because of the prevalence of tuberculosis among the inhabitants) by the East River. This block stood on the city's notorious Lower East Side, where Knickerbocker Village, one of New York's first public housing efforts, now stands (figure 3.3). "There are bricks and brownstone blocks and plaster and broken glass from hundreds upon hundreds of condemned tenements in the New Grounds," observes Mitchell:

> The ruins of the somber old red-brick houses in the Lung Block, which were torn down to make way for Knickerbocker Village, lie there. In the first half of the nineteenth century, these houses were occupied by well-to-do families; from around 1890 until around 1905 until they were torn down, in 1933, they were rented to the poorest of the poor, and the tuberculosis death rate was higher in that block than in any other block in the city. All the organisms that grow on wrecks grow on the hills of rubble and rubbish in the Subway Rocks and the New Grounds.[1]

Fig. 3.1. Jacob Riis, *The Mulberry Bend,* circa 1890. Museum of the City of New York, The Jacob A. Riis Collection.

Fig. 3.2. *(inset)* Jacob Riis, *Mulberry Bend, Park,* 1919. Museum of the City of New York, The Jacob A. Riis Collection.

The tenements, the purveyors of disease, were ripped down in a burst of government initiative, carted off to the Brooklyn coast and deposited on the shore. And like the ideal prison inmate, resolved to truly reform his ways, those tenements were serving their time well: The minerals in the old brownstone and brick, so condemned as sponges of disease, became blocks of nutrients for sea animals starving in the polluted harbor of New York. The tenements that brought so much sickness and death now offered new life to the sea.

The life of the Lung Block slums on the East Side is a wonderful image for understanding the politics of slum clearance in New York City. It suggests the dialectic between creation and destruction that animated efforts to reform housing conditions among New York's poor. Two opposite impulses have motivated different schools of "reformers" over the past century and a half. First is the impulse to provide better conditions for the worst-off citizens, by improving their physical environment, amenities, or services available to them. The second is the impulse to destroy what is "unhealthy" in the city, as a surgeon would eliminate a diseased part of the body in the interest of protecting the whole. These competing ideologies are manifested most clearly in the struggles over the neighborhoods of New York's Lower East Side.

Throughout the nineteenth century, the "creative" impulse dominated, as intellectuals and activists alike dreamed of ways to make city life more pleasant and healthy for all its residents. But by the end of the nineteenth century, the ramshackle wooden and brick tenements of the Lung Block began to be seen as spawning grounds for disease, vice, and social unrest. A generation of housing reformers began to advocate their elimination—by the slow and haphazard collective acts of a thousand real estate developers and the rapid machinery of government bulldozers—as the ultimate creative act. As surely as bad housing for the poor would destroy individual lives and corrupt the entire city, so would parks and a wholly different kind of housing redeem Manhattan. This focus on destruction as the goal would have grave repercussions for the future of New York City. The policies begun in the late nineteenth century shaped urban development politics and policy for the next hundred years.

This chapter traces the rise of the idea of slum clearance, from its haphazard beginnings at Mulberry Bend in the notorious Lower East Side "Five Points"—named for the intersection of five streets: Mulberry, Anthony (now Worth), Cross (now Park), Orange (now Baxter), and Little Water (which no longer exists)—to the beginning of the 1930s when the New Deal institutionalized programs of large-scale slum elimination and public housing construction. Over the first three decades of the twentieth century, New York pioneered not only institutional and public policy strategies that would pave the way for massive federal public housing and clearance programs,

but also the intellectual framework and cultural attitudes that were crucial to supporting an ethic of demolition. By the 1950s, New York had embraced an ethic of slum removal, under the leadership of Robert Moses, and had become a leader in urban renewal politics and techniques. Understanding the roots of this ideology, and the motivation of the government and private-sector elites who spearheaded it, is crucial to any evaluation of urban development in the twentieth century.

This chapter therefore describes the precedents to the massive slum clearance efforts of the 1930s and the even more extensive urban renewal efforts of the 1950s. Those efforts made up what one historian has called the "most important public policy undertaken by New York after World War II."[2] Despite the extensive literature on housing and housing reform in the United States and especially New York City, historians have never fully explained the intellectual and cultural dynamic that provided justification—and celebration—of an ethic of tenement destruction. Perhaps we have

Fig. 3.3. Cherry and Monroe Streets, 1932. In one of the earliest slum clearance efforts, this block was torn down to make way for Knickerbocker Village. Along Cherry Street are the early-nineteenth-century townhouses that Berenice Abbott would photograph in anticipation of their demise. Collections of the Municipal Archives of the City of New York.

too easily believed the assumption of some reformers that the removal of tenements
was an inevitable solution to the tenement house problem—that no matter what else
was tried, destruction was an ultimate step. Or perhaps the early history of urban renewal has seemed unconnected to later, larger-scale efforts. In standard histories of
housing, the roots of slum clearance are treated only tangentially and parenthetically,
as if the New Deal public housing and urban planning initiatives were a brand-new
strategy. In most accounts, slum clearance seems to emerge from nowhere, a radical
new reaction to problems that had long existed.[3]

In fact, the "tenement problem" had been debated since the early nineteenth century. The rhetorical exhortations of moral guardians at that time had brought piecemeal
housing regulations and moderate suggestions for model low-income housing. But in
the late nineteenth and early twentieth centuries, these efforts were supplanted by a far
more radical suggestion: the elimination of tenements by demolition. How did the
early-nineteenth-century reformer, who walked the streets, climbed the tenements,
and worked slowly to provide the slums with running water and parks give way to the
blunt vocabulary of the wrecking ball and bulldozer? How did the social reformer who
zealously explored the "shadows" of New York, returning from the "foul core" to appeal for tenement regulations, yield to planners who sat in a room with an aerial map
and felt-tipped pens, circling neighborhoods and labeling them "slum clearance"?

Slum clearance marked a sharp break with past practice and ideology. The twin
pillars of nineteenth-century housing reform were the inviolability of private property and limited government action. Slum clearance challenged both of these: it required that the government expend great amounts of money to remove the unacceptable products of a private real estate market. As a radical challenge to the status
quo of housing reform, the ideology of slum clearance becomes a far more complex story, revealing the fault lines in the beliefs of elite New Yorkers regarding the
role of public and private actors, the awkward adolescence of city government, and
powerful cultural dilemmas concerning the diversity of the modern city, all played
out over these vilified buildings.

The story has an ironic twist. Despite all the hand-wringing over the horrible
conditions of the tenements and the viciousness with which they were attacked by
almost everyone, the level of planned slum clearance was actually extremely small
until the 1930s. New York may have been known as the city that tore itself down
every ten years—more so even than Chicago, the true "phoenix" city that rebuilt itself out of the ashes of the 1871 fire—but when it came to the tenements it hated,
it hesitated and failed to act. Despite decades of acknowledgment of the problem,
destruction did not become the dominant method of coping with substandard hous-

ing until the 1930s. Thus, our story is as much about failure: Why did destruction of tenements take hold so late despite powerful political advocates and weighty European examples? What ideologies and cultural patterns encouraged elites—both governmental and private—to change course and begin a pattern of large-scale demolition of city neighborhoods?

Ironically, the impetus for this new paragon of urban development—the destructive model—had its roots not in change but in stasis. To Progressive reformers, slum clearance began to seem necessary because the Lower East Side had changed at a slower pace than other parts of the city. If Fifth Avenue epitomized the dangers and the destructive effects (in the eyes of some residents and retailers) of overdevelopment, the story of Mulberry Bend and the Lower East Side's slums was one of "underdevelopment." For a host of reasons, the area was consistently unattractive to private developers and remained, to the chagrin of reformers, a neighborhood of deteriorating housing. The history of slum clearance is therefore the mirror image of development along Fifth Avenue. While Fifth Avenue was wrestling with questions of preservation and neighborhood character, in the Lower East Side private developers were urged and government was employed to speed up the process of destruction for eventual rebuilding. Along Fifth Avenue, retailers and homeowners, with the aid of government, had sought to slow or even freeze development. In the Lower East Side, a frustration with the lack of change became fuel for the engine of creative destruction.

JACOB RIIS AND THE "LEPROUS HOUSES" OF MULBERRY BEND

If buildings could remember, the oldest tenement in New York would bear the memories of social reformers' passionate attacks. New York invented the tenement in the United States. Not long afterward, New York also originated the idea of a tenement house "problem" and then the tenement house reformer. The "old-law" (pre-1901) tenements came to define the words "tenement" and "slum." Earlier, "tenement" had an ideologically neutral meaning in English usage as "an abode for a person or for the soul, in which someone else owned the property."[4] In New York City, after the enactment of the 1901 housing law, "tenement" had a broadly defined legal meaning: it applied to all buildings housing three families or more—and it applied to nearly three-quarters of the city's residential structures. But even as the 1901 law defined tenements in this manner, ironically classifying such opulent apartment houses as the Dakota or the Ansonia on the Upper West Side in the same category with the most squalid housing projects, New Yorkers had come to associate "tenement" with "slum."[5] Mulberry

Fig. 3.4. Marketing at the
Five Points, 1869, from
Frank Leslie's Ill. News.
© Collection of The New-
York Historical Society.

Bend, even after it had been "cleared," would be the Platonic counterideal to which all housing for the poor would be compared.

The story begins at the start of the previous century, when the meager land of Manhattan Island and rapid land speculation brought wealth and poverty into close contact and pitted city builders, speculators, and workers against one another in an open conflict for space. Although since 1676 there were precedents for removal of "nuisances"—as dilapidated or vice-ridden housing was called—only in the early nineteenth century did such removal become a tool in the vocabulary of city policy. An 1800 law allowing for demolition by the city applied almost exclusively to abandoned buildings. In a few cases, however, the city used its power of condemnation for purposes other than street laying or other public works: against tenements.[6] Historian Elizabeth Blackmar describes in detail the battle to remove the Five Points that had by 1829 acquired the image as "ground zero," as we would say today, of sin and debauchery in New York (figure 3.4). Housing "horrors too awful to mention" in its tenements, brothels, saloons, and on its streets, where every sin in the Bible was acted out, the Five Points seemed beyond defense. After four years of legal wrangling, the city finally cleared out the triangle in 1833.[7] Through the 1830s, social reformers, retailers, and others who sought to enhance the value of their property supported further efforts to clean up the Five Points area.

Despite these few highly visible slum clearance efforts, most of the steps taken by the city were far more tentative ones. Although a continuous line of tenement house commissions, committees, boards, and departments all had included demolition as one of their strategies through most of the nineteenth century, destruction functioned mainly as a stock rhetorical device rather than a tool of public policy. Indeed, attacks on the most notorious tenements elicited fiery words and gave reformers a moral high ground from which to preach. But even the worst tenements lasted far longer than the volume of rhetorical bile heaped on them would have portended. Only the most decrepit and dangerous tenements were destroyed by government dictate, and only after many decades of protest and denunciation. Gotham Court, which was built in the 1850s and long stood as a symbol of tenement evil, lived—by New York actuarial tables—to a ripe old age of forty-five, before finally being destroyed in 1895 under the leadership of Jacob Riis. That it lasted so long was a shock and insult to tenement reformers, but was quite typical of the time. An 1853 tenement house committee had condemned the "crazy old buildings" and the Association for the Improvement of the Conditions of the Poor had attacked "these crying evils" and described in detail the horrendous living conditions offered in the court.[8] Declared Lawrence Veiller, the secretary of the 1901 Tenement House Commission:

It would seem that after such a revelation, no civilized community could tolerate such a condition of affairs for a moment, yet not till nearly forty years later was Gotham Court dealt with. In 1896 it was torn down, and no longer can it send forth its evil influences to pollute the stream of our civic life. But if one could reckon the evil that it has done in the sixty years of its existence, what a heavy sum it would be! Who can estimate the extent of the physical and moral disorder thus created by this one building, the loathsome diseases, the death, the pauperism, the vice, the crime, the debasement of civic life?[9]

Gotham Court owed its demise to the successful efforts a few years earlier to demolish the most notorious of New York's slums, Mulberry Bend. The "Clearing of Mulberry Bend," a three-acre site located a few blocks north and east of City Hall Park, was the first salvo in the battle against the slum, and "one of the first slum clearance projects on a modern scale in New York City."[10] Just north of the infamous Five Points, Mulberry Bend had long been known as one of New York's worst slum areas, and there had been repeated calls for its demolition. But only when Jacob Riis brought his camera there in the late 1880s was "The Bend" finally brought down. Through Riis's eyes, and through his words, New Yorkers learned about the nature of the "shadows" of New York (see figure 3.5).

Jacob Riis's writings and photographs were the effective tools of a fiery social reformer who provided a map of social degradation in New York. A Danish immigrant who came to the United States in 1870, he embraced his new country with a burning patriotism, which drove his intense efforts at tenement reform for more than thirty years. Better than any other housing reformer, Riis was able to bring to the homes of Broadway and Washington Square the lives of those within the Lower East Side tenements. He provided a guide to New York's underside, complete with the tragic dramas of young prostitutes, rampant diseases festering in overcrowded tenements, gambling, and violent encounters in the back alleys of the slums. He told the stories with the authority of an insider, having spent his days and nights exploring the basement saloons, catching sleeping boarders with magnesium flashes, and recording the sweatshop work of children.

Jacob Riis launched the modern attacks on tenements. His contribution exposed the depth of the tenement problem to those who had never been adventurous enough to explore the jungle of the Lower East Side. He was best known, then as now, for his photographs, some of the earliest and finest photojournalistic exposés.[11] Riis's strategies for reform, however, have been underestimated. His call for parks and model tenements have been considered simply part of the dominant vocabulary of social reform

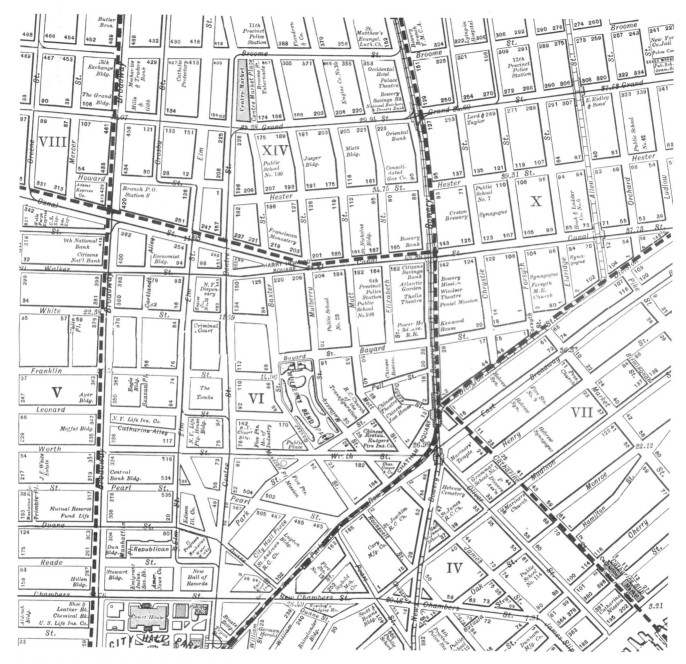

Fig. 3.5. Map from *How the Other Half Lives: Studies Among the Tenements of New York* (1890; reprint, New York: Dover Publications, 1971). Mulberry Bend, the "foul core of New York," was located just north and east of New York's City Hall.

of the time. What has been ignored is that it was Riis who gave powerful rhetorical and documentary justification for destruction as an essential tool of tenement reform. On the one hand, he supported model tenements and regulations—he helped found, for example, the City and Suburban Homes Company, one of the early private model-home developers in the city. On the other hand, he was most passionate when arguing that the solution for the worst tenements was removal. Riis had long chided the "optimists of the Health Department" who for so long advocated inspection and enforcement of regulations to improve conditions in the Bend. It was clear to him that "the more that has been done the less it has seemed to accomplish in the way of real relief, until is has at last become clear that nothing short of entire demolition will ever prove of radical benefit."[12]

For Riis, Mulberry Bend was the "wickedest of American slums," a place of unmatched physical and moral destruction. "Where Mulberry Street crooks like an elbow . . . is 'the Bend,' the foul core of New York's slums."[13] His photographs and text, rambling and anecdotal, amount to a description of the degradation inherent in the chaotic world of the tenements. Disheveled men sleep in a basement saloon, a bedraggled man looks up from his "cave-dwelling," children play baseball amid garbage. This run-down conglomeration of tenements held one of the highest densities of people in New York—upward of seven hundred per acre. It was filled with gangs of youths who committed crimes in such back alleys as Bandits' Roost and Bottle Alley, inspiring Riis to claim that "it is not exaggeration to say that there is not a foot of ground in the Bend that has not witnessed a deed of violence."[14] The Bend contained dozens of "stale-beer saloons" and brothels that were "prolific of untold depravities."[15] The death rate in the Bend, for example, was 50 percent higher than in the rest of the city. Especially tragic was the death rate for children under the age of five—the Tenement House Commission had counted 155 in 1882—which far outpaced the rest of the city.[16] The answer to the disaster of Mulberry Bend was, to Riis, simple: "I got a picture of the Bend upon my mind which as soon as I should be able to transfer it to that of the community would help settle that pig-sty according to its deserts. It was not fit for Christian men and women, let alone innocent children, to live in, and therefore it had to go."[17]

For Riis, Mulberry Bend was a place of destruction: lives were destroyed by disease, souls were destroyed by sexual sin, hope was destroyed by the weight of accumulated misery. Not all of this despair, he believed, was caused by poverty or other forces beyond the control of Mulberry Bend's inhabitants. Throughout his work, Riis, like many other reformers of the late nineteenth and early twentieth centuries, maintained an ambivalent relationship to the inhabitants of the tenements. Although he seemed to show sympathy for the subjects of his photographs, his revelatory images and articles were laced with words of condemnation and racist disgust. Riis's concern for the immigrants' living conditions was only matched by his loathing. He often blamed the inhabitants for their own environment, rather than focusing on, for example, city policy or the greed of landlords. The immigrants he observed were considered culpable for the unacceptable conditions of their neighborhoods. Nonetheless, Riis believed that people's behavior would improve exactly as much as did their living conditions. Tenement dwellers "are shiftless, destructive and stupid," wrote Riis. "In a word, they are what the tenements have made them."[18]

Riis was a product and a promoter of a renewed skepticism and disgust with cities at the end of the century. A long-standing American distrust of cities increasingly found receptive authors and audiences. Best-sellers such as Josiah Strong's *Our Country* (1885), Joaquin Miller's *Destruction of Gotham* (1886), and Edward Bellamy's *Looking Backward* (1888) bore testament to a deep-seated loathing of cities.[19] Perhaps most prominent in the litany of fears of the city were unrest, danger, and political upheaval. *The Destruction of Gotham*, for example, is a story of the burning of New York by an angry mob; *Caesar's Column*, by Ignatius Donnelly, portended a final, devastating conflict between New York's rich and poor, between what guidebooks had referred to as the "Light and Shadows" of New York.[20] Riis himself, in a remarkable, breathless conclusion to *How the Other Half Lives*, pointed to elite fears of political revolt by immigrant masses. He created an apocalyptic vision of social unrest of the inhabitants he had just portrayed in words and photographs. On a visit to one of New York's beaches, he drew a parallel between crashing waves in which the immigrants played and the potential for upheaval held in fragile check within the tenements:

> Once already our city, to which have come the duties and responsibilities of metropolitan greatness before it was able to fairly measure its task, has felt the swell of its resistless flood. If it rise once more, no human power may avail to check it. The gap between the classes in which it surges, unseen, unsuspected by the thoughtless, is widening day by day. No tardy enactment of law, no political expedient, can close it. Against all other dangers our system of government may offer defense and shelter; against this not. I know of but one bridge that will carry us over safe, a bridge founded upon justice and built of human hearts. I believe that the danger of such conditions as are fast growing up around us is greater for the very freedom which they mock. The words of the poet [James Russell], with whose lines I prefaced this book, are true today, have far deeper meaning to us, than when they were penned forty years ago:
>
> > Think ye that building shall endure
> > Which shelters the noble and crushes the poor?[21]

For many reformers the "menace of great cities" was encapsulated in and caused by the conditions of the slums.[22] They feared social unrest and resistance to assimilation if immigrants were ill-housed. Improved housing, argued E. R. L. Gould, a national advocate for slum clearance and decent housing, "is a powerful factor in good citizenship. . . . The genesis of 'isms most often takes place in the miserable tenements of a great modern city." These fears served equally to justify parks. Young people, offered "no opportunity for legitimate play, no rational outlet for an excess of animal spirits," naturally were drawn into gangs "for nocturnal maraudings."[23] The 1894 Tenement House Commission (discussed in a following section) insisted that "no one can become familiar with life in the most crowded districts of New York without the conviction that no greater immediate relief can be afforded the inhabitants than by letting in more air and sunshine by means of playgrounds and small parks, and furnishing thereby, near at hand, places for rest, recreation and exercise for young and old."[24] In the small area bounded by Mulberry, Bayard, Baxter, and Park Streets, Progressives could find an agglomeration of all the evils to which they addressed themselves in the city: drunkenness, youth criminality, prostitution, disease, and lack of light and air for children. Reformers were preoccupied as much with the social evils caused by the tenements as with the physical and emotional hardships affecting individuals. The tenements, with Gotham Court as the most wretched example, were "the cause of most of the problems in our modern cities."[25]

Thus for Progressive urban reformers like Riis, the slum was the breeding ground not only for the ills affecting the individuals but for the political fury that might consume the city. And since Progressive reformers saw in the city a series of physical settings for the diminution of the individual and community, they also, logically, believed that changing that environment would be the start of a solution to the problems of the cities. The reformation of Mulberry Bend might not only eliminate the "foul core of New York" but could create quite the opposite movement: homes where virtue could be promoted and healthful activities enjoyed. An ideology of "positive environmentalism," as the historian Paul Boyer has called it, accompanied Riis's powerful "negative environmentalism."[26] If a positive environment had the ability to transform persons and communities for the better, a negative environment had to be eliminated before it infected everyone within its reach.

Even as Riis sought to demolish history and its effects, he wanted to achieve a different future. Destruction of the tenements, in Riis's vision, would be followed by the building of parks, bringing the restorative powers of nature to those deprived of it. Following the tradition laid out by Frederick Law Olmsted, Riis held a nostalgic view of the countryside as the source of American virtues and productive citizenship.

Just as the tenements intrinsically held some elemental evil, "nature," in the pastoral form perfected by Olmsted in New York, magically diminished the desire of people to commit crimes, inspired them to hard work, and molded them into active, committed citizens.[27] Furthermore, pastoral parks were a symbol of order, of the steady, thoughtful domination of nature, which would serve as a reprieve from the chaotic street life of Mulberry Bend (figure 3.6).[28]

Fig. 3.6. Postcard: "Mulberry Bend Park," 1907. The crowded, decrepit tenements of "The Bend" are replaced with the clean curves of an Olmstedian park. Museum of the City of New York.

With this view, Riis salvaged a creative meaning from the destruction of Mulberry Bend. "So the Mulberry Bend had its mission after all," he wrote just after the park was dedicated. "The filth began there, and now that it is ended and won, we look upon smoothly paved and cleanly swept streets. . . . It is all the work of the decade that began the battle with the Bend. Its mission was not for New York only, but for the whole country; for by its lessons every American city may profit."[29] In the place of the "foul core" of New York's tenement district would be "trees and grass and flowers; for its dark hovels light and sunshine and air."[30] Where tenements sank their inhabitants into physical and moral disease, parks raised them up with their inherent restorative powers. Of course, in Riis's description, the people are entirely absent from the "after" picture. Where once hordes of filthy inhabitants crowded into slums, now only sunshine and open space take their place. It is unclear where all the people have gone.

In order to achieve this vision of "reform," Riis took the connection between environment and social condition, so central to Progressive reformers' beliefs, to a logical extreme. "There is," he insisted, "a connection between the rottenness of the house and that of the tenant that is patent and positive."[31] But even more than this, Mulberry Bend, and the other slums like it, not only created the crowded and dangerous conditions where human depravity could flourish, but became themselves generators of that depravity. Riis anthropomorphized the tenements, making these configurations of real estate into base participants rather than mere shelters for human activity. "Such a slum as this is itself the poison," he wrote about the Bend:

> It taints whatever it touches. Wickedness and vice gravitate toward it and are tenfold aggravated, until crime is born spontaneously of its corruption. . . . Recovery is impossible under its blight. Rescue and repression are alike powerless to reach it.[32]

Mulberry Bend "had to go" because it was so horrible, beyond redemption. When he was asked if the result of destroying Mulberry Bend was simply to scatter poverty, Riis insisted that "the greater and by far the worst part of it [poverty] is destroyed with the slum . . . something is gained in the mere shifting about; some of the dirt is lost on the way."[33] Riis's faith in demolition was passionate, highly emotional, but with little intellectual foundation or long-term vision. His intended solutions were unclear—what would happen to the immigrants displaced by destruction, and whose responsibility was this? Throughout his reform campaigns, Riis remained deeply critical of profiteering landlords and of political corruption that protected them. But rarely did Riis insist that the root cause of the slum problem was a system of property exploitation. In the end he always returned to the tenements themselves, as literal personifications of depravity.

What made Mulberry Bend utterly unredeemable? Although Mulberry Bend was by any empirical evaluation—density, disease, mortality rate—one of the worst slums in the city, it was not unique. Riis called it the "foul core" of slums, but it was also "typical."[34] Few other areas—Gotham Court, south of Mulberry Bend, was one; the Lung Blocks of Cherry Street another—had the history of Mulberry Bend. If *How the Other Half Lives* was an exposé that shocked, and perhaps titillated, upper-class New York, it was also a book of history, of tenements and the efforts over half a century to combat their evils. Riis opens *How the Other Half Lives* with a genealogy of the tenement, beginning with the "rear house." Tenement lots were often built up in several stages. Early-eighteenth-century single-family homes were altered

Fig. 3.7. Mulberry Bend, circa 1892, following the publication *of How the Other Half Lives* (1890). Already Jacob Riis's fascination with the Lower East Side was taking hold. Photographs, paintings, postcards, and etchings of the Lower East Side slums made famous by Riis proliferated in the years after *How the Other Half Lives* was published. This image shows the layering of building types in the Lower East Side: the early-nineteenth-century wooden townhouses of merchants and sailors (right, middle), the first tenements of the post–Civil War era, and the six- and even seven-story tenements of the last two decades of the nineteenth century. The Germans, who once dominated the Lower East Side (and were the most populous immigrant group in New York in the nineteenth century), are represented by the Shults Bread delivery wagon, while the newer Italian immigrants who would come to dominate Mulberry Street are in evidence with Peirano wines (right) and the hanging cloves of garlic (left). © Collection of The New-York Historical Society.

or replaced with apartments. Then, the front half of the lot was developed with five- or six-story tenements. The "rear tenements" were soon surrounded on three sides by other tenements and thus became the darkest and dingiest of all. It was in these rear tenements where the worst evils were found and sometimes sought after. "Nothing would probably have shocked their original owners more," wrote Riis, "than the idea of their harboring a promiscuous crowd; for they were the decorous homes of the old Knickerbockers, the proud aristocracy of Manhattan in the early days."[35] To reformers like Riis, the transformation of the early-nineteenth-century homes of "Knickerbocker" families into some of the worst, most congested housing in the city, was especially poignant; it was a perversion of history. Riis offered a narrative history of the tenements in which the first "rear houses," converted into rented buildings for poor immigrants, led steadily, as immigration increased, to the six-story tenements that were the fabric of the Lower East Side by the end of the century. Like the story of Fifth Avenue, the tenement narrative led from these old houses, to Five Points, to the present crisis, where the most sophisticated and committed of reformers confronted the worst slums yet imaginable. Calling to the "memory of man," Riis insisted that "the old cow-path [Mulberry Street] has never been other than a vast human pig-sty."[36] It was these buildings, the "crazy old buildings, crowded rear tenements," that had become the focus of tenement commissions and housing reformers (figure 3.7).[37]

The rear houses and the old-law tenements, and Mulberry Bend in general, were thus also a problem of historical inheritance, not just one of avaricious landlords, uncivilized immigrants, and corrupt politicians. To reformers, Mulberry Bend was the physical embodiment of the history of slums in New York because it bore the accumulated evils of half a century. Slum clearance has been described as a policy developed as a rational, final response to the problems of inhuman housing for poor people. But closer examination reveals how central the historical symbolism of these tenements was in contributing to their sought-after demise. Cultural understandings of the "leprous houses," images of danger and political unrest, and the construction of the old-law tenement as the scourge to be removed continued to animate housing reform efforts. Just as the recalled and invented memories of Fifth Avenue were utilized to create an image of a successful, "good place" that had to be defended, the awful history of Mulberry Bend—the "foul core" of New York—was repeatedly paraded before the public to offer a diagnosis of a "sick place" that had to be eliminated. It was no accident that the focus was always on efforts to eliminate the oldest and worst slums of the city, the "rear tenements" and so-called old-law tenements that were built previous to the Tenement House Act of 1901, or "new law." These "leprous houses," as Charles Dickens called them in 1842, came to define the two sides in the "battle with the slum" over the next several decades.[38] The power of these places in the public imagination, an imagination powerfully shaped by Riis's photos and writing, would continually reappear to shape not only attitudes but the actual choice of housing development sites and strategies.

The changing powers of city government in the late nineteenth century powerfully shaped the development of slum clearance as policy and ideology. Riis's efforts, beginning in the late 1880s and accelerating until Columbus Park was opened in 1897, revealed for him the problems reformers would face in forcing action from a recalcitrant city government, political machinery, and resistant private owners. Riis quickly recognized the middle ground in which reformers would find themselves, trapped between the inchoate powers of the city government and the fractured but vociferous resistance of real estate owners and speculators. Legal limitations on the powers of government and, perhaps even more important, the political skittishness of city government to initiate widespread slum clearance had created strong resistance to clearing Mulberry Bend.

Among the detailed recommendations of the 1884 Tenement House Commission—a set of very specific recommendations about lot coverage and access to air and light—was a call for the extension of Leonard Street to Pell Street, right through Mulberry Bend, the notorious tenement area. In 1884, the commission had recommended that the street be extended, "as has been recommended in former years."[39] While other recommendations of these commissions dealt with the regulation of present and future tenements, only this one so clearly advocated destruction. The commission's suggestion gained a huge boost when, in 1887, New York State passed the Small Parks Act, which provided aid for the clearing of slums and the creation of parks within poor areas. Over the next decades, New York created a number of parks in Lower Manhattan: Mulberry Bend Park, Seward Park, Hamilton Fish Park (see figure 3.8). By 1888, plans for the park had been drawn up; all that awaited was the purchase of the buildings and the "clearing" of the Bend.

But what appeared to be a relatively simple process became extremely complicated. Over the next seven years, the city battled within itself over the legitimacy of taking property for park uses. It also fought local property owners over the value of the lots. The situation reached farcical proportions when the city took possession of the properties of Mulberry Bend in 1894 but delayed the actual demolition due to lack of funds.[40] The city then became a slumlord, collecting thousands of dollars in rent from inhabitants of the Bend. The following year, Mayor Strong ordered the buildings vacated and then destroyed. Having paid the owners a total of $1.5 million to leave their properties, the city quickly auctioned off the buildings in June 1895 for a grand total of $800 to wreckers who would demolish the buildings and remove the ruins within thirty days; some buildings sold for as little as $1.50.[41] Despite this important step, the muddy lot remained empty for another year, aggravating Riis even further. Only after more pressure from Riis, and the tragic death of several children,

Fig. 3.8. Essex Street, looking north, 1936. Mulberry Bend Park was followed by the creation of a number of other small parks in the Lower East Side, such as Seward Park (right), bounded by Essex, East Broadway, and Grand Streets. The pushcart peddlers of Hester Street (the cross street in the middle of the photograph) would be removed later that decade by order of Mayor Fiorello La Guardia. Their replacement, the public Essex Street markets, required further demolition of tenements along Essex Street to the north. Collections of the Municipal Archives of the City of New York.

was the Bend finally transformed into a park, which opened to much fanfare in 1897. Ironically, because he had remained a constant critic of the city's incompetence, Riis was not invited to participate in the opening of the park.[42]

Jacob Riis marshaled and defined many of the arguments that would animate slum clearance for the next decades: Progressive belief in the instrumentality of the environment, the ineffectiveness of regulations, and the need for strong governmental intervention. But Riis also recognized how difficult slum clearance would be in New York, despite the small successes he had achieved at Mulberry Bend, in Gotham Court, and in the construction of other small parks. "Doubtless the best would be to get rid of it [the tenement] altogether; but as we cannot, all argument on that score may at this time be dismissed as idle."[43] What would change is that slum clearance would no longer require the enthusiasm of a single, vociferous champion but would become institutionalized in law, in government programs, and in state and federal budgets, driven forward not by revealing photographs but by planning logic. The transformation would take place over two decades of debate among planners, reformers, and other elites over how to rid the city of its slums.

Most nineteenth-century reformers had worked on two fronts in their battle with the slum: demanding improvements to existing tenements and regulating future tenement construction. The numerous commissions established to propose legislation for the improvement of tenement housing produced a long list of regulations through which they hoped to shape the private housing market. The 1879 Tenement House Competition resulted in a series of "model" plans for tenements in the hope of influencing future designs. The great achievement of this competition was to insist that all rooms have access to light and air—hence the air shafts between buildings that created their dumbbell shape. Hailed at the time as a humane answer to the airless, windowless tenements that were being replicated across Manhattan, the "dumbbell" tenements were not much of an improvement, and later they themselves became the scourge of housing reformers. Their air shafts provided very little ventilation, and the regulations had ignored the continuing problems of crowding, sanitation, and fire safety. The work of Jacob Riis and the tenement house commissions of 1894, 1901, and beyond was largely to undo the damage of the dumbbell tenement. Lawrence Veiller declared the dumbbell to be the "curse of our city. . . . [W]e are reaping the evils of that system of the prize plan of 1879, built all over the crowded wards of this city."[44]

The Second Tenement House Committee, which issued its report in 1884, recommended design regulations and enforcement powers to address the problems of the 1879 act. This committee sought to require 65 percent maximum coverage (previously, tenements typically covered 80 percent or more of a lot), provision of water supply on each floor, direct light to each room, and the elimination of privies. It also proposed that the city adopt methods of record keeping and inspection that would later be incorporated into a distinct Tenement House Department.[45] Most of these recommendations were not adopted or codified in any way. So in 1894, yet another Tenement House Committee was established by the state legislature. Despite its well-known chairman, Richard Watson Gilder (the poet and editor of *Century* magazine), and its dramatic investigations into the horrible conditions of such landlords as Trinity Church, the 1894 Committee changed little. It expanded the regulations of the 1884 commission and called for necessary enforcement authority to empower the city to uphold its own regulations.

The failures of the 1894 commission provoked a new commission, the 1900 Tenement House Commission, chaired by Robert De Forest and Lawrence Veiller. This commission would be different from all that preceded it. Out of their research, the commission produced a law that fundamentally affected the building of new tenements. The Tenement House Act of 1901 limited lot coverage to 70 percent and required that toilets be installed in each floor of all tenements, new and old, that all rooms have windows, and that fire escapes be installed in all buildings. The extent of these reforms and their enforcement by a newly created Tenement House Department were so fundamental as to make 1901 a dividing line between one age and another, between old-law and new-law tenements.

Riis's advocacy of demolition as creative reform found receptive ears. The ineffectiveness of tenement house regulations (especially the dramatic failure of the 1879 "dumbbell" regulations), the exponential growth in the immigrant populations and consequent expansion of tenement districts beginning in the 1880s, and the powerful example of urban reform in Europe spurred reformers to reconsider their strategies. But while most began to embrace wholesale destruction of tenement buildings as the answer, they did so for different reasons.

The developing calculus of destroying the old in order to build better tenements was deceptively simple. Reformers found themselves at odds with one another over the purpose and effectiveness of tenement destruction and creation. In essence, reformers divided on the purpose of destruction and what creative act would follow demolition of the tenements. One group of reformers, including Felix Adler, founder of the Ethical Culture Society and leader of the Charity Organization Society, advocated destruction as the first step toward public housing. Adler, writing in 1884 as chairman of the Tenement House Commission, stated the new position baldly:

> The evils of the tenement house section of this city are due to the estates which neg-
> lect the comfort of their tenants, and to the landlords who demand exorbitant rents.
> The laboring classes are unable to build homes for themselves, and the law of moral-
> ity and common decency binds the Government to see to it that these houses shall
> not prove fatal to the lives and morality of the inmates. If the houses are overcrowded
> the government must interfere. It must compel a reduction of the number of inmates,
> enforce renovation at the expense of the landlord, and where that is no longer possi-
> ble, must dismantle the houses and remove them from existence.[46]

Adler insisted that since the private market had failed to provide decent housing for the poor, it was the city's responsibility to step in to aid the helpless. The Charity Organization Society (COS), which essentially served as the social service and wel-fare wing of municipal government, was the earliest and most vocal advocate of mu-nicipal housing. Though it had to wait for years, the COS advocated from the 1890s onward large-scale demolition combined with model tenements. In 1896 and 1900 it sponsored design competitions for model tenements, and its exhibit of the winners in February 1900 was the inspiration for the work of the 1901 new-law commission. Indeed, many of the state and federal commissions on New York City tenements were peopled by COS members, often previous heads of the COS's own permanent ten-ement house committee.[47]

Other reformers were equally enamored of a vision of large-scale demolition of tenements. E. R. L. Gould, a lecturer on social science and statistics at Johns Hopkins University and expert witness for Gilder's 1894 commission, utilized medical metaphors that pervaded the housing reform discourse when he declared simply: "There is no cure for cancer except the knife. Neither is there any other satisfactory way of dealing with irremediable insanitary premises than to tear them down.... The first step in house-reform is to get rid of the bad houses."[48]

During the investigations of the 1894 commission, the philosophy of housing re-form through creative destruction was fully embraced for the first time. Gould, Gilder, and the members of the 1894 commission embraced destruction as a creative act in itself. The rear tenements, especially, were "an awful curse, destructive alike to health and morality . . . [and] should be the first to be destroyed, and its disappearance may be made the means of a positive benefit."[49] Adler found himself at odds with the com-mission because, in his mind, it was focusing too much on destruction and not enough on building new housing. Adler argued that demolition of tenements without re-placing them immediately, at least in another part of the city, was an essentially de-structive act, destroying desperately needed shelters. He favored the suburbanization of the population, the building of large model tenements in Harlem and beyond. But as that would not happen in the immediate future, Adler saw the value of parks—open space, fresh air—completely neutralized by the increased crowding in the remaining miserable tenements, while the displaced searched for new housing. In a lively ex-change with Richard Watson Gilder, Adler criticized the tendency to tear down ten-ements and replace them not with needed housing but with parks. Adler saw publicly funded housing as the only alternative if the city was going to destroy people's exist-ing homes. Gilder stridently resisted city-owned housing. He and the commission saw the movement for publicly funded and owned housing as dangerous, "bad principle and worse policy . . . an unjustifiable interference with private enterprise." Public housing would cost too much, would require rents too high for the poor, and would discourage the "natural" development of housing by the private real estate market.[50]

Although Adler and the COS failed to gain support for public housing, their ef-forts did bear the fruit of new legal powers given to the state Board of Health and the city Department of Buildings. For much of the century, the Board of Health retained limited powers to require demolition of tenements. As early as 1866, the act creating the Metropolitan Board of Health gave that board the power to "condemn buildings that were unfit for habitation" because of physical conditions that would cause dis-ease or other injury.[51] This new power was to be exercised only in extreme situations. These powers were elaborated in laws of 1867 and 1887, but were still restricted to those buildings that threatened immediate harm.

The Tenement House Act of 1895 substantially increased the legal powers of the Board of Health. Expanding the reasons for condemnation and demolition, and pro-viding a coherent process for implementing vacate and condemnation orders, the act gave new impetus to tenement reform by demolition. In what seemed like a minor semantic point, the act authorized the Board of Health to demolish a tenement if it were not considered fit for human habitation. Previously, the building had to be con-sidered a "nuisance" under the law, which did not permit the city to compensate the owners. With the new power came a system of compensation for virtually all owners of condemned property.

Soon after the Tenement House Act of 1895 was passed, the Board of Health ini-tiated a campaign against the fabled "rear tenements." The fertile ground of moral and physical degradation that galvanized reformers lay deep in the interior of tenement blocks, behind the street-facing facades. Considering the currency of rear tenements in the public imagination (enhanced by tabloid revelations about the condition of Trinity Church's tenement properties), the Board of Health must have felt confident that it could muster public support for an attack at the source of the tenement house evils. But whatever the general support for demolishing rear tenements, when the extent of the board's campaign became apparent, landlords and developers rebelled and challenged the board's powers. In *Health Department v Dassori*, the Court of Appeals held that demolition was to be a last resort, used only when no other method could effectively remove the "nuisance." In a pointed rebuff to the Board of Health's larger goals for tenement reform, the decision cited a previous case, *Myers v Gemmel*, which rejected the notion that owners or renters had a right to light and air.[52]

Thus, one major obstacle to slum clearance was simply the immaturity of the city's financial and legal mechanisms to spur and manage its growth. Condemnation powers were newly discovered and vaguely defined. Indeed, for most of the century, the state Board of Health had final authority over the regulations concerning housing conditions. Municipal bureaucracy was not yet able to handle the monumental tasks of record keeping and regulation enforcement. And, as we have seen, one of the biggest obstacles to a concerted municipal solution for tenement problems was the cost. Any condemnation without compensation—which would alienate the powerful landowners—was politically unacceptable, but any condemnation requiring compensation was fiscally dangerous. The case of Hamilton Fish Park, between Houston, Stanton, Pitt, and Sheriff Streets in the Lower East Side, is illustrative. The city spent almost $1.7 million to acquire the land in a poor district. To make matters worse, the property was owned by a number of different people, some of whom challenged the awards given by the city.[53]

The question in the legal challenges had seemed to be about semantics—what was a "nuisance"—and the meaning of the 1895 law. But it represented a much larger conflict. The Board of Health was in essence trying to exercise extensive police powers over the built environment, extending its protectorship to encompass far more than elimination of health hazards. The board was trying to radically shape the urban environment through powers of condemnation and demolition. Furthermore, the board, even though it relied on arguments and statistics attesting to the danger of disease in rear tenements, also operated from a position of moral outrage. The reputation of these places as sources of social evil motivated its campaign. What landlords saw as encroaching state power—defining "unfitness" in moral terms as opposed to the more narrow physical definition—the Board of Health saw as a logical, responsible extension of the 1895 law.

The new Tenement House Department that began its work in 1901 was built on several decades of advocacy for various new elements that would constitute a slum clearance program. But the contradictions inherent in the city's housing reform movement—a call for speedy action along with a hesitancy about government intervention, a dedication to regulations along with the tempting presence of new condemnation powers—would make the translation of rhetorical fascination with the simplicity of the slum clearance solution into coherent public policy far more difficult.

"NEW YORK'S REAL NAPOLEON III"

Jacob Riis's success at Mulberry Bend was the culmination of a rising tide of indignation at the conditions of the slums as well as a concerted institutional effort to provide regulatory powers for transforming tenements. But despite the clearing of Mulberry Bend, as well as new legislative imprimatur for tenement destruction, the Lower East Side was not remade by slum clearance in the first two decades of the twentieth century. De jure condemnation did not translate into de facto power. In the midst of the Mulberry Bend struggle, Riis had written a biting attack on the city:

> Let me ask you a simple question in arithmetic, if it took us eight years to get the Mulberry slum made into a dunghill, how long is it going to take us, with present machinery and official energy, to get the two tenement blocks over there, where people are smothering for want of elbow room, made into two parks?[54]

Reformers, government officials, and real estate developers did not divide neatly into three camps, but fractured along several lines. Reformers were split between those urging government-built and -owned public housing, and those seeking only strong regulations. Some government officials advocated extensive clearance as part of an interventionist city-planning ideology; others sought to leave redevelopment up to private business, with regulatory guidance provided by the city. Finally, real estate interests were fractured. Speculators saw benefits accruing to landowners who knew how to exploit the "improvements" made through government-sponsored slum clearance. Small-scale landlords (many of whom were themselves immigrants), on the other hand, depended on the rental income of old-law tenements.[55] The failure of slum clearance to take hold following Riis's advocacy and initial successes, then, was not a result simply of the lack of political will; rather, it reflected a sharp division among the interests of New York's city-building elites.

The failure of the 1895 rear tenement campaign cast a shadow for decades on the strategy of demolishing tenements. The Tenement House Department, established in 1901 by the Tenement House Act, lamented the failure of the board's "crusade" against the rear tenements. The department's annual report of 1902, essentially its manifesto, states that "the decision of the Court of Appeals . . . has made it unwise for the department to take steps looking toward the destruction of such houses."[56] Tenements could be "vacated"—evacuated for a period of time—but not permanently demolished, except in extreme circumstances. The department resisted advocates of large-scale demolition and sought to continue the more gradual elimination of tenements.

The Tenement House Department, in its first report, carefully balanced its far-reaching purpose of eliminating all "houses unfit for habitation" with the political resistance on the part of property owners against large-scale demolition. While claiming its task to be enormous and radical—"cleansing of the Augean stable was a small task compared to the cleansing of New York's 82,000 tenement houses . . . [some of which] surpass imagination"—the department carefully avoided zealously applying its newfound powers of condemnation: "Requiring a tenement house to be vacated is so extreme a measure that the department has naturally been unwilling to take this step except in the most serious cases."[57] Indeed, the department went out of its way to declare a détente with owners: "While recognizing that the department was created primarily to protect the health, safety and welfare of those classes of the population who are unable to protect themselves, it was felt that the department should exercise extreme care in enforcing the Tenement House Law, so as not to make it a measure of oppression to tenement house owners."[58]

In the place of a missionary zeal for demolition, the department substituted a philosophy of destruction through private development. Reformers observed the process of destruction and rebuilding of business and residential buildings in the rest of the city and assumed that the same process would occur in the tenement districts. In its 1914 report, the department noted that

> it is not an unusual sight to see a business building, erected only a decade ago, being torn down to give place to a new structure in keeping with modern demands. In the same manner, as soon as the old tenements have become sufficiently unpopular with tenants, wholesale demolition or reconstruction is bound to follow. That time is not far distant in New York City . . . the process of eliminating the old buildings is now not one of law but of competition, which is both surer and speedier in its results.[59]

Riis, too, had recognized that private commercial and real estate development would have to be at the vanguard of the push to remove slums. The transformation of the city "comes so quickly sometimes as to fairly take one's breath away. More than once I have returned, after a few brief weeks, to some specimen rookery in which I was interested, to find it gone and an army of workmen delving twenty feet underground to lay the foundation of a mighty warehouse. . . . Business has done more than all other agencies together to wipe out the worst tenements. It has been New York's real Napoleon III, from whose decree there was no appeal."[60] Thus, even Riis, who gave the movement for slum clearance of the worst areas its most powerful visual and rhetorical ammunition, also recognized the power of private real estate in the city.

Tenement house reformers were faced with a perplexing dilemma of their own making. They were committed to righting the wrongs of a private real estate market that had resisted change and profited from horrendous slums. But the reformers were still committed to finding the solution within that very system. Real estate owners and their organizations were skeptical. In the first decade and a half, various lawsuits challenging the Tenement House Department regulations and even the legal legitimacy of the Tenement House Law kept the department in the courts continuously. The most potentially damaging attack came from the United Real Estate Owners' Property Association, an eight-thousand-member group, which fought the law's demand that the "school sinks" and privies be removed and every building be hooked up to a public sewer. It hoped that by highlighting the costs to poor landlords, the department and its regulations might be abolished. Others challenged—in lower courts, successfully—that the definition of "tenement" should be narrowed, to exclude larger apartment buildings and, in Brooklyn, converted townhouses.[61]

Lawrence Veiller, the cochair of the 1900 Tenement House Commission and coauthor of the Tenement House Act of 1901, was the outstanding proponent of this strategy for ridding the city of its old-law tenements. After his work with Robert De Forest on the 1901 law, Veiller followed De Forest to the Tenement House Department as an assistant (his aggressive attacks on landlords prevented him from being appointed by Seth Low as the chair). He left the department when Tammany returned to power in 1904, but continued his housing advocacy, first as chair of the Charity Organization Society's Department for Improvement of Social Conditions and as director of the National Housing Association, which he founded in 1911.[62]

Veiller believed that victory against slums lay in investigation of slum conditions, the "education of the community," and a public exhibit of the results. Out of these efforts would come a movement for "legislation which will remedy . . . the evil conditions discovered, and will prevent their repetition in the future."[63] The National Housing Association, which published *Housing Betterment* (later *Housing*) magazine, was intended to be a clearinghouse of information for communities attempting to enact and enforce tenement laws, and to be an ongoing advocate for the enforcement of those laws.

Veiller was highly critical of government-owned and -operated housing. Although at times he believed government was necessary to provide subsidies and

price stability for the construction industry, overall Veiller believed that government had no place in building and operating public housing.[64] "No government—as governments are constituted in this country—is fitted to manage apartment and tenement houses or other dwelling units in which vast numbers of people reside."[65] As late as 1930, Veiller was proclaiming that "the United States is a land of private enterprise. . . . Government housing plays no part in the solution of its housing problems. The motto of the American people is to keep the Government out of private business and to keep private business out of government."[66] As PWA clearance efforts took hold and a movement in New York and nationwide to create public housing authorities expanded, Veiller had, by the mid-1930s, begun to move with the tide of reformers to embrace slum clearance. Overcrowding was, he admitted, "a problem as obdurate as that of the slum; and in some ways more intractable. . . . Tentative and fragmentary efforts to control it—by bylaws or otherwise—have so far

Fig. 3.9. Mulberry Bend tenements, 1998. Today on Mulberry Street, immediately across from the park, stand "rear tenements" of the type scorned by Jacob Riis and other reformers. (The housing development in the background is Chatham Towers.) The front tenement building at least offered light into front rooms; the rear tenements were almost entirely closed in. Photograph courtesy of Iguana Photo.

signally failed."[67] But he still saw New Deal housing as dangerously piecemeal, and not part of a large regional planning ethos.

Nevertheless, Veiller took some pride in his agency's accomplishments. While many tenement owners and speculative builders and architects had predicted that the Tenement House Law "would absolutely put an end to the building of tenement houses in New York City," in fact, quite the opposite was true. By 1916 one-third of the city's population (1,585,260) was living in new-law tenements; by 1931 the number would be approximately three million. Veiller proudly noted that by 1916 the Advisory Council of Real Estate Interests of New York City praised the law as a "desirable asset in real estate development."[68]

Nonetheless, despite Veiller's optimism, the old-law tenements remained. James Ford, whose *Slums and Housing* is the most comprehensive study of New York's housing conditions, lamented in 1936 that the department had been so hesitant to exercise its police power: "New York is often described as a city continuously in the making, in which comparatively young buildings are ruthlessly destroyed to make way for others of greater height and more modern equipment." In fact, tenements showed "astonishing longevity."[69] In an average year between 1918 and 1935, no more than three or four hundred individual old-law tenements were destroyed.[70] Considering the ultimate goal of ridding the city of the 82,652 old-law tenements that existed in 1900, this portended a hundred-year task. Reformers could not even congratulate themselves on steady, if slow, progress. In the middle-class housing boom of the 1920s, so much low-income housing had been lost that thousands of old-law tenements—having stood vacant for a decade, awaiting the tide of development—were used as housing for the poor once again (see figure 3.9). As late as 1936, some 67,000 of these old-law tenements were still in use.[71] Instead of a concentrated attack, the elimination of old-law tenements took place haphazardly, proceeding only when the "wave of fashion surges in their direction," as with the Upper East Side.[72] Ironically, the poorest neighborhoods experienced the greatest physical stability. For while business buildings marched up the island, and the wealthy repeatedly left their brownstones to be converted or demolished—nearly every decade—the older tenement districts were bypassed.

DECONGESTANT: EMBRACING SLUM CLEARANCE IN THE 1920S AND 1930S

A number of factors pushed the city government and reformers toward accepting and promoting a policy of slum clearance that would finally take hold at the end of the 1920s. First was the continuing example of European cities and their dramatic slum clearance efforts. Between 1880 and 1940, the more radical efforts of Europe—demolishing slums and building public housing—served as examples of both successful and dangerous methods for housing reform. Some observers positively dripped with envy at the powers granted London by the Cross Act of 1875 and its subsequent amendments. The London City Council could declare whole areas clearance districts and thus, with little legal delay, wipe out entire slums, compensating owners little or nothing for their unsanitary buildings. By contrast, the unwillingness to reward slumlords for their buildings in condemnation actions would stall slum clearance efforts in the United States for years.[73] Some reformers saw London's legal tool, duplicated in France and Germany, as a quick way to get rid of unacceptable tenements without costing the city enormous sums.

Lawrence Veiller, even in his protests against public housing, praised the comprehensiveness with which the British—especially in the midst of the post–World War I housing shortage—attacked the problem of slums:

> It must be admitted even by one who does not believe in the Government's undertaking enterprises of this kind . . . that the steps which have been taken in these government-built houses are so far in advance of anything that has been done in the past.[74]

Europe continued to be the yardstick by which New Deal efforts were measured. While American efforts at slum clearance were erratic and lacking a comprehensive city plan, European clearance and housing construction efforts were centralized and more efficiently achieved. James Ford lamented the fact that "the contrast between New York practice and English practice in ordinary demolition is one so striking that it cannot be passed by. . . . [I]n England, demolition appears to be brought about with a minimum of difficulty and friction, and no compensation is required if the building is judged by the public authorities to be unfit for human habitation."[75]

Europe also provided examples of model public housing efforts. The investments in public housing and the architectural work of J. J. P. Oud in Holland; Walter Gropius, Marcel Breuer, and Bruno Taut in Germany; and Le Corbusier in France were remarkable not only because of their innovational design but also for the financial backing for public housing provided by the national governments. European architects offered Americans two types of housing: the "apartment in a garden" approach, consisting of relatively low-rise buildings surrounding a courtyard or series of courtyards, and the "tower in the park," where huge residential towers would allow for extremely high densities, but with instant access to nature.[76]

Organizations began to look at model housing as a policy. As noted previously, the Charity Organization Society saw from the start the dangers of relying on regu-

lations or even slum clearance alone. The COS moved toward an advocacy of model
housing that had as an implicit component extensive slum clearance. "Ever since its
organization," the COS wrote on the fortieth anniversary of its Tenement House
Committee, "the Committee had realized that the problem of housing low income
families could not be solved merely by regulation of existing buildings, but that some
form of new construction would be necessary to rehouse those who were living in
substandard dwellings."[77] In 1896, the COS, along with the Improved Housing
Council, had formed the City and Suburban Homes Company to build model low-
income housing. With E. R. L. Gould, the economist and federal housing adminis-
trator, at its head until his death in 1915, City and Suburban became one of the first
and largest producers of model tenements in the country.[78]

The experience of World War I was crucial in ratifying the efforts of model housing groups and suggested, as it did in so many other areas of American life, the possibilities of large-scale investment and coordination of industry by the federal government.[79] Housing production had stalled—only 1,624 dwellings were built in
1919, compared to the high of 54,884 in 1906—and the vacancy rate had declined
to virtually zero.[80] The federal government, through the U.S. Shipping Board and the
United States Housing Corporation, began building housing for workers in war industries. Although New York gained few housing units from the war experiments,
the taboo of government involvement in funding, building, and operating housing
was broken. Young architects, such as Clarence Stein and Henry Wright, who would
be prominent in New Deal public housing, and housing advocates, such as Edith
Elmer Wood, found inspiration in the experience of the war. The federal government
had recognized that in certain conditions, and certain places, the private market simply could not provide for all housing needs.[81]

European experience with slum clearance was used by others as a cautionary tale.
Riis himself was skeptical—if not of the legitimacy of widespread slum clearance, at
least of its practical possibilities in the United States: "The drastic measures adopted
in Paris, in Glasgow, and in London are not practicable here on anything like as large
a scale."[82] Others faulted European cities for zealous destruction and weak commitment to building new housing. The Tenement House Department noted that the
"hardships produced through tardiness in replacement" of housing—the extensive
homelessness that it produced—spoke against this type of tenement house reform.[83]
Some also remained skeptical of the vast "police" powers exercised by the city governments in England, by which private property was taken with little compensation
or appeal. Moving into uncharted areas of eminent domain, these municipal powers
seemed at odds with American traditions. Indeed, the Supreme Court had, in the

1893 *Monongahela* case, raised a large obstacle against the exercise of condemnation power by requiring awards to property owners on the basis of fair market value, not on a government-determined amount. But it was also these condemnation powers that had sparked the first slum clearance efforts and that would be at the heart of the renewed slum clearance of the New Deal era. Despite the limitations imposed by *Monongahela*, New York State passed its first "excess condemnation" law in 1913. Excess condemnation was a process whereby the city would take by eminent domain an area "in excess" of what was absolutely required for a public project—a bridge approach, or street widening, for example—and then sell off the land to private developers. Excess condemnation allowed the city to recoup some of the cost of the public works project, get rid of noxious tenements, and plan for new uses.[84] The state law was passed in 1913, but the city did not use the right of excess condemnation for the exclusive act of slum clearance and park development until 1927.

Specific housing models and legal changes occurred within the rise of the modern city-planning movement, which boosted the idea of planning by destruction. New York produced some of the movement's most powerful proponents and was the site of its first experiments. Following Daniel Burnham's famous dictum from 1893, "make no little plans," architects and members of the young planning profession began imagining a wholesale rearrangement of Manhattan's gridiron layout. Comprehensive city plans—George B. Post's 1899 plan for Lower Manhattan was succeeded by the 1904 and 1907 plans of the New York City Improvement Commission and, later, the plans of the Regional Plan Association—all proposed to defeat the grid and its inefficiencies by slicing through large boulevards and laying out public plazas.[85] With the growth of automobile traffic, the need for more efficient traffic movement was paramount. Planners devised widened or new cross-cutting avenues through the Lower East Side. Although New York never achieved the City Beautiful ideals of interlocking boulevards and public buildings, the movement to reorganize and beautify the city brought extensive street widenings in the Lower East Side and the construction of the Williamsburg and Manhattan Bridges.

The more abstract result of this array of developments—lessons of Europe, new legal powers, federal experimentation in World War I, the rise of city and regional planning—was to give reformers a new sense of their abilities and a new set of tools to intervene in the real estate market. In essence, it represented a new notion of how places, whether they be individual homes, neighborhoods within the city, or the whole metropolitan region, were built and rebuilt. It provided, all at once, new tools and rhetoric both for protecting places as they were—such as on Fifth Avenue—and radically, speedily remaking them.

In New York's Lower East Side, the movement toward slum clearance gained intensity because of economic changes in the 1920s and then the Great Depression. In the wake of a rapid construction boom in the 1920s, the Lower East Side declined precipitously in population, from a high of 530,000 to 250,000 in 1930. Miles of new-law housing in Brooklyn, Queens, and the Bronx, close to the expanding network of subways and elevated trains, lured a prosperous working class.[86] Lower East Side landlords found themselves holding property in an area that lost over half of its population. The only solution to their financial problems was either to transform their property into middle-income housing or commercial buildings. Both of these solutions were aided by government investment.

Ironically, the first major slum clearance and public housing experiments sponsored by the PWA occurred outside of the Lower East Side, in Williamsburg and in Harlem. But a number of reformers urged a return to the Lower East Side, the "foul core" of New York's slums. Mary Simkhovitch, for example, the founder of Greenwich House and a member of the first Housing Authority, argued that "the public will not be with us unless slum clearance is done"—and done in the Lower East Side.[87] The clearance efforts in the Lower East Side in the late 1920s and 1930s—including the widening of Allen Street, the creation of Sara Delano Roosevelt Park between Chrystie and Forsyth streets (figure 3.10), and the building of the Amalgamated Dwellings along Grand Street—were the product of many forces. These forces included not only a rational evaluation of conditions, as well as the cynical advocacy of landowners in the area, but also the indictment of memory.

What would replace the lost homes? The first tentative steps in the direction of public housing were taken under the Reconstruction Finance Corporation (RFC). One of only two projects undertaken by RFC, Knickerbocker Village (designed by John S. Van Wart), was completed in 1933. For thirty years, the "Lung Block," located in the Lower East Side between Cherry, Catherine, Monroe, and Market Streets, was on the top of housing reformers' "most wanted" lists and certainly provided ammunition for the COS in its bid to have slums demolished rather than "improved" through regulations. As Jacob Riis described the "Lung Block" in *How the Other Half Lives*: "In the shadow of the great stone abutments [of the Brooklyn Bridge] the old Knickerbocker houses linger like ghosts of a departed day. . . . The years have brought to the old houses unhonored age, a querulous second childhood that is out of tune with the time, their tenants, the neighbors . . ." (see figure 3.11).[88] Robert De Forest, the head of the 1901 Tenement House Commission, took aim at the Lung Block in 1903 as earlier reformers had pointed to the Five Points, or Gotham Court, or Mulberry Bend: "I know of no tenement house block in this city which is so bad from a

sanitary point of view, or from a criminal point of view. Every consideration of public health, morals and decency require that the buildings on this block be destroyed at
an early date."[89] For the next thirty years, the new Tenement House Department
made one of its priorities the improvement of the Lung Block tenements.

Fred French, one of New York's biggest developers, assumed the task in the spirit
of both public service and private gain. Knickerbocker Village revealed how the conflict between reformers and property owners could be mended with the introduc-
tion of the federal government into the housing business. Suddenly, slum clearance
meant new profits. French gleefully shared with Princeton students in 1934 the discovery that destruction was as profitable as construction:

> Our company, strangely enough, was the first business organization to recognize that
> profits could be earned negatively as well as positively in New York real estate—not
> only by constructing new buildings but by destroying, at the same time, whole areas
> of disgraceful and disgusting sores. These sores, for more than a century, have been
> festering in our very midst, festering with disease and, what is worse, perhaps, fes-
> tering with crime.[90]

Fig. 3.10. Forsyth Street looking
northward from Grand Street,
1931. In one of the most dramatic slum clearance efforts, the
blocks between Chrystie and
Forsyth Streets, from the Manhattan Bridge to Houston Street,
were demolished to make way for
public housing. The failure of
that effort left the neighborhood
with a long parkway, Chrystie-
Forsyth Park. Collections of the
Municipal Archives of the City of
New York.

Fig. 3.11. Jacob Riis, *Old House on Cherry Street, "The Cradle of the Tenement,"* circa 1890. With this and other photographs, Riis footnoted the history of the Lower East Side as the nineteenth-century home of the middle-class merchants and sea captains. The Jacob A. Riis Collection, Museum of the City of New York.

As mentioned earlier, the remains of the Lung Block were finally carted off to provide nourishment to the New York harbor fish for decades after it was torn down.

Only in the 1930s, when the federal government became a crucial player, did slum clearance become the dominant method of improving New York's housing stock. The Depression and the subsequent New Deal legislation brought a fundamental restructuring of the system of housing in New York and across the country. With government funding and encouragement, New York established the New York City Housing Authority in 1934 and designated large areas for demolition and new housing construction (see figure 3.12). First Houses, built in 1935 at Avenue A and East Third Street, were the first products of the New York City Housing Authority; they were soon followed by massive projects such as East River Houses, the Corlears Hook renewal area,

Fig. 3.12. Thomas Airviews, Stuyvesant Town, 1943. Robert Moses and city planners of the 1930s introduced a far more radical version of reform through destruction. Stuyvesant Town, which lies on eighteen blocks bounded by Fourteenth and Twentieth Streets, First Avenue and C, was built by the Metropolitan Life Insurance Company in 1943 with slum clearance incentives from the state. Today it houses some twenty thousand people. © Collection of The New-York Historical Society.

and Williamsburg Houses. The commitment of the federal government to low-income housing construction came with the Housing Act of 1937. In 1937 alone, some 37,000 apartment units were torn down throughout the city. By 1938, "the greatest elimination of Old Law housing in the city's history had occurred."[91] Although old-law tenements persist to this day in the Lower East Side, by the end of the 1930s, the city had gone a long way toward winning the first round of the "battle of the slum."[92]

CONCLUSION: "CATACLYSMIC" REFORM

In 1938, as old-law tenements were being torn down at a pace that would have pleased Jacob Riis, the Federal Writer's Project looked back to the first slum clearance site:

> Every foot of the "Bend" reeked with abject misery, cruelty, shame, degradation and crime. By day a purgatory of unrelieved squalor, at night the "Bend" became an inferno tenanted by the very dregs of humanity. . . . Cleaning of the district was impossible; still less any kind of reclamation. It had to be destroyed utterly.[93]

It had taken Jacob Riis's eloquence and a decade-long campaign to force an antiquated municipal machinery to finally remove the slums of Mulberry Bend. For much of the early twentieth century, housing reformers were forced to use a slow-paced method of ridding the city of its tenements: the cyclical workings of the private speculative real estate market.

What the New Deal achieved, and urban renewal experts like Robert Moses perfected in the 1950s, was a means of speeding up the process of slum clearance. Through governmental leadership, a convergence of the interests of reformers, developers, and landlords was achieved and the bulk of the old-law tenements eliminated.[94] In the Lower East Side, the government intervened to facilitate change by providing fuel for the process of creative destruction of the hated tenements. Where private real estate developers would not be moved, the local housing authorities using federal dollars took over the job of removing and replacing the tenements. Distilled to its essence, the story of slum clearance is about managing the pace of creative destruction in the city. On Fifth Avenue, creative destruction had to be cooled to the point of freezing in order to protect what had become an important place for the city's past and future. On the Lower East Side, the legends and memories of reformers fueled the engine that would bring down most of the old-law tenements.

Jane Jacobs would later lead the revolt against the ideology of urban renewal. In her 1961 book, *The Death and Life of Great American Cities*, Jacobs called these massive interventions of government into the urban landscape "cataclysmic." They brought rapid, decisive, and irreversible physical and social change to neighborhoods previously characterized by an "organized complexity."[95] Already in the 1930s key critics had warned of the effects of these interventions. For example, James Ford, writing in the midst of the New Deal housing efforts, saw that the slum clearance efforts for which reformers had long hoped were often deleterious to cohesion of the city. Piecemeal demolitions, such as the elimination of Mulberry Bend, were frustrating to the larger vision of a planned city:

> The wiping out of old tenements . . . has been uneven in its effects. Some new structures have obliterated all evidence of their predecessors. Other clearance presents an untidy appearance on widened thoroughfares or has left gashes and raw wounds where buildings are only partly demolished.[96]

Jacobs also built on a long, if submerged, tradition of lamenting the rapid transformation of the city even if it eliminated some of the most horrible of housing. Indeed, Jacobs would lead a counterrevolution, a "modernism of the streets," which celebrated the very places condemned by reformers.[97] Even as the tools of urban renewal were being assembled, from Jacob Riis's campaign down to the establishment of the New York City Housing Authority in 1934, there were murmurs of discontent—and not only by those whose homes were being torn down—at the destruction wrought by these efforts. Even as Mulberry Bend was to be demolished, some artists and intellectuals suggested that something would be lost. Edward Townsend, whose *Daughter of the Tenements* (1895) was a widely read classic of the tenement-life genre, scoffed at the zealous destroyers of the picturesque:

> In the course of human events, as they are directed and advanced by municipal energy, Mulberry Bend is to be converted into a park. For the sunlight and air so introduced into that neighborhood we shall all feel appropriately proud of our share in the achievement, yet I cannot but regret that even with all the deliberation our rulers may exercise in this matter, the transformation of the Bend into the park will have taken place before any American painter shall have found time from working up his "Naples sketches" and elaborating his "scenes from Cairo streets" into ambitious canvases, to step over into the "Bend" and preserve its distinctive color and action for those of us who care. He might even conceal his indiscretion by labeling his picture "Street Scene in an Italian Town," and sell it, i' faith![98]

Other writers, like William Dean Howells in *A Hazard of New Fortunes* (1889) and James Huneker in *The New Cosmopolis* (1915), made almost identical lamentations, including the exhortation for painters to preserve the memory of the tenement areas. Indeed, already in 1915 Huneker was suggesting to those who ventured to the myth-

Fig. 3.13. George Wesley Bellows, *The Lone Tenement,* 1909. Bellows looked below the technological marvel of the Blackwell's Island Bridge (now known as the Queensboro Bridge) to the destruction it wrought on the immigrant neighborhood. Chester Dale Collection, National Gallery of Art, Washington, D.C.

ical Lower East Side that there was "no more East Side . . . it [is] only a fable."[99] Even Jacob Riis believed the Bend "had its picturesque, its humanly interesting side":

> With the perpetual market on street and sidewalk, its crowds of raven-haired women, bright kerchiefs adding grateful touches of gayety to the sombrest of garbs, its celebration of communal saints (imported, not domestic) on the flimsiest of pretexts, it was a study for an artist always; yet I never saw one there.[100]

Contemporary artists, especially those of the "Ashcan" school, flocked to the Lower East Side, drawn to a place in Manhattan where they hoped to find the irrational, the fantastical, and the chaotic (see figures 3.13 and 3.14).[101]

Fig. 3.14. A lone tenement on Essex Street between Stanton and East Houston awaits demolition to make way for the Essex Street Market, 1935. A quarter century later, similar images would be found throughout the Lower East Side, as public housing and slum clearance were embraced by city planners. Collections of the Municipal Archives of the City of New York.

As the Lower East Side's population declined rapidly in the 1930s, with many of the immigrants who had first settled there having fled to northern Manhattan, the other boroughs, and beyond, writers began to celebrate or at least memorialize life in the "immigrant quarter." In the works of Michael Gold and Anzia Yezierska, Abraham Cahan and Henry Roth, the memory of the Lower East Side was being "collected."[102] Michael Gold began his classic *Jews Without Money* (1930), to name just one example, with a memory: "I can never forget the East Side street where I lived as a boy. It was a block from the notorious Bowery, a tenement canyon hung with fire-escapes, bed-clothing, and faces." At the heart of virtually every tale of the immigrant East Side was the tenement itself, the historical starting point for the group's history. "Every tenement home was a Plymouth Rock," declared Gold.[103] The nostalgia for neighborhoods cleared to make way for new bridges and parks or, less commonly, public housing, grew in intensity as slum clearance and urban renewal accelerated. Alfred Kazin, writing about an urban renewal area that was once his neighborhood, noted that

> despite my pleasure in all this space and light in Brownsville . . . I miss her old, sly, and withered face. I miss all those ratty little wooden tenements, born with the smell of damp in which there grew up how many school teachers, city accountants, rabbis, cancer specialists, functionaries of the revolution, and strong-arm men for Murder, Inc.[104]

Thus, by the end of the Depression, the slums of New York—and the most famous slum area of all, the Lower East Side—became more important as a place of memory and less a living neighborhood. The slums had become, in Pierre Nora's terms, a *lieux de memoire,* a disembodied site of memory—and no longer a *milieu de memoire,* a living setting for a community's past. This trajectory would continue in the post–World War II era, and the Lower East Side would grow as a place of nostalgic tourism, usually for those who had never lived there.[105]

At the same time as immigrants and their children were memorializing the immigrant history of the Lower East Side, promoters of urban renewal were resurrecting a different, more distant past of the neighborhood and its tenements. Those who sought to draw capital and government investment into the neighborhood (most notably the East Side Chamber of Commerce) recalled the glorious seventeenth- and eighteenth-century histories of the Lower East Side as home to the great founders of the city—Delancey, Rutgers, Roosevelt—and therefore worthy of a better future to redeem an appalling present. The East Side Chamber of Commerce advertised the places where George Washington had lived (1 Cherry Street) or where famous families such as the Roosevelts had their first lands in America. The Chamber proudly reported that an enormous amount of real estate on the Lower East Side was owned by descendants of some of the "original" families, including names such as Astor, Goelet, Cheeseborough, and Fish.[106] "Nowhere in all the realty records of America would one find so many distinguished and socially prominent owners of a huge community's property as one does on the lower East Side." Virtually every issue of the *Chamber News* in the 1930s contained historical descriptions of sites in the East Side or personal reminiscences. "Be proud of the lower East Side," the *Chamber News* proclaimed. "It has as fine a history as any of our original colonies."[107]

Ironically, it was often the oldest buildings of all—the "foul core" of the Lower East Side—to which the boosters looked for their valuable history. The rear tenements, after all, were often townhouses of merchants dating back to the late eighteenth century, near descendants of the families whose names appeared on street signs—Rutgers, Delancey, Forsyth. Even Lillian Wald, the reformer who defined her work by the horrors of the Lower East Side, noted the historic homes she occupied. The Henry Street Settlement was housed in two early-nineteenth-century townhouses, she wrote, that "still bore evidences of its bygone social glory" deserving of "the restorer's touch."[108]

It was to the romanticizing of the tenements that Robert Moses reacted with such venom. In 1956, at a celebration of the United Settlement House's seventieth anniversary (just around the time Joseph Mitchell was tracing the contributions of the bricks from Cherry Street), Moses mocked the notion that the slums and the Lower East Side had produced great artists for the reasons of their density and communal life. Some "social scientists," Moses snidely noted, "say that since the slums have bred so many remarkable people, and even geniuses, there must be something very stimulating in being brought up in them." They make the "slum sound romantic." In fact, the "slum is still the chief cause of urban disease and decay," he declared. "It was bequeathed to us by unconscionable rascals . . . the old enemies are still with us." Moses derided any nostalgia for the destroyed swatches of tenements that surrounded the Settlement House on Rivington Street. Characterizing the Lower East Side as an "outpost," a "jungle," and a "waste," Moses reaffirmed the ultimate dream: to "eradicate" the "irredeemable rookeries."[109]

But even as Moses spoke, a countermovement was developing to challenge this dominant philosophy of housing reform through slum clearance. This movement had its roots not only in contemporary battles but in a growing concern with the historic fabric of the city that had begun over a half century earlier, as Manhattan's elites became increasingly preoccupied with the preservation or destruction of the physical symbols of the past.

4 PRICELESS

Historic Preservation and the Valuing of Space

To persons who see in such a relic something more than an inert mass of masonry, who are susceptible to the power of association which imparts to a lifeless object something of the life that has been associated with it in passing years . . . plain stone walls like these become graven tablets teaching an imperishable lesson of heroism and self-sacrifice, the destruction of this link connecting the present with a bygone generation will be a source of deep regret.

—Edward Hagaman Hall, *The Old Martyrs' Prison*

When a man has traversed the streets of a city for fifty years, certain buildings become familiar landmarks. He first saw them perhaps on trudging to school with his books, and has seen them nearly every day since. He experiences a slight shock whenever such buildings are destroyed. There appears something wrong in the general aspect of the town. Of late years these shocks have followed one another so continuously that he may well wonder whether he is living in the same place.

—*Old Buildings of New York City*

One of the "familiar landmarks" of New York was the old City Hall in City Hall Park (see figure 4.1). Just south and west of Mulberry Bend, where slum clearance had gotten its start, City Hall stood proudly since 1811, widely revered as one of the city's most beautiful and historic works of architecture. But at the end of the century, it was threatened with destruction to make way for a new complex of municipal buildings. The "shock" of demolition had often inured New Yorkers to the creative destruction of their city. City Hall's threatened destruction had the opposite effect: it mobilized an influential segment of New York society to fight aggressively to save one of the "treasures of the City." In the process, the specter of demolition boosted a fledgling historic preservation movement.[1]

The story of City Hall—one of the first major historic preservation battles in New York—reveals new perspectives on the rise of historic preservation. The power exerted by early preservation groups to stop the demolition of City Hall can serve as a corrective to a narrative of historic preservation in New York that locates the beginning of historic preservation much later, as late as the 1960s and the founding

Fig. 4.1. City Hall in 1998. Behind City Hall is the Tweed Courthouse; to the east is the Municipal Building; and farther to the north are the federal and state courthouses. Just beyond the courthouses is Columbus Park (formerly Mulberry Bend Park) and the tenements of the Lower East Side. Photograph courtesy of Iguana Photo.

of the Landmarks Preservation Commission following the demolition of Pennsylvania Station in 1963–66. From the early nineteenth century onward, commentators have waxed eloquent about New York's propensity to throw away remnants of its past. Blame has largely been laid on the domination of commerce over the island. William R. Taylor implies as much in his work on culture and commerce in New York. "Business and commerce," he argues, "had the run of the city. The result, in many observers' eyes, was the progressive creation of an ahistorical landscape of purely commodified land, an island without memories."[2] But this view is misleading. The common belief that New Yorkers cared little for their past has clouded the vision of historians and current historic preservationists. With eyes glistening in amazement at this "monster out of control," as Henry James wrote, we have failed to recognize that New Yorkers were in fact deeply concerned about their city's history.[3] The effort to keep a large space out of the land market and removed even from use for public needs is significant and revealing.

There is a widespread sense that the early twentieth century was an ineffectual, muddled period in the progress of the preservation movement. But, on the contrary, many of the arguments and institutions that would sustain the preservation movement throughout the century were founded and elaborated at this time.[4] In the early years of the century, preservation began to expand as a coherent cultural undertaking, and even an intellectual discipline. The ideas of how to preserve the physical past in the urban landscape were new and in flux. Some advocates of preserving the physical past in the urban landscape pushed the boundaries of how the past would be merged with the present. They linked Progressive housing and economic reform with protecting the past, attempted to broaden the fabric of the past that would be preserved, and even began developing a critique of the private real estate market that lay behind the speedy disappearance of old New York.

But to tell the story of the City Hall fight in this manner would be to frame historic preservation in early-twentieth-century New York as simply an oppositional force, a bulwark against commercial exploitation of land. In fact, the effects of a new interest in protecting the past were ambiguous. Indeed, by the end of the era the public and intellectual basis of preservation had become less fluid. While the 1920s and 1930s brought important developments in the preservation of historic structures around the country—the development of Greenfield Village and Williamsburg, the establishment of Charleston's historic district regulations, the creation of the federal Historic American Buildings Survey—the preservation movement promoted a strategy of segregating history from daily life, making it the object of patriotic veneration for school and tourist groups. The ultimate solution offered for City Hall and the many other historic structures was to set them apart from the city of private development, often within the confines of parks. This symbolic segregation of the historic from the contemporary, the "priceless" from the exchangeable, was as much imprisonment as protection. Those engaged in preservation had become fixated on a "masterpiece theory" of preservation—preserving the few outstanding examples of each era of the city's architecture. This framework would hold for the next quarter century after World War II, and even beyond. In doing so, preservationists paved the way for history in the form of buildings and landscapes to become less concerned with a wide range of historic associations and more valued for limited patriotic, nostalgic, and aesthetic reasons.[5] Preservationists who scored notable victories and eloquently tried to secure sacred, "priceless" objects in a city dedicated to commerce also did their part to support the tumultuous destruction and rebuilding of the city.[6]

"SACRED STONES": EARLY PRESERVATION IN NEW YORK

The fight over City Hall, which raged almost continually between 1888 and 1910 and intermittently to the end of the 1930s, was but one of numerous battles to preserve physical remains of the city's past. The struggle was initiated by a powerful coalition of institutions and individuals who used their influence throughout the city to save other historic structures in this era.

Many historians who deal with the historic preservation movement simply skip lightly over the whole period from 1880 to 1930. Others jump from the first efforts in the nineteenth century to the end of the 1920s. The standard narrative traces the movement from the saving of Independence Hall, the Mount Vernon Ladies Association, and perhaps the first period rooms of George Francis Dow. It then moves quickly to the end of the 1920s when Rockefeller's Williamsburg and Ford's Greenfield Village were initiated. Considered next are the establishment of Charleston's historic districting law in 1931, the involvement of the federal government in preservation with the Historic Sites Act in 1935, and the work of the Historic American Buildings Survey, the WPA, and the Civilian Conservation Corps.

Others recognize that many important preservation battles took place in the early years of the century. Reformers attempted to save buildings and use historic sites for a variety of purposes, from hagiography to collecting colonial arts and crafts to Americanization. Too often preservation is seen in isolation, as a focused movement of grumpy elites. In fact, preservation was part of a much larger resurgence of interest in the American past. New writings in the history of historic preservation are recognizing the importance of these early efforts in establishing the ethos of historic preservation; in establishing key organizations; and in linking preservation, planning, and social reform in addressing larger cultural concerns.

The majority of preservation efforts at the turn of the century were directed at saving homes and public buildings considered important for their Revolutionary War associations, or ones that had particular architectural merit. Fraunces Tavern, located at the bottom of Broadway not far from City Hall, was saved from demolition in 1904 through an intense campaign launched by the Sons and Daughters of the American Revolution. The Tavern was the object of great veneration and preservation efforts at the turn of the century largely because of its "one supreme memory" from the American Revolution: Washington's farewell address to his commanders, given in the "Long Room" in 1783. But other Revolutionary-era homes, with more or less important connections to the Revolutionary period, were saved by the initiative of local patriotic societies in conjunction with national groups such as the Daughters of the American Revolution. In 1885, Alexander Hamilton's home in what is now Harlem, the Grange, was moved to the safety of St. Luke's Episcopal Church, becoming in the process the church's parish house. In 1924 when the church threatened to demolish it, J. P. Morgan Jr. and George Baker Sr. contributed the funds necessary to have it saved. Archibald Gracie's mansion on the East River (later the home of the Museum of the City of New York, now the home of New York's mayors), the Lefferts Homestead in Brooklyn, the Morris-Jumel Mansion in Harlem, and the Dyckman House on Upper Broadway were all protected, restored, and used as museums. Other efforts moved beyond the purely patriotic. Poe Cottage, the slight home of Edgar Allan Poe, was saved despite the failure of the city to contribute money. Theodore Roosevelt's home, on East Twentieth Street in the heart of a neighborhood rapidly losing its residential character and becoming a center of business, had been remodeled into stores and restaurants, and was finally demolished in 1910. It was rebuilt after his death in 1919 to serve as a permanent museum of his life.[7]

In addition to patriotic organizations, ad hoc groups of citizens were involved in battles to save historic buildings (as would be the case with St. John's Chapel, discussed later). The Municipal Art Society, which would lead the effort to gain a landmarks preservation law in the post–World War II era, was weak in its support for preservation in the early years of the century. Although the society initiated a campaign to save the Colonnade Hotel (part of Andrew Jackson Davis's remarkable 1833 urbanistic row on Lafayette Street) and supported the campaign for City Hall, it ignored many efforts to save buildings of little architectural value. In its annual reports, the question of civic beautification and public art dominated, while preservation fights were rarely mentioned. When the society did participate in such fights, it reinforced a narrow focus on protecting buildings of special architectural merit.[8]

These apparently antiquarian efforts to save the homes of famous New Yorkers and Revolutionary Americans was not, however, all there was to the preservation movement. Indeed, as historic preservation found its intellectual and political footing at the end of the nineteenth and beginning of the twentieth centuries, its advocates hoped that past and future could coexist, that the city's perplexing creative destruction could be controlled in such a manner as to protect discrete elements of the past while not stifling the magnificent growth of the city. Those who sought to save historic structures hoped that they would serve as moral and physical "stabilizers" in the urban landscape, slowing if not stopping the chaotic transformation of the city according to market rules.[9]

The young preservation coalition was dominated by people firmly engaged in designing, building, and reforming the future city, not those reveling in nostalgic reveries for "old New York." The best example of the constituency of this new preservation movement is Andrew Haswell Green, one of the key figures in New York City's development in the latter part of the nineteenth and beginning of the twentieth centuries.[10] Green was born in 1820 and died of a gunshot wound inflicted by a deranged man on Park Avenue in 1903. He was best known for his central role in helping to propel the consolidation of Greater New York. Beginning in 1868, he advocated throughout the city and in the State Assembly for a single municipality to replace the separate cities and unincorporated areas of what is now New York City. At the same time that he was pushing for consolidation, Green helped create the New York Public Library, fought various preservation battles within the city, and also defended wilderness areas, such as Niagara Falls and the Palisades in New Jersey. Green's extensive work for the preservation of important buildings and natural places would not have seemed to him at odds with his work as a promoter of New York City's growth, physically and socially. Indeed, he saw these enterprises as wholly compatible.[11] Thus, even during the years he was heading the Consolidation Inquiry Committee in the 1890s, he would be the main voice to preserve the historic City Hall.

Green helped create, and was supported in his efforts by, a series of organizations dedicated both to protecting the city's past and promoting a glorious future. The City History Club—founded in 1896 to teach schoolchildren about their city's history through tours, research projects, and lectures—noted in its statement of goals that while the group hoped to "awaken intelligent and active interest in the traditions of our own city," it specifically did not intend to "make antiquarians of the members."[12] The club declared: "History is past politics, and politics future history." By "arousing

an interest in the picturesque history of Manhattan," the club would be resolutely dedicated toward the future, toward the "improvement, uplifting and civic betterment of
the community."[13] Similarly, the American Scenic and Historic Preservation Society
(ASHPS), one of the nation's first preservation groups, was organized around the belief that the past would be valuable for present-day city building. The ASHPS was incorporated in 1896 as a publicly chartered, private organization that would serve as
the custodian for historic properties in New York State and advocate nationally for
the preservation of historic buildings and natural landscapes. [14] The ASHPS was ahead
of its time—one of the most influential preservation organizations, the Society for the
Preservation of New England Antiquities, was established fourteen years later, in
1910. The early work of the ASHPS—histories of important sites, book-length annual reports—and its leadership by Green suggested that the organization would have
greater influence than it did. Despite Green's hope (echoed by Edward Hagaman Hall,
the long-time secretary of the society and author of the major reports) that the
ASHPS would mimic the work of the British National Trust, the group never attained
the power or scope of their European counterpart. The ASHPS leadership would help
New York State gain a large number of protected historic sites. Still, preservation remained largely a local battle.

Andrew Haswell Green epitomized a new set of city builders who were at least
rhetorically concerned with constructing a city in which the past and present coex-
isted comfortably. These preservationists tentatively proposed ideas that would challenge the driving force of private real estate development in the city. Ultimately, however, their vision was limited, as it had to be given the structure of the movement
itself. The preservation movement championed by these men and women would support the very processes that would doom much of the historic fabric of the city.

ST. JOHN'S CHAPEL

One of the most intense, and unsuccessful, campaigns to save a building was waged
over St. John's Chapel, a parish of Trinity Church standing on a park bounded by Varick, Beach, Hudson, and Laight Streets (see figure 4.2). The Chapel, designed in 1803
by the one of City Hall's architects, John McComb Jr., stood at the heart of one of
the few remaining genteel squares in Lower Manhattan, although the area had declined with the influx of warehouses and tenements.[15] In many ways, this was a
preservation battle of the simplest, most elitist kind: the church was admired for its
age and its architecture. But a dig beneath the surface reveals that St. John's defense
was launched not purely for antiquarian reasons.

Fig. 4.2. St. John's Chapel in the winter of 1866–67, when it stood alongside grand townhouses built around St. John's Park. © Collection of The New-York Historical Society.

The Progressive preservation of community and the more conservative preservation of architecture were conjoined in this battle. The fight over St. John's Chapel, which occurred contemporaneously with the City Hall conflict, reveals the broader possibilities for preservation—to be a part of a larger movement for economic reform, stability for neighborhoods in the face of speculation, and improvement of housing for the poor.

St. John's was a parish chapel and an offshoot of Trinity Church, one of the oldest and most wealthy churches in New York City. Trinity stands at the head of Wall Street, observing the heated work of the financial center of the world. Some New Yorkers believed that Trinity watched over Wall Street's morals, in some way standing in opposition to the obsession with money that reigned there. But others saw Trinity as completely conjoined with the materialistic work of that street, one corporation among many. It was as if Trinity sat at the head of the table, the host to the practices people loathed on Wall Street. Looking back, it is clear that Trinity Church's birth portended trouble. The vast land grant given by the British Crown in 1705 and its designation as the "sole" parish in the city would make it suspicious in the post-Revolutionary era. Since that time it was attacked repeatedly for its exclusiveness, its Tory leanings, and, most of all, its wealth. The Progressive attack on corporate conspiracy did not take long to find its way to the oldest of New York corporations. In 1894, Richard Watson Gilder undertook a study of the condition of Trinity's tenements, finding that this wealthiest of churches was also a slumlord. The long ground leases Trinity had offered on its extensive Lower Manhattan properties had resulted in dense streets of worker tenements. While Trinity asserted—largely accurately—that because of the ground leases, they had no legal rights over the condition of the buildings built thereon, the symbolism was too stark: the richest church in America, dedicated to Christian charity, turned out to be a purveyor of sin and disease to its own flock. "Is Trinity the church evangelical, benevolent and Christ-like, and Trinity the landlord avaricious, grasping and devilish?" was the question that enraged New Yorkers asked.[16]

The uproar subsided with the demolition of the worst tenements, but distrust lingered. Trinity did not help its reputation by fighting numerous regulations sought by tenement commissions. For instance, the church went to court to fight basic tenement house legislation allowing the city to force private owners to fix their properties for health reasons. Jacob Riis argued in *The Battle with the Slum* that "Trinity, the wealthiest church corporation in the land, was in constant opposition, as the tenement house landlord, and finally to save a few hundred dollars, came near to upsetting the whole structure of tenement law that had been built up, in the interest of the toilers and the city's safety, with such infinite pains."[17] The issue burst in 1908 when Trinity sought to close down St. John's Chapel, one of the many churches Trinity had spawned but retained administrative control over. The outcry was swift and overwhelming. A memorial signed by, among others, President Roosevelt, Secretary of State Root, New York Mayor McClellan, and former mayor Seth Low was presented to the church and published in all the major newspapers.

The defense of St. John's inspired overblown feats of literary protest. Richard Watson Gilder, the 1894 Tenement Commission chair and poet, wrote a poem mocking Trinity's disrespect for the "sacred stones" of St. John's:

> Guardians of a holy trust
> Who, in your rotting tenements,
> Housed the people, till the offense
> Rose to the Heaven of the Just—
> guardians of an ancient trust
> Who, lately, from these little ones
> Dashed the cup of water; now
> Bind new laurels to your brow,
> Fling to earth these sacred stones,
> Give the altar to the dust!
> here the poor and friendless come—
> Desolate the templed home
> Of the friendless and the poor,
> That your laurels may be sure!
> Here beside the frowning walls
> Where no more the wood-bird calls,
> Where once the little children played,
> Whose paradise ye have betrayed,
> here let the temple low be laid,
> Here bring the altar to the dust—
> Guardians of a holy trust![18]

St. John's parishioners and clergy organized a protest and brought their case to court, attempting to stop the closing order. Bowing to the pressure (exacerbated by continuing revelations about the condition of the tenements to which they held the ground leases), Trinity agreed not to destroy the church. It was, however, a short-lived victory. With the widening of Varick Street to make way for the dual subway system and more rapid automobile traffic to downtown, St. John's was finally done in (figure 4.3).[19] Critics charged that by destroying St. John's, Trinity had laid waste to a

Fig. 4.3. The former site of St. John's Chapel in 1937, as St. John's Park was cleared in the decade after the opening of the nearby Holland Tunnel. The post office pictured here had stood on the site since 1919, when the chapel was demolished in order to widen Varick Street. © Collection of The New-York Historical Society.

valuable monument of New York's past. Its audacity, wrote Ray Stannard Baker, was a relic of the "whole aristocratic, feudalistic system" that had no place in the "new democracy" of the twentieth century.[20]

Part of the fury over Trinity Church's willingness to let St. John's Chapel be demolished was rooted in these same sentiments. Trinity offended the sensibilities of elite New Yorkers by ignoring the squalor over which it was landlord, resisting the noble efforts of the tenement commissions, perpetuating an undemocratic institutional organization, and unjustly redistributing the wealth of the church to its uptown parishioners, away from the downtown poor.[21] The church was morally condemned, in essence, for acting like a big business and not a religious institution. Critics were enraged that the church evaluated its policy toward the tenements and St. John's according to economic calculations. Ray Stannard Baker accused Trinity of being no better than an insurance company in its monopolistic, controlling tactics.[22] Others accepted that Trinity had to act like a business: "Trinity the landlord," A. W. Halsey wrote in 1895, " is not a charity organization; rents are not given away; tenants not paying have to be ejected; the business is conducted like any other business."[23]

The loose coalition of individuals who rallied to save St. John's reveals how diverse were the individuals and organizations interested in preservation. The St. John's campaign was led in part by I. N. Phelps Stokes, who was, as we will see in chapter 7, both an antiquarian collector as well as an active housing reformer and real estate developer. Signers and participants in the fight included Reform and Tammany mayors, architects Charles Follen McKim and George Post, Metropolitan Museum of Art president Robert W. De Forest, and J. P. Morgan. Certainly, antiquarians saw in the Trinity conflict and other preservation efforts a chance to save the homes of their ancestors and to create—through a network of historic houses, battlefields, and monuments—a bulwark against the influx of foreign ideas. Preservation battles, however, came increasingly under the leadership of a group of upper-class reformers, city builders, professionals, and managers.[24]

The St. John's Chapel crusade reveals not simply a repetition of preservation campaigns following the patriotic model of Mount Vernon or the Jumel Mansion. Rather, it shows that possibilities for a broader notion of historic preservation were ripe at the end of the nineteenth and into the twentieth centuries. Even as some suggested that buildings might more properly be preserved for posterity by moving them elsewhere, away from the furnace of private real estate development and public works, others were beginning to argue that the historic building's power was intimately tied to its site and even its use. I. N. Phelps Stokes, for example, had urged that St. John's not be moved and that it continue to be used as a church. He produced statistics showing that while some wealthier parishioners may have been moving northward, there was still a sizable real and potential population for the chapel to serve. Others insisted that although the church no longer served its religious function it could at least be used as a public forum.[25] New York's elites, well in the grip of a fascination with history and with New York's past, experimented and fought for a potentially expansive notion of how and what of the physical past would be preserved in the urban landscape. The fight to save St. John's posed these issues; the battle over New York's infamous City Hall brought them to a head.

"LIFE-THREAD" OF THE CITY

When New York's City Hall was completed in 1811, only three of its sides were faced in marble. The back, facing north, was left with its bricks exposed. Since City Hall was at the extreme northern end of the city at the time (see figure 4.4), the builders assumed that few would ever see the cost-cutting measures the city had made. By the 1880s, this assumption had become part of city folklore, a humorous example of the

Fig. 4.4. N. Currier, *City Hall Park*, 1851 (lithograph). The dream of many planners and preservationists was to return City Hall to its pristine original state, where it stood alone, surrounded by lush vegetation and a flowing fountain, as pictured in this nineteenth-century etching of Broadway and Park Row. The park, however, never appeared this way—absent are the several other buildings that occupied the park, as well as the generally unkempt state of the park in its early, and busy, life. © Collection of The New-York Historical Society.

naiveté of the earlier inhabitants of Manhattan who were unable to foresee the explosive growth of the city in the nineteenth century. By 1890, the city was well developed up to Central Park, well on its way to filling in the grid laid out by the city commissioners in the same years during which City Hall was built. City Hall had been inadequate for years, requiring that the burgeoning municipal enterprise be distributed to various public and private office buildings in and around City Hall Park, at great expense to the city. Beginning in 1888, the city initiated no fewer than seven competitions and proposals to produce plans for new municipal offices and a civic center.

The fight over City Hall became the first and longest-running preservation battle because it was so immersed in both the city's history and its potential future. In

1889, standing on the steps of City Hall, one could see the future of the American city in one quick glance. To the east, the broad swoop of the Brooklyn Bridge, completed in 1883, dispersed its cargo into City Hall Park and stood as a stunning example of the possibilities of engineering and transportation systems.[26] Just south of the bridge, on Park Row, were the towers of the *Tribune* and *New York World* buildings, vanguards of a new commercial culture and a "vertical monumentalism" that would symbolize that modernity and dominate the city's skyline.[27] They would be joined in 1913 by the Woolworth, the world's tallest building. In 1900, beneath the eastern side of the park, would be dug the first of New York's subway lines; the West Side line would burrow beneath the southern tip a decade later. Thus, the dream of a City Beautiful, of parks and majestic vistas, and of grand public buildings at the ends of boulevards and efficient transportation lines all were to be found in and around City Hall Park. City Hall thus lay at the center, geographically and psychologically, of the future city. It and the park in which it stood were greatly valued for what they symbolized about the past and what they promised for the future. By 1940, when the shape of City Hall and its surrounding park was essentially set for the rest of the century, the controversy over the historic site had become a touchstone for debates over the place of the past in the urban landscape.

The almost continuous City Hall debate over the course of four decades blurred competition with competition, proposal with proposal. Indeed, later commissioners and citizens found themselves returning to the morgue of civic center plans repeatedly, offering pieces of past proposals attached to new ones. The basic options of a grand municipal building or series of buildings in or around City Hall Park remained constant. What did change was the attitude toward City Hall and the park. At the start of the movement for new public buildings in 1888, the city readily sought to build in City Hall Park. By 1914, when the Municipal Building that now stands at the eastern end of Chambers Street was completed, City Hall was safe from demolition; gone too was the idea of encroaching on the park at all. In fact, the city followed the advocates' wishes to clear the park of all smaller buildings that had been placed there over the past century. This was a very different outcome from what was expected when the process began.

In 1888, Mayor Abraham Hewitt proposed that two wings be added to the old City Hall, connecting it with the Tweed Courthouse of 1878, just north, fronting on Chambers Street. Hewitt's plan, using Charles B. Atwood's winning competition scheme, was quickly rejected by the city council, but it was followed in 1889 by the Municipal Building Commission's plans for a totally new building that would require

Fig. 4.5. Chambers Street, looking east in 1907, to the recently
built Hall of Records
(1897–1905, John R. Thomas;
completed by Horgan and Slattery), with older structures in its
shadow. Within ten years, the
Municipal Building would tower
over this spot just to the south,
and the new courthouse complex
would occupy the sites to the
north and west. © Collection of
The New-York Historical Society.

the demolition of the old City Hall. The Commission, working under new rules set
by the state legislature that removed City Hall Park as a site for the buildings, found
no other suitable site. With a new state legislature voting in 1892 to allow the use of
City Hall Park, 1893 brought a highly publicized architectural competition, attracting 134 proposals to design a building on the site of the old City Hall.[28] The competition was, however, rendered moot. First, the jury could not decide on a single
winner. Then, the fickle legislature acceded to protests and reversed itself, now refus-
ing the use of City Hall Park for the courthouse and municipal building.

City leaders retained the hope that some combination of the plans from the 1893
competition could be utilized for a municipal building. In the meantime, John R.
Thomas, one of the finalists in the 1893 competition, was hired in 1897 to design a
Hall of Records—the most desperately overcrowded building—for the corner of
Chambers and Centre Streets. Thomas conceived of his building as the first of an even-

tual line of French classical structures that would create a grand civic center around City Hall Park. After his death, the building was completed by the firm of Horgan and Slattery in 1905 (figure 4.5). Earnest civic center master plans were put forward in 1899 by George Post and in 1903 by Post and Henry F. Hornbostel; their plan anticipated the general recommendations of the 1907 Civic Improvement Commission. The cost and magnitude of the project doomed the master plans, but one important element, a major new municipal office building, became a reality. In 1907, a competition for an office tower at the corner of Chambers and Centre streets was won by McKim, Mead and White. By 1914, the twenty-story building was complete (figure 4.6).

Only with the competition of the Municipal Building did the focus of city and state officials shift away from building on City Hall Park. Several courthouse designs—later developed in Foley Square, immediately north of City Hall and west of Mulberry Bend—were proposed for City Hall Park, but were soon rejected. The city's office needs were never completely satisfied, nor was a monumental civic center created. Nonetheless, City Hall Park was never again considered for such plans. In the end, the advocates for the preservation of City Hall and the park were victorious: City Hall was saved, the park improved, never again to be seriously threatened. City Hall and its park were removed from the endless political calculations about what land could be used for municipal projects. City Hall had become priceless.

What accounts for this transformation? What arguments were marshaled to make City Hall and its park elevated above the market, what Georg Simmel called the "frightful leveler"?[29] During the preservation battle, advocates for protecting City Hall articulated a wide range of reasons for the value of the historic building. More interesting is the opposite question: What stalled the building of a new courthouse and city hall? Why could the nation's largest city not produce a civic center commensurate with its explosive growth, especially after the consolidation of the five boroughs in 1898? For all the potent rhetoric that would be deployed to protect City Hall, powerful forces and individuals resisted the preservation of the building. What was the calculus of publicly initiated destruction? How did city policy makers persist in trying to demolish public and private buildings to make way for new public buildings?

The story of the twenty-year battle over City Hall and the attempt to design a new municipal civic center have all the elements of municipal farce: bungled design competitions, a meddlesome state legislature, bizarre design proposals from individuals and institutions, biting editorial commentary, bureaucratic infighting, and eloquent defenses of the city's past and idealistic visions of its future. As early as 1889, in response to new delays and requests for site legislation from the state assembly, the *New York Times* declared that "This vacillation and hesitation is getting to be

Fig. 4.6. The McKim, Mead and White Municipal Building, completed in 1914. Photograph courtesy of Iguana Photo.

childish. The Legislature would be justified in assuming that the people and authorities of this city do not know their own minds and cannot be relied upon to hold the same opinion for a year at a time."[30] This brief overview concerning the various plans could indicate that the *Times*, on the surface, was correct.[31] But if we disentangle the various battles, we can see more clearly the conflicting attitudes toward creative destruction and the pressures that shaped the market for space. In the City Hall debate, historical values conflicted with public needs—the necessity of a new municipal office complex—as well as with pure market prerogatives. The fight was so intense because preservation advocates urged the city to consider City Hall and its park "priceless" in the very arena where the "pure" market for rentable and developable space reached its apotheosis.[32]

Influential cultural institutions, such as the New-York Historical Society, the American Scenic and Historic Preservation Society, the City History Club, and later the City Club of New York, began in the late 1880s to articulate an attitude toward the preservation and dissemination of city and national history that focused on the instrumentality of historic monuments. History was the currency that would buy a healthy future for the city: homogenous social relations and a respectful and responsible citizenry. But history in books was not enough. History and historical education needed monuments from the past. For young historic preservationists as well as those who fought the slums, it was the "aura" of the past, as Walter Benjamin has called it, the "authentic" link to the past that gave old buildings their power.[33] When Edward Hagaman Hall, the president of the American Scenic and Historic Preservation Society, fought the destruction of the colonial-era Debtors' Prison in City Hall Park to make way for the first subway station, it was self-evident to him that the building was something more than "an inert mass of masonry." The "power of association," he wrote, "imparts to a lifeless object something of the life that has been associated with it in passing years."[34] The development of this idea marked a crucial shift in the popular attitude toward history and toward the urban landscape.

In the eyes of the historic preservationists, historic buildings and places served as ready spurs to the collective memory of the city in ways that books could not. The American Scenic and Historic Preservation Society wrote in its 1910 annual report of the "storied Park" that it sought to defend. The park was indeed a place of stories in the writings of these early historic preservation advocates. New Yorkers used City Hall and the few other remaining historic buildings to tell stories about the past.[35] Buildings are, ultimately, mute messengers of collective memory. The history within them is revealed through the telling of their history. Memories are not so much recalled as retold, and in the process remade. Each defense of City Hall (or other historic buildings) was accompanied with long recitations of the important events and persons who had passed through the building or across the park. "History" was a repetition of stories, located in particular places, which told the crowning myths of the city and nation. Thus, a mention of City Hall was usually accompanied by a note of the great events of the building: the reading of the Declaration of Independence in the park, the meetings of the Sons of Liberty, and Lincoln lying in state beneath the famous curved stairway of City Hall. Historic buildings were the "life-thread" of the city, as Melusina Fay Peirce (philosopher Charles Peirce's first wife and a fierce fighter for preservation) observed. They connected the past with the present, the city's beginnings with its future. In a city where the past was destroyed so rapidly, where the main "story" was one of pastiche and fragment, and forgetting was dangerously easy, historic buildings provided narrative threads over time. Speaking of Fraunces Tavern, Peirce wrote that it was "not strange that it should be forgotten by the now almost wholly un-American—by the almost wholly foreign—City of New York."[36] Historic buildings in their actual connection with the past could restore through the telling of their stories the American virtues held within their walls.

For New Yorkers enamored of historic buildings, City Hall held a more sacred, almost spiritual, meaning. Perhaps the most eloquent testimony came from Green. Although he was instrumental in ushering in the vast metropolitan government through the consolidation of the five boroughs in 1898, he fought plans that would have demolished the old City Hall to make way for a larger municipal complex. In 1894, as it was becoming more and more likely that a master plan for the City Hall Park area would require the demolition of City Hall, Green organized—under the auspices of his new organization, the ASHPS—an intense protest that resulted in the halting of a widely publicized competition. About this first organized protest to defend City Hall, Green wrote:

> While Independence Hall in Philadelphia no longer answers its original purpose, who in that City would have the effrontery to propose its removal and thus wipe out all visible insignia of its precious memories? Or who in Boston would consent to the destruction of Faneuil Hall . . . adorned with memorials of that City's history?
>
> How long will it be before some, careless of the conservative influence of distinguished achievements, will want to remove Bunker Hill Monument or destroy the home of Washington at Mount Vernon? Are the principles and the works of our fathers wholly forgotten? Is that subtle, refining sentiment dissipated that delights to preserve what is left of the material environment of Shakespeare and Milton?

Are the achievements of the past to fade into oblivion? The moral power of association can scarcely be overestimated. It arouses as well the slumbering chord that responds to the inspiring strains of the "marseillaise," awakens tender memories at the sympathetic melodies of "Sweet Home," and will always attract the thoughtful to scenes made memorable by deeds worthy of remembrance.

It is not wise to destroy the monuments that keep alive these lessons.[37]

City Hall was certainly admired for its architecture: it had long been considered a masterpiece of the French classical revival style, and advocates dutifully noted its place atop the pantheon of New York buildings. But far more important was that City Hall was a crucial bearer of the city's past, and through that past the valuable lessons of earlier, presumably more virtuous, generations could be passed on. It was, to start with, one of the oldest buildings in the city. "Where in New York," Green rhetorically asked the 1893 Building Commission, "is there left a public building or monument of historic value?"[38] Part of the preservation instinct, then, was to hold onto the few remaining buildings of the early nineteenth century and before. In 1894, *Harper's* agreed with the "general opposition to the demolition of the old City Hall":

> It is not only a creditable piece of architecture, but it is the most important historical monument of the city. In New York an existence of nearly a century quite suffices to make a building venerable. The majority of cultivated persons in New York would regard the demolition of City Hall not only as a municipal calamity, but as an act of vandalism.[39]

Commentators associated City Hall with a more virtuous era, free from the commercial values that they saw everywhere around them. At one of the early meetings of the Board of Commissioners for the Erection of a New Municipal Building in 1889, George Rose lamented the surrender of the city to commercial interests: "What a sorry spectacle for a great and rich people to confront in the extended area of Manhattan Island south of Union Square! Nothing but piles of brick and mortar. Clear evidence of a vast population's parsimony and a care only for material things."[40] Saving City Hall and its park was for many advocates one final effort to spare at least one area from the rolling avalanche of private real estate development. Herbert Croly, the architecture critic and Progressive author, while praising City Hall, lambasted the city for allowing commercial interests to dominate the landscape: "Private, special and business interests have been dominant in New York ever since the Revolution, and have left an indelible mark upon the public life and appearance of the city. . . . [T]he streets have been made a gift to real estate speculators and builders to deform as suited their interests; and they have done and are doing their worst."[41] For some, City Hall and its park constituted one of the final resting places of the Revolutionary generation's glowing example. Although City Hall was built after the Revolution, the park itself was the setting for readings of the Declaration of Independence, meetings of the Sons of Liberty, and an important speech about the Tea Party by Alexander Hamilton. Furthermore, prisoners of war were kept in the old prison—called the "Martyr's Prison"—which now ill-housed the city's department of records.

If the shortcomings of unrestrained commerce were illustrated for the benefit of the city's elite, the most important lessons were aimed at the millions of immigrants who were flooding into New York. The City Hall debate, which featured eloquent but rarefied discussions about the sanctity of the building, seemed to have little to do with the question of overcrowding in tenements, the stale air of so-called rear tenements, and the rampant prostitution in the backrooms and basements of Mulberry Bend. But, in fact, in Mulberry Bend and City Hall Park, destruction and preservation were different means to the same Progressive end: the successful—as defined by the reformers—assimilation of the millions of immigrants flooding into New York and its notorious Lower East Side. In the eyes of reformers, Mulberry Bend's history of crime and degradation could only perpetuate vice; buildings with a noble history, such as City Hall, with their "authentic" connection with heroic events of the early Republic, could battle vice with the examples of American ideals.

Historic buildings could speak to the illiterate and to those not fluent in English or unschooled in the governing myths of the city and the nation. Andrew Haswell Green, as head of the ASHPS, argued that "visible historic memorials are objects to attract the attention and to gratify the finer feelings of every class." But he lamented that "Young as our country is, the actuality, so to speak, of our founders is already losing itself in the mists of the past; so long, however, as we can preserve the material objects left to us which those great men saw, [used], or even touched, the thrill of vitality may still be transmitted unbroken." The unwritten message was, If we, the descendants of the founders, cannot deign to remember, how will the "illiterate or however refined" immigrants adopt the values of the Revolutionary generation?[42]

But it was not unwritten elsewhere. In the work of the city's history organizations, the social implications of preserving historic buildings were clearly stated. The City History Club, for example, one of the steady players in the "history industry" in New York, recognized the value of early buildings for the education and assimilation of the new immigrants who were flooding into the country. In fact, the City History Club, founded in 1896, bound itself to educate newcomers to the city and nation's heritage. It included as one of its fundamental purposes "to help the immigrant's child and the child of generations of loyal Americans alike to feel the duties of social service and the privileges and responsibilities of being 'citizens of no mean city.'"[43] But what is striking in its programs—slide lectures, "history clubs" set up in schools and settlement houses, printed walking tours, books on New York City history—is the emphasis it placed upon using historical sites as a tool of assimilationist education (see figure 4.7). In Mulberry Bend, demolition was needed to eliminate the worst excesses of an exploitative real estate system and the immigrants' own moral failings, and thus stem, in Jacob Riis's words, the "resistless flood" of immigrant disaffection. In City Hall Park, the dangers of the immigrant revolt were to be eased and possibilities of assimilation achieved through preservation rather than destruction. Thus, the value of specific buildings and spaces for a reform program was powerfully influenced by collective memories that were attached to the place. In the minds of preservationists and tenement reformers alike, collective memory was a newly effective currency, adjusting value and shaping development.

Fig. 4.7. Cover of the 1917–18 annual report of the City History Club. United States History, Local History & Genealogy Division, The New York Public Library, Astor, Lenox and Tilden Foundations.

The impassioned arguments of Green and others reveal the beginnings of a more subtle philosophy compared to the hagiographic overtones of the earliest preservation arguments. Certainly, like the first preservationists (who sought to preserve Mount Vernon and Revolutionary battlefields), Green emphasized the Revolutionary heritage of the site. But already he had moved beyond purely Revolutionary themes. He argued that the later history of the city and nation was captured in the history of City Hall. By its very age and stature, Green argued, the building bore all the memories of nineteenth-century New York. Just as the buildings of Mulberry Bend held the harmful essences of past sin and crime, and therefore had to be physically destroyed, so the very walls of City Hall retained the valuable lessons of New York's remarkable growth, and therefore must be preserved. "Its presence tends to keep alive associations that are near to very many of our citizens, a visible landmark, an object lesson to the people, that should not be destroyed."[44]

The fight over City Hall also brought historic preservation advocates together

with those who fought for parks. This alliance took advantage of the same 1887
law authorizing funding for small parks that had supported the demolition of Mulberry Bend. Throughout the debate, the park itself was seen to equal—if not surpass—the value of City Hall itself. The 1910 annual report of the American Scenic
and Historic Preservation Society quoted historian Henry B. Dawson's 1865 elegy
to the park:

> It must not be forgotten that the Park is still the refuge of the people. . . . Here they
> have met Lafayette and other friends of freedom and their country, making the welkin
> ring with their joyous shouts; and here they have mingled their tears over the mem-
> ory of Jackson, Clay and other departed worthies. On all occasions, whether of joy or
> sorrow, of prosperity or calamity, of welcome or of separation, the Park is now, as it
> ever has been, the resort of the people. Nor does it possess much less interest to oth-
> ers than to us. The past—the common property of all—shows the Park to have been
> *the Fantail of New York*, the cradle in which the much-lauded "cradle of liberty" in
> Boston was itself rocked in its infantile years.[45]

The ASHPS had been founded on an ethos that valued scenic and historic natural
landscapes almost as much as historic structures. The ASHPS had steadily worked to
save important scenic areas such as the Palisades in New Jersey and Niagara Falls; it
even reported on the ruin of scenic landscapes in Europe during World War I.[46]

The linkage of historic preservation and land conservation was not a coincidence.
Green had first been prompted to initiate his protest against the City Hall development plans when the option of moving City Hall was being embraced by several cultural institutions. Both the New-York Historical Society, which was moving to Central Park West and Eighty-first Street, and the Tilden Trust, which was establishing
the New York Public Library at Forty-second Street in Bryant Park, responded favorably to the idea of moving City Hall out of the park as a way of saving it. Green
entered the fray to protest even moving City Hall: "The building is indissolubly connected with its site and surroundings. Remove it and interest in it vanishes."[47] The
land was literally sacred by virtue of the historical events that had taken place there.
In opposition to the commodification of the earth that all around City Hall was
achieving its most frictionless movement, Green sought to remove City Hall and its
park from the real estate market's grasp.

However, deep splits within the historic building and park preservation coalition
ultimately weakened the effort to save City Hall Park and its historic buildings. While
these groups often overlapped and clearly supported one another, at times their purposes collided. Park advocates, while pleading its historical importance, were primarily interested in preserving City Hall Park as open space in an increasingly crowded

downtown. Despite having a road cut through it, a post office placed at its southern tip in 1875, and several other buildings built upon it, City Hall Park remained one of the very few open spaces downtown. Park advocates repeatedly noted the contradiction in city priorities. "While we are condemning property in the lower wards for park purposes," the *New York Times* wrote in 1889, "it would be very absurd wantonly to destroy or impair an existing park."[48] Green reiterated the attack in his 1894 protest: Since the city was spending a million dollars every year to build several small parks, including Mulberry Bend—"within a stone's throw of the City Hall Park"—it seemed patently insane "practically to close that already existing and greatly used and needed" park.[49] The City Club of New York, fighting once again to keep buildings out of the park, stated the problem plainly: "The only way to preserve the parks is to preserve them, and to accept the fact that they have been stricken from the list of possible building sites. We hold the parks in trust for future generations."[50]

For park advocates, the goal was not only to prevent further encroachment, but actually to eliminate all buildings, except City Hall, and restore the park to its supposed original condition (see figures 4.8 and 4.9).[51] The "original intent" preservationists, however, articulated a historically weak argument. For, in fact, the park had from early on in its history been home to a variety of public buildings and activities. The notion of a recreational park was a relatively recent attitude. At times, this found historic preservationists in conflict with their park colleagues who argued that many of the small buildings scattered around the park had important historical associations. For example, the old Hall of Records, on the northeast corner, had been a prison during the Revolutionary War, but in 1902 was threatened with demolition to make way for the IRT subway station. Edward Hagaman Hall argued that the eventual gain of a few yards of open space—which he admitted the "City is in need of"—"would not be adequate compensation for the loss of this, the oldest municipal building in the City, and a building that represents as no other in New York the sufferings that were endured and the sacrifices that were made by American patriots for the cause of American independence."[52] But in the main battle to save City Hall, preservationists often used the blunt instrument of law to halt all new construction in the park. The *New York Times*, generally a strong advocate of preservation and of parks, mocked the bill pursued by Green and other preservationists: "The worst of what has been called the bill to 'save the old City Hall' is that it took away the power to remove the old eyesores from the eastern side of the park, including this brownstone building and the engine house in the corner. . . . It not only 'saved' the old City Hall but it saved the rest of the old buildings." For the *Times*, City Hall alone was worth saving; all else only interfered with the use of the park as a leisure and recreation area. For others, such as Hall, these "eyesores" were in fact important relics with significant civic lessons.

Fig. 4.8. "Uncle Sam," Old New York Sketches by John Di Mariano. Postcard of City Hall Park from Broadway and Park Row, 1922. "Uncle Sam, please let us remove the smoke screen (P.O.). We want the Old Colonial Gate to the most beautiful city in the world restored as it was over one hundred years ago. 1812." Museum of the City of New York.

Beyond the contention between park and historic building advocates was an intense debate within the preservation community and the press more generally over which buildings in City Hall Park deserved to be saved. Park advocates and protectors of historic buildings each saw a threat of destruction from incursions to the park. But they valued the buildings and spaces of the park differently; even those who saw great merit in saving City Hall were divided. Not everyone agreed with the highblown rhetoric of the preservationists, although they certainly wielded enormous influence in the state assembly. While no one advocated the demolition of City Hall simply to get rid of it, many criticisms of City Hall were expressed. There were many who openly agreed that the old City Hall was inappropriate for the vast municipal enterprise New York had become. Even the *New York Times*, which had praised the exterior building in 1893 and wanted the building saved—"one of the handsomest buildings in the country" the newspaper had called it—criticized the building as totally unsuitable as the administrative heart of a modern municipality.[53]

Fig. 4.9. Postcard: The Civic Center, New York, circa 1920, featuring City Hall with the Tweed Courthouse and post office removed. Throughout the 1920s and 1930s images of a "restored" City Hall Park proliferated. Museum of the City of New York.

Reverence for antiquities, especially for beautiful antiquities, is a noble and ennobling sentiment. But reverence for the old City Hall that takes account only of its exterior beauty and ignores its internal loathsomeness is not a noble, but a discreditable sentiment. The City Hall is not fitted for any modern business or public purpose.[54]

Furthermore, the *Times* questioned the historic associations so cherished by preservationists. "The City Hall has other historical associations in which the patriotic citizen does not take pride. . . . Here foul-mouthed, illiterate, be-diamonded Aldermen divided plunder wrested from the taxpayers of the city. In the light of the disreputable associations which cling to the City Hall, it is a question in the minds of many good citizens whether these unpleasant memories of a great city's shame do not overshadow the dim recollections of the patriotic and remote past."[55] The architectural press, though it offered great praise for the merits of City Hall, urged that the courthouse be demolished and City Hall demolished or removed in order to provide adequate room for a new civic building. With those buildings out of the way, there would be "nothing to hamper architects" in their effort to build a grand public building. Appeals to sentiment about City Hall were brushed aside. The architectural advisors to the 1893 building committee "are quite as capable of appreciating the undoubted beauty of the old building as most people, but it seemed from the first utterly impracticable to incorporate it with the new one, and the wisest course is certainly in such cases to avoid sacrificing both buildings to unreflecting sentiment."[56]

If there were quibbles about saving City Hall, no one seemed to want to preserve the Tweed Courthouse, located just behind it. A symbol of municipal corruption since its completion in 1872 at a cost some twenty times its budget, the Tweed Courthouse played an important role in shaping how city leaders approached the expensive construction of municipal buildings. "The city of New York still suffers," the *Times* wrote early on in the process,

> and for years to come will continue to suffer, the penalty of the official wrongdoing of the past. The enormous municipal plunder of the Tweed ring and the continuance of the political methods that made it possible fill the people with distrust and fear whenever there is any great public work to be done. This feeling has been a terrible check upon the progress and improvement of the city, and the chief obstacles in the way of securing for its authorities full control over its local interests.[57]

There was little positive that anyone could say about the Tweed Courthouse (pictured in figure 4.10). Building the courthouse and giving up the land for the federal post office (in 1875) represented "one of the worst sins against public decorum and aesthetic decency which any city of metropolitan pretensions ever committed."[58] The Tweed building was a daily reminder of the dangers of municipal corruption and civic scandal. In 1889 the *New York Times* declared its opposition to plans that would remove all buildings but save the Tweed Courthouse. "This proposal," the editors wrote, "contemplates the demolition of the City Hall, the most creditable public building belonging to the city, and now also a historical monument in a city which has altogether too few of such monuments."[59]

Ironically, the symbolic power of the Tweed Courthouse was its best protector. Successive city administrations, daunted by the prospect of heaving a wrecking ball at millions of dollars of taxpayers' money, planned around it. Indeed, so powerful was this recent memory of municipal corruption that at several points in the twenty-year odyssey of City Hall it was proposed that the Tweed Courthouse—despite its hated appearance and associations—be saved while the revered City Hall was slated for removal or demolition. For instance, in 1893, despite the recommendation of the Architectural Advisory Committee (composed of some of the most important architects of the day—Napoleon Le Brun, William Robert Ware, and Richard Morris Hunt)[60]—the

Building Commission agreed to a misshapen, awkward ground plan: the new building would wind its way in an asymmetrical manner around the Tweed building, creating in effect a long thin alleyway between it and the courthouse and, to the south, leaving only a two-hundred-foot-wide swatch of park land between the new building and the post office. The plan would for "all intents and purposes, destroy the City Hall Park. . . . All of the 'park' that is left will be a strip of ground a hundred feet wide from Park Row to Broadway, far from enough for even a spacious foreground for a great public building and utterly insignificant and worthless as a public breathing place."[61]

This paradox did not go unnoticed by the *Times:*

> There is no good reason why the Court House should be preserved. It is not of any architectural value, it is practically the subject of complaint from everybody who is forced to inhabit it . . . and there are no associations connected with it that are not disgraceful to the city. The municipal authorities must now see that it is unreasonable to insist upon a condition that will destroy the City Hall Park and greatly mar the effect of the new City Hall, for the sake of keeping a building that is practically a blunder, architecturally an eyesore, and historically a disgrace.
>
> Historically, every instructed New-Yorker must be as much ashamed of the Court House as he is proud of the City Hall.

Fig. 4.10. Postcard: Broadway, south from Chambers Street, circa 1925. City Hall Park (seen here from the roof of one of the nation's first department stores, A.T. Stewart's) was a crowded place and had long been occupied by buildings, including the Tweed Courthouse (in the foreground), City hall, and the Alfred Mullett post office (at the southern tip). Museum of the City of New York

And yet, Mayor Gilroy sensed political disaster if he provided his opposition with such a powerful symbol of municipal waste.[62] An exasperated *Times* attacked Mayor Gilroy's logic with venom:

> The only argument that has ever been heard in favor of keeping the Court House is that it cost a great deal of money. It is true enough that an enormous amount of money was paid ostensibly on account of the building, but it is not in the building [most was sheer fraud]. . . . To insist that it should be kept, to the manifest detriment of the new City Hall, is merely to insist upon throwing good money after bad.[63]

The Tweed debacle taught municipal administrations to avoid any appearance of a municipal boondoggle:

> Mindful of the scandals and disasters that followed the discoveries relative to the building of the Tweed Court House, the managers of Tammany have long been determined that the new Municipal Building shall be built without inviting opposition and without resulting in scandals that would furnish material for their opponents.[64]

Thus, mayors sought every means possible to eliminate costs. With land in the City Hall area skyrocketing—as the debate crawled on from 1889 to 1910, the cost of building on land on the north side of Chambers Street increased two or three times from an estimated $3–4 million in 1893 to upwards of $13 million in 1910—city officials turned easily to the "free" option of building on public land. Cost surfaced as a compelling force in the valuing of space in another manner: the amount of money spent on rent for municipal offices threatened to become a scandal in itself. The city was spending over $300,000 for office space in buildings along Chambers Street and in several other buildings scattered throughout the area.[65] From the start, the purpose of putting the new City Hall and courthouses in City Hall Park was done to avoid having to pay enormous amounts to condemn private land in Lower Manhattan. And as the years went on, the value of the land grew, and it became ever more difficult.

Some groups mocked the city's cost-cutting measures. It seemed to be an ominous sign that the greatest city in America could not spend the money to build a grand civic center. Others insisted that the taxpayers would eagerly accept increased taxes in order to pay for a City Hall worthy of their city's stature. Finally, more savvy observers assured a hesitant Building Commission that the increase in property values due to the presence of City Hall and the refurbished park would in the long run more than offset the added expense of acquiring the land.

It was against the very idea that the "free" land of the park was the best option for a financially strapped city that park advocates reacted most vociferously. As we have seen, as early as 1889, one of the prime protests against the demolition of City Hall was that a new building would ruin the park. By 1910, advocates had developed a very clear notion of the "pricelessness" of park land. "The question thus narrows down to the old one," the *New York City Globe* wrote, "of whether park space as park is worth to the public what it would bring in the open market. The judgment of the community, on many occasion expressed, is that it is worth that and much more."[66] As the latest plans for the civic center were debated in 1910, the *Times* scoffed at the calculations made by the city about the "savings" realized by paying a low price for the land in City Hall Park:

> In fact the land in the park is priceless. . . . To part with a square yard of it for a new building would be the worst kind of improvidence. . . . To build on the two blocks north of the park will be expensive, especially the grand scheme of a monumental group of related buildings is accepted, but not nearly as expensive as the destruction of park land. . . . To build in the City Hall Park would be to erect a monument to stupid municipal improvidence, to keep before the eyes of future generations a lasting reminder of the perversity and nearsightedness of their forefathers.[67]

The quest for "free" space was rooted in the fierce negotiations over the value of space between the city, private owners, civic institutions, and citizens. The high cost of creating a civic center was a result not simply of an explosive real estate market, but also the designs proposed by the city and the architectural profession. While it might seem that design questions were separate from the equation of creative destruction, in fact the prevailing ideologies of design powerfully influenced how and whether land was to be redeveloped. The desire to plan a unified civic center was itself an artifact of the time, an influence of the City Beautiful movement and, more generally, the work of Haussman and the Beaux Arts movement. Creating a civic center with grand vistas, open space, and boulevards was a financially expensive aesthetic choice that would play an important role in determining the city's plans.

The history of the designs proposed for City Hall and the civic center is the history of the City Beautiful aesthetic and Beaux Arts planning ideas. A slide show displaying the designs for the civic center from 1888 to 1910 presented numerous variations on a preferred architectural order. But it is important to note that though the Beaux Arts is often identified with the classical revival style, this was hardly its defining feature. Indeed, though the winning designs in the 1893 competition were all certainly Beaux Arts, their facades ranged from the French Chateau to elaborate neoclassic styles. The concern of the Beaux Arts was with planning, procession, and spatial arrangements—not primarily "style." That preference, urged by architects and the young planning profession, and adopted by many members of social and cultural institutions, was repeatedly invoked in the discussion about City Hall and its park. Over the two decades that a new City Hall was debated, the questions of spatial arrangements, of views and vistas, and of symmetry—not specific historic style—dominated the arguments of all sides.

The 1888 plan of Mayor Hewitt was partly rejected because its tall "wings" would unnaturally tower over City Hall, in an ungainly, spliced-together monumental gesture. Similarly, the 1893 competition, though efficient until run aground by the legislature, was a sad excuse for a comprehensive civic center. The ground plan was an awkward U shape, squeezed in between the courthouse and the post office. In 1910, one of the proposals—again, to save money—was to place the new City Hall directly behind the old City Hall. Although it was symmetrical, its nearness to the old City Hall and sheer size was oppressive. The *New York Times* complained that "The old City Hall, one of our few architectural landmarks of recognized worth, will stand dwarfed and obscured. . . . The Court House will tower above it, ten stories in height. . . . [T]he effect will be ludicrous." And the *Evening Post* insisted that the new building would "make City Hall look like a little white dog crouched at the feet of a stern master."[68] Herbert Croly, writing in 1903, had nothing to say about the style of possible municipal buildings. He instead ranted about the failure of the city to protect the space around its center:

> The municipal government degraded one of the most spacious and delightful squares with which any City Hall in America was surrounded into an insignificant little park, over-run with buildings, with no approaches, no vistas.[69]

This final image, of a uniform group of buildings, symmetrically organized around a monument—in this case the historic City Hall—was the Beaux Arts ideal (see figure 4.9). What is striking is how different that image was from the images of downtown Manhattan from the period: spiked skyscrapers desperately seeking to be visible in the sky because at the street level, traffic was too busy and buildings crowded too closely together. To accomplish this contrast was expensive. The Beaux Arts was a spatially luxurious architectural philosophy: it depended on the free expenditure of space to achieve its effects. Achieving symmetry in an assembly of buildings in downtown Manhattan would have been a radical task, a costly fight against the chaotic current of real estate development. Symmetry among buildings and open spaces was unnatural in the individualistic free real estate market of Manhattan; the call for "vistas" and "foregrounds" was an almost absurd notion for private developers. For the most visionary planners, meaningful space was achieved through the expenditure of space, the most valuable commodity in Manhattan.

The City Hall design battles of the late nineteenth and early twentieth centuries reveal, on the one hand, how age and historical significance conferred cultural value on a place and thus spurred a movement to stop its demolition. However, it was also the idea of creating, writing, and building a common history that propelled visions of clearing City Hall Park and creating a new civic center complex. Beaux Arts visionaries were not always in alliance with historic preservationists; architects and planners who imagined a grand civic center were willing to sacrifice the old City Hall to make way for their designs. Nonetheless, it should not be surprising that the Municipal Art Society, which fought alongside the ASHPS and others to protect City Hall, was also the main author of the city's comprehensive plans for creating a Beaux Arts city plan. If some planners envisioned a wholly new civic center, cleared of the old buildings of City Hall Park, and preservationists stoutly defended their historic monuments, on one fundamental point both groups were in agreement: they were planning for history. If preservationists lamented the destruction that came with this greatness, they never rejected the city's stature. While some sought to hold onto pieces of the past, others, who would consider themselves equally historically minded, looked to the creation of pasts in the future, of creating monuments that would enshrine in "masses of masonry" New York's glory.

"PRICELESS"

Little changed in the public acceptance of City Hall as a sacred historic site to be preserved forever. There were a number of proposals for solving the municipal office crisis throughout and after the City Hall fight. In an 1889 Board of Commissioners for the Erection of a New Municipal Building hearing, George Rose had argued that Mulberry Bend itself was the appropriate setting for municipal offices: "There are acres of tenements crowded to repletion within five minutes' walk of the Mayor's Office which ought to be bought up and converted into municipal buildings, for sanitary reasons as well as from the need of the city for more land for public purposes."[70] James Harder offered a plan in 1903 for building a massive complex on Union Square. While City Hall Park was the obvious choice, over the years city officials and private citizens had suggested that the civic center be moved to Union Square (James Harder's 1903 plan), Washington Square, and north of Central Park (proposed by the Police Commissioner Richard Enright in 1924).[71]

The City Club's most powerful image in its campaign against a municipal building in City Hall Park in 1910 was an outline elevation, where the meager City Hall was dwarfed by a massive new building behind it to the north. They offered an alternative that was widely embraced: the city would buy up, over a course of years, the whole Chambers Street frontage and up Elm Street. A large municipal building would line Chambers Street, with an even larger building hovering further north on Elm

Street. This way, City Hall would not be overshadowed and would in fact be emphasized. It would sit like a jewel in a jewel box of civic buildings. Proposals in the 1920s and 1930s followed this basic idea. One of the most widely viewed and celebrated plans was offered by Francis S. Swales and the American Institute of Architects' New York Chapter in 1924, proposing that a massive, setback skyscraper be built along Chambers Street and that the post office at the point of the park be removed.[72]

In the late 1920s, Foley Square was developed as a center of municipal, state, and federal courts, a partial answer to the need for more office space. Guy Lowell's New York County Courthouse of 1926 was followed by the 1928–30 New York State Office Building, Class Gilbert's modern classical U.S. Courthouse, and the 1939 massive new "Tombs" prison, on the site of John Haviland's original from the previous century. The intensive investment in these government buildings north of City Hall Park attests to the solidity of the principle that the park would not be disturbed. Thomas Adams, the British planner who would be a key figure in the Regional Plan Association (RPA) in the 1920s, argued for the place of City Hall in the futuristic, regional city that he, Lewis Mumford, and members of the RPA envisioned. Their plans for the city were produced in *The Building of the City*, a volume of the 1931 Regional Plan that offered several plans for a new civic center. By 1940, however, the decision had been made, not through consensus or open debate, but through political machinations and the vicissitudes of the real estate market. City Hall would be saved, but the broader ideas posed in the intervening years disappeared. In his dramatic images and discussion of the civic center, Adams argued that City Hall—"this gem of early American architecture"—be given a "better setting and more dignified surroundings that it now has."[73] Adams proposed, following what many had been arguing for years, that the post office be removed and a much grander, towering municipal building be built along Chambers Street, from Broadway to Centre Street, directly behind City Hall (see figure 4.11). In 1939, following Adams's advice, the park was finally cleared of its last "encroachment," the Alfred Mullett–designed post office, and an ethic of preservation was solidified.[74] The sanctity of City Hall would never again be challenged, but neither would private real estate's prerogative on developing the vast majority of the rest of the city.

By the end of the 1930s, the preservation movement in New York City had slipped into a quiet slumber. The next big fight, beginning just as the World's Fair closed, would be led by George McAneny, the wide-ranging borough president of Manhattan and head of the Regional Plan Association in the 1930s. Against the future "powerbroker" of New York, Robert Moses, McAneny sought to save Fort Clinton, at the southern tip of Manhattan. Though victorious—the half-destroyed fort was ul-

timately saved only to remain to this day a shell of its former self, a gateway to the Ellis Island ferries—McAncny and other supporters (such as the Municipal Art Society) only reinforced what had come to be the accepted practice of preservation: the protection of individual buildings—"a few gems" as Adams or the Municipal Art Society would say—amid a sea of green grass (figure 4.11).[75] This "masterpiece theory," championed by preservationists in the postwar era, came to dominate ideas about the physical past in the city.[76]

In response to the failure of the preservation movement outdoors, in the midst of the rapidly changing city, those concerned with protecting and using the city's past embraced a new strategy. Starting in the early years of the century and gaining steam into the 1920s and 1930s, preservation-minded New Yorkers seized one of the few options left to them: saving historic structures and objects by bringing them indoors.

Fig. 4.11. The "priceless" City Hall. In this plan from the early 1930s, City Hall stands alone, with the Tweed Courthouse and the post office removed. The new courthouse buildings of Foley Square lie to the north (left), with Mulberry Bend behind the hexagonal courthouse building. Collections of the Municipal Archives of the City of New York.

5 "A VANISHED CITY IS RESTORED"

Inventing and Displaying the Past at the Museum
of the City of New York

If there is one building on Manhattan that has a reasonable chance of being
permanent, it is the Museum of the City of New York, which has just flung
open its doors. . . .

Paris, London, Rome and Vienna have no need of such a museum. To
see antiquities there, all one has to do is look about one. But New York is
practically rebuilt anew every generation. Nothing of the past remains to
remind us of how those lived who came before us.

—*New York American*

In 1915, because of a need for greater space at the Bank of the United States on Wall
Street and the pressures of property values in downtown Manhattan, the century-old
Assay Building was taken down. With the invitation of Borough of Manhattan President George McAneny, several preservationists, led by I. N. Phelps Stokes, drew the
facade of the building and had it carted away stone by stone to the rear of the Metropolitan Museum of Art. There it sat, disassembled for eight years, before being rebuilt in 1923 as the southern facade of the American Wing, the Metropolitan's elaborate series of period rooms chronicling American arts and crafts (figure 5.1).[1]

This was not the first time that proposals had been made for uprooting and reassembling a landmark building. City Hall, the object of New York's first great preservation fight, had been sketched speedily by architecture students at Columbia University in anticipation of its proposed demolition in the early 1890s. The New-York
Historical Society (NYHS) and the organizers of the not-yet established New York
Public Library offered to move the building and incorporate it into their new institutional homes. Other notable buildings had been eagerly carted away to be used as building materials or historic relics. The detritus of New York's creative destruction gained
in historical importance even as it was removed for its declining economic value.

But the removal of the Assay Building so that it could be used as the doorway into
a museum of Americana is a remarkable symbol. It marked a recognition of the weakness of the young historic preservation movement to accomplish it goals "outdoors."

Fig. 5.1. The facade of the Assay
Building, which was installed as
the entrance to the American
Wing of the Metropolitan Museum of Art in 1924. The Metropolitan Museum of Art, Gift of
Robert W. de Forest, 1924. All
rights reserved, The Metropolitan
Museum of Art.

Fig. 5.2. Construction of the Museum of the City of New York, taken from the neighboring Academy of Natural Sciences by its reference librarian, Frank Place, 1929. Museum of the City of New York.

When St. John's Chapel on Varick Street was threatened with demolition beginning in 1909, a huge outcry was made to keep the church where it had stood for close to a century.[2] But the Assay Building elicited no such interest. Despite their fervent efforts beginning in the late nineteenth century, preservationists had had little success in saving more than a few historic sites. The mistakes of the past would indeed be repeated, often in far more destructive and governmentally supported ways. The effort to preserve Manhattan's physical past "outdoors" had lost much of its energy as well

and would not regain it until after World War II. Even as a cult of all things colonial was being revived in the second decade of the century and would bring unprecedented efforts to literally rebuild that colonial world in places like Greenfield Village and Williamsburg, preservationists in New York City were able to save only a few threads of colonial and early national life. They turned, instead, to bringing the physical remnants of the past indoors.[3]

The Museum of the City of New York (MCNY) was the most energetic institution in this "indoor preservation" movement. When the MCNY's new building on Fifth Avenue was opened in 1932, the preservation community greeted it with high hopes because it seemed, to those who had spent years fighting for the preservation of landmarks, that finally the tide had turned (see figures 5.2 and 5.3). The MCNY symbolized to some observers that New York had finally recognized the importance

Fig. 5.3. The Museum of the City of New York, 1998. Photograph courtesy of Iguana Photo.

of protecting its past, thereby providing a line, a flow between past, present, and future. Edward G. Robinson, the director of the Metropolitan Museum of Art, supported the MCNY in part because he felt that it offered the final opportunity to preserve New York's disappearing material culture:

> The material for its collections now exists in abundance in and about the city, mostly hidden away in private possession waiting for an opportunity to be permanently taken care of and displayed, but with the rapid disappearance of the old homes of New York this situation cannot last long and we should take advantage of what lies at our hands before it is too late. It is a responsibility which we owe both to the present and to future generations.

The MCNY would prevent the loss of "a constantly increasing source of inspiration and enlightenment."[4]

The *Springfield Republican*, reporting on the laying of the cornerstone in 1929, saw the MCNY as the culmination of a tide that had begun to turn "20 or 30 years ago." The MCNY would inspire a new respect for New York's landmarks:

> Influences flowing from this new institution should make easier the preservation of ancient landmarks, of which, unfortunately, few remain in and around the city. For New York, with its zeal for modernization and its constant shifting of residential and business districts, has been ruthless in obliterating traces of its past. This indifference cannot be attributed to alien hordes or to crooked politics; nor has it been confined to New York, though it has been most apparent there through the intense pressure of modern economic growth on sentimental and artistic values.[5]

Helen Appleton Read, the art and architecture critic for the *Brooklyn Eagle*, lamented that the MCNY had not been built earlier:

> Had the interest which the Museum of the City of New York symbolizes been of longer standing it would have been possible to have rescued some of the typical phases of the various periods which characterized the city and which today are as lost as any of the seven cities of Troy. . . . The move from dwelling house to apartment has caused the destruction of innumerable relics that would have immeasurably enriched the museum collections.

Nonetheless, "with the growing consciousness of a native tradition, this ruthless scrapping of the past is over. What is left will be carefully preserved and the mistake not repeated. Today is, after all, tomorrow's past."[6]

The message of the museum was conveyed both in its specific teachings and in the

Fig. 5.4. Museum of the City of New York, Auditorium, 1932 (before exhibits were installed). Museum of the City of New York.

very fact of its existence. In 1930, under pressure to open the new museum (which was behind schedule) and to elicit the necessary $100,000 to complete and install the costly exhibits, the Board of Trustees, with great fanfare, opened the museum in December 1930 for viewing by members. (It would not open to the public until early 1932.) In the space of three days, several thousand members and guests walked through the empty building (see figure 5.4) and came away exuberant. One visitor, Anson B. Moran, wrote James Speyer immediately after his visit:

> I cannot let my visit to the Museum yesterday pass without sending you a few lines of my enthusiasm for your achievement. . . . In the first place the building is restful and delightful, and so much more attractive to me than the larger museums that I have been in the habit of going to . . . the building gives an air of rest unlike most museums. . . .[7]

For many New Yorkers who had invested in the goals of the museum, the existence of the building itself was the victory. The MCNY represented, in its emptiness, the possibilities of writing and preserving New York's history, and therefore, its future. "If there is one building on Manhattan that has a reasonable chance of being permanent," the *New York American* editorialized soon after the first opening, "it is the Museum of the City of New York, which has just flung open its doors."[8]

Unfortunately, the optimism of these first visitors was unfounded. While ostensibly standing as a bulwark against the widespread disregard of the city's material past, in fundamental ways the MCNY supported the project of destructive city planning and development. The MCNY codified the transformation of the city as natural and in the end benevolent. It enshrined the notion that New York's growth and development benefited all. Finally, the MCNY served to quell the movement toward legal protection of New York's historic fabric "outdoors."[9] By becoming the storehouse for the heirlooms of New York's elite, it in a sense sanctioned the booming demolition business. The real estate industry could continue its work at a rapid pace without the obstacle of guilt, because the MCNY, along with other historical institutions, would save the most important remnants of "old New York."

The MCNY did not do this alone—it could not. Rather, the MCNY was but one of an already extensive and booming "history industry" that comprised other institutions dedicated to preserving the history of the city's material culture, historians intent on writing the city's history, and public events dedicated to arousing new interest in the city's past. When the MCNY was founded in 1923, an extensive network of institutions were already dedicated in various ways to preserving New York's past: through the NYHS (founded as the nation's first historical society in 1804), a network of historic house museums, the American Wing of the Metropolitan Museum of Art (opened the year after the MCNY was founded), and the Municipal Art Society (founded in 1895), New York's elite had heartily embraced and led a national movement toward a colonial revival and a fascination with American arts and crafts.[10] Building on a long tradition of collecting the physical past in museums and private collections, New Yorkers had collected in new institutions the finest works of American art as well as more mundane but historically revealing material fragments. In the first decades of the twentieth century, New York's elite had become more sophisticated in their philosophies of collecting and displaying. Preservationists had begun to arrange period rooms, inspire and then mimic techniques used by department stores, and build a body of knowledge about long-neglected American material culture.[11]

The MCNY represented a distinctive addition to New York's growing history institutions. More than any other institution in New York, the MCNY emphasized the physical development of the city as the core of its history. The MCNY was the first museum in New York and perhaps in the nation dedicated to chronicling the physical transformation of a single city. Through period rooms, models, and dioramas—relatively young techniques for museums—the MCNY tried to create, out of a landscape subject to "constant restless reconstruction," a usable past.[12] The end result, however, was a past that supported the city's developers, rebuilders, and an ethos whereby the "constant restless reconstruction" of the city became its natural process of growth.

Early on in its history, the museum adopted as its motto a saying attributed to Abraham Lincoln:

> I like to see a man proud of the place in which he lives, I like to see a man live so that his place will be proud of him.[13]

The MCNY was, at its base, an effort to secure a sense of New York as a place, a city with a history and therefore a capacity for "community"—the elusive goal of elite reformers. Why and how elite New Yorkers chose to preserve and codify the record of the transformation of New York's landscape tells us much about their attitudes toward city building and rebuilding. Behind the silent rooms where "relics" of New York's past were collected were turbulent debates about the progress of the city. As happened repeatedly in various arenas of civic debate in this era, the politics surrounding real estate development and the city's history were transposed into the politics of place.

NEW YORK'S "ATTIC"

The MCNY grew out of murmuring dissatisfaction with the NYHS that exploded in the form of a relentless campaign of criticism launched by Mrs. John King Van Rensselaer around 1915. A life member and critic of the NYHS since 1898, she declared the NYHS to be "dead or moribund. Instead of being in the front rank of similar organizations in the United States, it is in the rear." The lack of attendance at annual meetings—at the 1917 meeting only 20 of its 839 members appeared—she attributed to the simple fact that these meetings were "uninteresting and dull."[14]

After a failed effort to take control of the NYHS board, Mrs. Van Rensselaer lived up to her threats and left the NYHS to found her own organization, the Society of Patriotic New Yorkers, in 1920. The goal of the group—which was composed only of people who could prove ancestral links to New York State prior to 1776—was to "launch an educational campaign to teach the inhabitants of the city and State just what New York really is and its importance in relation to the Union." "What we want to do," said Mrs. Van Rensselaer,

> is to introduce New Yorkers to our New York heroes—the men of great names who have aided in making New York what it is. . . . We want a house of the year 1800, of which there are still half a dozen in the city. There we will install figures of men and women—call them wax figures, if you like—dressed in the costumes of their times, and surrounded by the furniture they knew.[15]

Mrs. Van Rensselaer's organization did not survive, but its deeply antiquarian ethos did. Following the Patriotic New Yorkers' example of housing the material wealth of "old New Yorkers" in a historic house, a small group of leading New York collectors and antiquarians sought, and was granted, a charter for a Museum of the City of New York on 21 December 1923. The MCNY's Certificate of Incorporation granted by the state shows that its mission had expanded beyond Mrs. Van Rensselaer's narrow purposes. The museum would "collect and preserve all documents, prints, books, photographs, portraits . . . relating to the culture and history of the city of New York"; in essence, the museum would be a clearinghouse for any and all activities relating to the city's history. They had grand notions for the museum—it would organize a photographic project recording the entire island for the city's three hundredth birthday in 1926, sponsor lectures on city history, and create period rooms. The MCNY would even lead "outdoor" preservation efforts: one of the museum's charter goals was to "lease, acquire, preserve and maintain buildings and sites in the City of New York of historical and/or cultural interest."[16]

The museum was led in its first few years by a worthy antiquarian successor to Mrs. Van Rensselaer (who died in 1925). The indefatigable Henry Collins Brown was active in virtually every effort to preserve and promote New York history in the first decades of the twentieth century. He had supported the preservation of City Hall and its park in one of the first preservation efforts in the city. In 1916 Brown had begun *Valentine's Manual,* a revival of the work of David Valentine, the Clerk of the Common Court, who until 1870 had included with the city's annual *Manual of the Corporation* notes and images relating to New York City history and folklore. Among Brown's many chatty books on "old New York"—including such titles as *In the Golden Nineties* (1928) and *Brown and Saratoga Trunks* (1935)—was a commemorative book on Fifth Avenue's history, completed in time for the Avenue's centennial.[17]

Brown and his group soon secured from the Department of Parks the long-neglected Gracie Mansion along the East River at Eighty-eighth Street to house its small but growing collection.[18] The 1799 mansion, owned by Archibald Gracie, a wealthy

merchant and, incidentally, the great-grandfather of Mrs. Van Rensselaer, had the distinction of having hosted such illustrious guests as Washington Irving, Josiah Quincy, and Louis Philippe of the French royal family.[19] Brown, interested in creating a historic preservation organization as much as a museum, called Gracie Mansion "exactly the place in which to establish an enterprise of this kind."[20] In the years immediately following the establishment of the museum, the Parks Department, which maintained ownership of the building, restored the building to its early nineteenth-century condition: several coats of white paint covered up the green color added in recent years, and electric lights were taken down to eliminate vestiges of the late-nineteenth- and early-twentieth-century changes (figure 5.5).[21]

Despite the apparent advantages with which the museum began—a restored historic mansion, some of the earliest period rooms in New York, wealthy backers—in its first three years it was known by few and visited by fewer. "Who even knows that

Fig. 5.5. Gracie Mansion, first home of the Museum of the City of New York, circa 1915. The 1804 Archibald Gracie mansion on the East River had been radically altered and "Victorianized." The museum, in its first years, returned the building to the conception of its original design and appearance. Museum of the City of New York. Gift of Samuel Landsman in memory of Stephen Jenkins.

New York has this museum?" one writer asked. Located amid tenements along the East River and offering a hodgepodge of furniture, prints, and models, the museum drew few to its doors. Brown was an energetic promoter of New York's history, but lacked both fund-raising skills and a creative imagination for museum design and display. Under Brown, the museum remained little more than a private storehouse for "relics" donated by New York's wealthy.

The question that always lurked in the background of the MCNY's activities was why such a museum was necessary at all. With the NYHS and its vast collections of books and manuscripts relating to the city's early history, and the Metropolitan Museum of Art, which had begun in 1909 to collect an unrivaled collection of early furniture for its future American Wing (opened in 1924), the MCNY seemed to some superfluous.[22]

Brown and his followers sought, from the very start, to define their museum as unique in New York's ever-expanding museum world, complementing rather than competing with other museums in the city. The MCNY would, most importantly, be focused exclusively on New York City. In contrast, the NYHS emphasized the colonial history of the city, and its extensive collection included material on all of New York State and the nation, along with works of art such as its famous Audubon prints, the paintings of Thomas Cole, and Tiffany glass.[23] Mrs. Van Rensselear had acidly attacked the "deformed monstrosity" for its badly organized, random assortment of objects, some of which did not even relate to New York.[24] The NYHS was, in a sense, an American historical society based in New York. The MCNY, on the other hand, was to focus on "visualizing the history of an American City, and the lives of its famous men and women."[25] In the first annual report, Brown wrote, "There is no other institution covering the field which we intend to occupy. . . . Ours is wholly and exclusively devoted to the greater City of New York and its Boroughs."[26] In its charter, the MCNY insisted that it would not seek to compete with the work of other institutions: "Nothing that does not pertain to this particular metropolis is solicited by our Museum, and under our by-laws nothing can be received that does not directly pertain to our old city."[27] The MCNY worked hard to gain the support of other history organizations. For example, while the NYHS remained conspicuously absent from the MCNY's annual reports and early exhibits, the MCNY was quite successful in gaining the assistance of the Metropolitan Museum of Art. Its director, Edward Robinson, wrote in support of the MCNY, provided regular loans for exhibits, supplied the MCNY with its second director (Hardinge Scholle), and served as trustee from 1926 until his death in 1931.[28]

The MCNY was not designed to be an archive or research center (like the NYHS), a museum for the collection of high art (like the Metropolitan), or an elite club of an-

tiquarians. The MCNY boasted that it would be built "entirely by voluntary subscriptions"; it would be the city's most "democratic" museum.[29] That the city contributed
the land on which the current museum was built and that the vast majority of the
MCNY's building fund and endowment came from a handful of donors did not deter
the Board of Trustees from trumpeting the numbers of contributors—1,328 by 1929—
who gave to the MCNY's fund-raising campaigns.[30] Finally, and most importantly, the
MCNY developed a vision of New York's history and devised methods of communicating that history that differed markedly from other museums in the city. The museum
would soon abandon its mediocre period rooms and instead try—not always successfully—to tell a visually engaging chronological story of New York's development.

Most of this program, designed to make the MCNY distinctive, came several years
after the museum was founded. It was only in 1925, when James Speyer, a founder
and a guiding hand for two decades, was able to oust Brown, that the MCNY gained
a new life.[31] Born in New York in 1861, Speyer had spent much of his youth in
Frankfurt, home of the prosperous Speyer financial empire. He returned to New York
in 1899 to lead the investment firm established by his father, Gustave Speyer. The
firm, which dealt first in foreign exchange, moved by the beginning of the century
into foreign bonds and railroad securities. Although it would not be able to compete
against such houses as J. P. Morgan, Loeb, or Kidder, Peabody, Speyer's firm nonetheless remained one of the ten largest investment firms for much of its life.[32]

It is unclear precisely why Speyer became so deeply committed to the cause of the
MCNY. Along with his highly popular and equally energetic wife, Ellin Prince Speyer,
Speyer was extremely active in a number of New York reform activities. He founded
the University Settlement Society on Eldridge Street in the Lower East Side, the
Speyer Hospital for Animals, and the Speyer School of Teachers College at Columbia,
and he was active in the Charity Organization Society, the United Hospital Fund of
New York, and the Provident Loan Society. A large portion of his estimated twenty to
thirty million dollar fortune was spent supporting these various social endeavors.

Speyer chose, however, to give the greatest single sum—over half a million dollars—and a large portion of his time to building the MCNY.[33] His fascination with
the American past may have been influenced by his wife, a descendant of Puritan settlers of New England.[34] It is also likely that, because of his strong continuing ties to
Germany, Speyer was especially worried about the suspicions that fixed so powerfully
on Americans of German background. Speyer's investment firm was able to prosper
in Europe because it collaborated with the German branch of his family. Speyer's
strong German connection made the experience of World War I, as one article later
euphemized, "an uncomfortable period."[35] Before the war, Speyer visited Germany
often, was a regular guest of Kaiser Wilhelm, and served, at times, as unofficial coun-

selor to German government officials in peace efforts; after the war he helped fund Germany's rebuilding.[36] During the war he worked exceedingly hard to escape the wrath that was visited upon the German community throughout the country. He retreated to his country house, where he immersed himself in war preparedness efforts, allowing the local army reserve to use his home as a training camp—after he had taken down the sign bearing the name of the estate: "Waldheim."

Under Speyer's leadership, the MCNY gained financial security and professional curatorial direction, and would by 1932 have a substantial building on Fifth Avenue. As a powerful, respected financier and a philanthropist of incredibly wide range, Speyer was well connected to New York's financial and cultural elite.[37] He quickly gathered commitments from major donors, such as William K. Vanderbilt and John D. Rockefeller Jr., as well as large numbers of regular memberships.[38] He also hired a new director to replace Henry Collins Brown.

If Brown was the archetypal antiquarian collector of New Yorkiana, Hardinge Scholle, who succeeded Brown as director, could hardly have been more different. Born in St. Paul, but educated from age twelve to eighteen in Germany, France, Spain, and Cuba (as he followed his father Gustave, a diplomat), Scholle was far from being a "native New Yorker." After attending Harvard and fighting in World War I, he began work as a curator at the Chicago Art Institute. Lured by the offer from the museum (which was promoted by Edward Robinson, the director of the Metropolitan), Scholle suddenly found himself in charge of telling New York's history. "I knew just about as much about the history of New York," said Scholle years later, "as I knew about the history of Timbuctoo [sic]."[39]

The contrast between Brown and Scholle suggests the diverging philosophies behind the MCNY. The division seems simple: Brown, the antiquarian, surrounded himself with period furniture and clothing and like-minded old New Yorkers; Scholle, the professional curator, embraced innovative methods of communicating history to a broad audience. There is no doubt that the lasting importance of the MCNY lies in the innovations made and collections acquired by Scholle and his staff.[40] But even though Scholle and Speyer, who remained the guiding force behind the museum for fifteen years, sought to create a professional museum of city history, based on the models in Europe and on the latest curatorial techniques, they could not and would not fight the pressures imposed by individual trustees and the limitations of their collections. The museum became a storehouse or "attic" for the treasured or simply discarded furniture, clothing, silverware, and dollhouses of the wealthy in New York.

With Speyer's financial backing—beyond his larger gifts, he also supported the museum at crucial moments with small grants—the MCNY put on its first major exhibit in 1926. Held at the Fine Arts League Building on Fifty-seventh Street (chosen

in part to highlight the inadequacy of its present home), the "Old New York" exhibit displayed furniture, paintings, and period costumes loaned by New York families and collectors, as well as the Metropolitan Museum. The exhibit was a stunning success. In its three-week run—all that the museum could afford—more than twenty thousand visitors attended. "The attendance at the exposition," Hardinge Scholle, the new director, gloated, "seems to refute the common assertion that New Yorkers are too busy with the present to bother with the past" (see figure 5.6).[41]

With a new energy provided by Speyer, Scholle, and Speyer's money, the museum's membership increased rapidly and donations began to flood in.[42] With Speyer and Scholle leading, the museum developed a plan for its future home in a new building. Beginning in 1929, the MCNY launched a $2 million campaign to build a museum to

Fig. 5.6. Harding Scholle, James Speyer, and others at Gracie Mansion (circa 1927). Speyer, the financier behind the Museum of the City of New York, is seated on the left; Scholle, its first professional director, is standing. Museum of the City of New York.

equal its projected collections and endeavors. Gracie Mansion, though too small and in-accessible from public transportation, originally had seemed a perfect setting for a history museum. One of the few remaining early homesteads in New York, it could also boast an appropriately illustrious connection with important figures in New York. Gracie Mansion would combine "indoor" and "outdoor" preservation of New York's physical past. The building itself would become a landmark for recalling early nineteenth century life, and indoors, the artifacts gathered from old families who were busy demolishing their homes would round out the story of New York's material life by supplying the furnishings, paintings, and clothing of at least a segment of New York's past.

Nevertheless, for all its apparent appropriateness as a setting for the display of New Yorkiana, Gracie Mansion was soon deemed inadequate. Even Brown, who had fought diligently to gain control of this neglected historic building, soon realized that a serious museum would need far more space than Gracie Mansion could provide. The needs of the museum would soon eclipse the limitation imposed by the competing desire to preserve and restore the building to its "original" condition. Furthermore, the practical problems of the building were immense. It lacked a good heating system, or any climate control mechanism at all, and, most important, was highly susceptible to fire.

And there was something more: while the new leaders of the museum—particularly Speyer and Scholle—believed wholeheartedly in historic preservation, they were more dedicated to the new, more professional vision of history collection and interpretation. Gracie Mansion could not escape being the home of antiquarians. To make the MCNY a truly modern museum of New York's past, it would need a modern building.

But first it would need a site. Although Gracie Mansion was on the Upper East Side, and would remain an adjunct museum and storage facility into the 1930s (when it became the home of the mayor), the Board of Trustees favored a site for the new museum building far downtown, on Washington Square. The site was chosen in part because James Speyer owned a portion of the land (the city owned the rest), but also because the directors hoped that a more central location would bring more visitors and attract new members.[43] Although it supported the museum, the city refused to grant the MCNY the prohibitively expensive site.[44] Instead, the city donated a lot adjacent to a high school on Fifth Avenue between 103rd and 104th Streets. This swayed the board, which agreed at the end of 1927 to build on the new site.[45] The MCNY trustees felt they could justify the site because they assumed that the development of wealthy homes—primarily apartment houses by the 1920s—would continue up the Avenue. In a sense, the MCNY was speculating on Fifth Avenue, as had so many others. But the

MCNY had entered the market in Manhattan real estate just as it was changing. The rise of the luxury apartment building and the slow decline of population on the island left the MCNY relatively isolated from elite society near the top of Central Park.[46]

The design of the building itself reflected a tension between a celebration of New York's future and an antiquarian immersion in its past. Soon after taking control of the MCNY Board, James Speyer began efforts to build the new home for the museum. In 1928 the MCNY held a limited competition for the design of the new museum to be built on Fifth Avenue. Joseph Freedlander, an architect of clean, if uninspired, neo-classical forms, ultimately won the commission.[47] For the MCNY, Freedlander de-signed an elegant and utilitarian building based on Georgian precedents. To architec-tural critics, the style, variously called "colonial," "late Georgian," and "American Georgian,"[48] was altogether appropriate. "Just as the exhibitions within indicate an ap-preciation of the wisdom and fortitude of our ancestors, so does the pure colonial character of the building acknowledge graciously the debt that current architecture owes to Seventeenth and Early Eighteenth Century America," *Architectural Forum* wrote in 1932. The style chosen by Freedlander "results in good architecture . . . it contributes a sympathetic atmosphere to the relics of the past that are housed in the museum."[49] Freedlander successfully offered a design that was spacious enough inside to allow for permanent and changing exhibits, but, on the outside, small enough to be seen as a successor to the mansions of Fifth Avenue, then quickly disappearing.

But Freedlander went further than merely copying a historic style. If the building could not be a true historic landmark, it could at least remind visitors of important New York buildings. Accordingly, the columned portico at the center of the main fa-cade made direct reference to the portico of the Federal Building on Wall Street where George Washington had been inaugurated—one of the signposts in New York's his-tory. To emphasize the connection, the opening of the building was scheduled for the anniversary of Washington's inauguration. The insistence of Freedlander and the Board of Trustees on visually linking past and present can be seen in a remarkable ren-dering that shows the near-final design of the MCNY with the original Stadt Huys in the background, a ghostlike figure watching over its descendant (figure 5.7).[50]

Thus, even though the museum was billed as a record of New York's development up to the present and into the future, and inside the MCNY staff intended to con-tinue its work of recording New York's continuing history, on the outside the build-ing bowed to the colonial revival wave of the period. The antiquarian motives of the museum's founders reemerged to enshrine a particular time in New York's history and to recall the homes and families of an elite group of "native" New Yorkers.

Completed in 1932 and built on city-owned land on Fifth Avenue at 104th Street,

A true Perspective View of the Southwesterly Prospect of the Proposed
MUSEUM of the CITY of NEW YORK
presenting as the Central feature of the Facade a Fac-simile of the "FEDERAL HALL" as that Edifice was completed by Major L'Enfant in 1789 with the portico where HIS EXCELLENCY GEN. GEORGE WASHINGTON took the oath as First President of this Republic. In this building was then established by the Saint Tammanys or Colombian Order, the First Museum in the City of New York ~ In the background is found the COURT OF NEW AMSTERDAM with the original STADT HUYS restored as it was in 1654, the first seat of our city government the "Community of the Manhattans" subsequently New Amsterdam.

Fig. 5.7. Museum of the City of New York: Architect's proposal, "A True Perspective View of the Southwesterly Prospect of the Proposed Museum of the City of New York" (circa 1931). In this near-final plan, the intended links between the museum and the city's history are made abundantly clear. The central portion of the building is a copy of Federal Hall, where George Washington was inaugurated as president in 1789. In the background is a sketch of the Stadt Huys from New Amsterdam in 1654. Museum of the City of New York.

the museum opened with great fanfare. Not only was the building an attractive addition to Fifth Avenue's line of museums and remaining mansions, it also answered the very practical failings of Gracie Mansion. First, it had far more space, including extensive office and exhibit workshop areas, as well as a courtyard in the rear that could be used for future expansion, when funds permitted.[51] Second, and equally important, the building was a steel-skeleton construction, including fire-resistant materials and a brick facade. The danger of fire had long plagued New York's cultural institutions and their potential donors.[52] Accordingly, the MCNY had from its opening contemplated how to safeguard its collections. The lack of a truly fireproof repository had worried the MCNY officials from the opening of the museum, and it would plague other institutions, such as the NYHS, well into the 1930s.[53] Indeed, the fireproof construction of the MCNY may have a been a large reason why the museum received so many donations from wealthy New Yorkers who might otherwise have left their furniture, clothing, silver, and art work to other institutions—or not donated them at all.

The MCNY was heralded, by its staff as well as by the New York press, as a first attempt to create in the United States this type of "civic museum."[54] The MCNY was to be modeled after the great city museums of Europe, especially the Carnevalet in Paris and the London Museum. At the same meeting at which Scholle was hired to be the new museum director, he was also given a six-week leave to travel to Europe and inspect its city museums.[55] Certainly, part of the goal of emulating European city museums was to give New York one more institution that would rival Europe. "London, Paris, Berlin, Stockholm and other European cities have museums to show their development from early days and to perpetuate important events in their history," James Speyer wrote in 1926. "We have no museum devoted to such a purpose."[56] But while Speyer and Scholle hoped to equal the stature of those city museums, they also wanted to improve on them. The London Museum, like the NYHS, had collected much that had little relevance to relating the history of the city. And the Carnevalet in Paris, while admirably recording the physical development of Paris, was a frozen museum: it had not continually updated its collections. "It could never become a museum of the Paris of today," remarked one writer.[57]

Central to the MCNY's mission, then, was bringing the history of the city up to the present and speaking to current concerns. The museum would sponsor a host of activities that would make it a center for the discussion of New York's future development. A representative schedule of talks in 1932–33 included "Planning New York's Future," "Traffic Control and Street Safety in New York," and "Civic Beauty in New York City," as well as "Early New York on Staffordshire Pottery" and "New York in the Nineties."[58] Furthermore, it was Scholle and Speyer's hope that the MCNY would continually add to its collections—which centered on the nineteenth century—to portray the changing city. Their efforts were only partly successful. To begin with, the museum lacked funds for acquiring collections. A larger obstacle was that so little remained even of the recent past, creating in the portions of each exhibit devoted to the twentieth century "many lacunae."[59] New York's growth, noted one reviewer, "has been so swift and so destructive as to leave few of the old shop fronts, old signs and utensils, pieces of furniture and paneling which are important items in the London collection."[60] Nonetheless, while all history museums—from Williamsburg down to the smallest house museum—expected their work to be relevant to the present, the MCNY distinguished itself by the extent to which it emphasized the role the museum would play in the unfolding of New York's future. As John Van Pelt declared in his study of the educational goals of the museum in 1932, "the Museum is not primarily historical, rather sociological."[61]

One of the central ways the MCNY hoped to be "sociological" was in its education of its young people, especially immigrant young people. The MCNY was from the start, like so many cultural institutions, oriented strongly toward educating immigrants about their city and nation. The state charter had declared that the MCNY would be established "for educational and patriotic purposes."[62] "The museum," emphasized a reviewer, "is conceived throughout as an educational institution, not a storage place. The models and other exhibits will do their teaching independently but great emphasis is to be laid on the educational staff."[63] James Speyer had a number of reasons for investing time and money into the MCNY; but whatever else motivated his love for the American past, he firmly believed that a good historical sense was necessary for the exercise of citizenship:

> There are hundreds of thousands of people living in New York who have come here from other parts of our country and abroad. Such a condition does not exist in European cities. It seems to us particularly important to give to these newcomers and to their children, some knowledge of and pride in the history of New York, to stimulate love for our City and help to make good citizens.[64]

James Speyer was deeply aware and enamored of the American past but also alert to its cultural divisions, which could take ugly forms. He brought to the MCNY a highly "patriotic" attitude, but also a belief in more subtle methods of assimilation of foreign peoples to the American creed. On the evening after the museum officially opened in January 1932, Mrs. Barclay Parsons expressed a common view among the early donors of the museum. She congratulated James Speyer on the realization of his decade-long effort to build a new home for the museum. "I cannot go to bed tonight and so close the day without sending you a line to try to tell you something of how I feel after seeing the first day of *your* museum. . . . It was deeply moving." Mrs. Parsons was especially impressed that it was Speyer, a Jew of German descent who had spent much of his youth in Germany, who was behind this "source of inspiration for good citizenship":

> For one who had been born New York and who had New York as a background the Museum would have been a priceless gift to make. Therefore how much greater is it when this great gift comes from one who has made New York his city by adoption.
>
> As an old New Yorker . . . thank you from the bottom of my heart for what you have done. The Museum that you have created will grow and grow and be a source of inspiration for good citizenship in the generations to come.[65]

Mrs. Parsons' congratulation highlights a central goal of the MCNY: to aid in the assimilation, using American history, of new immigrants (and ignorant "native" citizens) into American society. That Mrs. Parsons's ideal example of the possibilities of immigrant economic and cultural assimilation had in fact been born in the United States and had lived in New York for over three decades seemed irrelevant.

The MCNY was like so many other cultural institutions of the time in its goal of aiding in the assimilation of immigrants. History had long been used as a crucial step in assimilation programs; Progressive Era schools, settlement houses, and other institutions pioneered new ways of presenting American history to the waves of new immigrants.[66] The MCNY also shared with similar organizations a distaste for the immigrants they purported to be serving. W. T. H. Halsey, the curator of the American Wing, for example, insisted that the American Wing was necessary to defend the nation against the "influx of foreign ideas utterly at variance with those held by the men who gave us the Republic."[67] Although few at the MCNY were as openly dogmatic, the museum was certainly not free of this creed.

In order to assist others who had made New York their "city by adoption," the MCNY established links very quickly to a number of organizations dedicated to teaching New York schoolchildren about the city's history. The City History Club, which dated back to 1896, provided guided tours of the city and had established a network of clubs throughout the city's public schools. Beginning in 1933, the club was based at the MCNY, along with its large collection of lantern slides and guidebooks to the city. The museum developed a "trips and trails" program that provided guide sheets for children and their families to visit different parts of the city, a Sunday lecture series, and a Saturday "Junior Museum" for children.[68] In 1931 the MCNY was given a $50,000 grant from the Carnegie Foundation to study the educational efforts of other museums around the country and develop its own programs. John V. Van Pelt, an architect and trustee, led the research effort and offered a long-term vision for the educational work of the MCNY: "The old conception of the museum as a place to house valuable collections to be examined by the public, or even not to be examined, has been so displaced that it seems reasonable to project the possibility of many future museums that will be merely store houses for material to be distributed to various educational centers and replaced in rotation."[69] While recognizing the "lack of funds," Van Pelt hoped that the MCNY would drastically expand its educational efforts and coordinate itself carefully with the curriculum of New York's schools.[70] Furthermore, the MCNY would loan its collections to schools, as the American Museum of Natural History was doing; it would set up branch museums to bring the museum closer to young people; it would sponsor radio shows on city history; and it would produce plays, children's fairs, and even movies of important events in the city's future development.[71] Writing from the depth of the Depression and the potential for political upheaval it portended, Van Pelt was blunt in his belief that the goal of the MCNY should be the "formation of good citizens":

> Children should be taught that a beautiful building not only enhances the value of surrounding property, but elevates the morale of those who pass it. They should learn who are the great men of the City, living as well as dead. Not deceived by charlatans,

they should become able to evaluate their fellow citizens and be filled with desire to emulate those of real worth.

Herein lies the true mission of the Museum.[72]

Speyer and his staff certainly agreed, in principle. But for all the rhetorical and even real commitments to educating the city's youth, especially its immigrant youth, the MCNY was more dedicated to creating a storehouse for the city's architectural and material treasures and, simultaneously, a new method for telling the story of the city's history.

A "VISUALIZED BIOGRAPHY"

The MCNY was to be "not a prosaic, historical account of the city's development," one critic suggested in 1930, but a "visualized biography" of New York.[73] Indeed, Henry Collins Brown, as early as 1924, noted that the MCNY was a direct product of his pet project of photographing "all that remains of Old New York." It was, he wrote, "a natural step from a Museum of *Photography* to a Museum of *New York*."[74] More specifically, the museum was intended to give a visual history of New York's physical development, to "show the metropolis in an uninterrupted series from the wigwam to the skyscraper."[75] At the laying of the MCNY's cornerstone, Governor Al Smith spoke fervently about the value of the "visual conception of progress" that the museum would offer: "Today is the day of the pictures," he declared. To give "future generations a knowledge of the imperial city of their own world" required a use of the visual dimension.[76]

In this effort, photography and other printed and painted images of the city proved important. Especially after the gift of J. Clarence Davies' enormous collection of images of New York, the MCNY would come to house one of the major collections of views of the city, along with the New York Public Library and the NYHS. By 1948, under the leadership of Grace Mayer, the curator of prints and photographs, the museum had over five thousand photographs, and thirty-eight thousand other miscellaneous pictorial materials, from postcards to prints and maps.[77]

At the real heart of the MCNY's exhibitions, however, were not photographs and views but a series of dioramas and models. Beginning with dioramas of Henry Hudson and crew aboard the Half Moon, Peter Minuit purchasing the island from the Indians, New Amsterdam in 1660 based on the Castello Plan, Peter Stuyvesant submitting to British officers demanding surrender of New York, and Nathan Hale facing General Howe in the Beekman House during the Revolution, the museum produced 153 models and dioramas by 1948.[78] The museum invested a large amount of money and time into producing these first models and dioramas. Working from a studio at the top of the

New York Life Insurance building on Madison Square, Dwight Franklin, the main cu-rator, and his assistant Ned Burns, spent two years producing the first five scenes.[79] In order to make the models "as accurate as humanly possible," Burns and Franklin and their staff extensively researched the people and settings, even traveling to Holland to inspect original views of early New York.[80] The dioramas were intended to be the clos-est thing the MCNY ever had to a permanent exhibit on New York's past, traced in twenty-five-year increments using key scenes in the city's history to mark the passage of time. Many of the dioramas dealt directly with architectural and "topographical" his-tory; but even dioramas that commemorated specific events were designed to feature "changing aspects of the city" in the background (figures 5.8, 5.9, and 5.10).[81]

While many of the models seem rigid and fake to today's sensibilities, early visi-tors were impressed by their "authenticity" and their ability to conjure up past events and places.[82] "Though they are miniature in size, these groups have all the color and

Fig. 5.8. Museum of the City of New York: Charles Capehart (left) modeling the "Castello Plan" (New Amsterdam in 1660, one of the earliest views of Manhattan Island), New Amsterdam Group, 1931. Museum of the City of New York.

Fig. 5.9. Working on the Model of the Museum of the City of New York, circa 1931. Museum of the City of New York.

intensity of living events and are executed with the utmost fidelity to the truth." When the building was first shown to the public in 1930, Virginia Pope predicted in the *New York Times Magazine* that "visitors will have the feeling of peering down the centuries through the large lens of an opera glass."[83] In a city so lacking in daily reminders of its past, the models and dioramas took on added importance. Another reviewer noted that "Such a display is far more living history than in shelves of books on old New York. The details are in colors and textures no historian's words can capture so well. A vanished city is restored."[84] In many aspects of its work, the museum was shaped by the same philosophy that had inspired period rooms and historic house museums. The museum's directors recognized, however, that individual objects, or even wholly reconstructed rooms and historic homes, were not enough to bring back the "vanished city." Because of the lack of landmarks to spur memories, the museum's directors recognized that New Yorkers would need more help to enter the past. The models and dioramas, wrote one reviewer, "have recaptured the long past of the greatest city of the world . . . breathing a sudden life and vitality into the dead relics about them. . . . In the model those times are as alive as last night's supper club."[85]

Fig. 5.10. Diorama: The Great Blizzard of 1888. Modeled by Ned J. Burns. Museum of the City of New York.

What exactly was the history, then, that was collected and exhibited in the MCNY? First, and most important, is the focus on the landscape. The MCNY supported an obsession with the physical appearance of the city, and the process by which its appearance changed, as the measure of the city's social and cultural progress. Second, the implicit argument throughout the museum was that the city's growth and development were to be celebrated. The dioramas always led from primitive Dutch and colonial conditions to modern, sophisticated buildings and technologies. Naturally, with this tacit optimism, the inequities and the diverging experiences of the city's minorities were all omitted. The museum stated its intention to exhibit the "contributions by descendants of different Nationalities to the growth of the City."[86] But, as we have seen, the primary method of "inclusion" was to persuade the immigrants that they had joined a clear and mightily flowing river of progress. The focus on physical "improvement" served to mask the diverging experiences of the city that had spawned at once the most glorious and most squalid products of urban development.

The MCNY emphasized creating a clear pathway from 1626 and the founding of New Amsterdam to the present. The constant changes in Manhattan's physical landscape had rendered a visible link between past and present—between the "beginning" (i.e., 1626) and the future—impossible. Henry James's "provisional city" would be made permanent, at least in one controlled setting, through a miniature portrait of New York's historical physical presence. Numerous commentators on the museum's development praised its exhibits for offering to visitors a quick overview of the city's history. Instead of being an activity of those who had the time, energy, and ability to read heavy tomes of history, New York's "three centuries of civic progress" would now be an "afternoon's occupation."[87]

This "afternoon's occupation" worked as well for "old New Yorkers" who came to visit their material pasts as for the young immigrants who came to the MCNY. The goal of forging out of New York's diverse population a single community was to be achieved at the MCNY by anchoring the sense of community in a sense of place with a common history. In a city of "all immigrants," as one commentator said, the MCNY used the history of the city's landscape as the vehicle for its assimilation program.

A photograph from 1935 shows a group of young children, members of the "Junior Museum" who participated in Saturday morning activities related to New York City history, with the product of several weeks' work: a copy of the model made of the 1660 plan of New Amsterdam (figure 5.11).[88] It is a powerful symbol: the effort to educate these children—many new to the country and city—took the form of charting New York's physical development. For these children, "constructing" early New York was to be a means of connecting them to a common history. The avowed centrality of the educational mission, and its focus on New York's physical history, shows how the constructed memory of place, as displayed and interpreted in the MCNY, was seen as a political tool, to educate an uninformed citizenry and shape the new immigrants who would become citizens.

Despite the praise offered for the innovative models and dioramas, and for the educational programs the MCNY pursued, many criticized the "tattered letters, odd maps and prints, time-darkened portraits and other fragmentary memorabilia" that constituted a large part of the museum's collections and exhibits.[89] Throughout its history, and even to this day, the MCNY has vacillated between two diverging purposes for the museum. On the one hand, the MCNY tried to use modern curatorial and exhibit techniques, avoiding sentimentality and emphasizing the educational role the museum could play. On the other hand, the MCNY continued to act as the city "attic"—a reputation that has been hard to relinquish. Partly because of its limited funds, the MCNY accepted virtually anything donated by New York's upper classes. Pens used in signing

contracts for the first subway; "Americus 6," the fire engine from William Marcy "Boss" Tweed's volunteer fire-fighting company; old dresses—they all were accepted graciously by a Board of Trustees desperately trying to play "catch up" with other museums. Speyer himself offered his Gilbert Stuart portrait of Washington on the condition that "from time to time" he be allowed to bring the painting back to his home.[90]

While Scholle and his staff hoped to tell a serious, carefully arranged chronological story of New York's development, the models and dioramas composed only one piece of the museum's exhibits. In order to lure donors of money and collections, the MCNY had freely changed its program and philosophy of exhibitioning. When the museum opened in 1932, it contained a hodgepodge of exhibits, the haphazard result of material donations, obligations to large donors, and the absorption of the City History Club and the Marine Museum. The first floor contained J. Clarence Davies' collection of views of New York (which I discuss in the following section), the collection of the Marine Museum (consisting primarily of models and images of ships), and a room devoted to the history of retail selling (funded by the descendants of F. W. Woolworth). The gift by May Davenport Seymour of her theatrical collection inspired a room dedicated to the history of theater in New York on the second floor. On the same floor were the rooms dedicated to the history of transportation and

Fig. 5.11. Museum of the City of New York: Students with the model of "The Castello Plan." "New Amsterdam Modeled in Sections—A Project of the Junior Museum," published in *Museum of the City of New York: Its Collections and Activities* (New York, 1935). Museum of the City of New York.

clothing of different periods (donated by Sarah Cooper Hewitt). The third floor would contain a room dedicated to the history of "communication" in New York, with models chronicling the town crier standing in front of a Dutch tavern, the 1867 stock ticker, and finally the Democratic Convention of 1924, which utilized telegraph, radio, and telephone. The room was paid for by a $50,000 donation by AT&T, NBC, and RCA and their subsidiaries.[91] Despite the goals of Scholle and Speyer, the MCNY remained in large measure simply a series of extra closets for New York's elite who were rapidly leaving their grand mansions and townhouses for suburbs or for smaller apartments. In 1931, in a benefit for the new Town Hall theater, descendants of some of the city's oldest families participated in a pageant, dressed as their ancestors. Their costumes were borrowed from the MCNY for the event.

COLLECTING AND SELLING A CITY

In 1929, J. Clarence Davies, one of New York's most successful real estate moguls and foremost collector of city views, donated his collection of over fifteen thousand maps and plans of New York to the MCNY. The collection consisted of a whole range of images from every era of the city's history, from 1626 and the city's official founding to a "modern photograph, made only several days ago showing the old block of English dwelling houses in Twenty-third Street that are coming down to make way for a sky scraping apartment house."[92] Worth over half a million dollars, Davies' collection equaled the largest gifts given to the museum and represented its first major acquisition.[93]

This magnificent collection was not the product of a dedicated "old New Yorker" but rather a savvy real estate speculator. Born in 1867, Davies had begun managing large estates and speculating in land in the Bronx in 1889, making him one of the early developers of that borough. He became perhaps the leading speculator and promoter of real estate in the Bronx, buying and selling properties and advising banks and developers—including railroad companies and the federal government.[94] For Davies, the images of old New York and, more specifically, the change in New York to the present, provided an invaluable tool in his efforts to attract investors. His first purchase came when he saw prints in a store showing "farm land and a cottage at Fifth Avenue and Forty-second street":[95]

> I was selling real estate in the Bronx and it occurred to me that these old prints were the finest arguments I could have. They showed the growth and changes in Manhattan in a few years and I bought them to show to clients, in order to stir their imagination as to what was going to happen in the Bronx.

"My collection," he stated baldly, "started, therefore, with the purchase of prints to illustrate real estate arguments."[96]

The story of Davies and his collection highlights an important point about the MCNY: although it was essentially a museum for the preservation and interpretation of New York's past, especially its physical past, it was deeply intertwined with the contemporary development of the city. Davies' open and triumphant link between his nostalgic desires and his real estate interests suggests that the effort to squeeze profit from space was inseparably bound up with the production of memories of New York's landscape.

The whole shape of the MCNY and its collections was linked to the rising and receding waves of development in the city. Many supporters and contributors to the MCNY saw the museum almost as a repository for their material wealth for which they no longer had space. But even beyond the content of the donations made to the MCNY, the very fact of those donations is integrally related to the real estate development of the city. Inside the museum, the collections that were rapidly donated in the late 1920s and 1930s were the result not only of elite New Yorkers' generosity. Much of this material was donated as wealthy New Yorkers abandoned their mansions and townhouses and settled in smaller apartments or fled to suburbs as commerce and manufacturing enterprises came to dominate Manhattan. The development of manufacturing and retail north of Forty-second Street marked the end of "Millionaire's Mile." In 1926, the Vanderbilts, despite valiant efforts, finally fled and allowed their row of mansions to be slowly dismantled. They offered to the MCNY the stonework, which was duly stored at the Arsenal in Central Park. At the same time, the Board of Trustees accepted the offer of the Consolidated Gas Company to take pieces of the old Academy of Music, which was slated to be demolished. The MCNY also investigated taking pieces of the Collis P. Huntington mansion at Fifty-seventh and Fifth.[97] The most comprehensive "indoor preservation" effort came in the mid-1930s when the Rockefeller family offered the MCNY the right to preserve as period rooms the home of John D. Rockefeller Sr. on Fifty-fourth Street (figure 5.12).[98] Thus, as Fifth Avenue's mansions came tumbling down, pieces of them were preserved at the MCNY. Preserved, paradoxically, in the MCNY is the record of the city's creative destruction.

By telling a narrative history in images of New York's development, J. Clarence Davies knew that he would be helping to write the next chapter. Just as J. P. Morgan helped to shape the canon of art history through his donations to and leadership of the Metropolitan Museum of Art, so too, on a smaller scale, did Davies' collection—and those given by others—shape the story of New York's transformation.[99] The impact of the museum's particular historical slant is not abstract: the MCNY has served

Fig. 5.12. Bedroom of John D. Rockefeller Sr., from residence at 4 West Fifty-fourth Street. The residence was demolished to make way for Rockefeller Center, but the rooms were reinstalled on the sixth floor of the museum. Museum of the City of New York.

as a major clearinghouse for images of New York, utilized by historians of New York and cities in general, artists and businesses, government agencies and antiquarians. Grace Mayer declared proudly in 1948 that the MCNY was

> the window dresser's best friend, the pictorial adviser of the public relations counsel, the background of banking brochures, the designer's delight, the author's background of the factual, the refuge of the nostalgic . . . [100]

Thus, with Davies' gift, the MCNY launched its development of a collection that would reinforce a particular account of New York's past and envisioned future.

CONCLUSION: "NEW YORK'S MEMORY"

With the completion of the building, the MCNY was launched. But despite its grand edifice, the MCNY never achieved its goals of becoming a center for the study of

New York history, nor as a primary educator of young citizens. Too inaccessible to most New Yorkers, underfunded, and its exhibitions limited by the antiquarian collections of its donors, the MCNY struggled throughout its early years to increase attendance and influence the cultural life of the city. The MCNY presented an exhibit of the latest photographs of Berenice Abbott and Samuel Gottscho, a real estate photographer, in 1934, but this was the exception. Most of the exhibits in the 1930s and onward would have pleased the antiquarian founder, Mrs. Van Rensselaer, including "Costumes Worn at the Prince of Wales Ball, 1860" (1933), "Late Nineteenth Century Brocade Dresses" (1935), "Historic New York China" (1934), "Dining in Old New York" (1937), and "Dressing for the Ball" (1946).[101]

In 1940, the WPA's *Guide to New York* stated that the museum was the city's "family album."[102] The phrase was an apt, and perhaps slightly critical, summary of what the MCNY became in the minds of many New Yorkers—an entertaining nostalgic journey. But it also suggests the more abstract goal of the museum: to create, through the telling of a common history, a unified "family" of New Yorkers. But in fact, New York was composed of more different and far-flung families than ever before. John Finley, speaking at the cornerstone-laying ceremonies in 1929, could truthfully say "we are all immigrants."[103] By 1930, when the MCNY was in the midst of its campaign and the development of its exhibits, much of New York's population had been born elsewhere.[104] The MCNY's leadership reflected this fact: the primary force behind the museum was a Jew of German descent who maintained strong ties to Germany; the museum's first director in its first crucial decade was another German-American who had spent much of his youth abroad and virtually no time at all in New York City; and one of its first and largest donors— J. Clarence Davies—was a first-generation Jewish real estate developer.[105] The MCNY was not simply, as one historian has argued, a breeding ground for the "New York pedigree" and a meeting place for the "old guard" who "circled the social wagons" in response to the influx of immigrants.[106] Contrary to this long-held belief that old families established cultural institutions—especially those detailing American history through buildings and material culture—as a means of communicating American history to ignorant immigrants, the MCNY was led by a group of new wealth and "new" New Yorkers. These leaders had a different strategy from the elite of the "history industry" who desired simply to transmit a particular narrative to New York's oldest and newest citizens. Instead, the MCNY's director, curators, and donors were hoping to create a "common" history at the same time they were teaching it. They saw New York's history and its future as intimately connected to the physical development of Manhattan Island. They hoped to create in the

MCNY, "New York's memory," a common history that might also provide a convenient past for their present city-building activities. [107]

Grace Mayer, the MCNY's famed curator, called William Faulkner's "Shall Not Perish" the "best description of a museum I have ever read!"[108] In that story, which takes place during World War II, a mother and her son take a trip to the town of Jefferson. They stop, before their return to the farm in Frenchman's Bend, in a museum built by an "old lady born and raised in Jefferson . . . built for nothing else except to hold the pictures she picked out to put in it." The museum contained

> pictures from all over the United States, painted by people who loved what they had seen or where they had been born or lived enough to want to paint pictures of it so that other people could see it too; pictures of men and women and children, and the houses and streets and cities and the woods and fields and streams where they worked or lived or pleasured, so that all the people who wanted . . . could come without charge into the cool and the quiet and look without let at the pictures of men and women and children who were the same people that we were even if their houses and barns were different.[109]

The MCNY would, like Faulkner's museum, describe

> the places that men and women have lived in and loved whether they had anything to paint pictures of them with or not, all the little places quiet enough to be lived in and loved and the names of them before they were quiet enough, and the names of the deeds that made them quiet enough and the names of the men and women who did the deeds, who lasted and endured and fought the battles.[110]

Faulkner's small town, with its museum so steeped in a universalizing nostalgia, seems dramatically different from the New York in which Grace Mayer worked and sought to record in the museum. In fact, however, it is not surprising that the MCNY's curator should be drawn to such a nostalgic image of a museum. For despite its concerted effort to become something more than a home for remnants of "old New York," the MCNY also perpetuated its founder's vision of a place where "our New York heroes" would find a home, "surrounded by the furniture they knew."

The MCNY, like Faulkner's fictional museum, was anchored in the belief that the "pride of place," as Lincoln allegedly said, would be the glue fusing an increasingly diverse and overgrown city. The pictures on display, the dioramas set into the walls, and the models in glass cases would create at least a veneer of a communal history that celebrated New York's accomplishments. It is no accident that the first works given the most care and completed for the museum's opening included the 1660 model of New

Amsterdam and a model of the Empire State Building under construction (figure 5.13).[111] The pair aptly summarized what the museum was trying to accomplish: to tell the continuing story of New York's growth, which had no limits in height or time, while also preserving the memory of the first buildings and landmarks that inevitably would disappear.[112] Thus, even as the MCNY would serve as booster to the city, it would be founded on nostalgia, on an attempt to preserve—at least indoors, in a glass case or a lifelike model—the city left behind by Manhattan's development.

Fig. 5.13. Museum of the City of New York: Diorama of the Construction of the Empire State Building, 1932. Museum of the City of New York.

6 "USES OF THE AXE"

Toward a Treeless New York

> . . . nearly ruined for the want of courage with the axe.
>
> As the trees grow, the weaker are pushed aside, and finally destroyed by the more vigorous, and the plantation is gradually thinned. This is the operation which is always going on in the forest when man does not intervene. . . . Thick planting is but following the rule of nature, and thinning is only helping nature do what she does herself too slowly, and therefore too expensively.
>
> —J. M. Forbes and C. S. Sargent, *Observations on the Treatment of Public Plantations, More Especially Relating to the Use of the Axe*

> "Oh dear, I'm so hot and thirsty—and what a hideous place New York is!" She looked despairingly up and down the dreary thoroughfare. "Other cities put on their best clothes in summer, but New York seems to sit in its shirtsleeves." Her eyes wandered down one of the side-streets. "Some one has had the humanity to plant a few trees over there. Let us go into the shade."
>
> "I am glad my street meets with your approval," said Selden as they turned the corner.
>
> —Edith Wharton, *House of Mirth*

Lily Bart, the tragic heroine of Edith Wharton's *House of Mirth* (1905), begins her long fall from the heights of New York's "new" wealthy society with a moment of respite in the company of Mr. Lawrence Selden beneath the trees of a small street just north of Grand Central Station. The moment offers a brief but wonderful foreshadowing metaphor for the rest of the novel. For Lily soon finds little respite from the raw heat of 1880s New York's vicious social world. She realizes only too late that it is Lawrence Selden, the aloof bachelor, who can provide relief from this world. In the end, she finds peace in the calming influence of sleep medicine, which lulls her into a never-ending slumber.

Lily Bart, as well as the young Edith Wharton, would have found little respite from the very real heat of the city. For when Wharton wrote the novel, and even when Lily Bart sought a husband and financial security on Fifth Avenue in the 1880s, few trees could cool the stone and asphalt streets of New York (see figure 6.1). Even though the island had not many years before been home to immensely rich and diverse forests and vegetation, virtually all that remained of that natural world that had

Off of Park Avenue, 1929. Collections of the Municipal Archives of the City of New York.

Fig. 6.1. Alfred Stieglitz, *Spring Showers—The Street Sweeper,* 1901. Alfred Stieglitz Collection, National Gallery of Art, Washington, D.C.

so captivated the early Dutch and English settlers were street names: Mulberry, Orchard, Pine, Cedar. As the city grew, one city historian observed in 1899, "the public gardens, the private lawns and flower beds and the street shade trees gradually disappeared, until the brownstone and red brick of the house walls, the gray of the pavement, expelled the remembrance of the restful green of fields and grove, and love of Nature was stifled in the dirt-laden air by the bustling life of the human ants."[1]

By the end of the nineteenth century, New Yorkers were well on their way to effectively segregating nature into park lands, suppressing it beneath the straight streets of the city's 1811 grid plan, and wiping it away from the daily lives of citizens in order to make way for the accelerating spin of destruction and rebuilding. As Luc Sante, one of the city's most incisive observers, concludes, "Manhattan's identity as a natural site is particularly irretrievable—the fact that it once contained two substantial ponds, was crisscrossed by streams, possessed marsh lands and flats, hills and valleys, was ringed by a coastline alternatively rock-ribbed and swampish. The great work of excavating, leveling, and reclaiming has left the island on its southern portion almost flat, with only a few gentle rises in the avenues to mark any sort of topographical ancestry."[2] One may now look at New York and think of the natural landscape of the city in terms of a few obvious features: the infamous black bedrock that juts out in Central Park and makes possible the city's skyscrapers (see figure 6.2), or perhaps the enviable deep har-

Fig. 6.2. Fifth Avenue and northeast corner of 118th Street, looking eastward, 1891. United States History, Local History & Genealogy Division, The New York Public Library, Astor, Lenox and Tilden Foundations.

bor that promoted New York's rapid rise to economic preeminence in the early and mid–nineteenth century. And yet it is almost impossible, except in a few places in the larger parks of the city, to be visually reminded that the island of Manhattan was one of the richest natural environments in North America, a product of an explosive past of volcanic activity producing a mountain range to equal the Rockies, glacial movements leveling those mountains and creating an extremely hard bedrock beneath a surface of fertile tillage soil, and oceans slowly fracturing the rock, carving out the Hudson and East Rivers that now define the island.[3]

In this chapter I describe how a city of remarkably rich and diverse natural landscapes was transformed almost exclusively into a setting for real estate transactions and commercial enterprise, and how a vocal group of social reformers sought to resist this transformation. However, rather than recounting the many stories of how Manhattan's builders covered over natural waterways, remade the swampy coastline, or leveled the natural hills of the island, I focus on one aspect—the elimination of street trees—in order to approach the larger question of the meaning of nature in the turn-of-the-century city.[4]

Street trees—as opposed to trees and vegetation within the city's parks—posed difficult and fascinating questions for Manhattan's residents. While parks, as Elizabeth Blackmar and Roy Rosenzweig have effectively argued, represented an important shift in the role of city government in removing space from the real estate market, they were clearly demarcated as the public realm.[5] Street trees, however, were ambiguously placed at the cusp between private and public, extramarket entities planted within the heart of commercial Manhattan. The fight over their removal, preservation, and renewed planting allows us to watch the tug of war between real estate developers, a growing government apparatus, and individual home- and landowners as they built and rebuilt the city. The result—as with other branches of the city-building enterprise, including slum clearance, historic preservation, and private real estate development—was a piecemeal policy that offered Manhattan a reprieve from becoming a truly treeless city but did not transform how New Yorkers conceived of nature in the city. Indeed, the anemic efforts of the private tree-planting groups and the city Parks Department only reinforced what New Yorkers seemed to know without ever having thought about: that, like oil and water, nature and New York could not mix. Just as the few historic structures saved in the early years of the century, or exhibits in a museum high up on Fifth Avenue, only hastened the "restless renewals" of Manhattan, so too did the few trees become reminders of nature's inability to survive in the overheated capital of capitalism.[6]

The vision of the booming metropolis as somehow "beyond" nature was a construct that served particular purposes: for commercial real estate developers, it slowed efforts to plan a park, parkway, and street tree system that in other cities took root, and thus justified their relatively free and rapid development and redevelopment of the land. For reformers, the image of a wasteland of commerce also supported the work of reformers who raised their work of reintroducing parks and street trees to Manhattan to a crusade. For those who interpreted New York's growth as a measure of the nation's development, the removal of nature was deeply troubling and a potent metaphor for more fearsome social calamities. "Nowhere in the world has the process of subduing nature progressed farther, become more highly developed," observed Ernest Gruening in a 1922 issue of *The Nation*. "Here man has been not merely in conflict with nature. Here nature has been not merely checked, tamed, and converted to his service. Here nature has been fully conquered and is now being destroyed. . . . New York [has] proceeded to suppress all traces of its heritage to will nature to conform to its error."[7]

The street tree movement, despite its enthusiasm and widespread support among leaders of the city's social reform movements, was always limited by the lack of government control and financial support, the dependence on fickle and unmanageable individual initiative, and the resistance of the business world. Stemming the tide of destruction of nature within the heart of the commercial city turned out to be much more difficult than the rhetoric of the reformers suggested. Street tree advocates, unlike their earlier park designer comrades, were never able to create a safe place removed from the field of real estate development. In part they were doomed because their focus was neither undeveloped land on the outskirts of the city nor overbuilt tenement areas but rather built-up avenues in the heart of the commercial district. But also, they were never a truly oppositional force. Tree advocates billed their work not as a sharp challenge to the city's rapid growth but merely as a way to soften and smooth over the chaotic debris—in terms of architectural cacophony and an unhealthy environment—left by the city's mode of growth.

The destruction of the natural landscape—like the destruction of tenements and the slow but sure elimination of historic buildings—was a lens through which New Yorkers viewed and interpreted their changing city. The elimination of street trees differs, however, from other sites of destruction and rebuilding because of the unique ways in which nature's devastation resonated with New Yorkers. Slum clearance taught some about the evils of immigrants and of speculative housing for the poor, and others about the unfairness of expanding city regulations. Historic preservation alerted New Yorkers to the social and cultural dangers of losing the city's architectural heritage. But nature, which offered powerful metaphors of the cycles of death and life, slow but inevitable change, and a foil to the manufactured world, provided more intangible tools through which New Yorkers interpreted other aspects of the city's constant building and rebuilding. Destruction of street trees, and the unsuccessful efforts to replant them, provided a powerful symbolic link between physical destruction and a perceived larger cultural crisis.

NATURAL NEW YORK

If other cities failed to become *urbs in horto*—cities in the garden—New Yorkers' suppression of nature from Manhattan Island proceeded with startling thoroughness, especially considering the richness of that landscape. Henry James and other chroniclers of early-nineteenth-century New York were not guilty of their usual exaggerations when they spoke of the full rows of trees that lined the streets of Manhattan and the extensive forests that covered the upper island. The fall from such a height was all the more striking to late-nineteenth-century writers.

The bedrock for which Manhattan Island is so known was formed by the crushing pressure of a mountain range that stood on the area some 400 million years ago. Where we now speak of the peaks of Manhattan's skyscrapers, 400 million years ago stood a mountain range of "alpine proportions" composed of rock deposits laid down some 300 million years earlier at the bottom of the ocean; these were pushed up by the volcanic activity beneath the surface of the sea.[8] The mountain range was slowly whittled down by the water and the scraping of glaciers from the north, leaving, after several hundred million years, only the bedrock close to the surface. It is the Manhattan schist, the youngest layer of the bedrock, which supports the new mountain range of skyscrapers in midtown and downtown, where it lies closest to the surface. New York was imagined by the city's developers and is today pictured by observers as a smooth, flat city made interesting by the spectacular variation of its skyline. At one time it was, however, "one of the most geologically diverse" regions in the United States.[9]

While the bedrock made the island hospitable to skyscrapers of the past hundred years, it was the water and rich soil deposits left by the melting glaciers—a thousand feet thick over the area—that gave Manhattan its rich natural environment. Colonists found lush forests of oak, hemlocks, walnut, and chestnut trees in such profusion that it made settlement difficult. Furthermore, New York lies at what is now identified as the dividing line between two climate zones. Thus, New York possesses not only trees and plants of the New England zone—such as New England maples, beeches, and birches—but also those of the mid-Atlantic region. Dutch settlers quickly complemented the rich native vegetation with fruit trees such as the peach, almond, cherry,

currant, and apricot, creating what one chronicler called the "perfumed" air of the island. Naturally, animals of all types were drawn to the forests and vegetation, and fish
were lured to the abundant salt marshes that rimmed the island.[10]

The ancient natural history of Manhattan reminds us that part of the story of nature in New York is one of simple destruction by humans. It is not inaccurate to see in
the late nineteenth and early twentieth centuries a progressive drive to rationalize the
physical island of Manhattan, creating a Cartesian grid of capitalist development. The
natural landscape, which most blatantly and obviously seemed to oppose the designs
of real estate speculators and city officials, had, literally, to be brought into line. Hills
were leveled to make the landscape match the lines on the grid plan, water was drained
from ponds where speculators had bought plots, streams were submerged into pipes,
marshes were filled, and trees were torn down. Colonists began the process by rapidly
cutting down the supposed "limitless" forest.[11] The rapid expansion of Manhattan in
the nineteenth century accelerated the change as eager developers leveled the bedrock
outcroppings to ease development; farms and forests were eliminated to lay out the
ubiquitous 100-by-25-feet lots of the grid established in 1811. Marshes and ponds
were filled in, rivers were submerged and channeled through pipes. The bedrock itself
was bored through with tunnels to create subways and water mains; the rock and soil
were then hauled away to expand the width of the island and the coastlines of other
boroughs. Not only was the green surface eradicated, but the earth itself was literally
dug up and carried away.[12] New Yorkers at the turn of the century recognized that in
the course of creating the largest city in the nation, they had destroyed a large part of
their natural heritage. The Tree Planting Association sadly noted in 1897 that

> Nature has done a great deal for Manhattan Island to make it attractive as a place of busi-
> ness, as well as for residence. Surrounded as it is, by rivers on every side and with the
> ocean breezes to cool the atmosphere, it should be ideal. But we live in a utilitarian age;
> the hills have been leveled and the hollows filled up, while the native woods have been
> cut down, and in their places we have straight streets and rectangular building plots.[13]

Of course, nature was not destroyed, nor would it be "recreated" uniformly in Manhattan. As with real estate development along Fifth Avenue, the image of a "wave" of development, or growth, belies the uneven distribution of natural amenities in the city.
Thus, nature might have been eliminated almost completely from the incredibly dense
Lower East Side (receiving only little relief from the Small Parks Act of 1887), but it remained much more prevalent in the small streets of Greenwich Village, which avoided
the intense development despite its proximity to the downtown (see figure 6.3).

Furthermore, what becomes clear in the late nineteenth century is that despite

Fig. 6.3. Berenice Abbott, *Patchin Place with Jefferson Market Court in Background*. November 24, 1937. In this tiny protected square off of Sixth Avenue near the Jefferson Market in Greenwich Village, the trees flourish amid the nineteenth-century townhouses. Museum of the City of New York.

humankind's remarkably rapid elimination of nature from view, submerged beneath asphalt and stone, its deep structures persisted. The suppression of nature was, in fact, only skin deep. Much like the false facades of commercial buildings that hid their internal steel structures, Manhattan appeared outwardly to have destroyed natural features of the island or at least kept them on a tight leash. If trees could simply be ripped out, just beneath the surface the stream still ran, and the veins of soil and rock still shaped how and where buildings could be built. Wind and fire, water and disease would continue to pose challenges to city builders and social reformers. Nature was unwilling to cooperate with—or at least registered silent protests to—the speculative ventures taking place on unnaturally straight roads and uniform subdivisions.

The rich glacial soil deposits that produced the attractive setting for settlement were simply covered by asphalt or superficially dug up for the bases of skyscrapers. The climate of the region, the wind and rain and snow, the attempt to capture sunlight, the flow of tides in the harbor—all these aspects of the natural environment are changed much less readily by humans. Thus, the ancient natural history of Manhattan does not come to a close at the end of the nineteenth century, even though we can clearly mark that time as a radical change in the balance of power between people and their environment. We can see the subsequent interactions with nature as the attempts of humanity to control nature, to rid it from certain parts of the city, and to preserve it in a certain manufactured state in other parts, such as Central Park. As one student of nature in New York has concluded, "Transformed, depressed, subdued, nature has by no means been eradicated in New York."[14]

Despite the persistence of natural processes and natural forms, the sense of ceaseless change in the natural just as in the human-made worlds (Henry James's "restless renewals") was established during this era.[15] The remarkable changes of the late nineteenth century, while clearly destructive of the centuries of natural environment, mimicked nature in the violent transformation that had always dominated in Manhattan. William Beebe, a student of natural New York in the early part of the twentieth century, aptly summarized the distant past as well as the conditions at the turn of the century:

> If New York's past could be compressed, the island would appear, to an onlooker, considerably like a frenzied fever chart. What was destined to become a supreme Urban Center has been tossed about, raised high in the air, lowered until it was at the bottom of a mighty sea; it has more than once been hidden beneath a half mile of solid ice.[16]

This is a useful metaphor for understanding New Yorkers of the turn of the century who called upon this image of their city to understand the human changes occurring with equal force and with a seemingly inevitable and "natural" progression. For if ever the clichéd phrase—"the only real permanence is change"—were true, it was so when applied to New York, both in its natural and manufactured environments. New Yorkers recognized that they had destroyed much of their natural heritage but also saw, based on the example of the natural history of the island, that nature was resilient and persistent and would, if aided or freed, reassert itself. This logic undergirded a curious crusade to replant street trees on the resistant streets of Manhattan.

"A BIT OF GOD'S COUNTRY": CENTRAL PARK TREE BATTLES

According to Frederick Law Olmsted, some well-to-do New Yorkers went crazy in 1889. In response to necessary "thinning" of trees in Central Park, the department had found itself faced with a barrage of criticism by neighboring citizens. Appalled at the sight of park workers felling their treasured trees, citizens had organized to stop the atrocities. Sure that this was the work of some corrupt park officer (there had been many in the Tweed years), citizens had taken the case to the press and lobbied in the legislature and even in Congress for the removal of the responsible park officials. Some, Olmsted reported, "have hastened to stand before a partly felled tree and have attempted to wrest the axe from the hand of the woodsman."[17] Olmsted, along with J. B. Harrison of the American Forestry Congress, was hired by the West Side Improvement Association to study the true merits of the case. Although there was little love lost between Olmsted and the Board of Commissioners of Central Park—he had been relieved of his duties in January 1878—he wholly backed the practices of the recently rehired Samuel Parsons and Calvert Vaux in their efforts to initiate widespread pruning of trees.[18]

Ironically, while he had for years attacked the park leadership for inappropriate removal of shrubs and trees, in this case Olmsted turned his ire on the riotous citizens. He calmly, if not a little condescendingly, proceeded to show how every landscape architect knew that it was necessary to periodically thin groups of trees, that the death of some trees was a necessary aspect of forest growth. He scoffed at the unprofessional attitudes of citizens, who "though well-meaning" had no understanding of the care of trees. He used most of the space of his report to quote from various authorities in the field of horticulture and landscape design, proving the unanimous support for the park department's methods. He concluded that public-spirited citizens would have to temper their enthusiasm with a good "degree of respect for the technical responsibility involved that few have yet begun to realize to be its due."[19]

This episode of civil unrest died quickly. And, despite the dramatic descriptions to which Olmsted was prone, it would be inaccurate to describe the 1889 protest against tree thinning as a major public dispute.[20] The Parks Department minutes and newspaper reports show only a bare mention of the protests—certainly nothing on the scale of the protests against the 1892 proposal for a speedway to be built along the entire west side of the park. Newspapers reported the event and Olmsted's report, but as much to mock the elite ignorance of the protesters as to highlight any mismanagement by the Parks Department.[21]

Nevertheless, it was not an isolated incident. Olmsted himself had repeated run-ins with the board over the thinning of trees, resulting at one point in the Board of Commissioners' passing an order forbidding him to cut trees without a specific order for each tree.[22] Citizens repeatedly complained to the Parks Department or the mayor about trees being cut down or inappropriately pruned on their streets or in parks throughout the city.[23] Finally, professionals dealt extensively in their professional journals and in reports on the condition of park and street trees with the methods and need for thinning. Superintendent of Parks Samuel Parsons responded in 1887 to a complaint about tree thinning in the park:

> it is the fear of public criticism that has prevented this necessary course from being followed out as it would have been under similar circumstances long ago on any private gentleman's place. The thinning out which has been done on Mr. Cyrus Field's country place during the last two or three years, and on various other country places that I know of in the neighborhood of New York, is far more radical than similar work done in Central Park.[24]

Thinning of trees was thus an important issue that had a persistent influence over public policy relating to trees. Indeed, the lamentation for a fallen tree, or a mistaken removal of one, continues to provoke a strikingly large response from park advocates and the general public.[25]

It was no accident that the first major battles over trees in New York occurred in Central Park. Central Park was created, very consciously, to be an almost sacred resting place of nature. It was a particular kind of manufactured nature, to be sure, but to park advocates it was the vital means of bringing the country to the city. Standing in stark opposition to the constant change and superficial values of Fifth Avenue, Central Park symbolizes for most historians a creative public spirit intentionally divorced from the destructive values that held sway across the street. Thus when it appeared that the landscape was being subjected to the same kind of destructive logic as Manhattan's commercial areas, both the citizens and the bearers of Olmsted's vision protested.

Central Park was a remarkable effort to preserve nature within the city, but it came from a context where a rich natural environment was being plowed under with stunning rapidity. It was only when New York had begun to expand quickly in the early to mid–nineteenth century that the first efforts were made to set aside land for parks. The 1811 plan had provided very few sites for parks, and the few that were built in the first half of the century were privately initiated, such as Gramercy Park. By the late 1830s, the city had recovered from the panic of 1837 and developed rapidly. The expansion of the commercial and industrial activity swallowed up the serenity of elite residential areas such as Washington Square, sending those families looking for escapes from the noise and crowds of business. At the same time, civic leaders became more alarmed by the crowding of Lower Manhattan, which they were sure had caused the 1832 and 1849 cholera epidemics. The belief that public parks could serve as "lungs" for cities, not to mention provide desperately needed recreation space, had a strong following. Rural cemeteries, such as Mount Auburn in Boston and Greenwood in Brooklyn, were ample evidence enough of the value of bringing "rural sights and sounds in[to] the midst of the city itself."[26]

Purchased in 1856 and transformed into the pastoral park by Frederick Law Olmsted Sr. and Calvert Vaux over the next decade, Central Park was the first "naturalistic" city park in the nation. By removing over eight hundred acres from the market, the city had fundamentally "altered its relationship to both public and private land."[27] Radically shifting the direction of unrestrained competition for land embodied so graphically in the 1811 grid plan, the city now initiated an "experiment in city planning," in which it in essence "sacralized" a large portion of northern Manhattan by making it "priceless."[28]

In opposition to the then-accepted notion of parks as places of organized sports or associational life, Olmsted envisioned the park as a place where the laborer as well as the professional would be reinvigorated after a week in the degrading business arena, where class tensions would be transformed into class sympathy, and where the stifling regularity of work would give way to spontaneity. Thus beyond securing a permanent, unchanging physical landscape amid the destructive transience of the city, Olmsted hoped to produce a setting for psychological re-creation.

But if Central Park defined itself in opposition to the city, the physical creation of Central Park required enormous destruction. This creative venture in fact required the removal of more than sixteen hundred renters and squatters; the demolition of homes, churches, and farms; and the massive, even violent, manipulation of the land. Northern Manhattan was not a frontier absent of human settlement in the early nineteenth century, but rather a series of compact settlements totaling some sixty thousand people. Thus, stone walls were dismantled, pig yards were cleared, and the houses and fences of the inhabitants were torn down. Once "stripped of its social and physical history," the land was subjected to an intense transformation at the hands of some 20,000 men, armed with pickaxes, hammers, shovels, and 166 tons of gunpowder. Archibald Watt, the largest owner of park land, had in 1855 spoken of "conquering the park" as an act of "war." Few would deny that the army of men and materials that attacked the rocks, the swamps, and the barren fields were engaged in battle. Horace Greeley, visiting the park in the early 1860s, commented, "Well, they have let it alone better than I thought they would." [29] He could not have been further from the truth: Central Park was as planned as the grid that covered the rest of the island. What the smooth lawns and curving pathways and pastorals views had hidden was a decade-long legacy of destruction in the service of creation.

The rapid pace of change to the environment that brought Central Park's naturalistic scenery into being did not slow to a halt, as if freezing itself for a landscape painting. In fact, Central Park could never be called "finished" and was always in a state of flux, either internally because of the dynamics of the natural environment, or externally by man's continual reshaping and additions of museums, monuments, and roads. In the first decade of its existence, Central Park had become a playground for the wealthy. Distant from the working-class neighborhoods, and conducive to the carriage-driving pleasures of the rich, Central Park in its early years had lived up to Olmsted's hopes of creating a place of "spaciousness and tranquillity . . . thereby affording the most agreeable contrast to the confinement, bustle, and monotonous street-division of the city."[30]

But new political leadership dictated changes in the shape of the park. For one, the park became more democratic: Greater numbers of workers and new immigrants flowed into the open spaces. "Untrained" in behavior appropriate to a pastoral park, these visitors seemed to be at odds with the passive recreation envisioned by Olmsted.[31] Rather than being uplifted by the moral inspiration of nature or by the example of their social betters, these visitors transferred their own ethnic and working-class culture of boisterous recreation to the park. The demands of these new visitors, and the control of the city by Tammany Hall, which was receptive to those demands, led to a democratization of the park. The new administration encouraged more active recreation and musical entertainment, and added several new buildings to the park. As the influence of Olmsted and Vaux over park policy waned (Olmsted was dismissed as landscape architect of Central Park in 1878), the power of the original ideal of the pastoral park dimmed.[32]

By the end of the century, Olmsted's original vision was being destroyed by the forces of time and neglect. The pastoral landscape Olmsted developed first in the very different ecological and climatic conditions of Britain was enormously expensive to maintain and would have required a consistent commitment unattainable in New York's notoriously fractious politics and the fiscal retrenchment of the 1870s and 1880s.[33] Since the official opening of the park, little of the essential maintenance had taken place, thereby jeopardizing the long-term health of the park's vegetation. Olmsted argued in his 1889 report that if thinning and pruning was avoided for too long, it was useless to start again: fixing the problem required "clean cutting" of entire groves of trees. This frustrated him immensely: groves of trees that had grown for several decades had to be simply ripped down and saplings planted.[34] During the Tweed years, beginning in 1870, the Parks Department did invest significantly in the maintenance of the park—but in ways completely different from Olmsted's plans. The Parks Department embraced a program of thinning with a vengeance, not to enhance Olmsted's designs but rather to open up views and allow for new buildings for the enjoyment of working-class visitors.

Responding in 1882 to the latest round of tree cutting to open up views and provide for "healthful circulation of air," Olmsted wrote his famous tirade, "The Spoils of the Park," in which he attacked at great length what he saw as political corruption of the park leadership and pointed to the state of disrepair to which the park had fallen since his dismissal four years earlier.[35] To Olmsted, who as official landscape architect and later as frequent consultant to the park commission opposed every effort to change the use and design of Central Park, these new encroachments and the failure to maintain the park—that is, to constantly re-create the pastoral landscape—was a sign of the slow destruction of his original vision. While Olmsted had long believed that the park was a "democratic development of the highest significance," he had an ambiguous faith in democracy. To him, the arrival of crowds of immigrants to the park and the advent of an elected parks board (it had been an appointed group) signaled the victory of the destructive side of democracy. Olmsted truly wanted people of all classes to enjoy and benefit from the park, but he wanted them to do so according to his ideals. Anything less represented the "spoiling" of the purpose of the park.

Olmsted was not alone in his attacks on the mismanagement of the park. New homeowners and developers of the Upper East and West Sides recognized that the value of their property was closely tied to the condition of Central Park, and they had come to accept Olmsted's landscape philosophy. Thus, the experience of the 1870s had taught them to be suspicious of the Parks Department projects for "improving" the park. This suspicion fell as equally on Olmsted and his followers as it did on political appointees of the Tammany administrations. Thus, the outburst of 1889 was not an irrational response to necessary maintenance, but an understandable skepticism of wary uptown citizens protective of their beautiful park as well as their investments.

Samuel Parsons, who became the parks superintendent in 1885 and remained associated with the park for two decades, continued the defense of Olmsted's original vision into the twentieth century (when it faced serious decline) in a 1911 article titled "Central Park and Its Destroyers": "For a park is more than mere greensward and shade. It is a bit of God's country set down in the midst of the busy and sordid city, to which the weary and jaded can resort and find renewed vitality and joy of living in utter forgetfulness of daily cares and depressing surroundings." But, Parsons insisted, "Most emphatically it is not a drill-ground, running-track, baseball and football field, site for public buildings, children's nursery, and general public playground upon which tens of thousands of people may sport at large and wreak their will upon trees, shrubs, and flowers."[36]

Parsons, Olmsted, and other tree experts turned to Darwinian language as they decried the distinct possibility of a "treeless city." Throughout his report on the tree-cutting controversy, Olmsted defended thinning using a distinctly Darwinian argument about the fundamental cycles of death and rebirth in nature. The model of repeating cycles of decline and rebirth through "natural selection," and of some inexorable logic guiding what seemed to be a horribly violent and chaotic process, served to explain the necessary destruction and replanting of trees.[37] Human intervention, by way of landscape architecture and street tree planting, would accelerate nature's own process of creative destruction, in order to benefit all. Frederick Franklin Moon, the dean of the New York State College of Forestry, explained that "Nature, while producing superb timber in her virgin forests, is reckless of time. . . . When tending the forest, man plans greatly to reduce this time by shortening the struggle for existence." Moon described the cycles of death and rebirth that constituted the "epic of the forest."[38] Olmsted, too, tried to explain the need for thinning, and even "clean-cutting," by way of Darwinian metaphors. The argument in his 1889 defense of thinning was that protecting trees from thinning crews would in the end kill far more than it would save. It was necessary to kill some trees so that others could live and prosper.

Olmsted merged in his writing the physical decline of the park with its social decline, transposing his view of nature's transformation into social terms. For Olmsted, Parsons, and increasingly the upper- and middle-class homeowners of uptown Manhattan, the pastoral landscape—made complete with strolling couples and genteel carriages—was symbolic of the "uptown utopia" the elites hoped to create.[39] So just as the rowdy recreation of the laboring classes and the "democratizing" of the park marked a clear shift from the paternalism of the pastoral park, so equally did the decline of the landscape itself   by building encroachments, lack of maintenance, and destructive cutting—symbolize a social declension. Even as he urged citizens to respect nature's cyclical ways, he saw an opposite cycle occurring: instead of a progressive advancement of the park's landscape and its visitors' behavior, he saw a distinct decline, a slow decay of his original vision. From the state of nature in the city, Olmsted judged the condition of human progress. It was a rhetorical strategy that many New Yorkers would later employ.

Central Park has never lived down to its advocates' worst fears. Indeed, even at the turn of the century, it managed to adapt to a new constituency with new ideas about how to use a park without losing its basic form. Olmsted, disgusted though he might be by the ball fields and band shell, would still be able to find his way around the park today. Ironically, however, by its very success, Central Park eased the way for the sacrifice of nature in the rest of the city. Once reformers had secured Central Park and the other large parks, it became much harder to intervene in the overheated real estate market to secure parkways, small parks, and street trees. Like the Museum of the City of New York, which had provided a haven for a few pieces of New York's material past, Central Park became as much nature's prison as its nursery.

In 1872, Olmsted predicted that

> The time will come when New York will be built up, when all the grading and filling will be done, and when the picturesquely-varied, rocky formations of the Island will have been converted into formations for rows of monotonous straight streets, and piles of erect buildings. There will be no suggestion left of its present varied surface, with the single exception of the few acres contained in the Park. Then the priceless value of the present picturesque outlines of the ground will be more distinctly perceived. . . .[40]

Nonetheless, even Olmsted was not satisfied with the "priceless" park. From early in his career he had advocated the development of park systems consisting of riverwalks, boulevards, large parks, and small neighborhood parks linked together in an "Emerald Necklace," as he called his Boston park system. But bringing the ideals of Central Park—which had been so contested—into the streets of the city would be far more difficult.

TREE CULTURE: THE DECLINE AND REBIRTH OF STREET TREES

If Killian van Rensslaer and his West Side Association members were unsurpassed in the fervor with which they protested the cutting down of trees, they were not alone, nor were they simply obsessed with their valuable park. For the decline of trees from the streets of New York was precipitous, almost complete, and one of the most visible changes in the city's physical landscape. A bird's-eye view of New York in 1830 would have been dominated by trees covering three- and four-story brick homes and businesses. Fifty years later the bird would have found few opportunities to land, although the artist would have had far less trouble drawing the buildings.

"The City is approaching a period when it will be without trees if its present policy of tree culture is continued," intoned the Tree Planting Association of New York City in 1914. The association had been working since 1897 to promote tree planting by the city and by private owners. In offering statistics of trees planted and trees removed in order to spur action, they essentially acknowledged defeat. Between 1908 and 1911 they surveyed Brooklyn and Manhattan and concluded that 9,000 trees had been removed and 584 planted. Carefully surveying six small sections of Manhattan, they found a declining number of removals—350 in 1908, 185 in 1909, and 75 in 1910—but none planted.[41] Laurie Davidson Cox, a professor at the Syracuse College of Forestry, surveyed Manhattan in 1916 and found only 5,400 street trees up to 110th Street, most of them in bad condition.[42] In Brooklyn the situation was even worse: They estimated that possibly 200,000 trees had been removed since the turn of the century.[43] Brooklyn's rapid expansion, especially after the consolidation of the city in 1898, saw wholesale removal of trees from what would become the vast expanses of working-class and middle-class housing. By 1880, even though some side streets and a few avenues had street trees, the elimination of street trees from the downtown was largely complete. The disappearance of street trees was all the more striking because within a short ride north of the dense downtown—to the Upper East and West Sides and the "annexed districts" of northern Manhattan and the Bronx—large tracts of fields and farms sustained heartily growing shade trees.

To some, the uniformly bad news about street trees in New York at the turn of the century illustrated the sad truth that trees and cities were not meant to grow together. The needs of commerce and the actions of city government combined to usher along the decline of street trees. Avenues were widened, sidewalks and curbstones were laid to separate pedestrian and road traffic, and gas and water mains were placed beneath the street. Workers chopped mercilessly at the tops and branches of trees to make way for telephone and electric posts and their wires that crisscrossed city streets. Gas leaks, electrical wires, and horse-biting wounds ranked among the major causes of death among trees. The tree that shaded Lily Bart survived against great odds: it required sunlight, a deep well of soil for its roots, and a wide surface opening to enable oxygen to reach the roots. These were all scarce. What the tree did not need it had in overabundance: pollution, excessive shading, and numerous injuries from people and animals.

Observers and advocates of a healthy "tree culture" repeated the litany of offenses New Yorkers had committed against trees in their midst and concluded that

> the history of tree planting in New York City shows that there has been no definite and systematic plan of work and as a consequence streets have been planted promiscuously with all kinds of trees and with little or no regard to the width of streets, nature of soil, nor to the artistic effect of certain trees in relation to the height of buildings upon those streets. No other city the size and importance of New York in the civilized world has paid less attention to the proper development of the planting of its streets and parks.[44]

Though other cities also faced similar problems and had seen great rows of elms disappear long before the Dutch Elm disease decimated them, New York's elimination of trees was far more rapid and complete. Some cities, like Washington, D.C., were cited repeatedly by advocates and professionals as having long maintained their trees. Other cities were well on their way to replanting. Newark, for example, established the Shade Tree Commission in response to a state law and began a program of planting 27,000 young trees on 180 miles of streets, creating a city nursery, hiring expert foresters, and disseminating "fruitful educational propaganda concerning trees."[45]

The short life span of trees, which remains virtually unchanged, served as a poignant symbol of the failure to reserve places for nature within the city.[46] The few trees that survived on Manhattan's streets appeared to be shackled escapees from Central Park. Street trees—in their various states of sickness and finally death—were thus usually barometers of negative change in the city. "The great elms that adorned the Mall a generation ago are dead," wrote Ernest Gruening in 1922. "A tree forty feet high in the lower half of Central Park is a rarity. Everywhere the forces of nature are shriveling, perishing before the relentless advance of stone and steel and poison gas."[47] Rather than advertising the prosperity of the city, trees came to be mocking symbols of the failure to maintain a place for nature within the city.

In the face of powerful forces that seemed to direct the elimination of street trees from the city, a variety of actors in the city development drama reacted with an organized, if only partly successful, effort to replant street trees. Though Frederick Law Olmsted and urban visionaries of the nineteenth century had long seen street trees as an essential design tool, it was only in the last decade of the nineteenth century, with the rise of City Beautiful planning ideals allied with Progressive social reform organizations, that street trees merited earnest defenders.

It was the establishment of Arbor Day that originated the street tree movement. Begun in 1874 in Nebraska under the inspiration of Sterling Morton, later a secretary of agriculture under Grover Cleveland, Arbor Day's popularity had spread quickly. New York adopted the holiday relatively late, in 1888, but with eagerness. Mainly focused on the schools, Arbor Day celebrations were full of pageantry, including speeches on such topics as "What the leaves do" and "The most useful tree."[48] The focus, however, was on the planting of trees. New York State planted some 24,000 trees in 1889, the year of the Central Park tree-thinning controversy.[49] From 1889 to 1909, 317,166 trees were planted in New York State on Arbor Day. But despite this apparent enthusiasm, it was short-lived: a report in 1909 noted that only 60,944—approximately one in five—trees still stood in 1909.[50] Most of the trees planted on Arbor Day were not in the heart of Manhattan: the obstacles posed by the city's forbidding environment precluded the one-day frenzy of planting from taking place there. But the wide publicity that accompanied the Arbor Day celebrations boosted the efforts of private tree-planting organizations.

It was these organizations—especially the Tree Planting Association of New York, founded by Cornelius Mitchell in 1897—that spurred the street movement in the city. The Tree Planting Association led neighborhood organizations, botanical societies, flower societies, and garden groups in organizing efforts to replant the city's streets. In fact, given the Parks Department's limited role, the Tree Planting Association was more than an advocacy organization; in a way, it served as a wing of the Parks Department, just as the Charity Organization Society's Tenement House Committee served as the precursor to the city's own Tenement House Department and the Fifth Avenue Association served as planning board and private police department to the Avenue. It was a classic Progressive social organization, blending religious fervor with a belief in the importance of environment for shaping behavior, a strong faith in professionals and their scientific knowledge, a continued paternalism toward the poor, and a new insistence on government involvement.

The Tree Planting Association was founded with the intent of completing Olmsted's work: creating a "complete plan for beautifying the city" by systematically planting trees along streets and avenues.[51] Cornelius Mitchell appealed to the nostalgic pangs of his members by reminding them of "their pleasurable reminiscences, the aspects of many of the streets and the small parks [below Fourteenth Street]. Here were to be found on every hand, thriving, vigorous trees in considerable variety. . . . A luxuriant foliage and often beautiful blossoms in season."[52] Mitchell would have agreed with the jeremiad of Carl Bannwart, who moved from nostalgia to a chastisement of the past generation and applause for the work of the current one:

Not so long ago, as men not yet old remember, Manhattan Isle as to many of its residence streets was a veritable grove of trees. What "old New Yorker" can forget the glory of the verdure of the olden East Broadway, or of Elm street that took its name from the towers of spreading green that lined its walks, or of old Marion street with its maples, or Prince street, or Lafayette place, or Waverly place, or Washington place, and so many, many thoroughfares of the fine old town all "awave with trees." But a perverse generation came upon the scene, and in the name of progress the "practical" man had his benighted, Philistine way with the trees.

New York has begun to repent, and to lament its folly, and the first stirrings of a purpose to make reparation are manifest. Private individuals and civic organizations are at work and successfully so—reviving the ancient New York spirit that loved and fostered trees.[53]

The Tree Association did not itself plant trees nor fund the planting of trees. Rather it considered itself a vocal advocacy group and clearinghouse for information on tree planting. It advertised the value of trees and provided, to individual property owners, information on what trees should be planted, how to plant and maintain trees, and city tree nurseries.[54] And in many ways it was an effective organization: through its advocacy, some hundred thousand trees were planted between 1900 and 1910 in all of New York City; on the other hand, it was less effective in preventing the hundred thousand trees removed during the same years. [55]

Although parks represented early attempts of city governments to control urban development, they shied away from extending this control beyond the boundaries of parks, parkways, and squares. Regulation of street trees is first recorded in New York City as early as 1708, but over the next two hundred years it had changed little: the City Council acted merely to allow private owners to plant street trees or to fine those who willfully destroyed trees.[56] An 1869 New York state law gave tax breaks for individuals who planted trees along public roads.[57] Legal cases around the country had established at least minimal protection of trees from attacks, whether by malicious individuals and their animals, or by companies seeking to lay gas lines or electric wires.[58]

The Tree Planting Association had immediately recognized its own impotence to replant Manhattan's streets. From its founding in 1897, therefore, the organization had called for city government control of street trees in the hopes that the Parks Department could then initiate a long-term, coherent planting program. "The growth of the greater city," argued Steven Smith, one-time health commissioner and head of the Tree Planting Association in 1912, "is far too rapid in every direction to await the slow movements of the people under the pressure of voluntary organizations."[59] With its urging, in 1902, the state legislature added Chapter 453 to the New York state laws, giving the Parks Department official jurisdiction over "all the trees and vegetation upon the streets, parkways, and public places of the city."[60] The law made no provision for funding this massive new responsibility for the agency—and, since the city's Board of Estimate refused to provide local funding, the law became, almost immediately, a "dead letter on the statute book."[61] In its first decade of legal control over street trees, the Parks Department regularly reported no new trees planted in Manhattan. In its best years in the first half of the century, the department planted five hundred trees in Manhattan and some two thousand in Brooklyn, but these years were the exception rather than the rule. The department spent as much time removing dead trees or trees damaged by land development and commerce as they did planting new ones. In most years, an equal or greater number of dead trees were removed than were planted—for example, 296 were planted in Manhattan in 1914 while 274 dead trees were removed—effectively negating any effort of the department to expand the tree population. Even these statistics of tree removal and planting reveal only part of the story. Not only were trees being ripped out of the ground by the thousands, but the remaining few and even the newly planted ones were doomed to short life spans. Surveys by Cox and the Tree Planting Association noted that of the existing street trees, even newly planted ones, many were dying or only barely surviving. J. H. Prost, one of the premier urban foresters in the country, insisted that even in Chicago, where conditions were more conducive to street trees, he estimated that for every ten trees planted three to five would die within ten years; in his survey of the trees of Chicago's streets in 1910 he found more than three thousand dead trees.[62] Dead trees, tree advocates reminded citizens and city officials, were worse than no trees at all: They were dangerous, looked bad, reflected negatively on the city's image, and cost a great deal to pull down.[63] Through World War II, then, the Parks Department exercised only limited authority over street trees, offering advice and assistance and approving applications by private organizations and individuals to plant trees. The Parks Department's efforts to plant trees on Manhattan's streets were less than overwhelming, due largely to the lack of funding. Planting and maintaining street trees remained a largely private affair.

The call for city control and funding for street tree planting came not simply from financial considerations but also from a frustration with the reliance on individual property owners. The ways in which individual owners who planted trees went wrong were innumerable: some planted trees too close to one another, others planted "inappropriate" trees (ones that required too much water or were not resistant to pollution), and most failed miserably in maintaining trees over time. The last problem was to be expected: with the rapid turnover in land and property ownership, it seemed inevitable that trees planted by one owner would be ignored by the next, and perhaps destroyed by the third. The Tree Association had to rely on the abilities and good judgment of citizens to accomplish the task of creating tree-lined streets, even as it insisted on the standards of new professional tree experts.

Tree advocates and park planners had tried to ban from Central Park the restless pace of New York politics and urban development. They engaged in a propaganda campaign or decades-long educational programs to show New Yorkers that the building of a park required a wholly different expectation about the pace of development than a new office building. In 1911, Parsons reminded New Yorkers that

> A park in a crowded city is the fruit of long, patient, expert cultivation; it is a picture painted in living growths by careful hands during many years, for the mental and moral uplifting and the physical recreation of man.[64]

Olmsted and Parsons were not alone in this frustration. Professional landscape architects and foresters, who were increasingly important in the parks and street tree movements, were especially frustrated by their continued reliance on individual citizens to accomplish important public work. Olmsted, in his 1889 tree-thinning report, chose to mostly cite experts on tree maintenance techniques. He concluded that private citizens would simply have to listen to professional tree experts if they wanted to have beautiful parks with healthy trees. In 1895, Olmsted complained bitterly that citizens had an extremely short vision of time:

> The average respectable citizen thinks of a tree as a tree; a piece of public property like a wall, a building, a bridge. He does not see a tree as an element of a future landscape any more than he sees it as an element of a forest. It is a piece of goods. It has cost public money. It represents public money. He cannot resist any ignorant public clamor against the destruction of it.[65]

This kind of angry defense of professional landscape architects and tree experts was not unique to Olmsted; it only stands out from the otherwise genteel tone of reports and articles about street tree planting.

Why this fury? Why did professional landscape architects and urban foresters find themselves so at odds with the "well-meaning" goals of citizens who wanted to plant trees? Part of the tension came from the rise in professional standards of tree planters and landscape architects that paralleled the much broader professionalization movement. By the end of the century, landscape architecture and forestry required professional degrees earned at proliferating schools of architecture and forestry.[66] The question of street trees was especially frustrating for tree experts. Planted and maintained by private owners, but placed along the primary public forums of the city, street trees held an ambiguous place in the urban landscape. Just as professional engineers were beginning to plan subways and architects were starting to build steel-skeleton sky-scrapers, landscape designers saw their contribution of parks, parkways, and a network of street trees as essential to the development of the modern urban landscape. But in-stead of finding themselves hovering above the public, drawing aerial view drawings of street trees, professional landscape designers and tree specialists found themselves encouraging, cajoling, and berating individual homeowners to plant trees correctly.

Although their power was limited, and they fought against enormous obstacles of bad environmental conditions, municipal indifference, budgetary constraints, and citizen apathy, tree-planting professionals and their allied organizations were fiercely committed to their work. "The love of trees has come to stay," insisted Carl Bannwart of Newark's Shade Tree Commission. "The conviction is strengthened that we must have them in our cities."[67] What motivated the founders of the organizations or the professionals who argued so fiercely for trees, and painstakingly described how trees could be reintroduced to forbidding cement and asphalt cities?[68]

One set of arguments for street trees centered on their value for the health of the city. Trees cooled the city; they produced oxygen while removing pollutants from the air; they moistened the air and eliminated dust; and they purified the soil and elimi-nated disease. Edith Wharton's Lily Bart sought shade to protect her from the heat as she waited for the train that would take her to an estate along the Hudson. For New Yorkers who could not leave, the heat of the city was far more insidious.[69] Stephen Smith insisted that many of the three to five thousand summer deaths in New York could be avoided if trees were planted throughout the city. Smith mustered extensive data he had assembled as health commissioner to prove what others simply believed as a matter of almost religious principle: trees could clean the air and absorb the dis-ease of the city.[70]

Despite their insistent claims that trees were crucial for saving the lives of the poor tenement dwellers by cleansing the air, water, and earth, the Tree Planting Associa-tion was primarily interested in planting trees along avenues and in wealthier resi-dential areas. The association had asserted that with "skilled management" trees could be reintroduced to Manhattan's streets; in 1914 they argued that the six sections in which they found 738 trees could contain as many as 10,500.[71] Laurie Cox suggested a goal of planting 200 trees per mile, thus increasing the number of street trees to 17,000 in Manhattan.[72] But perhaps they protested too much: Even the optimistic leadership accepted that "a large portion of the streets of the Borough of Manhattan presents conditions which do not warrant the cultivation of street trees."[73] In essence, despite arguing fervently for widespread planting of trees, they were willing, out of pragmatism, to sacrifice a large portion of the island—and always the poorest areas—to "complete denudation."[74]

The association's Tenement Shade Tree Committee struggled valiantly, and perhaps vainly, to plant trees in tenement districts. Even though the middle class and wealthy had fled farther and farther north in Manhattan, or into the outer boroughs, the poorest New Yorkers lived in the Lower East Side, which became, in the first decade of the twentieth century, the densest place in the world. The Small Parks Act of 1887 had brought some relief in the form of a series of small parks such as Mulberry Bend, Stuyvesant, and Corlears Hook. But anything more than small pockets of grass and trees was elusive.

Tree advocates noted the paradox that where trees were most needed, they were most absent. The Tree Association argued that something should be done to ensure that the new tenement areas of Brooklyn should be planted with trees, and the older ones of Manhattan given at least the consolation of a few trees: "From both an aesthetic and a hygienic standpoint, the tenement house districts offer an encouraging field for the outlay of the comparatively small sums of money and the effort necessary to provide sheltering and life-giving foliage where it is needed vitally."[75] But even the humanitarian plea was rejected by downtown businesspeople, who argued that "effort in this direction . . . is wasted. . . . The fewer trees they plant where they have no other function than to temporarily obstruct the sidewalks, the better for the success of the movement."[76] By the second decade of the twentieth century, tree advocates had relented: The most comprehensive plan for tree planting in New York essentially suggested no tree planting below Washington Square, with the vast majority limited to the Upper East and West Sides.[77]

Perhaps more important, at least to those who had the power to actually affect the number of street trees, were the arguments for trees in the beautification of the city. Trees would offer the "element of beauty and relief to [the] usually commonplace rigidity of line and barrenness."[78] Following Olmsted's arguments for a system of parks and parkways, tree advocates believed that trees offered visual foils to the monotony of the city and its crass commercialism. In a city dominated by an architecture of spectacle, where historical styles were crudely recycled, the purifying presence of nature's beauty could, critics argued, soften the deleterious effects of commerce.[79] Second, street trees would be the closest approximation to a park network that New York could afford. For Laurie Cox, the Forestry School professor who prepared plans for a street tree system, lines of trees along streets and avenues would serve as a substitute for an absent park system: "Due to intensive use of all available real estate, a park system by means of these ordinary forms of park connections would appear to be practically impossible. We must make use in some form of the existing streets."[80] Finally, many planners saw an even more grandiose role for street trees. By laying out single or double lanes of trees along both sides of streets, planners hoped to succeed where the City Beautiful movement had failed: creating a system of connecting boulevards organizing the city around monuments and public buildings. Street trees offered one last chance to achieve visual order.[81]

Beyond its aesthetic, health, and recreational value, nature in the form of parks— and even street trees—had long been recognized as valuable to property, useful in attracting investments and shoppers, and a general improvement in the image of the city. Tree-planting advocates noted—usually as the first, most important "good" of planting trees—the value of trees to property. Carl Bannwart, a tree expert, asserted in 1915 that "The appearance of a city is its chief material asset. The calibre of a city's people, as a whole, is exactly expressed in the outward and visible aspect of their municipal home. Now there is nothing that gives tone to this aspect like well-kept parks and well-treed streets."[82] Just as Central Park had sent the land values around it skyrocketing, advocates insisted that trees almost automatically increased the value of real estate. Cox bypassed this issue in his report: "It will not be considered necessary in this report to discuss the many ways in which trees on city streets affect the health, the beauty and even the real estate values of the community. Everyone has heard of these things, everyone believes them and nearly everyone is willing to pay his share in securing them . . . there are few questions of municipal life upon which the average citizen is more unanimous in his opinion than in the desirability of shade trees on the streets of his city."[83] The financial value of trees to adjacent property was not mainly practical—their cooling effects, for example—but more intangible: trees offered variety in the visual landscape and gave a sense of the street or neighborhood as being "well kept."

Despite the financial argument for trees, many developers and property owners fought the imposition of street tree systems. Their power and the image of Lower Manhattan as predominantly commercial and industrial led many to turn the tables on tree advocates and proclaim that, in fact, trees on the streets were destructive of the city. What tree advocates lamented as unfortunate, but remediable, conditions for trees, others saw as clear evidence that trees would only cause problems in places they did not belong. Editorialists argued that tree roots were bad for building foundations and sidewalks, and got in the way of laying out gas mains.[84]

The problems of having enough soil or water were secondary to the driving force of real estate development that rendered low-density uses, such as parks, gardens, or trees in front of townhouses, obsolete. The minute construction of the city for speculation and development—laying out the grid of streets and dividing plots of land into speculative space, demarcating street and sidewalk with curbstones, and expanding access to electricity and water—worked against street trees. By the time tree advocates could launch a real effort, it was necessary to essentially create "artificial" opportunities for trees to grow.[85] Those who criticized the planting of trees and even welcomed the removal of street trees from business areas had accepted and thus perpetuated the change in city structure that had been accelerating in the second half of the nineteenth century. From the antebellum "walking city," New York was quickly becoming a city of segregated activities: downtown for business, uptown for residences. There would remain—in New York especially—more mixing of uses than in other cities, but the goal, enshrined in the 1916 Zoning Resolution, of separating commercial and industrial areas from residential ones became dominant. Those who criticized tree-planting efforts in the downtown, and tree advocates who were willing to sacrifice the downtown to a treeless future, had adopted an attitude toward urban structure that would come to dominate American city planning for much of the century.

If trees were to be the park system New York never had, street tree advocates had to balance their design goals with the limitations of the dense, commercial city. On the basic issue of survival, trees were an extremely risky endeavor. On all sides—below-ground obstructions, ground-level pollutants and horse-bites, above-ground pollution and electric wires—trees faced enormous obstacles to healthy growth. Carl Bannwart, of the Newark Shade Tree Commission, displayed the frustrating limitations with a long tirade against the common curbstone, which prevented water from reaching tree roots: "The greatest enemy of the shade tree is the curbstone. Whoever invented the curb did a good thing for his time—a time when the question of 'utility' was first, and that of city beautification by means of trees was not in the race at all."[86] He offered detailed plans for redesigning curbstones to allow for grills and for root expansion. Much of the energy of park advocates and professionals was spent figuring out low-cost methods of providing soil, water, and protection so that trees had a fighting chance simply to survive.

The tensions between the hopes of tree advocates and the limitations of the commercial city were most clearly felt as tree advocates debated how best to plant trees within a larger urban design vision. Tree advocates had to carefully balance an image of the ideal street—of towering elms and maples creating a cathedral-like effect—with the constraints of the city. Even if Olmsted complained about the limitations placed upon him by the width of Central Park and the continued proposals for "encroach-ments," within the park he was largely free to design a sophisticated pastoral landscape. But street tree planners had to consider the rights of individual homeowners, the needs of businesses, and the requirements of traffic. For instance, while trees were themselves "advertisement[s], helping to attract shoppers or house-hunters," they could not be allowed to overshadow the real advertisements on the sides of buildings, nor darken shop windows, nor slow the drying of shoppers' sidewalks after storms.[87] The Fifth Avenue Association was particularly aggressive in combating the introduc-tion of street trees, which it was sure would block the view of pedestrians and bus rid-ers into the now-famous shop windows along the Avenue.[88]

In order to balance the competing constituents along New York's streets, trees would have to be "suppressed."[89] Instead of the flamboyant elms, Manhattan needed straight, thin trees, which spread high above traffic, but required little soil and could survive New York's pollution and human and animal attacks. Some urged that only shrubs and very small trees be used on Manhattan's streets. Pruning, which so bedev-iled Olmsted, had to be vastly stepped up to hold back the growth of trees. Like Bon-sai trees, street trees in Manhattan had to be restrained, stunted in their growth so that they would "decorate" rather than "form" their surroundings (see figures 6.4 and 6.5). According to one tree expert:

> it will probably be necessary to clip the trees, in order to restrain them from too large growth, as well as to maintain the compact growth and regular outline which are most appropriate to trees which must necessarily be dominated by architecture.[90]

Tree advocates and park officials, as they sought to balance a nostalgic and idealistic vision of lush avenues with a realistic assessment of the financial, bureaucratic, and environmental conditions, fought over what trees could be planted. The vast major-ity of trees to be found in Manhattan in the first two decades of the twentieth cen-tury were poplars, maples, and sycamores.[91] The ideal tree species thus had to be at-tractive (according to long-standing criteria of beauty) and tough enough to withstand the harsh environment of the city, but also malleable enough to comply with the design limitations of the busy and increasingly crowded business districts.[92]

The ailanthus, the "tree of heaven" that would grow in Brooklyn, had at one point in New York's history seemed to be the answer to the city's dilemma. It was extremely hardy, flourishing notoriously on tenement roofs and right through the asphalt. It had been a popular city tree in New York, primarily for its tenacity in surviving the dif-ficulties of life in the city for generations. But the ailanthus was less attractive because it grew irregularly and gave off a bad odor during certain times of the year. What had

Fig. 6.4. *Last Tree on the Avenue*, from a 1913 series of photographs showing the sole remaining tree at Fifth Avenue and Thirty-seventh Street. © Collection of The New-York Historical Society.

Fig. 6.5. Off of Park Avenue, 1929. A single man stands not far from the lone tree on an Upper East Side Manhattan street. Sixteen years after the alarm of the "last tree on Fifth Avenue" little had changed on neighboring streets. Collections of the Municipal Archives of the City of New York.

once been "considered a suitable embellishment for the finest homes and boulevards," according to Oliver Allen, "had fallen from grace and been condemned as a weed."[93] The ailanthus may have been good for one age and one type of city, but for the city of skyscrapers and congestion, its smell, tendency to split, and overexuberant growth were precisely the wrong attributes. So what had once been one of the most popular urban trees now became a hated species and was permanently banned from use by the Parks Department.[94]

Tree advocates and professionals recognized that certain traditions surrounding trees were difficult to overcome. For example, throughout the tree-planting literature, professionals expressed a concern that uninformed citizens and local tree-planting organizations were always overcrowding trees in an effort to create thick shaded corri-

dors like those in the main streets of small towns. The elm, the favored tree in the
United States, was also the strong aesthetic favorite among citizens and professionals.
But for city streets the elm was "expensive": it required a large amount of soil and regular pruning to prevent its branches from blocking too much light from adjacent store
windows or getting in the way of wires and traffic. It was, however, difficult to restrain
private owners from pursuing a traditional ideal of trees and towns. "The truth seems
to be," theorized Elbert Peets,

> that we are trying to apply our traditional village ideals of tree-culture, tree-form, and
> tree-species to our present entirely different urban conditions. As soon as we learn that
> we cannot grow in the heart of a city the elms and sugar maples which shade so many
> village roads, . . . nor grow them with as little care as they need along a moist country
> road between rich fields, we shall be able to bring trees back into the crowded parts
> of our cities.[95]

Even as the Parks Department pursued trees that were most appropriate for Manhattan—Norway maples and sycamores especially—officials, including Robert Moses,
also acceded to demands for American elms.

THE SPIRITS OF THE TREES

For planners and developers, street trees may have been just another urban design tool.
But if street tree planners were satisfied with the smooth look of a row of trees along
both sides of an avenue, many others revered trees on a far more individual basis. We
need only to think back to that curious little event in 1889, the critique of the uses
of the axe, to imagine that New Yorkers' relationship to their natural environment was
perhaps more powerful than we might have imagined. What could make the people
of Edith Wharton's Fifth Avenue, who so carefully circumscribed their actions so as
not to cause alarm, suddenly splay themselves in front of a tree to protect it against
the axe of the pruners? Why the obsession with trees? Beyond the value of trees for
health-related reasons, or as tools for urban design, trees held far deeper, intangible
meanings for New Yorkers.[96]

Like City Hall, which had given rise to a historic preservation movement, some
trees were celebrated as historic monuments virtually on par with the city's historic
buildings. The same groups that watched over City Hall, Fraunces Tavern, Hamilton
Grange, and the Jumel Mansion also kept tabs on the Hangman's Elm in Washington
Square Park and the trees around Hamilton's Grange.[97] The rhetoric they used in
speaking of the historic value of trees was similar, too:

Treasures, indeed, though too seldom appreciated! Intimately associated as they are in many instances with our National life as well as with local events, much of the history of America is written in the story of her trees, living or otherwise, and can be traced through a study of the part they have played in connection with its development. Living Links in the chain of human interests that spans the centuries, such trees possess a unique historic value, and should be carefully preserved.[98]

A 1938 study of "famous trees" by the Department of Agriculture summarized this view of the historical value of trees:

Trees by their very nature are landmarks and memorials. They are therefore identified with human happenings. Also, trees, having more than the allotted life span of man, carry their associations through generations of men and women. Thus they often figure not only in biography but also in history.[99]

As with historic buildings in New York, as the years passed there were fewer and fewer trees to preserve and celebrate. The American Scenic and Historic Preservation Society, established to protect historic buildings and landscapes, reported regularly on the state of New York's historic trees and tabulated the yearly losses. In 1913 it recounted the celebrations for the "Inwood Tulip," the "oldest and biggest tree in Manhattan"; lamented the passing of the De Lancey Pine from the New York Zoological Park "on account of old age"; and urged that city planners consider altering the street plans in order to save historic trees.[100] City historians recalled with special sadness the passing of the last of the Stuyvesant pear trees on Third Avenue and Thirteenth Street, which had stood for more than two hundred years. The Historical Society was so struck by this loss that it took pieces of the dead tree and preserved it in the society's new building on Central Park West (figures 6.6 and 6.7)[101]

This kind of dedication to individual historic trees suggests that though treated much like historic buildings, trees resonated as historic landmarks in very different ways. Though "useless" compared to historic buildings that could be adapted for different needs, trees were in other ways more powerful landmarks from the past. Where buildings were mute objects that had simply withstood the weathering effect of time and humanity, trees were living organisms that had continued to grow and develop. City Hall's classical columns reminded onlookers of the architecture of the early nineteenth century. Washington Square townhouses could speak to the memory of those who, like Henry James, had lived in the city awash in a sea of red brick. Trees, however, were alive and therefore could truly connect the present with the past, and suggest the shape of the future. As one chronicler noted in 1909,

Section of the "Old Stuyvesant Pear Tree," four feet from the Ground. Presented by Rutherfurd Stuyvesant.

Fig. 6.6. This cross-section of the Stuyvesant Pear Tree (planted by Peter Stuyvesant near Third Avenue and Thirteenth Street) was mounted on a base and preserved by the New-York Historical Society. © Collection of The New-York Historical Society.

[Arbor Day] holds quite as rich possibilities of spiritual growth as of merely physical development. It is a symbol of progress. It is the only one of our American holidays which turns its face toward the future rather than toward the past. . . . Our young cities have too often been ruthlessly sacrificed to a brutal, hideous materialism; and a large number of our city children have never known the beauty of places devoted to "green things growing."[102]

More effectively than historic buildings, trees could symbolize the passing of time.

Preservationists anthropomorphized historic buildings, speaking of the buildings as if they had been conscious in the past, and therefore carried with them the "memories" of great events and people. While the rhetoric in defense of historic buildings could be quite melodramatic, it rarely struck such a personal note as could individual trees. De Long Rice wrote in *The Spirits of the Trees* that trees seemed like members of one's family:

Fig. 6.7. Stuyvesant Pear Tree, Third Avenue at Thirteenth Street, 1863. © Collection of The New-York Historical Society.

But there is a nameless tree, the most sacred and beautiful that waves from the green landscape of memory—nameless because it is not the same with us all. It may be an oak, a poplar, a chestnut, an apple tree, or any of the others; it is the tree that stood at the door of the old home. Our childish feet passed in and out beneath its boughs; it gave welcome asylum to sweet songsters that dwelt with us in poverty or in wealth; it spread its shadows for our plays and pranks, and for our lazy dream-filled hours.

It is no accident that tree planting grew enormously in the years around World War I, when families used trees as memorials to their fallen sons.[103] Rice found some consolation, as did families of war victims, in the immortality guaranteed trees by their use as furniture and building material:

Great trees, like great men, must live on in service after death, some to sweeten memory with flowers and fruits that vanished with our better years, others to know more serious duties in the march of human life. The whirling saw which parts the fallen bodies of the oak and the pine, sings to them a song of immortality, and sends their timbers of strength and beauty to while away the centuries in the fairest abodes of men—to wall and shelter happy homes; to be a table in a house of plenty; to be a chair beloved of weary beauty; to be a fiddle and carry the soul of melody; to be a desk and hear a poet's thoughts.[104]

John Flavel Mines, a flaneur of New York in the late nineteenth century, poignantly described the removal of trees behind St. John's Chapel on Varick Street to make way for a freight depot:

The only public execution I ever witnessed was the slaying of those great trees under which my sisters and I had played, and I would as soon have seen so many men beheaded. A fatal fascination drew me to the spot. I did not want to go, but could not help going out of my way to pass it by. The axes were busy with the hearts of the giants I had loved, and the iron-handed carts went crashing over the flower-beds, leaving a trail of death. The trees lay prone over the ploughed gravel-walks, and a few little birds were screaming over their tops, bewailing the destruction of their nests. It was horrible. As I looked upon the scene, I knew how people must feel when an army passed over their homes, leaving desolation in its wake.

For Mines, the trees had been removed not for something equally valuable—"a block of homes"—but rather for a "coarse pile of bricks for use as a freight depot, to make it a centre of ceaseless noise and riot." The destruction of this site of repose, an "earthly paradise," for an "abomination of desolation" did not speak well to the city's priorities.[105] And on the Lower East Side, where trees and parks were more scarce than anywhere else on the island, inhabitants complained to housing reformers Lawrence

Veiller and Robert De Forest about the rapid removal of the few trees in their neighborhood. One woman eloquently commented on the meaning of the trees that had
been cut down after her family had moved to a new home:

> This house had rather a refined, quiet aspect, and was well kept and clean. . . . But best
> of all, our scenery had changed. Actual trees grew before us and green yards and pretty
> flowers. In the street next ours, right opposite, were two small, low, private houses,
> and to the people in the tenements around, the open space and lovely green were like
> a veritable oasis in the desert of down town. The Brooklyn Bridge was also a part of
> our view, and could be distinctly seen from end to end. How often by night we would
> watch the lights twinkling like stars in the distance. It was a very happy change, and
> we were permitted to enjoy it for a little while, indeed a very little while.
>
> Lots, I understand, are very valuable, and soon the beautiful trees were cut down.
> It was a barbarous thing. The green yards and flowers went next, and then we knew,
> though at first we mourned and wondered, that all this digging and uprooting mean
> new houses of greater height and depth. Once more we were to have the high, for-
> bidding walls before us. Nor did it take long. In little over a year it was all accom-
> plished, and even our beloved bridge was completely hidden from view.[106]

Arbor Day celebrations, too, were augmented with lamentations for lost trees
that, like Rice's elegies, emphasized the powerful personal attachment trees could
promote. "Woodman, Spare that Tree," by George P. Morris, was read in schools
on Arbor Day, 1909:[107]

> Woodman, spare that tree!
> Touch not a single bough!
> In youth it sheltered me,
> And I'll protect it now.
> 'Twas my forefather's hand
> that placed it near his cot;
> There, woodman, let it stand—
> Thy ax shall harm it not!
> That old familiar tree,
> Whose glory and renown
> Are spread o'er land and sea—
> And wouldst thou hew it down?
> Woodman, forbear thy stroke!
> Cut not its earth-bound ties;
> Oh, spare that aged oak,
> Now towering to the skies!

Trees, as living organisms that grew slowly and steadily, and then could die of "old age," meant more as symbols of the flow of time than as monuments from specific moments in history. Where Fifth Avenue blocks could change dramatically in a decade, with sturdy buildings coming down in a day, trees could stand for decades or centuries. Trees offered few clues to the specific time in which they lived; their thick trunks and gnarled roots and branches simply spoke of great age, of the passing of time. Trees were celebrated not only because they stood in such stark contrast to the "unnatural" city around them, but because they represented a wholly different pace of time. Where the city moved to a molto allegro pace, trees followed an adagio tempo.

That, at least, was the image. But in Manhattan, even the trees were being caught up in the "restless renewals," the yearly pulling down of the old to make way for the new, which had come to characterize the city's growth. Instead of "having more than the allotted life span of man," trees that would typically have outlived their planters died a virtual crib death in Manhattan. Trees were simply no longer standing, to serve either as traditional historical monuments or as more abstract symbols of time. "The trees," Ernest Gruening said bluntly, "shadowed by great structures, their leaves withered by the noxious exhalations of the city, are dying."[108]

The use of trees and the axes that cut them down as metaphors for decrying the ills of the city resonated with a long-standing trope in American culture. Dating from the beginning of the new nation, artists (such as Thomas Cole) and writers (like Thoreau and Cooper) had used tree stumps and, implicitly, their exterminating axes as visual and literary symbols of the destructive side of the American character. But the metaphor went further: the stumps of ancient trees, felled in an instant, posed a "temporal crisis," as Barbara Novak has called it. They suggested that humans—and especially Americans—were promoting "extraordinary accelerations" in the pace of change, literally unsettling notions of time itself.[109] In the city, and in Manhattan in particular, the disparities in the movement of time, between humans and nature's representatives, was all the more striking and troubling. The "hurricane of the axe," which Thomas Cole had condemned nearly a century before, ravaged not only trees in Manhattan but also the invented idea of a cohesive, consensual community.[110]

Near the beginning of Betty Smith's *A Tree Grows in Brooklyn*, published in 1943, the presence of the ailanthus serves as a warning of a neighborhood's decline. If there was an ailanthus growing, the narrator writes, "you knew that soon that section of Brooklyn would get to be a tenement district. The tree knew. It came there first."[111] A few years later, in 1950, E. B. White offered an equally cautionary lament about nature in New York. He noted that outside his bedroom window an ailanthus seed had found the "perfect conditions for ailanthus growth": " solid rock . . . two dead vine leaves, a cigarette butt, and a paper clip." For White, the ailanthus's ability to survive and thrive—"a stalwart forest giant"—spoke as much to the frailty of New York's environment as to the hardiness of the tree of heaven. For this "soil" was the best that "the fairest city in the world can scrape together to take care of its own."[112] In 1955, White returned to this theme, seeing trees as bastions of creative energy amid an often destructive city. Sitting beneath a tree—perhaps that same ailanthus—White noted that

> All day the fans had sung in offices, the air-conditioners had blown their clammy breath into the rooms, and the brutal sounds of demolition had stung the ear—from buildings that were being knocked down by the destroyers who have no sense of the past.

The lone tree offered some solace and more of a "sense of the past" than existed in the world beyond its shade (see figure 6.8).

White's lamentations, like Betty Smith's sad reminder and those melancholy notices about the Stuyvesant pear tree or the passing of Hamilton's thirteen sweet gum trees, may seem to come from very different places than the worry about the increased temperature, the rising mortality among tenement children, or the quest to harmonize the chaos of styles of building forms. In fact, all these motivations for preserving and planting trees were complementary. For just as the diseases and heat of the city literally killed people and destroyed the city, so too did the absence of these living beings suggest the intangible decay of the city as a social community. Thus physical destruction and social destruction were easily conjoined in the crisis around street trees. The inability of the city government and private citizens, working individually and together in reform organizations, to protect and plant trees portended a tragic future: disease, heat, and dust would make the city physically unbearable, and bleak avenues of commercial buildings would sap the spiritual life and beauty from the city. New York would become simply a marketplace, not in any sense a community or the civilized capital city of the nation.

Trees served as compelling examples of the cycle of destruction and rebuilding that had come to be one of the defining features of the city. At the same time, they were metaphors for the process whereby intangible bonds of community, association, or economic stability were broken down, destroyed, and then started up again. What were the stories people told themselves about change in the city? What were the "urban baedekers," as William R. Taylor has called them, that helped city dwellers un-

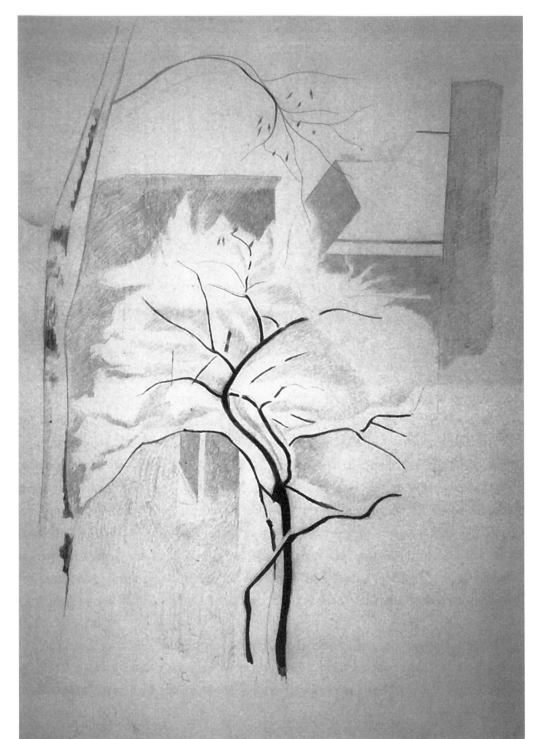

Fig. 6.8. Joseph Stella, *Tree and Houses*, 1915–17. Stella, an 1896 immigrant to New York City, is perhaps best know in New York for his images of Brooklyn Bridge, a symbol of the modern city. But he also turned his eyes to the fragile persistence of nature, as embodied by this tree, perhaps an ailanthus, surviving in the cracks of the pavement.

derstand the new forms of the commercial city?[113] Taylor would certainly agree that there were many "guidebooks" to the city, many experiences that could provide ways of comprehending New York. Trees provided one metaphor, one scenario for understanding and perhaps accepting more readily the cycle of destruction and rebuilding that was coming to be "second nature" for urban inhabitants. The experience of urban tree planting—where the story almost always ended in failure and where only the tough and scrappy trees like the ailanthus persevered—may have helped established the truism that nature cannot survive in Manhattan, that the tumultuous cycle of destruction and rebuilding is the "natural" and inevitable way to build cities.

PRO URBIS AMORE

I. N. Phelps Stokes and *The Iconography of Manhattan Island*

Every passion borders on the chaotic, but the collector's passion borders on the chaos of memories.

—Walter Benjamin, "Unpacking My Library"

In 1932, Isaac Newton Phelps Stokes completed the most personal work of recollection in a life that had been preoccupied with commemoration. A few years earlier, in 1928, he had concluded his monumental work of two decades, *The Iconography of Manhattan Island*, a six-volume collection of prints, maps, and views of the island; a massive chronology of the city's history; and a microscopic analysis of its physical transformation. Now he published *Random Recollections of a Happy Life*, a memoir of a life spanning nearly seventy years in New York City. At one point, Stokes recorded a series of dreams of old New York that filled his nights after the days of work on the *Iconography*:

> Speaking of Old New York reminds me: I have always been a dreamer of dreams—by day as well as by night—although of late years day-dreams have not played so important a part in my life as they once did, but at night I still, occasionally, wander through unknown lands, and accomplish impossible feats. I have long specialized in dreams of Old New York, and they are the most delightful of all my dreams. I usually start out from some point in the modern city, and on my way—perhaps to keep an appointment at some other well-known point—I am tempted to try a short-cut, and soon find myself in strange and impossible surroundings—from the modern point of view. The houses are those with which I am familiar from the prints and other pictures of the eighteenth or nineteenth centuries, or, almost as often, belong to still earlier times.
>
> I wander over the hills and valleys, and often through virgin forests, and sometimes come out on the shore of the Hudson or the East River, where I recognize the topography from the old maps, and take great pleasure in searching for landmarks which I know exist—or at least existed at the time pictured in my dream. Sometimes I find them, and am thrilled by the discovery, but curiously enough they are almost never inhabited. Although the streets are sometimes populated, I generally pass unnoticed—apparently unseen!

On waking and returning to his research, Stokes found it

> a source of much pleasure often to be able to recall something of their ancient appearance, but a constant source of regret to reflect that so many interesting old landmarks have been destroyed, and that so little actually remains from the past—so much less than in many of our other early cities.[1]

Stokes's dreams can be read as the sweet confessions of an antiquarian, so immersed in his work of history that his nights were filled with fantasies of exploring the past. But this interpretation would not correspond well with the life Stokes led beyond the *Iconography*. For while he is best known now by historians of New York as the author of the ultimate biography of the place, he was in his time at the forefront of modern ideas of city planning and housing reform, an important Progressive reformer who developed city-building strategies that would bear fruit in the second half of the century. Indeed, Stokes was at the vanguard of virtually every type of city-building endeavor of early-twentieth-century New York City. He was immersed in the speculative real estate business as head of his own real estate company and as an architect of corporate skyscrapers. At the same time, he invested enormous energy and time into the improvement of low-income housing, both by advocating slum clearance and by designing and building model low-income housing complexes that incorporated open spaces. Finally, he was an ardent antiquarian collector of old views of the city, and a fervent advocate of historic preservation. There were few for whom the motto *pro urbis amore*—"for the love of city"—took such active and wide-ranging forms (see figure 7.1).[2]

On one level, Stokes's *Iconography* is important for the simple reason that it has shaped generations of students of New York and American urban history as well as a range of developers, preservationists, and planners. Since it was written, the *Iconography* has been considered the ultimate sourcebook on the history of New York City. "No other city in the world," wrote R. W. G. Vail in an obituary for Stokes in 1945, "can boast of having such a complete record of its growth from trading post to metropolis."[3] And yet, while historians, architects, and urban planners interested in Manhattan's physical history use the *Iconography* in their work, returning to it as an indispensable reference tool, few have considered it to be an important document in the city's cultural history.[4]

Studying the *Iconography* allows us to probe the psychological and intellectual responses to the creative destruction of Manhattan by one man who played so many roles: reformer, historian, antiquarian collector, and "native" inhabitant. Through I. N. Phelps Stokes we can see how abstract transformations in the city were translated into private memory, how public acts provoked emotional responses and, rever-

Fig. 7.1. John Singer Sargent, *Mr. and Mrs. I.N. Phelps Stokes,* 1897. The Metropolitan Museum of Art, Bequest of Edith Minturn Phelps Stokes, 1938. All rights reserved, The Metropolitan Museum of Art.

berating back into the public sphere, led to intellectual and cultural shifts in the way New Yorkers understood their city's development. Stokes reveals the essential elements of a dominant set of attitudes toward city building in the twentieth century: a celebration of urban transformation accompanied by a lamentation for an invented "golden age," a measuring of this change in the physical alterations of the urban landscape, and a belief in social reform through physical reform—especially the radical intervention of government, not merely by regulation but by bulldozers. Thus, the *Iconography* is not the product of one eccentric "old New Yorker." Quite the opposite: the *Iconography* reveals the complex attitudes of elite New Yorkers toward urban creative destruction, memory, and the politics of place. Stokes reflects quite purely the sharp tensions that have come to define attitudes toward the urban landscape. Stokes's modernist notions of city development and redevelopment, as well as his deeply antiquarian, obsessively nostalgic side, can be seen as extreme manifestations of increasingly common attitudes in the first third of the twentieth century. In many ways Stokes encapsulates what Michael Kammen has called the "nostalgic modernism" that defined the intellectual atmosphere of the interwar years.[5]

Stokes's dedication to the history and imagery of the city was not an "aside" to a life of housing reform, but rather a different manifestation of a commitment to building Manhattan. One set of his activities reached backward in time for ideals to redeem the future city, while another pointed forward to redeem the reform work of past generations. These two aspects of his life were not, however, unconnected or antagonistic; indeed they supported each other. Stokes, the historian and antiquarian, assisted Stokes, the city builder. The reverse was also true: in remaking the urban landscape, through speculation, building, and reforming, Stokes made the anguished cries of the preservationist seem inevitable.

"SPEAKING OF OLD NEW YORK . . ."

For the life and work of Stokes to offer insights into the attitudes toward urban development in the twentieth century, we must return to the history of the Phelps family. Stokes's attitudes toward city development and preservation grew in part from his own family's deep roots in New York, not only as residents but as highly committed social reformers.

If the *Iconography* was the most comprehensive study of a single city, and if few others could more tenaciously seek out the history of the city than Stokes, it was in large part due to his family heritage. Residents of the city from the end of the eighteenth century, the Phelps and Stokes families, brought together by the marriage of James Boulter Stokes (1804–1881) and Caroline Phelps (1812–1881), were active in social welfare issues from the early nineteenth century onwards. The list of the family's involvement in social reform is a capsule history of philanthropic efforts in nineteenth-century New York, especially those relating to the education of African-Americans and the creation of model low-income housing. Anson Green Phelps (1781–1853), the patriarch of the family (it was his partnership in the Phelps, Dodge mining company that provided the family's original wealth), had been an active abolitionist, an advocate of colonization, and a supporter of the founding of the Republic of Liberia in 1825. His son and daughter-in-law continued his work by founding the Colored Orphan Asylum and providing money for educating black students in the United States and in Africa. James Boulter Stokes was a founder of the Association for Improving the Condition of the Poor, established in 1843; both he and his wife were active in the earliest efforts to build model tenements in the Lower East Side. In the twentieth century, led by Newton—the son of Anson Phelps Stokes Sr. and Helen L. Phelps—various family members pursued the work of ameliorating the conditions of the poor and uneducated, in all aspects of New York city life.[6]

These combined interests—in the education of African-Americans (and, to a lesser degree, Africans) and in developing new approaches to housing—were given institutional form by Caroline Phelps Stokes, the youngest daughter, who established in her will the Phelps-Stokes Fund, founded in 1911. The fund, a relatively small philanthropic foundation as compared to those established by Carnegie, Ford, Rockefeller, and Russell Sage in the same period, split its work between the "education of Negroes both in Africa and the United States, North American Indians and needy and deserving white students" and the "erection of tenement house dwellings in New York City for the poor families of New York City."[7] While his brother Anson Phelps Stokes Jr. immersed himself in the educational side of the fund, becoming secretary of Yale University and serving as trustee of the Tuskegee Institute and the Hampton Institute, Newton dedicated himself to leading the fight for model low-income housing.[8]

Stokes inherited from his family two important commitments. As one of the few "native New Yorkers," from a family especially committed to recording its history,[9] he was immersed in New York's past from early on. But equally important, Stokes could not help but be influenced by his family's dedication to social reform, especially housing reform, in part because he came of age when housing conditions became one of reformers' greatest concerns. What is remarkable is the way in which Stokes joined these two aspects of his life.

Born in 1867, Stokes grew up in the midst of New York's greatest growth and upheaval. He graduated from Harvard in 1891 and pursued banking for a year, but he quickly returned to his passion: architecture. In 1893, the year of the World's Columbian Exposition in Chicago, he attended architecture school at Columbia University, but he was dissatisfied with the school's lack of emphasis on planning and housing. With the urging of important reformers and family friends E. R. L. Gould, Josephine Shaw Lowell, and Robert W. DeForest, the latter with whom he would remain a close collaborator throughout his life, Stokes went to Paris to study at the École des Beaux Arts with the intent of returning as an architect and advocate of model low-income housing.[10] While in Europe, Stokes traveled extensively in order to inspect the more advanced social housing efforts in France, Germany, and England.

On returning to the United States in 1897, he founded an architectural firm with college friend John Mead Howells, the son of novelist William Dean Howells. Stokes had on his own submitted plans for the Tenement House Competition of 1896 (whose result was the revolutionary City and Suburban Homes development), and with Howells won the commission for the University Settlement House on Rivington and Eldridge Streets in the Lower East Side.[11] The firm of Howells and Stokes, which lasted until 1917, focused its work on public and university projects, and participated regularly in architectural competitions that emphasized housing.[12] At the same time, the firm was active in building the settings for elite New York's visual infrastructure: office towers for insurance companies and homes for corporate leaders.[13]

It was, however, Stokes's public advocacy of low-income housing that had the most public impact. The list of his involvements in New York City low-income housing activities is impressive. After failing to win the 1896 Improved Housing Council's competition, he became a member of the Tenement House Committee of the Charity Organization Society, led by Lawrence Veiller, and he successfully urged the committee to sponsor an exhibition of model low-income housing. This exhibit resulted in the formation of the New York State Tenement House Commission, which included Stokes, and the passing of the landmark "new-law" tenement legislation of 1901.

Although he helped draft the 1901 law, Stokes quickly moved away from Veiller's commitment to regulations. In 1912, he quit the Charity Organization Society's Tenement House Committee in frustration over Veiller's focus on ever-more microscopic regulation of tenement house construction.[14] From very early on, Stokes pushed the boundaries of the housing debate by arguing, as Jacob Riis had in the 1890s, that mere regulation of the building of new tenements could never solve the problem of old slums or truly create more economically healthy neighborhoods. Instead Stokes urged massive slum clearance and much more comprehensive physical and economic planning of whole areas. Perhaps inspired by his visits to London where the Working Classes Acts of 1885 and 1890 had allowed for extensive slum clearance with few bureaucratic delays, Stokes urged that New York City government be allowed to move quickly to rid the city of its slums.[15] Like Riis, he supported demolition of slums as an end in itself—as a way simply of removing the hated "rear tenements" and providing more open space in dense neighborhoods—as well as a means toward creating model housing.

And yet, Stokes remained deeply skeptical of the city's involvement in redevelopment. His support for "excess condemnation," the holy grail of city planners, suggests his ambiguous attitude toward public intervention in the real estate market.[16] While excess condemnation meant new powers for municipal government, it also presupposed a close involvement with private real estate developers. As committed as Stokes was to low-income housing, he remained suspicious throughout his life of permanent state- or federally owned public housing. The federal government's role was an important one: it could afford to "prepare" a site by purchasing, taking, and clearing land. But private developers should retain, he believed, a primary interest in the land.

Perhaps the most extensive example of the type of planning that Stokes favored, and perhaps the most ominous example of what could go wrong, is the 1929 Chrystie-Forsyth project. In one of the city's first major excess condemnation projects, the city paid to take and demolish five blocks of tenements between Chrystie and Forsyth Streets in the Lower East Side, only a few blocks from Riis's first slum clearance campaign at Mulberry Bend Park. Problems arose after the city had completed its demolition and the private developer coalition fell through, leaving "seven blocks of rubble" and no new housing.[17] Only by virtue of the intervention of the Works Progress Administration was the strip of urban desert transformed into the park that exists today. But the housing was lost forever. It was this pattern of publicly initiated demolition and infrastructure building followed by private development that would come to predominate in postwar cities, often to the same destructive ends.[18]

Stokes saw no contradiction in his advocacy of radically new redevelopment powers for the state and his belief in the efficacy of private developers to bring about progressive urban development. His various careers—as architect and housing advocate, as collector and historic preservationist—had presumed some merging of government and private initiative. Howells and Stokes, while founded by two idealistic young architects, was active in building the modern commercial city, gaining commissions for office buildings in New York, the Baltimore Stock Exchange, and apartment buildings.[19] The firm moved freely from designing St. Paul's Chapel at Columbia University, where Stokes and his wife Edith are buried, to the Bonwit Teller department store on Fifth Avenue. Nor did Stokes acknowledge the conflicting nature of his own various activities. In fact, his firm's architectural projects on Fifth Avenue and his personal real estate investments were part of the "compelling force" that spurred the rise of dense tenements and led to the demolition of many historic landmarks.[20]

Throughout his life, Stokes remained deeply involved in real estate speculation. Especially after the dissolution of the Howells and Stokes architecture firm, real estate speculation and development constituted Stokes's major income-producing work. As with many others, Stokes did well in the boom years of the real estate market after World War I—but, also like others, he overextended himself and found himself stuck with devalued property when the market plummeted. In the midst of the Depression, which his wealth could not escape, Stokes himself moved out of a townhouse on Twenty-second Street near Madison Square (which had become the headquarters of the Metropolitan Life Insurance Company) and into a two-room apartment at 953 Fifth Avenue, a building he had designed. Following the script of so many in Manhattan's wildly fluctuating real estate market, he soon moved into a cheaper apartment on less exclusive Madison Avenue.[21]

Stokes's skill as a social reformer lay in his technical expertise and attention to detail. He brought a new level of sophistication to the growing field of low-income housing, and always insisted that housing and planning required the highest level of professionalism.[22] The architectural competitions he participated in and sponsored offered novel ways of bringing a professional approach to designing low-income housing.[23] This questioning of age-old methods of regulating height and lot coverage, light and air access, allowed Stokes to consider and develop far more interventionist methods of improving low-income housing. But he never questioned the basic system under which space in Manhattan was developed. His conviction that publicly assisted private development could yield a more egalitarian urban environment "diverted his attention," historian Roy Lubove has asserted, "from the limitations of economic planning in a speculative, entrepreneurial real estate system."[24]

Even as he pursued diverse activities of city building that fueled New York's rapid transformation and the city's apparent disregard for its own past, Stokes participated actively in the early efforts to protect the historical landscape. He tirelessly fought to save St. John's Chapel from the widening of Varick Street and drafted the passionate appeal to the leaders of the Trinity Corporation, which was signed by officials from the mayor on up to President Theodore Roosevelt. As was discussed in chapter 5, he also was instrumental in saving the facade of the Assay Building, a United States branch bank built in 1823–24, which had stood adjacent to the U.S. Treasury Building on Wall Street. Having failed to secure the building as a clubhouse for the Grolier Club, Stokes had the building moved stone by stone to a lot behind the new Metropolitan Museum of Art building in Central Park. In 1923 it was re-erected as the south facade of the new American Wing.[25] Finally, beyond entering the competition for the new Municipal Building, he had in 1910 proposed a way of building a new civic center that would not require the demolition of the old City Hall.[26]

The Howells and Stokes architectural practice strongly advocated the adaptation of historical styles to modern forms. Stokes's municipal building proposal adapted the Gothic style (also used by Cass Gilbert for the Woolworth Building, completed in 1913) to the setback skyscraper that would come to dominate New York's skyline. While he freely adapted historic styles to modern buildings, he also showed a strong interest in building "authentic" historic buildings. His chapel at Columbia University presented a "rare" opportunity "not only to design, but to construct a church in close conformity with the principles and traditions of the country and period to which the design belongs. . . . The Chapel is one of the few American churches in which the dome, as well as the vaulting, is constructed entirely of masonry."[27] In his private life, too, Stokes showed a strong desire to literally live with the aura of the past around him. In 1910, when his real estate fortunes were at their height, Stokes read an article in the British *Country Life* magazine about a half-timbered Tudor manor house that was to be sacrificed for "some projected municipal 'improvements.'" Like the Assay Building a few years later, Stokes had the whole house taken down, brought over to his property in Greenwich, Connecticut, and re-erected.[28]

Stokes remains a fascinating figure because he so intensely embraced the different extremes of the development of New York City, alternately immersing himself in its distant past and its utopian future. He lived his life neither as a crippled antiquarian, unable to participate in contemporary political debates—indeed quite the opposite is true—nor as a single-minded modernist, fully embracing the dawning "megalopolis." He seemed to move fluidly from the Grolier Club and the Society of Iconophiles to the Tenement House Commission and its proposals for model housing in the Lower East Side, from the city's Art Commission to the Phelps-Stokes Fund's educational programs in Africa.

REMEMBRANCE OF THINGS NEW YORK: PRODUCING *THE ICONOGRAPHY*

Stokes's commitment to low-income housing development, as well as his other work relating to the design and planning of the city, was extensive. Nevertheless, it would

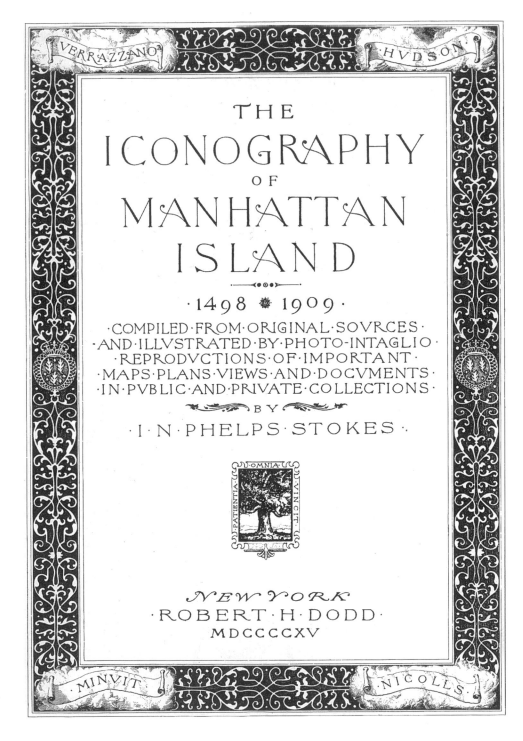

VERRAZZANO   HVDSON

THE
ICONOGRAPHY
OF
MANHATTAN
ISLAND
·1498 ✸ 1909·

COMPILED·FROM·ORIGINAL·SOVRCES·
·AND·ILLVSTRATED·BY·PHOTO-INTAGLIO·
·REPRODVCTIONS·OF·IMPORTANT·
·MAPS·PLANS·VIEWS·AND·DOCVMENTS·
·IN·PVBLIC·AND·PRIVATE·COLLECTIONS·
BY
· I·N·PHELPS·STOKES ·

·OMNIA·
PATIENTIA   VINCIT

NEW YORK
·ROBERT·H·DODD·
MDCCCCXV

MINVIT   NICOLLS

Fig. 7.2. *The Iconography of Man-*
hattan Island, title page.

be the *Iconography* on which Stokes's "lasting fame as an author" would rest (see figure 7.2).[29] In its structure, its philosophy of history, the process by which it was produced, and its final statement about the nature of Manhattan's development, the *Iconography* was closely linked to Stokes's other work. For at the very root of Stokes's interest in city history and the project of charting its physical transformation was his recognition that Manhattan's history was being removed by the wrecking ball. The shape and substance of the *Iconography* reveals a powerful tension between a sentimental antiquarianism and a rational, deliberate record of Manhattan's miraculous growth.

Beginning in 1909, amid the city's Hudson-Fulton celebration—the starting point of an exuberant new interest in the city's history—Stokes began collecting and assembling images for the *Iconography*. The work was intended to be a one-volume compilation of the most important prints, views, and maps of New York from its discovery to the present (that is, 1909). Stokes soon found that the number of images he wanted to include would far exceed the space of one volume. But more importantly, his interest moved beyond merely reproducing images but in using those images to tell the history of Manhattan. With each image—a document from which Stokes read a piece of the city's history—the work expanded to three volumes, then four, and finally six.

The *Iconography* as it finally evolved over two decades of work is a hybrid of several book genres: it is at once an encyclopedia, art book, history textbook, guidebook, and timeline. On one level it is simply a coffee-table book of wonderfully reproduced images of New York City. But its extensive historical summaries and analyses of each view also make it an imposing history of Manhattan Island. With its detailed index volume, it became the standard reference encyclopedia of the city's history, where dates and names could quickly be identified. Stokes enlisted a small army of researchers to assist him in locating, acquiring, and photographing the images; researching the background history and providing a historical analysis of each print; writing historical sketches of each period in New York's history; assembling entries for the two-volume chronology; and—most importantly for future researchers—assembling the 677-page index volume.[30] Stokes was not modest about his goals: he believed that the *Iconography* would be a "comprehensive history" of the city.[31] In 1926, when he received an award from the New-York Historical Society for the completion of the six volumes, he insisted that he had included "all procurable information of real significance" to the history of the city.[32] Stokes could make this hubristic claim with some sense of security because he had drawn from a spate of city histories produced during the previous four decades.[33]

Stokes's effort to document the images and history of New York City was extraordinary in its range and microscopic detail, and in the personal commitment by which it was created. Just as New York is defined as the place where one finds the extremes of American life, so Stokes was the "New York" of city imaginers. Stokes was, however, joined by many others in this era in his attempt to encapsulate or comprehensively describe the city. Though it was only in 1995 that the *Encyclopedia of New York City* was published, throughout the early twentieth century various encyclopedic surveys of New York were undertaken. Photographic surveys—by the Wurts Brothers and by the Bryon Company, to name just two—provided, mainly for the benefit of the buyers and sellers of real estate, a detailed snapshot of Manhattan's streets. Collectors, as we have seen at the Museum of the City of New York, assembled a plethora of engravings and lithographs of New York views into portfolios of Manhattan's development. Pure booster books, like W. Parker Chase's *New York, The Wonder City, 1932*, which documented all that was great and magnificent about New York's physical development, abounded. As Stokes was writing his *Recollections*, the Regional Plan Association was busy preparing its vision for the future of the New York metropolitan region. *The Building of the City* (1931), a volume of the *Regional Plan of New York and Its Environs*, written by Thomas Adams, was a mammoth undertaking on par with Stokes's. It surveyed the entire history of Manhattan and the larger region to offer its regional planning solutions to the problem, as Adams put it, of "City Building in a Democracy."[34]

Finally, just as Stokes was completing his most personal of encyclopedias, perhaps the most widely read of all encyclopedic portraits of New York was initiated: the Works Progress Administration *Guide to New York City*, completed in 1939.[35] Stokes provided the model for the WPA writers and photographers. Indeed, the WPA *Guide* researchers and writers often consulted Stokes, especially using his massive chronology to document particular aspects of the city's development, such as the record of housing reform laws.[36] But Stokes's more personal effort is important not simply because it influenced the WPA *Guide* but because of what he suggested about the times. Stokes's effort, if seen in light of the WPA's monumental, nationwide effort to describe the history and transformation of the key cities of the nation, suggests a larger trend of encyclopedic attempts to define a place in time.

To what end was Stokes's massive project undertaken? What first inspired Stokes to begin assembling images of Manhattan and, year after year, to dissect each image and display "all of the available worth-while material" on Manhattan's physical history?[37] The *Iconography*'s roots lie not, paradoxically, in a public-reforming ethos, but in the more intangible personal reactions to the creatively destructive city.

Stokes certainly saw the images of old New York as having educational value. He donated his own collection to the New York Public Library in part to give it the widest possible audience, so it would "not only give pleasure to the eye and educate the mind, but stimulate civic pride and patriotism."[38] Early on in his collecting and researches for the *Iconography,* he offered the Metropolitan Museum of Art his collection of prints for five years in order to "give the greatest pleasure to the greatest number. . . . In this country, or at least in New York, the general public has no opportunity to see the pictorial record of our past, which certainly has an educational value."[39] Stokes's model of history taught through visual imagery was utilized, if not actually copied, by the Museum of the City of New York, the City History Club, and other institutions. He served on the boards of the MCNY and the New-York Historical Society and supported their efforts to make the history of New York accessible to students and "embryo citizens."[40] Beyond these largely rhetorical efforts, however, Stokes did little to develop the educational uses of the *Iconography.* The book itself could only be acquired by a very few: it was printed in very limited quantities and its cost—$100 for the set—was prohibitive. Stokes, like the Society of Iconophiles, limited the number of printings, even while stating that he hoped to spark interest in old views and promulgate the lessons contained in those views.[41]

If Stokes believed in the power of history—especially visual imagery of the past—to shape citizens, it was certainly not the animating force behind the *Iconography.* Much more important were the personal, psychological reasons behind his work, specifically the nostalgia for "old New York." Despite his at times highly technical, rational, and forward-looking approach to tenement reform and city planning, Stokes was equally enamored of journeying as a tourist to the foreign country that was New York's past. Writing in the latter part of his life, during the Depression (when his financial standing had dropped considerably), Stokes laments the passing of the city he saw in his vast collection of American prints:

> What person of average intelligence, possessed of a modicum of imagination or sentiment, could fail to be moved by the contemporary picture of some seventeenth-century settlement constructed by our forefathers . . . or by the awe-inspiring appearance of "Ye great town of Boston," or of Philadelphia, or New York, as portrayed in that rare trio of Brobdingnagian early eighteenth-century "prospects," the envy and despair of all advanced collectors. . . . Or what modern mind could refuse to be impressed by the early "portrait" of some tiny hamlet which has since become an important city, or by a comparison, for example, of the sky-line of New Amsterdam with that of the modern city of New York? . . . Can there be anyone so callous, and so lacking in romance . . . ?[42]

Although the *Iconography*'s narrative propelled New York, inexorably, toward new achievements and new heights, Stokes's sentiment often rested on pure sorrow for a past gone forever. Writing in 1933, Stokes lingers over a seventeenth-century view of New Amsterdam, noting the quaint homes and neat garden plots:

> Indeed, we cannot escape a feeling of envy, mingled with regret, when we consider how calm and peaceful life must have been in those charming little old eighteenth- and early nineteenth-century towns, where our forefathers lived under the shadows of the church steeples:—how different from that which we lead to-day! The railroad, the automobile, the skyscraper, and others of their ilk, which are chiefly responsible for these changes, are indeed doubtful blessings: they have robbed us of much that was worth while in life. Where can we find to-day such attractive cities, such alluring villages, and such charming rural and river scenes, as are portrayed in many of these early views?[43]

The average New Yorker, Stokes commiserates, "sadly admits . . . that the city is not what it once was."[44] Stokes used the *Iconography*, at least in part, as an escape hatch from the present into past worlds.

It was the personal reaction to these old views that drew Stokes to them, not any abstract, formal notion about their value as art. "In most higher forms of collecting," notes Stokes, "beauty is the ideal towards which the collector strives, the one essential characteristic which guides his choice. . . . Not so with the collecting of historical prints, which, for the most part, must be judged by a different standard":

> Few of the prints of Old New York can justly be called beautiful, but many possess other qualities which endear them to the heart of the intelligent collector, who regards them almost with reverence and awe as the frail documents of a by-gone age,—silent bearers of many a half-read message, which perhaps his alert eye is destined to decipher. In themselves admittedly incomplete and unsatisfying, if judged by the standards of the average picture lover, as contemporary illustrations of successive steps in the physical growth of our great city, they render more real and vivid our written history, and become at once instructive and intensely interesting.[45]

The insistent quest for Stokes was, if even for a brief moment, to return to the New York of years earlier, to authentically recreate in his mind the city of his youth. The two decades' work of collecting, researching, and writing the *Iconography* was in part an ensemble of "authentic" images of Manhattan's past that could serve as spurs to memory.[46]

It had been, after all, a transcendent encounter with an old print that had started Stokes on his journey. In 1909, in the year after his interest was first sparked by an exhibit of old New York views, Stokes dined at the home of W. T. H. Halsey, the renowned collector and founder of the American Wing at the Metropolitan Mu-

seum of Art. It was one view on Halsey's wall—a print of Manhattan from the Livingston farm in what is now the Lower East Side (figure 7.3)—that in particular caught his attention:

> I remember that it was while examining his beautifully drawn and colored pair of St. Memin engraved views (probably the finest pair in existence) that something in the aspect of the little group of houses clustering along the river bank at the foot of Mt. Pitt, combined with something in the attitude of the two figures in the foreground, and in the appearance of the coach hurrying along the road in the middle distance, suggested to me the idea of writing a book on the history of New York prints.[47]

The leap into the past that the print allowed inspired Stokes to undertake the project of preparing "under one roof . . . a comprehensive and balanced collection" of the most important Manhattan maps, plans, and views.[48]

Fig. 7.3. St. Memin, "View of the City and Harbour of New York, Taken from Mount Pitt, the Seat of John R. Livingston, Esq.," 1796 (*Iconography* I, plate 6).

The *Iconography* was clearly something different from the scores of books on New York history being produced in the early years of the century. While those histories had placed at the very center of the historical stage the personalities who had made New York—Peter Minuit and his bargain purchase of the island, "peg-leg" Peter Stuyvesant and his angry resistance to the British, DeWitt Clinton, Boss Tweed, the millionaire moguls of Fifth Avenue, and the political and social reformers of the more recent years—Stokes expressly stated that his work would make "special reference to [the city's] topographical features and to the physical development of the island." The work would in the end be a chronicle "dealing with the physical rather than . . . the personal side of the city's history." Though Stokes recognized that "legends or myths," which were the heart of traditional city histories, were the "poetry of history," he gave little space to those aspects of the city's history. The *Iconography* would be the work of a "historical scientist," a book "illustrating the physical development of the city."[49] The normal view of a "history" was in Stokes turned upside down: illustrations, usually decoration for heavy tomes, became his centerpiece, with the written accounts serving almost as ornament. For Stokes, Manhattan's physical change embodied, metaphorically and literally, all other aspects of the city's history. Stokes would "read" from the maps and views of the city—from colonial times to the present—the political, economic, social, and cultural development of the city. The story of Manhattan—which he celebrated, ending on a positive vision of political and economic reform in 1909—was the story of the building, unbuilding, and rebuilding of the city. The *Iconography* was first and foremost a visual history of the city's transformation, an unprecedented effort to encapsulate visually the development of a physical place and human settlement over time.

The focus on the physical transformation is not only emphasized by the primacy of images in the *Iconography*. Its fourth and fifth volumes consisted of the Chronology, a daunting year-by-year listing of key events in the city's history. The Chronology was dominated by notes of the physical development and redevelopment of the city. Stokes was vigilant in reporting important fires, demolitions of historic buildings, the death of old trees, and street-widening plans. Except for notes on political battles and the policy acts of mayors, the Chronology comprised little beyond a listing of the physical transformation of the city. Some 1906 listings, for example, include the following events:

No date: Henry James's "rambling reflections" are published under the title "New York
    Revisited" by *Harper's Magazine* in February, March, and May
No date: Long description of closing of Thames Street and opening of wide street—
    all done by negotiation with a private corporation

Jan. 1: Mayor McClellan's annual message

Jan. 10: City acquired by condemnation proceedings land bounded by Broadway, Hamilton Place, and 138th Street. Montefiore Park is developed (see Prendergast, *Record of Real Estate*)

March 26: State legislature stops use of steam locomotives at grade level

April 18: San Francisco earthquake—New York sends $2 million in aid

April 24: City agrees to Columbia filling in land under waterfront upon Riverside Park from 116th to 120th Streets to be used for athletic fields

April 25: City acquires land for municipal playground at 59th Street and Tenth Avenue

April 26: City acquires land for municipal playground at 184 Cherry Street

June 20: Table "marking the site of the provost prison, which was unveiled in 1901 in the old hall of records and which since the tearing down of that building has been lying in storage, is re-erected" by Daughters of the American Revolution

June 22: "Excavating" for Singer Building at 149 Broadway begins[50]

One can almost imagine Stokes combing through pages of old issues of the *Times, Tribune,* or *World* for all notices of demolitions and important new constructions. He doggedly, obsessively scoured the city for records of the tangible transformation of New York's physical form.[51]

His final chapter, "The Modern City and Island," the period from 1877 to 1909, offers a virtual year-by-year account of the city's political and physical developments with brief notes on the establishment of important institutions. Corruption scandals of the Tweed Ring and the efforts to reform the political system are central, as is the establishment of Greater New York City in 1898. Stokes proudly relates the building of parks, such as at Mulberry Bend, the improvement to the waterfront and docks, and the rise of skyscrapers and the glorious mansions along Fifth Avenue. For a work that sought to be a "comprehensive history," the overview offers no overarching interpretation of the city in this era, no concern with truly coming to grips with the massive changes—especially social and cultural—experienced by the city during this era. The most significant omission is the vast impact of immigrants on the social, cultural, and political life of the city. Stokes does note, in the preface to the *Iconography,* the importance of immigrants to New York's history, but his only mention in the era of the greatest immigration in the city and nation's history concerns the establishment of Ellis Island as the immigrant headquarters.[52]

The prospect of interpretation appears to have been much too difficult a task for Stokes.[53] He begins the Chronology with the following caution:

> If the historian's knowledge of his subject were complete, and his judgment unerring, the writing of history would be a simple matter, depending only upon the writer's power of expression, and the amount of space available. As, however, these ideal conditions practically never exist, his task usually resolves itself into an attempt to draw conclusions from too meagre records, and to reconcile or explain contradictory, or seemingly contradictory, statements.[54]

The answer, for Stokes, was to "allow the facts and the myths, together with the interpretations of competent authorities, and even the casual comments of intelligent observers, to speak for themselves." The Chronology, therefore, would provide "all procurable information of real importance or interest relating to the history and development of Manhattan Island, special emphasis being placed on information regarding the physical growth of the city of New York."[55]

This "ideal method of presenting history"—that is, of assembling, in chronological form, as much information about Manhattan's landscape—pervades all parts of the *Iconography*. While they could have been organized by subject matter, or visual form (prints, maps, engravings), the views are organized chronologically. The historical summaries offer little more than a distillation and translation of the chronological listing into prose form. The Index volume, too, is an abridged version of the Chronology, providing a brief chronological outline of the important issues relating to a particular place, event, or figure.

Most striking, however, is that the analyses of the views—the real heart of the *Iconography*—are not used to build a sweeping understanding of Manhattan's past and its transformation, but rather to serve merely as skeletons for a microscopic study of individual plots of land. For example, the analysis of a 1796 view of the city, which shows Lower Manhattan from the Hudson River, constitutes eleven small-print pages. One paragraph offers an example of Stokes's style:

> The large residence with well-defined string-courses, seen just at the left of No. 6 State Street, occupied the lots nos. 9 and 11 State Street. According to title records there lots belonged to Carey Ludlow, and were, by his will dated 1814, bequeathed to his wife. A very good picture of the Ludlow house is found in Lamb's *History of the City of New York*, II: 445. No. 9 State Street appears first in the 1797 directory, where it is given as the address of J. Watson and Carey Ludlow, although, during the following three years, Joseph Corre, the tavern-keeper, seems to have occupied the building. The properties at Nos. 9 and 11 had a frontage of 55 feet, more or less, and adjoined, there being at the time no No. 10. . . .[56]

The level of detail in the *Iconography*, and the clear commitment to completely reconstruct pieces of the city, is not unlike the work of Marcel Proust, whose *Remembrance of Things Past* was begun at precisely the same time. Where Proust tried, partly through sheer volume of memories, to recover his personal past, so too did Stokes try to capture the totality of New York's past. But the two works are also radically different. Stokes's compendium is a rational, deliberate organization of the tangible, observable physical past into bound volumes. Much of what Proust saw as essential—the fleeting rush of memories, the flood of emotion—was banned from the *Iconography*.

But, in fact, these two attitudes toward the urban landscape—between rational study of the city's development and the affective, sentimental appreciation of city life and its past—were warring within Stokes, and within New Yorkers more generally. Stokes felt powerfully the emotional pull of the past even as he pursued a strategy of the "historical scientist." It was, in fact, the more personal reaction to the prints, and to a vanishing city, that had provoked Stokes's work.

FROZEN CITY: PHOTOGRAPHY AND MEMORY IN THE *ICONOGRAPHY*

The place of photography in the *Iconography* is particularly revealing of Stokes's personal beliefs as well as more general attitudes toward city building and remembrance. Stokes chose to limit the images in the *Iconography* to prints, maps, and engravings, banishing perhaps the most vital of the arts in the early decades of the century. Like other collectors of old views, Stokes supported the efforts to reinvigorate etching, steel engraving, and other older arts. In the preface to the *Iconography*, Stokes gives a brief history of printmaking processes, noting that "with the introduction of photography, in the early '50's, engraving by hand and lithography as an art virtually ceased."[57] One of the hopes that animated his efforts was that "in the not too distant future, the new beauty and charm of our city will again find some even more worthy form of permanent expression."[58] He also was deeply skeptical of modern art, of which photography was perhaps the most vital form. The "modernistic movement in art," Stokes wrote in 1933, comprised "young, and generally mediocre, artists" who were bent on producing only "novel and striking effects, often with very little training, and even less effort."[59] The *Iconography* does include a number of photographic plates, mainly to illustrate the final period of the work, 1877 to 1909. But these photographs in the *Iconography* are not artistic in any sense; they are purely reference images that he uses to discuss certain important buildings; there is not a single image produced by an important photographer of the era, such as Alfred Stieglitz, Lewis Hine, or Jacob Riis. [60]

His general exclusion of photography from the *Iconography* was in some ways a remarkable choice for Stokes, considering the fact that he was hardly as absolutist as his fellow collectors, some of whom virulently opposed photography. Stokes himself was an avid photographer from his childhood onwards. In the late 1870s, he worked with some of the early wet-plate developing and continued to experiment with the latest photographic methods and cameras in his later years, even as he became obsessed with prints.[61] He also later edited a catalog of daguerreotypes that he had rescued and helped Berenice Abbott get funding for her classic series of photographs on New York in the 1930s.[62]

Ultimately, however, Stokes committed himself to challenging photography's growing importance as a powerful tool of memory. For those who saw great danger in New York's disregard for its physical past, photography was, in fact, considered an obstacle in that it corrupted memory more than it preserved it. Thus, just when New York's landscape was undergoing furious "cycles of demolition and construction," as William Dean Howells called them, the technology and art form seen as most able to "freeze" a moment in time was maturing and coming to dominate the interpretation of the modern city.

Stokes was not alone in fighting photography's growing importance for telling the history of the city. Stokes worked closely with the Society of Iconophiles, a small but influential organization dedicated to producing a "visual biography" of the city without the aid of photography, to which they were adamantly opposed. The dialogue between Stokes, the Society of Iconophiles, and their anonymous enemy called "photography" reveals how Stokes and his friends conceived of the place of memory in the modern city.

The city, and Manhattan in particular, became the subject par excellence of photographers in the first decades of the twentieth century. It was the encounter of the photographer—now far more mobile and versatile because of the development of handheld cameras—with the city that inspired one of photography's most creative periods. Out of the urban crucible came the central themes in photography: the pictorialism of the late nineteenth and early twentieth centuries; the realist social photography of Jacob Riis, Lewis Hine, and others; and the modernist abstraction of people such as Paul Strand in the 1920s.

While scholars have long recognized the centrality of the urban environment in shaping the methods and attitudes of modern photography, the theme of the city's physical transformation has been less recognized. In fact, the replacement of old with new, townhouses with skyscrapers, and tenements with towers remained a leitmotiv through the first decades of the twentieth century. Nonetheless, it is safe to say, as a number of scholars have argued, that photography moved further and further from recording the city, and instead sought out the city's abstract forms and patterns of movement.[63] Photography's project became an increasingly feverish effort to capture not specific places or moments in urban life but the essence of the modern city in abstract portraits. The city became, as Wanda Corn has put it, "no longer a series of discreet 'views' but a certain state of being." In essence, New York dissolved from a place into an idea.

While photographers were most interested in the abstraction of the city and in charting the process of change, seeing these as symbolic of the modern city, many elites were deeply invested in the substance of the past. It was precisely the tangible city of the nineteenth century that they sought to save.

Founded in 1894 when William Loring Andrews brought together at the Grolier Club several friends from his real estate, collecting, and printing circles, the Society of Iconophiles was dedicated to "issuing a series of engraved views of New York." Choosing as its motto *pro urbis amore*—for the love of city—the organization published limited editions of past and present views of New York, focusing especially on historic landmarks, important early views, and significant figures in New York's history. Society members (the membership grew up from twelve to fifty regular members and fifty associate members) were given the privilege, and obligation, to purchase the yearly production of images. With Andrews as the president for much of the group's life (he died in 1920; the organization lasted into the 1930s), the group produced 119 different images, ranging from a reproductions of some of the most famous views of the city from the seventeenth and eighteenth centuries to commissioned engravings by such well-known engravers as Joseph Pennell, Sydney Smith, and E. D. French (figures 7.4 and 7.5).

The Society of Iconophiles, like so many of the other "history industry" organizations, was formed as a response to the turbulent creative destruction of New York. In a familiar refrain offered in his annual messages to his iconographic compatriots, Andrews remonstrated:

> Tearing down and building up, only to tear down again within a decade or two of years, has been the fad and fashion of the times during the last half century in many parts of this Knickerbocker town, and no city has needed more than ours the Chronicler and the Artist to note and picture the shifting scenes its streets present from year to year.[64]

Fig. 7.4. E. D. French, *City Hall,* 1896, copper engraving. Society of Iconophiles Collection, The Grolier Club.

Andrews deplored the destruction of old New York that was proceeding with such lack of a sense of loss. "The busiest man in our midst, in these days," he told the society in 1913,

> is the stalwart, heavy handed house wrecker. Nothing stays his pick-ax, his crow-bar and his shovel in their iconoclastic work of wiping piles of brick and mortar off the map of the city, and when his work of destruction is accomplished, he surveys the scene of ruin and devastation he has wrought with as much pride and complacency, as the builder before him experienced in the erection of the edifice.[65]

Despite the tone of these laments, the society was not a group of curmudgeonly antiquarians determined to stall modernity from their leather armchairs at the Grolier Club. Indeed, most of the members were active in endeavors such as real estate de-

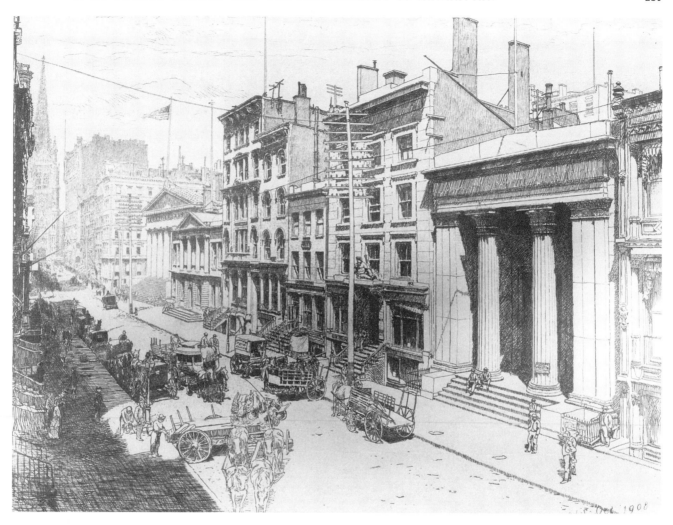

Fig. 7.5. Sidney L. Smith, *Wall Street in 1883,* 1909 etching from photograph. Society of Iconophiles Collection, The Grolier Club.

velopment and banking that supported the engine of creative destruction. Andrews himself celebrated the new city even as he urged that pieces of its history be saved:

> The rebuilding of this city as it is going on with breathless rapidity before our eyes, is a Titanic work, and I am glad that I have lived to witness it. I only hope that a few of the narrow, crooked lanes in the lower part of the city, with their antiquated buildings . . . will outlast my time.[66]

In its desperate effort to record New York landmarks, the society avoided photography, the most versatile medium for its work. Indeed, the society "religiously avoided" the use of photographs.[67] As Andrews said in a 1901 address to his fellow Iconophiles, the society was dedicated to "act the part of foster-mother to the moribund art of engraving as it was practiced from the invention of photography."[68] Despite the society's best efforts, however, Andrews suspected the project would yield only minor success: "[A]ncient and honorable crafts one and all succumbed to the pressure exerted by the camera with its numerous progeny of processes. . . . There seems to be little interest for our prints. Our usefulness has passed."[69]

While Stokes, Andrews, and the society were not blind to photography's advantages, they generally looked at the camera with disdain. "To whatever degree of excellence photography may attain," argued Andrews, "its limitations we claim are as defined and immutable as those of any other mechanical art."[70] The Iconophiles objected to photography on two grounds. First, despite its apparent fidelity to recording a place, photography, the society argued, lacked a crucial element: the obvious mark of human investment. An engraving required time: messy pencil sketches made on site, days of painstaking work on a copper plate. The Iconophiles viewed photography as a purely mechanical art. It was all too easy, a bit of industrial "magic" that required no emotional investment, neither to create nor to reproduce the image. The photographer was almost an assembly-line worker, in an increasingly anonymous factory called New York. As Andrews commented in his 1897 *Journey of the Iconophiles*:

> That the most highly perfected photographic process yet invented is capable of producing a work of art in the high sense of the term, we are not willing to admit. . . . [T]he camera will continue to perform its appointed tasks like the obedient but senseless automaton that it is, and nothing more.[71]

Visual memory, the Iconophiles seemed to suggest, was attainable, but only at a cost of physical and emotional labor that photography did not require.

The society had no illusions that their engravings were somehow more accurate, in an objective sense; for example, the society's correspondence with artists is filled with references to the way the scenes would be altered to make them more appealing. The unadulterated record of a building or street was never the goal of the Iconophiles. Indeed, photography's alleged capacity to accurately record a place and a time was a fatal drawback. What Iconophiles sought was something that was, in their minds, more authentic: a personal rendition of historic sites living comfortably in a modern city.

The society also objected to the sheer abundance of photographs. Not only did photography produce images with no power to trigger memory, but there were too many of them. The democracy of the camera, which made New York the most photographed city in the world, yielded few useful memories, complained the Iconophiles. They walked a fine line: the society wanted to sponsor reproducible art, but its members were frightened by the uncontrollability of photography. Engraving was a perfect compromise, one of the "purest forms of reproduction": it was true art and yet could be reproduced in quantity.[72] But to demonstrate its exclusivity, the society made great fanfare of its regular cracking of copper plates used to make the hundred imprints of each image.

The critique of photography made by this small organization resonates with much deeper cultural dilemmas concerning city building. Photography, in the end, came to embody all that the Iconophiles found so disturbing about the modern city. They saw the endless reproduction of photographs (not only as prints but also as photogravures in books) as pernicious profit-making, another example of the materialism of the modern city. Further, photography's new processes seemed inscrutable and suspicious; they seemed to emanate from the same inexplicable source as the city's miraculous development. Like the city "swiftly rising," photographs appeared almost as if "by the wand of a magician."[73] Finally, neither photography nor the city that was increasingly its private subject held the possibility of imagining a different time. The city itself, all so new, had not yet, observed Andrews, "felt the softening touch of time" that would allow for the record offered by the "artist's pencil."[74] The twentieth-century city was, like the photographic image, "too new and spic and span." An art that did not hold within it the possibility of spurring a recollection was "sham art—a delusion and a snare." And "cheap art," Andrews intoned, "is a misnomer."[75] We live, Andrews said, in a barely veiled stab at photography, in a "day of cheap reproductions."[76]

Photography's exponential growth had made the possibility of bounding the place, of collecting every conceivable image of Manhattan into a book, impossible. Photography's very presence problematized the question of collective memory in Manhattan. The characteristics of photography as defined by Stokes and the Iconophiles— its democratic nature, replicability, and supposed ease—were unsettling to anxious elites eager to control the historic iconography of their city.

Scholars have long focused on the messages contained in photographic images themselves to study photography's impact: the shock of Jacob Riis's Mulberry Bend photos, Stieglitz's portraits of immigrants coming to Ellis Island, Strand's cool modernistic interpretations of the skyscraper city. But equally important was the theoretical challenge offered by the method itself. In response, the devotees of older forms of illustration desperately sought to hold onto a different notion of place, organized around the cherished persistence of historic buildings and landscapes.

Stokes tried to balance the Iconophiles' roles as antiquarians and historians, alternately exhibiting the sentimental responses of the former and the allegedly dispassionate, "scientific" responses of the latter. But Stokes also played a third role, as the collector. If Stokes moved uncomfortably between soberly describing New York's ascent to present heights, and lovingly recalling the vanished past, he never swerved from his devotion to the marketability of "old New York."

ACQUIRING NEW YORK

Stokes's history of New York, like the city of legend, began with a purchase. In 1908, he happened upon an exhibit of "old New York City Views" on Fourth Avenue, probably set up in anticipation of the Hudson-Fulton celebration that would begin in the fall of 1909. He emerged an hour later "the proud and happy owner of a full dozen respectable, if not very valuable prints."[77] These first purchases spurred an enthusiasm for collecting New York City views that did not abate for twenty years. Stokes's pursuit of old views of New York bordered on the obsessive, as all true collecting must. After his encounter with the exhibit of New Yorkiana, he reported that his "enthusiasm now rapidly increased, and soon knew no bounds." What had started as a hobby and then became a narrowly defined project of cataloging key views of New York finally produced six volumes and, admitted Stokes, "would occupy somewhat more than my leisure hours during almost twenty years."[78] "I rushed from dealer to dealer and spent every spare moment feverishly delving through portfolios [and] drawers of old stock."[79]

"I think I was born acquisitive, and a collector," observed Stokes in his 1932 memoirs.[80] What began with postage stamps developed into a passion for Manhattan views, then city views more generally, and then, at the end of his life, sculptures of the human body. Beyond any educational purpose or a personal link to the past that the views and history in the *Iconography* offered, Stokes was taken by the collector's pursuit, especially the financial risk and return that accompanied the trade in prints. "One of the greatest pleasures" of writing the *Iconography*, he revealed, "was the search for and, if the chase proved successful, often the acquisition of rare items for my collection. . . . The pursuit of this usually illusive game often led far afield, and sometimes resulted in romance, once or twice almost in tragedy."[81] It is Stokes the collector, not the historian or architect or housing reformer, who most powerfully shows himself in the *Iconography*. The *Iconography* was intended as much for book and print collectors as it was a reference book for historians, antiquarians, and students in the city.

Stokes was at the forefront of a new "industry" in old New York views, for which there had actually been a market since the 1830s and 1840s. Stokes, the Society of

Iconophiles, and other groups modeled their books after such nineteenth-century collections of city views as Bourne's *Views in New York* (1831). Stokes, in letters to collectors and friends, expressed his hope to emulate these earlier collections as well as a similar book, *New Amsterdam, New Orange, New York,* by William Loring Andrews, his friend and fellow collector.[82]

In producing the *Iconography*, Stokes was quite clear in his focus on the interests of collectors of New York views: "My ambition is to produce a book which, although probably supplying little . . . new or original matter, will, from its character and from the manner of its arrangement, be of distinct interest and value to the collector as well as to that larger and growing class of intelligent book lovers who take an interest in all that relates to the early history of the city."[83] The desire to enhance New Yorkers' interest and understanding of their city's development was submerged beneath the more important goal of creating a collector's book. It was logical then that Stokes would limit the number of copies printed and would downplay the extensive historical summaries preceding the views, which he

> prepared with the object of supplying in the briefest readable form, an outline of the more interesting events. . . . They are intended primarily for the information of the general reader and the collector who are interested in knowing something of the history contemporary with the illustrations, but who may not have the time or the inclination to consider the subject in detail.[84]

Thus, what the reader might normally expect to be the centerpiece of a history book is in fact secondary in the *Iconography*.

In his preface, Stokes quickly dispenses with the educational purposes of the *Iconography* and focuses intently on describing the work's relationship to the pursuit of collecting. After briefly explaining the *Iconography's* organization, Stokes quickly moves to a discussion of the history of print collecting, especially as it became a profitable venture: "Print collecting has long been considered one of the most profitable and alluring of hobbies, as well as one admirably suited to the enthusiast of moderate means."[85] The very language he uses to describe his work in assembling the images for the *Iconography* is that of the consumer—the careful, savvy shopper. Stokes had entered the "land of desire," as William Leach has called it, where the "temptation" of a good deal always triumphs over financial prudence.[86] Stokes discussed with great relish the book and print catalogs of the early years of the century, when but a few hardy collectors found innumerable "bargains which make the mouth of the present-day collector water."[87]

More telling is how closely the language with which Stokes speaks of print collecting mirrored that of the real estate developer and the *Real Estate Record and Builders' Guide*. The writings of Stokes as well as other collectors include discussions of the mysterious reasons for the rise and fall of the market and stories of remarkable acquisitions, savvy investing, and dramatic losses. Stokes warned, for example, that "print collecting is no longer the poor man's hobby," but urged the potential collector to have no fear:

> although the time is past, at least temporarily, for bargains in the shops and auction rooms, there is still an ample reward in store for his perseverance and his discriminating knowledge, along unbeaten paths, farther afield; and that the greater effort required to bag the elusive game only adds new zest and pleasure to the quest.

But, he suggested, as "in almost every form of collecting it is a wise rule to buy the best."[88] He urged caution especially since the "high prices realised during the past few years [before 1915]" were bound to drop. "Whether present values will continue or not, no one can foretell. . . . I am disposed to think that they will not."[89]

And then there were the collectors' yarns: stories of spectacular "finds" and inflated values. Just like the common newspaper features that traced the miraculous increase in the value of a plot of land, Stokes offered stories of extraordinary increases in the value of New York prints. Early on in his career as a collector, for example, Stokes bought from a man "forty minutes' ride by trolley from the Brooklyn end of the Bridge" for $400 a fragment of one of the most famous early views of New York, the Burgis View of 1716–18. With the sale of the Edwin Holden Collection in 1910, which released into the market some extremely rare items and spurred a new excitement for New York views, the "value of New York City prints took a sudden jump" and he was able to sell the fragment for $1,800. Stokes was stung by the guilt of having made a killing from the poor man from Brooklyn, saying "my conscience smote me, and I seriously considered sending my Brooklyn friend an additional cheque." But, alas, "I am ashamed to acknowledge that I never did this."[90]

Stokes's contrition toward his "Brooklyn friend" is odd, because his good fortune was in fact a "natural" outcome: to make a "killing" was compensation for the risk of being "killed" in the market. Stokes later found himself, if not killed, at least tossed violently as the market curve swooped downwards. And in an ironic twist, Stokes was essentially priced out of the market: in the 1920s he moved into collecting prints of other cities "largely because of the steadily mounting price of New York City views."[91] Stokes, like his experience in the real estate business, overstayed the market for views. When his real estate business began to flag in the late 1920s, he tried to unload his prints only to find few willing buyers. Only when his financial situation had recovered did he donate the collection to the New York Public Library.[92]

It should not be surprising that so many of the most important collectors of city views were active city builders. Though dominated by some of the few "old New Yorkers" as well as those involved in the publishing trades (such as Theodore De Vinne), a startling number of collectors were deeply immersed in designing, developing, and planning the city of the future. Stokes's extensive searches for views to purchase or at least photographs for the *Iconography* brought him into contact with a number of seemingly unlikely collectors, such as John Crimmins, the head of public works for the Borough of Manhattan and the main inspiration behind the widening of Fifth Avenue (among other radical planning efforts).[93] Robert De Forest, president of the Metropolitan Museum of Art and a long-time tenement reformer, was an ardent collector, as was J. Clarence Davies, one of the most powerful real estate moguls of the time, and, of course, James Speyer of the Museum of the City of New York.[94] The cultivation of the past and the protection of its visual memory was in fact the serious pursuit of many important city builders at the forefront of developing modern New York.

The work of these collectors of Americana can and should be seen as representing a new interest in the American past, a profound nostalgia that gripped the nation even as it entered its most "modern" period.[95] The *Iconography* is, in this way, the greatest achievement of an early-twentieth-century renewed interest in New York city and state history.[96] This fascination about the development of the largest city in the world occupied a whole range of city dwellers and builders: obsessive antiquarians and profit-seeking collectors as well as budding historians, planners, and real estate developers. The strength of the movement to collect, interpret, and reproduce American arts and crafts, architecture, and folklife suggests that contrary to standard views, New Yorkers—and Americans more generally—were caught in the first decades of the twentieth century between looking forward and backward.

Certainly Stokes pursued his collection of city views out of strong personal and emotional desires to recreate and preserve the past. The very act of collecting these old views suggests a powerful psychological engagement with the changing material world. In the sometimes odd, obsessive manners of the collector, John Elsner and Roger Cardinal have argued, lie "desires for suppression and ownership, fears of death and oblivion, hopes of commemoration and eternity. Collections gesture to nostalgia for previous worlds."[97] It is the life of Stokes the collector that reveals his deepest anxieties about the changing urban condition and the tale it told about American society in general.

Virtually all collectors of Americana—Stokes included—were also collectors willing to sell their cherished possessions. The financial aspect of the collecting fever was not simply an "underside" to the phenomenon, but an essential feature of it. The tight connections between the language of real estate and the language of collecting images of Manhattan's transformation is clearly no accident. Private real estate development has been at the heart of the city's economy and the central engine in its physical transformation, and that logic came to prevail in the efforts to write the biography of the place. The world of collecting images of the city—and the newer business of sketching, painting, and photographing its transformation—was a derivative industry of creative destruction. In essence, the commodification of Manhattan's space now extended to the commodification of images of that space. For Stokes and others, images of the city offered a way to literally purchase the city and "acquire" New York. Not surprisingly, the number and popularity of prints expanded precisely at the moment that the city was demolishing its physical past with the most startling efficiency. It was those prints of buildings now gone or threatened by the wrecker's ball that proved most popular and profitable. Stokes and his fellow collectors made money from the creative destruction of Manhattan, even as they fought to preserve its past in books as well as in the actual landscape of the city.

A "CHAOS OF MEMORIES"

Isaiah Berlin's famous essay on Tolstoy uses the Greek poet Archilochus's saying— "The fox knows many things, but the hedgehog knows one big thing"—to analyze Tolstoy's writing. Tolstoy was, according to Berlin's interpretation, a fox who wanted to be a hedgehog; he was by nature a writer fascinated with the infinitely varied ways individuals thought and acted, but he desperately wanted to find a single, overarching set of principles to explain the progress of history.[98]

This dichotomy also applies to Stokes, but in a different way: Stokes hoped that by being a fox he would become a hedgehog. In other words, Stokes hoped that his sheer drive to include "all relevant information" would somehow produce a deeper understanding of Manhattan's transformation. Stokes wanted to write a "comprehensive history" of the city but had no interest in propounding a thesis and understanding of what had fueled the city's growth and development. His implicit expectation was that by pure accretion of image, narrative, and facts, a sense of the place would emerge.

Stokes's dreams of "old New York" now can be seen as the dreams of a man caught between the nineteenth and twentieth centuries, or more accurately, between two conceptions of place. These dreams were "authentic" trips back to a nineteenth-

century city. They were, in a way, Stokes's reward for the *Iconography:* his painstaking work of visual and factual reconstruction of "old New York" gave him the resources to literally "re-walk the walking city."[99] It is striking, however, that people are of little importance in Stokes's nocturnal Manhattan. Almost gleefully he notes that "Although the streets are sometimes populated, I generally pass unnoticed—apparently unseen!" This partly reflects Stokes's focus in the *Iconography* on topographical and architectural developments in New York. But it also demonstrates the anonymity that is the hallmark of the modern city in which Stokes lived. What characterized twentieth-century Manhattan—at its economically and culturally most vibrant in the 1910s and 1920s, when Stokes did the bulk of the work on the *Iconog-*

Fig. 7.6. Reginald Marsh, *People Seated and Standing in Subway,* circa 1928. Bequest of Felicia Meyer Marsh, Collection of the Whitney Museum of American Art, New York. Photograph copyright © 1998: Whitney Museum of American Art.

raphy—was the crowd, the fragmented interaction of diverse peoples, as portrayed in works like Dos Passos's *Manhattan Transfer*, or in the swirling street images of the Ashcan school, or the more humorous paintings by Reginald Marsh of packed subways, the crush of people at Coney Island, or a mixed crowd waiting for a twenty-cent movie (see figure 7.6). New York was the most modern of cities not only because of its skyscrapers, but because of the crowds of people who inhabited that modern landscape, a city of people anonymous and yet connected by the fleeting bonds of urban living. The question posed by the modern metropolis, which Stokes was unwilling and unable to confront, was how the increasingly diverse city would assimilate, bend, and change to accommodate its population.

Toward the end of his life, Stokes recognized the impossibility of pursuing and capturing a fixed sense of place. In his memoirs, he noted that the *Iconography* had had "a narrowing influence" on his life.[100] Backing away from his early assertions that he would write a "comprehensive history" of the city, Stokes called the *Iconography* nothing more than a "useful compilation."[101] Perhaps the failed attempt to fully grasp the sense of place of Manhattan, which had continued to change rapidly in the few years following the final volume, turned Stokes away from collecting prints. He began collecting sculptures of different body parts—heads, torsos, feet. He hoped, in the same orderly manner as he had pursued views of the city, to gain a complete record of how artists had portrayed the human body over the centuries.

While Stokes resembled Marcel Proust in the scope of his collecting passion, and the pure breadth of his effort, he diverged sharply from Proust's vision of history and memory. For Proust believed that memory could not actively be recovered—it was by its nature "involuntary."[102] Proust was first moved, as was Stokes, by a chance encounter with memory. Halsey's St. Memin print was to Stokes what the *madeleine* was for Proust. But where Proust succumbed happily to these waves of memory, Stokes resisted and sought instead to engage his memories and the past in a rational, orderly fashion. That first, emotional reaction to the St. Memin print strikingly yielded to a dispassionate description when Stokes finally came to analyze the print years later in the *Iconography*. The analysis identified the contemporary places (Grand, Clinton, and Division Streets) shown in the prints, discussed the history and quality of the print itself, gauged its value, and synopsized St. Memin's career. The personal response Stokes had had or the larger meaning he hoped readers would draw from the print were absent. Apparently, Stokes the historian and chronicler ultimately shied away from the intangible emotional meaning of the print.

"Every passion borders on the chaotic," Walter Benjamin remarked, "but the collector's passion borders on the chaos of memories."[103] Although the spark of sentimental memory first inspired Stokes to begin collecting and compiling the *Iconography*, the "chaos of memories"—their ultimate unmanageability and elusiveness—moved Stokes to despair. In attempting to be the "totalizing collector" of Manhattan's transformation, Stokes led himself into what John Elsner and Richard Cardinal have called the "less cosy aspects of collecting, where envy, frustration, depression and despair" lurk.[104] He tried to tether the slippery past through a scientific method, or more accurately, pure stubbornness. His endless notebooks, in which he scrawled minuscule notes as he ventured around the city and country and to Europe in search of details to add to his microscopic portrait, attest to this frenetic attempt to capture the sense of the city. It was not merely the obsessions of the collector that occupied him, but the particular obsession of the collector of place who sought to truly capture in pictures and words its essence.

What Stokes ultimately reveals is the virtual impossibility of capturing the sense of place in the modern city. We are left with a passionless record of Manhattan's seemingly inevitable, miraculous growth, a chronicle of building, reforming, improving. The *Iconography* is a rational, careful, and, in the end, desperate attempt to capture the "sense" of Manhattan as a place by the sheer persistence of the collector. The *Iconography* evokes no spark of excitement; it exhibits what Walter Benjamin called the "mild boredom of order."[105]

8 LANDSCAPES OF MEMORY AND AMNESIA

Out for a walk, after a week in bed, I find them tearing up a part of my block
And, chilled through, dazed and lonely, join the dozen
In meek attitudes, watching a huge crane
Fumble luxuriously in the filth of years. . . .
As usual in New York, everything is torn down
Before you have had time to care for it.
Head bowed, at the shrine of noise, let me try to recall
What building stood here. Was there a building at all?
I have lived on this same street for a decade.
Wait. Yes. Vaguely a presence rises
Some five floors high, of shabby stone
—Or am I confusing it with another one
In another part of town, or of the world?—

   —James Merrill, "An Urban Convalescence"

Although it became "usual in New York" that "everything is torn down," the experience of this normal process of destruction and rebuilding had a profound impact on New Yorkers. The question that plagued New Yorkers for a century, and that is asked with increasing fervor in cities undergoing similar processes, is "How can spatial memories find their place where everything is changed, where there are no more vestiges or landmarks?"[1] In the background of this story lie two theoretical principles that help illuminate the links between collective memory and the city. First, collective memory is stored and preserved in physical landscapes. The work of Maurice Halbwachs, whose writings in the 1920s and 1930s inaugurated the scholarly investigation of collective memory, is an important starting point. Halbwachs argued that the phrase "collective memory" is redundant. Since all memories are social constructions of individuals creating and recalling the past through telling, writing, and celebrating with others, all memories are collective. But, second, not only are collective memories "socially" constructed, they are also literally constructed. Memory is built into the physical landscape and individual encounters with buildings, natural sites, and whole regions. Landscape and memory are codependent; memories are literally impossible without physical landscapes to store and serve as touchstones for

Fig. 8.1. Berenice Abbott, *Wall Street, South and DePeyster Streets,* November 26, 1935. These small buildings—a union headquarters and tobacco warehouse, formerly a prison—seem of a very different place than 60 Wall Street, center, and the slightly smaller (though it looks much smaller here) Bank of Manhattan (left). Like the Little House, the buildings on South Street seem oblivious to the office towers in the distance. Museum of the City of New York.

the work of recollection. While Halbwachs's essential theme may seem self-evident, it is a theme that has only lately been explored by historians.[2] We have tended to focus on written and oral histories as the main sources of collective memories; even the history of historic preservation is a subfield in its infancy. Halbwachs forces us to reckon with the intimate connections between collective memories and the physical landscape.

The linking of collective memory to the physical landscape was not accidental but, rather, institutional. The invention of a new understanding of how cities would be built was accompanied, and propelled, by a new set of historical institutions founded in the early twentieth century, which made up what might be called the "history industry." I use this phrase to suggest three points about the links between landscape, memory, and creative destruction in Manhattan during this period. First, the recovery and communication of local history—a fascination with the history of place—was a national phenomenon, an intellectual and cultural "industry" that occupied writers and teachers and concerned old and new institutions such as historical societies and art museums. Second, the history of place was manufactured. History was a product, if not made out of whole cloth then at least powerfully imbued with missions rooted in the social issues of the day. Finally, the pairing of "history" with "industry" supports my larger argument that there was a tight link between the pursuit of commercial profit—especially profit from the development and speculation in space—and the search for New York's history. The dominant force behind Manhattan's creative destruction—commerce and real estate development—was also the force that shaped its written and displayed history. History, as it was socially constructed and used, became the servant of the development and redevelopment of the city.

Concepts as slippery as "collective memory" and "place" make historians nervous. Place has long been a central category of analysis in geography, philosophy, literature, psychology, and architecture, and social and cultural historians have mastered sophisticated methods to understand the "lifeworlds" of historical actors. Yet historians have generally been skittish about rigorously exploring how people assigned meaning to their physical surroundings, how those meanings were shaped by society, and how those meanings in turn shaped society. Preferring to focus on events in time, historians have usually treated places as mere sites or settings for human action.

The phrase "politics of place" is meant to suggest that the concern for place should not be seen as some hazy, sentimental, nostalgic, and perhaps intrinsic attachment to a set of buildings. The politics of place in Manhattan suffused contemporary battles over arenas of profit making, efforts to control and assimilate immigrants, the development of a democratic commercial culture, and competing visions for government activity. Indeed, one of the central drawbacks of the literature of "place" is that it has been dominated by a phenomenological approach in which landscapes are assumed to have intrinsic, universal meanings for people in all places and all times. Thus, just as historians have rarely brought the concept of place into their narratives, geographers, psychologists, and sociologists have tended to gloss over the particular meaning of a place at a particular historical moment.[3]

Viewing urban development through the lens of the politics of place means that this book cannot neatly be categorized as a historiographical account of Progressivism, city planning, or even New York. It lies instead in the rich zone between social, cultural, and urban history. This study of destruction and rebuilding contributes to a renewed effort in the past decade to define the world of ideas and actions in which reformers of this era operated. Progressive "environmentalism" took a range of forms, including regulating and demolishing slums, building parks and planting trees, devising Beaux Arts city plans, and protecting historic buildings. All were efforts to build one aspect of the Progressive vision, what Daniel Rodgers has called the "language of social bonds," into the landscape of the city, and thereby into the minds of its inhabitants—especially those with new and weak ties to the United States.[4] But rather than perceiving attitudes and cultural forms as flowing neatly from the stream of capitalism or Progressive political alliances, I have charted the return trip as well, showing how cultural attitudes shaped land values, setting agendas for preservation and demolition, and influencing the nature of zoning.[5] Thus, this book has moved from a discussion of the economic calculus of real estate speculators on Fifth Avenue to the emotional attachment to street trees, from the assimilationist goals of historic preservation advocates to the antiquarian collecting habits of "old New Yorkers."

An emerging consensus argues that Progressives of various types were unified under a common set of attitudes toward the instrumentality of history in politics and public policy.[6] Rapid destruction and rebuilding of the physical reminders of the past created the prospect of a society with little respect for history. New Yorkers did not accept this outcome. In each urban reform effort I have discussed—slum clearance, tree planting and construction of parks, historic preservation, zoning—the question of how to protect and perpetuate the best buildings and architectural values of the past was central. One of the Progressives' main goals in preserving his-

Once upon a time
there was a Little House
way out in the country.
She was a pretty Little House
and she was strong and well built.
The man who built her so well said,
"This Little House shall never be sold
for gold or silver and she will live to see
our great-great-grandchildren's
great-great-grandchildren living in her."

I

Fig. 8.2. Illustration from *The Little House* by Virginia Lee Burton. Copyright © 1942 by Virginia Lee Demetrios, renewed 1969 by George Demetrios. Reprinted by permission of Houghton Mifflin Co. All rights reserved.

tory was to educate New Yorkers, especially new immigrants, in the skills of American citizenship. William Taylor has argued that aspects of popular culture—in the form of movies and cartoons and newspaper stories—were the "urban baedekers" with which immigrants learned about their new country.[7] Progressives and their followers in the 1920s attempted to write narratives in brick, steel, and stone, to build a "baedeker" of civics into the landscape of the city. In this effort, they had to employ destruction, preservation, and creation to eliminate the wrong memories and preserve the right ones. But the Progressive reformers were not opposed to the healthy, and profitable, growth of the city. Indeed, Progressives sought to manage the process of destruction and rebuilding that engulfed Manhattan in order to create a history that would aid in the assimilation of immigrants and, equally, promote the vibrant development of the city. They would rarely maintain the balance, tipping ultimately in favor of supporting the city's turbulent development.

In 1942, Virginia Lee Burton won the Caldecott Medal for what would be her most enduring picture book for children, *The Little House*.[8] Burton was born in 1909 and lived much of her life around Boston until her death in 1968. By 1940, she had already established her fame with *Mike Mulligan and His Steam Shovel*. That children's story chronicled the heroic efforts of Mike and his brave steam shovel, Mary Anne, to dig a foundation for a new town hall in a single day.

In *The Little House,* Burton turned from the romance of construction to what she portrayed as the tragedy of urbanization. The story was based on the author's own experience of having to move her north Boston home to Folly Cove near Gloucester to clear the way for the building of a new highway. *The Little House* tells of a contented nineteenth-century home in the countryside and its experience with a big city, which her illustrations show to be unmistakably Manhattan. The house rests on a gentle hill and watches, smiling over the activities of the family it shelters. The children enjoy the seasons in their full glory—skating in the winter, planting in the spring, swimming and gardening in the lazy summer days, picking apples and attending school in the fall. Nothing upsets the steady pace of life for the family nor for the Little House (figure 8.2).

But trouble is in the distance. The lights of the city appear at first as just a yellow haze on the horizon, easily mistaken for the rising sun. Slowly the glow becomes brighter. Suddenly, with Mary Anne the steam shovel making a dramatic return to dig up the hills, a road is cut through the fields behind the Little House. Cars and power lines are followed quickly by scores of identical white suburban houses.

Fig. 8.3. Illustrations from *The Little House* by Virginia Lee Burton. Copyright © 1942 by Virginia Lee Demetrios, renewed 1969 by George Demetrios. Reprinted by permission of Houghton Mifflin Co.

Within a few short pages, even these are gone. In their places have sprung up tenements, an elevated train, and crowds of people. The Little House, finding itself engulfed in the midst of the metropolis, inexplicably abandoned by its family, loses its smile and awaits its fate. The tenement buildings are replaced by taller skyscrapers, the crowds grow thicker, the cars more numerous. The Little House is boarded up

and lies abandoned in a dark canyon of skyscrapers, ignored by passersby. Finally, by chance, the great-great-granddaughter of its builder happens upon the Little House. Once reminded of the past, she becomes entranced with the idea of living in the house, and arranges to have it moved. For a brief moment, the bustling city stops to observe the odd ritual of a little wooden house being wheeled through the streets. But once it is gone, city life resumes at its same hectic pace, with people moving ever faster and buildings climbing ever higher (figure 8.3).

The house is brought back out to the countryside, a place very much like its original site, and rooted again into the hillside. A new family, that of the great-great-
granddaughter, moves in and begins once again the activities with which the Little
House began its life, updated for the mid–twentieth century. Burton concludes with
the lesson learned by the Little House: "Never again would she be curious about the
city. . . . Never again would she want to live there" (p. 40).

Burton describes an urban condition of unstoppable and inscrutable development
and redevelopment, destruction and rebuilding with no apparent end. It is the
Little House's very innocence about the nature of urbanization in which she is engulfed that serves as a sign of her virtuousness. She is the quiet hero not only because
she is rooted in the country but also because she stands above the commerce in space.
The Little House, the original builder and owner declares, "shall never be sold for
gold or silver" (p. 1). Furthermore, even after it had been forsaken by its owners, the
house was not demolished like all the buildings around it; it was a "holdout" against
the march of development that enveloped the rest of the city.

In Burton's tale, as in the writings of real estate owners, sellers, and observers, real
estate development is an a priori fact, something to be apprehended with awe as well
as fear. For Burton, the only solution is to flee, because the effects of urban development are so disruptive and its sources so inscrutable. But even young readers must be
bothered by the easy ending. What is to prevent the city from continuing to expand
and devour the new home in the country, what the great-great-granddaughter calls
"just the place" (p. 37)? New Yorkers wondered and worried about the same question. What generated the "restless renewals"? Could they be controlled?

The Little House watches the urbanization drama unfold from a tiny plot of land
that appears to be the only piece of green in the entire city. Like many city builders,
Burton reinforces the belief that cities were not intended to, nor could they, support grass, trees, and animals. The plot of land, complete with a picket fence around
it, symbolically separates the Little House from its tenement neighbors. Burton pro-
motes in primary colors and simple drawings what housing reformers increasingly
advocated in the 1920s and 1930s: decongestion through slum clearance, the building of parks, and inducements to private home ownership in suburbs in order to
solve the social problems of the slums—even those in the "foul core" of New York.

The Little House serves as a convenient primer about the battles surrounding city
development in the first half of the century. But at the heart of the story, and the
heart of this book, is the role of memory. *The Little House* contrasts the world of the

country, where memory and tradition are strong, with the city that only lives for to-morrow and has no concern for the past. In the country, the Little House "watched the moon grow from a thin new moon to a full moon, and then back again to a thin old moon" (p. 4). But as the city and its accelerated ways spread to the Little House's doorstep, "everyone and everything moved much faster" (p. 16). In the city, there are no seasons, no differentiated times of the day or year, no sense of links across time. As the bearer of family history and memory, the Little House stands in stark contrast to what Burton portrays as the city's lifeless buildings. That landscape elicits no attachment and supports no memories. Indeed, the great-great-grand-daughter must be shaken out of her city-induced stupor before she remembers the Little House. In Burton's New York, there could be no *urbis amore*, "love of city," as I. N. Phelps Stokes might have said, because there was no time for memories or physical sites in which to invest them. For Burton's Little House, life in the city is literally timeless—and, hence, meaningless.

The *Little House* is a deeply nostalgic story of pastoralism lost and joyfully regained. But such fables are not merely children's fairy tales. Many of the pivotal transforma-tions in city building—zoning, slum clearance, historic preservation, and tree plant-ing—were rooted in and supported by the stories, especially the histories, New York-ers told themselves and others about how cities grew, developed, and changed.[9] As the preceding chapters have shown, the stories people told themselves about urban transformation were calculated efforts to shape the city—for good or ill, personal profit or public benefit (see figure 8.3).

This book has explored the cultural meanings attached to the fundamental process of urbanization, which I have characterized as creative destruction. Virginia Lee Burton clearly joined forces with "declension" critics who saw in the rise of the modern city only loss. She fought the "progressives" who celebrated the city as a new setting for community and she defended the "antiquarians" concerned about the disappearance of the physical past. I take neither side. Rather, I have tried to ex-plain the shape of the tensions and contradictions that elite New Yorkers encoun-tered when they tried to build a city—physically and metaphorically—out of con-tinuous upheaval.

The cultural consequences of a city that gained nourishment by repeatedly de-stroying and rebuilding itself are profound. All people in all places make their way in the world with some nod to the past and with an eye to the future. But in few places was the tension between looking backward and gazing forward greater than in Manhattan in the first decades of this century. One of the primary ways people link themselves, however weakly or fleetingly, to the past has always been through attachments to relatively stable landscapes. Constant change made this connection highly problematic, but also potentially useful. Some saw an opportunity to sever the restrictive ties the past imposed. The city builders of New York, however, struggled to make history a value and a tool in the marketplace for space. In their effort to "make time visible," as Lewis Mumford said, they knowingly or unknowingly helped to fuel Manhattan's creative destruction.

NOTES

CHAPTER ONE

1. Henry James, *New York Revisited* (1906; reprint, New York: Franklin Square Press, 1994), p. 34.

2. *Diary of Philip Hone* (1845), quoted in William Cole, ed., *Quotable New York: A Literary Companion* (New York: Penguin, 1992), p. 50; and Luc Sante, *Low Life: Lures and Snares of Old New York* (New York: Random House, 1991), p. x.

3. David Ward and Olivier Zunz, "Between Rationalism and Pluralism: Creating the Modern City," in *The Landscape of Modernity: Essays on New York City, 1900–1940,* ed. Ward and Zunz (New York: Russell Sage Foundation, 1992), p. 3.

4. Dramatic examples of destruction—natural and human—such as the Chicago fire of 1871 and the San Francisco earthquake of 1906, the radical replanning of Paris under Baron Haussmann, and the urban renewal efforts of Robert Moses are highlights in the history of cities and their physical transformation; they have also proven to be fruitful opportunities for historians to study social change. My focus, however, is on the "ordinary" sources and effects of creative destruction. For examples of some fine works focusing on destruction in the city, see Christine Meisner Rosen, *The Limits of Power: Great Fires and the Process of City Growth in America* (Cambridge: Cambridge University Press, 1986); Karen Sawislak, "Smoldering City: Chicagoans and the Great Fire, 1867–1874" (Chicago: University of Chicago Press, 1995); Ross Miller, *American Apocalypse: The Great Fire and the Myth of Chicago* (Chicago: University of Chicago Press, 1990); David H. Pinkney, *Napoleon III and the Rebuilding of Paris* (Princeton: Princeton University Press, 1958); and Carl Smith, *Urban Disorder and the Shape of Belief* (Chicago: University of Chicago Press, 1994). There is an extensive literature on the San Francisco earthquake, as well as important floods such as those in Galveston, Texas, and Johnstown, Pennsylvania, at the turn of the century.

5. See Joseph A. Schumpeter, "The Process of Creative Destruction," chap. 7 in *Capitalism, Socialism and Democracy* (1942; reprint, New York: Harper and Row, 1976).

6. Marshall Berman, *All That Is Solid Melts into Air: The Experience of Modernity* (New York: Simon and Schuster, 1982), p. 99.

7. In doing so I am building on a generation of work by urban geographers, mostly notably David Harvey, who have explored the urban process under capitalism. These scholars have "respatialized" urban studies, showing how urban space itself becomes a reflection and generator of capitalist innovation, and is a powerful engine shaping social and cultural development. I use this theoretical work to explore a particular historical moment in the history of capitalist urbanization. For an excellent overview, see David Harvey, *The Urban Experience* (Baltimore: Johns Hopkins University Press, 1989). For an overview of recent Marxist studies of the city, including the work of Harvey and Manuel Castells, see Ira Katznelson, *Marxism and the City* (New York: Oxford University Press, 1993).

8. Aldous Huxley, "Usually Destroyed," in *Tomorrow and Tomorrow and Tomorrow, and Other Essays* (New York: Harper, 1956), p. 225.

9. In his path-breaking *Fin-de-Siècle Vienna: Politics and Culture* (New York: Vintage Books, 1981), Carl E. Schorske argues that in their efforts to be free of the past and its constraints, artists, intellectuals and politicians of *fin de siècle* Vienna were in fact more deeply engaged in the past than ever before.

10. Quoted in Nathan Silver, *Lost New York* (Boston: Houghton Mifflin, 1967), p. 9. Ironically, for some, such as E. B. White, the city's essence was to be found in the very invisibility of time, in the absence of physical links to particular moments in the past. Paradoxically, White argues, this quality gave Manhattan a greater claim on the past: The city "carries on its lapel the unexpungeable odor of the long past, so that no matter where you sit in New York you feel the vibrations of great times and tall deeds, of queer people and events and undertakings" ("Here Is New York," in *Essays of E. B. White* [New York: Harper, 1977], p. 118).

11. For an excellent discussion of the changes in the perception of space and time wrought by technological developments, see Stephen Kern, *The Culture of Space and Time* (Cambridge: Harvard University Press, 1983).

12. Although the concept of collective memory—both the notions of an identifiable collective community and of fixed memories—is fraught with definitional potholes, a number of historians have found it a fruitful area of study. The starting point of such a study is the work of Maurice Halbwachs, who remains the most influential theorist on the subject. For an overview of his work see Maurice Halbwachs, *On Collective Memory*, ed. and trans. Lewis A. Coser (Chicago: University of Chicago Press, 1992). See also Michael Kammen, *Mystic Chords of Memory: The Transformation of Tradition in American Culture* (New York: Knopf, 1991); David Lowenthal, *The Past Is a Foreign Country* (New York: Cambridge University Press, 1985); and "Memory and American History: A Special Issue," *Journal of American History* 75 (March 1989): pp. 1117–1280.

13. In *Nature's Metropolis: Chicago and the Great West* (New York: W.W. Norton, 1991), William Cronon uses "second nature" to describe an "artificial nature that people erect atop first nature," the original prehuman nature (p. xvii).

14. Several fine recent works on the social and political history of New York City's physical development at the turn of the century anchor this book. Some of the most useful include David Hammack, *Power and Society: Greater New York at the Turn of the Century* (New York: Columbia University Press, 1982); John Mollenkopf, ed., *Power, Culture, and Place: Essays on New York City* (New York: Russell Sage Foundation, 1988); Ward and Zunz, eds., *The Landscape of Modernity*; and William R. Taylor, *In Pursuit of Gotham: Culture and Commerce in New York* (New York: Oxford University Press, 1992).

The closest historical work to my own is David Moisseiff Scobey, "Empire City: Politics, Culture, and Urbanism in Gilded-Age New York" (Ph.D. diss., Yale University, 1989). Focusing on New York City in the Gilded Age, Scobey describes the first great wave of creative destruction that accompanied New York's rise to prominence from the middle of the nineteenth century through the first three decades of the twentieth. He argues that the upheavals of New York City's economic and social life were not "growing pains" or "natural" symptoms of excessive growth that would be progressively (and Progressively) ameliorated by a rising civic consciousness, but rather the inherent, unavoidable flip side of capitalistic prosperity and economic expansion. The "uptown utopias"—the aristocratic residential areas of the Upper East and West Sides—were the direct response by elites to the chaos of Lower Manhattan.

15. The population of New York City grew from 2.33 million in 1910 to 7.89 million in 1950. See George Lankevitch, *A History of New York City* (New York: New York University Press, 1998), p. 146.

16. "The Building of New York," *Architecture* 56 (December 1927): p. 324, quoted in Robert A. M. Stern, Gregory Gilmartin, and Thomas Mellins, *New York 1930: Architecture and Urbanism Between the Two World Wars* (New York: Rizzoli, 1987), p. 19.

17. In a recent architectural history of the city in this era, Stern, Gilmartin, and Mellins note that

"for the first time in the city's history, many significant buildings were demolished to make way for buildings of lesser distinction" (*New York 1930,* p. 19).

18. William Dean Howells, *Their Wedding Journey* (Boston: Houghton Mifflin, 1871), p. 27.

19. Ann Douglas, *Terrible Honesty: Mongrel Manhattan in the 1920s* (New York: Farrar, Straus and Giroux, 1995), p. 17.

20. White, "Here Is New York," p. 121.

21. Ibid., p. 118. The population of New York City in 1910 was 41 percent foreign born. Lankevitch, *A History of New York City,* p. 146.

22. White, "Here Is New York," p. 121.

23. Ibid., p. 118.

24. Ford Madox Ford, *New York Is Not America* (New York: Albert and Charles Boni, 1927), p. 107.

25. Daniel J. Boorstin, "The Landscape of Democracy," in *Democracy and Its Discontents: Reflections on Everyday America* (New York: Random House, 1974), p. 68.

26. "The Vanishing of New York's Social Citadels: Four Great Establishments on Fifth Avenue That Have Unwillingly Given Up the Ghost," *Vanity Fair* 25 (October 1925): p. 51, quoted in Stern, Gilmartin, and Mellins, *New York 1930,* p. 20.

27. Gutzon Borglum, "Our Ugly Cities," *North American Review* 228 (November 1929): pp. 548–53, quoted in quoted in Stern, Gilmartin, and Mellins, *New York 1930,* p. 19.

28. Despite the enormous theoretical achievements of David Harvey and other urban geographers, their work has often verged toward a deterministic view of urbanization that leaves little room for the influence of cultural values on the understanding and transformation of place. The focus on New York City is an implicit argument that it is only through a concrete example of a single city that the process of capitalist urbanization can be studied. Harvey himself returned, in a recent work, to the close study of Paris under Haussmann. See Harvey, *Consciousness and the Urban Experience: Studies in the History and Theory of Capitalist Urbanization* (Baltimore: Johns Hopkins University Press, 1985).

29. The absence of a separate chapter titled "the rise of city planning" is a conscious choice, reflecting my own critique of the historiography of city planning. First, city planning does not "rise" from nothing in this era; a number of recent works have made plain the truth that city planning has long roots in the nineteenth century, dating at least to Olmsted and even before. Second, the city-planning movement was hardly unified in approach and in its supporters. My argument is reflected in the fact that "city planning" is addressed in each chapter: Each case study describes a different set of efforts to shape the city according to rational, planned means. See, for example, Scobey, "Empire City"; and David Schuyler, *The New Urban Landscape: The Redefinition of City Form in Nineteenth-Century America* (Baltimore: Johns Hopkins University Press, 1986).

30. See "Le Corbusier Scans Gotham's Towers," *New York Times Magazine,* 3 Nov. 1935.

31. Le Corbusier, *When the Cathedrals Were White: A Journey to the Country of Timid People,* trans. Francis E. Hyslop Jr. (New York: Reynal and Hitchcock, 1947), p. 45. See also Silver, *Lost New York,* p. 11.

32. Le Corbusier, *When the Cathedrals Were White,* p. 45.

CHAPTER TWO

1. Henry James, *New York Revisited* (1906; reprint, New York: Franklin Square Press, 1994), p. 45.

2. Ibid., p. 40.

3. Fred Rothermell, *Fifth Avenue: Twenty-Eight X-Rays of a Street* (New York: Harcourt, Brace and Co., 1930). "Spine of Gotham" is the title of the frontispiece poem.

4. Especially insightful are Charles Lockwood, *Manhattan Moves Uptown: An Illustrated History* (Boston: Houghton Mifflin, 1976); M. Christine Boyer, *Manhattan Manners: Architecture and Style, 1850–1900* (New York: Rizzoli, 1985); Ronda Wist, *On Fifth Avenue: Then and Now* (New York: Carol Publishing Group, 1992); Kate Simon, *Fifth Avenue: A Very Social History* (New York: Harcourt Brace Jovanovich, 1978); and Theodore James Jr., *Fifth Avenue* (New York: Walker and Company, 1971).

5. Elizabeth Blackmar, "Uptown Real Estate and the Creation of Times Square," in *Inventing Times Square: Commerce and Culture at the Crossroads of the World, 1880–1939,* ed. William R. Taylor (New York: Russell Sage Foundation, 1991), p. 53.

6. Quotations from Louise Frances Reynolds, *The History of a Great Thoroughfare: A Few Facts Concerning Fifth Avenue and Its Adjacent Streets* (New York: Thoroughfare, 1916), no pagination; "The Fifth Avenue," *Real Estate Record and Builders' Guide* (hereafter cited as *RERBG*), 15 June 1878, pp. 515–16, quoted in Robert A. M. Stern, Gregory Gilmartin, and John Massengale, *New York 1900: Metropolitan Architecture and Urbanism, 1890–1915* (New York: Rizzoli, 1983), p. 307; "Middle Fifth Avenue: The Evolution of the New Piccadilly," *RERBG*, 20 April 1901, p. 694; A. C. David, "The New Fifth Avenue," *Architectural Record,* July 1907, p. 2; and J. F. L. Collins, *Both Sides of Fifth Avenue* (New York: J. F. L. Collins, 1910), p. 50.

7. The 1993 confrontation between the organizers of the 25th Anniversary of the 1969 Stonewall Riot and Mayor Giuliani over the celebration's parade route suggests how important the image of Fifth Avenue remains. A renegade parade defied the city's agreed-upon route up First Avenue, and instead proceeded up Fifth. Herbert Muschamp, the architectural critic, astutely notes the impression of Fifth Avenue today as being "at once privileged and doomed" in "Seven Miles with the Power to Transform," *New York Times* (hereafter cited as *NYT*), 25 June 1995, sec. H, p. 34.

8. For an exemplary theoretical discussion and historical account of consumers' separation from the agricultural products they consume, see William Cronon, *Nature's Metropolis: Chicago and the Great West* (New York: W. W. Norton, 1991).

9. For a discussion of legal rulings on land valuation, see Joel Schwartz, *The New York Approach: Robert Moses, Urban Liberals, and Redevelopment of the Inner City* (Columbus: Ohio State University Press, 1993), chap. 1.

10. "Imageability" is the term used by Kevin Lynch in his classic work on the design of cities, *Image of the City* (Cambridge: MIT Press, 1960).

11. I discuss the problem of locating the "birth" of city planning in chapter 1.

12. David, "The New Fifth Avenue," p. 4.

13. Ibid. Numerous such "lists" were published during this period. See, for example, American Scenic and Historic Preservation Society, *Twenty-Fourth Annual Report* (1919), pp. 154–55; and William Pedrick, "Fifth Avenue To-Day" in *Fifth Avenue Old and New, 1824–1924,* ed. Henry Collins Brown (New York: Fifth Avenue Association, 1924), pp. 99–100. Pedrick noted that the value of property along Fifth Avenue from Fortieth to Eighty-sixth Streets had grown from $397,000 in 1841 to $259,611,000 in 1924. The 1924 figure did not include, he quickly added, the $53 million of property exempt from taxes, such as the New York Public Library ($23,600,000).

14. Measurements from insurance maps in George W. and Walter S. Bromley, *Atlas of the City of New York, Borough of Manhattan* (Philadelphia: G. W. Bromley and Co., 1902, 1921, 1930). For an outstanding visual documentation of the Avenue, see *Fifth Avenue, New York, from Start to Finish* (New York: Welles and Co., 1911).

15. "Middle Fifth Avenue: The Evolution of the New Piccadilly," *RERBG*, 10 April 1901, p. 694.

16. Reynolds, *History of a Great Thoroughfare*. As early as 1855, Henry Tappan, the chancellor of the University of Michigan, had suggested that Fifth Avenue would develop this way: "The city has not only advanced in magnitude, it has also been rebuilt. The palaces of the last generation were forsaken and turned into boarding-houses, then pulled down and replaced by warehouses. He who erects his magnificent palace on Fifth Avenue to-day, has only fitted out a future boarding-house, and probably occupied the site of a future warehouse." Quoted in Seymour Toll, *Zoned America* (New York: Grossman, 1969), p. 83.

17. David Schuyler, *The New Urban Landscape: The Redefinition of City Form in Nineteenth-Century America* (Baltimore: Johns Hopkins University Press), p. 78.

18. Schuyler, *The New Urban Landscape,* p. 64, quoting Henry Tappan.

19. Stern, Gilmartin, and Massengale, *New York 1900*, p. 307.

20. Burton Hendrick, "The New Fifth Avenue," *Metropolitan Magazine* 23 (1905): p. 244.

21. In 1927, for example, only five new single-family homes were built in Manhattan. Stern, Gilmartin, and Massengale, *New York 1900*, p. 444.

22. Theoretically, a skyscraper could go infinitely high, as long as the tower did not cover more than 25 percent of the lot. This synopsis comes largely from Kenneth Revell, "Regulating the Landscape: Real Estate Values, City Planning, and the 1916 Zoning Ordinance," in *The Landscape of Modernity: Essays on New York City, 1900–1940,* ed. David Ward and Olivier Zunz (New York: Russell Sage Foundation, 1992), pp. 19–45. The literature on the creation and effects of the 1916 Zoning Resolution is, needless to say, enormous. For a good overview, see S. J. Makielski Jr., *The Politics of Zoning: The New York Experience* (New York: Columbia University Press, 1966).

23. *The WPA Guide to New York City: The Federal Writers' Project Guide to 1930s New York* (1939; reprint, New York: New Press, 1995).

24. Phrase is from a draft chapter for the *WPA Guide.* See WPA Federal Writers' Project—NYC Unit, "Architecture of New York," series 32, roll 117, MN# 21116 Municipal Archives (box 2, folder 2, "Miscellaneous").

25. *RERBG*, 7 and 14 February 1920.

26. In "Empire City: Politics, Culture, and Urbanism in Gilded-Age New York" (Ph.D. diss., Yale University, 1989), David Moisseiff Scobey discusses the "market in space" in the post–Civil War period: "Manhattan land was no longer merely a site of activity or a repository of wealth, but a fund of capital from which surplus-value could be—had to be—extracted" (p. 91).

27. "Present and Future of Union Square," *RERBG,* 8 October 1904, p. 718.

28. F. Scott Fitzgerald, "My Lost City," in *The Crack-Up*, ed. Edmund Wilson (New York: New Directions, 1945), p. 25.

29. Kenneth T. Jackson, "The Capital of Capitalism: The New York Metropolitan Region," in *Metropolis, 1890–1940,* ed. Anthony Sutcliffe (Chicago: University of Chicago Press, 1984).

30. Emanuel Tobier, "Manhattan's Business District in the Industrial Age," in *Power, Culture, and Place,* ed. John Hull Mollenkopf (New York: Russell Sage Foundation, 1988), p. 85.

31. The peak immigration year was 1907, when just over one million immigrants were processed at Ellis Island (but that number was nearly matched in several other years as well).

32. Edward Ewing Pratt, "Industrial Causes of Congestion of Population in New York City," *Columbia University Studies in History, Economics and Public Law* 43 (1910): p. 45.

33. Ironically, however, Manhattan's greatest growth in manufacturing capability occurred in the final decades of the nineteenth century. The first three decades of the twentieth century saw Manhattan gradually lose its manufacturing empire, as the new borough of Brooklyn eclipsed it. In the first few decades of the twentieth century, manufacturing did continue to grow, but at a much slower rate than previously, particularly in comparison to Brooklyn.

34. Leybl Kahn, "The Loft Building in the Central Business District of Manhattan" (Ph.D. diss., Pratt Institute, June 1963).

35. The stores' dependence on their factories may explain why the Fifth Avenue Association never pushed for an outright ban on factories or a retroactive removal of the industries. The FAA after 1915 was in part led by executives from B. Altman and Bes and Co. See Gregory Gilmartin, *Shaping the City: New York and the Municipal Art Society* (New York: Clarkson Potter, 1995), p. 192.

36. Gail Fenske and Deryck Holdsworth, "Corporate Identity and the New York Office Building, 1895–1915," in *The Landscape of Modernity: Essays on New York City, 1900–1940,* ed. David Ward and Olivier Zunz (New York: Russell Sage Foundation, 1992), pp. 129–59.

37. *RERBG*, 21 February 1920, p. 247.

38. Tobier, "Manhattan's Business District," p. 91.

39. Tobier, despite providing a fine summary of New York's development, falls into this logical trap.

for example: "As befits a commercial city built for profit and not for glory—be it of state or religion—its real estate market has exhibited little patience for nonpecuniary considerations. Yesterday's valued locational advantages of a given structure and use can never rest on their laurels in Manhattan, but must prove themselves at each new turn of the economic wheel. Failure invites the wrecker's ball and redevelopment, or worse, foreclosure for tax arrears" ("Manhattan's Business District," p. 79).

40. Scobey, "Empire City."

41. *RERBG*, 24 March 1900, p. 497.

42. *RERBG*, 8 January 1910, p. 56.

43. See Elizabeth Hawes, *New York, New York: How the Apartment House Transformed the Life of the City, 1863–1930* (New York: Knopf, 1993).

44. John Flavel Mines, *The Island of Manhattan, a Bit of Earth* (New York: Real Estate Loan and Trust Company of New York, 1890), p. 9.

45. *RERBG*, 4 June 1910, p. 1191. See also letters on the subject on 28 May 1910, pp. 1137 and 1140.

46. Pratt, "Industrial Causes of Congestion," p. 24.

47. Ibid., p. 93.

48. Blackmar, "Uptown Real Estate and the Creation of Times Square," p. 51.

49. Mines, *The Island of Manhattan*, p. 19.

50. Kinahan Cornwallis, "The Bixby Fortune: A Romance of Land Values in New York City," *New York Sun*, 2 October 1906.

51. Mines, *The Island of Manhattan*, p. 10.

52. See Scobey, "Empire City," pp. vi–viii, for a discussion of the mythology surrounding this first real estate transaction.

53. Mines, *The Island of Manhattan*, pp. 6–7.

54. Pratt, "Industrial Causes of Congestion," p. 106.

55. Reynolds, *History of a Great Thoroughfare*.

56. Pedrick, "Fifth Avenue To-Day," p. 101.

57. Collins, *Both Sides of Fifth Avenue*, p. 50.

58. Ibid., p. 53.

59. Ibid., p. 54.

60. Moses King, *King's Handbook of New York City* (Boston: 1893; reprint ed., New York: Benjamin Blom, 1972), p. 153.

61. King, *Handbook of New York City*, pp. 150–52.

62. Hendrick, "The New Fifth Avenue," pp. 241–42.

63. James, *New York Revisited*, p. 40.

64. Ibid., p. 110.

65. Ibid., p. 232.

66. David, "The New Fifth Avenue," *Architectural Record*, p. 4. It was the early-nineteenth-century redbrick townhouses that drew the sentimental praise of critics. These homes, like those remaining on the north side of Washington Square, had an "elegance of simplicity and fine proportions," wrote Helen W. Henderson in *A Loiterer in New York* (New York: George H. Doran Co., 1917), p. 201.

67. David, "The New Fifth Avenue," *Architectural Record*, p. 2.

68. Ibid., p. 11.

69. Reynolds, *History of a Great Thoroughfare*.

70. Hendrick, "The New Fifth Avenue," p. 244.

71. Henderson, *Loiterer in New York*, pp. 236–37. For another example of this genre of lament, see F. S. Laurence, "On the Passing of Delmonico's, an Architectural Landmark," *Architecture* 52 (November 1925): 419–21. Laurence noted that rarely in New York were buildings torn down because of structural weakness due to age: "[W]e do not revere [our buildings] sufficiently to allow them to remain standing

much more than a few years, twenty or thirty years at most. Madison Square Presbyterian Church, Madison Square Garden, and now Delmonico's! Will it be the Century Club next, or what other example of our good earlier architecture which yet survives, hinting of a traditional culture and a civic background of more than yesterday's origin?" (p. 419).

72. As I discuss in chapter 1, the reformers who have been included in the world of "Progressivism" varied radically in their philosophies and strategies. In the case of Fifth Avenue, reformers followed few rules, utilizing a whole range of strategies. For a discussion of how the term "Progressive" might still have relevance, see Daniel T. Rodgers, "In Search of Progressivism," *Reviews in American History* (December 1982): 112–32.

73. Hendrick, "The New Fifth Avenue," pp. 233, 241. Hendrick, who began his journalistic career as a writer for *McClure's* during the heyday of such muckrakers as Lincoln Steffens, Ida Tarbell, and Ray Stannard Baker, later became a biographer, or perhaps more accurately, a hagiographer. Ironically, in 1932 he completed a long biography of Carnegie, funded by Carnegie's widow (*Dictionary of American Biography*, supplement IV [1946–50], s.v. "Hendrick, Burton Jesse," pp. 367–68).

74. Edith Wharton, *The Age of Innocence* (New York: D. Appleton Co., 1921), pp. 24–25. This passage was the basis for one of the more startling images in the 1993 film version of *The Age of Innocence*: a view of Mrs. Manson Mingott's mansion in the middle of unsettled land around Central Park.

75. "The New Mayfair of New York City's Society," *NYT,* 6 September 1908, sec. 5, p. 4.

76. The most comprehensive collection of "holdout stories" can be found in Andrew Alpert and Seymour Durst, *New York's Architectural Holdouts* (Mineola, N.Y.: Dover, 1984).

77. See G. W. Bromley, *Atlas of the City of New York, Borough of Manhattan*, plate 17, for a real estate map of the Herald Square district. It shows how Macy's failed to get the tiny corner piece in assembling eight convoluted parcels for its building site. Macy's struggle highlights one of the most difficult issues in New York real estate history: assembling lots necessary to build large buildings.

78. Reynolds, *History of a Great Thoroughfare.*

79. The seminary did finally sell the property in the 1930s. Today, imbedded in the base of a relatively new skyscraper, stands a brass relief sculpture of the Wendell home.

80. Discussed in Wist, *On Fifth Avenue, Then and Now.*

81. Andrew Alpern and Seymour B. Durst, *Holdouts!* (New York: McGraw-Hill, 1984), p. 12.

82. Ibid.

83. *NYT,* 29 May 1920, p. 1.

84. Although the Vanderbilts led the battle to prevent development along the Avenue, they were hardly alone. As late as the 1920s, the Rockfellers were buying up lots adjacent to their mansions at Fifty-fourth Street in order to preserve the neighborhood. See *NYT,* 30 December 1925, p. 4.

85. For a discussion of the use of covenants in antebellum New York City, see Elizabeth Blackmar, *Manhattan for Rent, 1785–1850* (Ithaca, N.Y.: Cornell University Press, 1989), pp. 100–101.

86. For a report of the influence of restrictive covenants (and the ending of their twenty-five-year validity) on the development of the Upper West Side, see "Upper West Side Building Tendencies—A Reconstruction Movement Imminent," *RERBG*, 1 January 1910.

87. See Patricia Burgess Stach, "Deed Restrictions and Subdivision Development in Columbus, Ohio, 1900–1970," *Journal of Urban History* 15 (November 1988): 42–68 (on the appeal of covenants, see p. 66). In the increasingly dense area of midtown Manhattan, owners used covenants to protect access to light and air before the 1916 Zoning Resolution regulated building heights. For example, the Fifth Avenue Hotel held covenants on the abutting property to the rear in order to protect the hotel's access to light and air. See *RERBG*, 21 April 1900, p. 677.

88. Ironically, very little has been written about the use and effect of restrictive covenants, especially nonracially based covenants. See Stach, "Deed Restrictions," for a listing of existing works.

89. Aymar Embury II, "From Twenty-third Street Up—Part Two," *Brickbuilder* 25 (November 1916): 281.

90. "Fifth Avenue—From Forty-Second to Sixtieth," *NYT*, 13 September 1908, part 5, p. 5.

91. Discussed in Stern, Gilmartin, and Massengale, *New York 1900*, p. 312.

92. *NYT*, 13 September 1908, sec. 5, p. 5.

93. *NYT*, 31 January 1909.

94. Collins, *Both Sides of Fifth Avenue*, pp. 61–63.

95. John Foreman and Robbe Pierce Stimson, *The Vanderbilts and the Gilded Age* (New York: St. Martin's Press, 1991), p. 43.

96. *RERBG*, 13 March 1920, p. 340. Just as the rise of Millionaire's Mile was not a steady, linear process, neither was its demise. Even the removal of private homes along Fifth Avenue was not a steady process. For example, after World War I began and the whole real estate market slowed, pressure on Fifth Avenue residents to convert their mansions into high-rises or office buildings declined. Latercomers to the "age of gold" quickly marched in to gain a foothold on the Avenue. See Embury, "From Twenty-third Street Up—Part Two," for private homes built in the first two decades after 1900.

97. *RERBG*, 8 January 1910, p. 51.

98. Hawes, *New York, New York*, p. 222. The lawsuits are discussed in "Upper Fifth Avenue's Future," *RERBG*, 12 April 1924 and in the months thereafter. See also Stern, Gilmartin, and Massengale, *New York 1900*, p. 387.

99. James, *New York Revisited*, p. 242. Several commentators saw this development as a "democratization" of the Avenue. See, for example, Mines, *The Island of Manhattan;* and *RERBG*, 12 April 1924.

100. Hawes, *New York, New York*, p. 195.

101. Ibid., pp. 199, 222.

102. Pedrick, "Fifth Avenue To-Day," p. 103.

103. See Fifth Avenue Association (hereafter cited as FAA), *Report for the Year* (1916), cover. The FAA is discussed extensively in Toll, *Zoned America*.

104. FAA, *Fifty Years on Fifth, 1907–1957* (New York: International Press, 1957), p. 36.

105. FAA, *Report for the Year* (1912), p. 3.

106. FAA, *Fifty Years on Fifth*, p. 36.

107. Fifth Avenue Commission, *Preliminary Report of Fifth Avenue Commission* (New York: R.L. Stillson Co., 1912), p. 2.

108. See *NYT*, 11 December 1994, city section, p. 6, for a comparison of the value of the land on Fifth Avenue with elite retail corridors worldwide.

109. For a discussion of the number and powers of BIDs in New York City today, see *NYT*, 20 November 1994. An almost apocalyptic portrait of America's future, especially the "fortress" mentality of elites, can be found in Mike Davis, *City of Quartz* (New York: Vintage Books, 1990).

110. Minutes of the FAA, 30 April 1907.

111. At times critics attacked the existence of these private police forces, over which the public had no control. These same accusations are made about business improvement districts (BIDs) today. In 1995, the Grand Central Partnership was found guilty of beating and forcibly removing homeless people from the area of Grand Central Station (see *NYT*, 7 July 1995, p. B1).

112. Scobey shows the centrality of the "arterial sclerosis" problem to public policy debates of the Gilded Age city ("Empire City," chap. 3).

113. The FAA leadership strongly advocated widening the Avenue, although on this issue they found themselves opposed to a large portion of their members. The process of widening brought great destruction to the elite homes, stores, and restaurants of the Avenue. Repeatedly, newspapers and magazines offered updates on the widening work, with complete catalogues of what was lost in the process.

114. See FAA, *Report for the Year*, (1922) for a discussion of the gift of the towers to the city.

115. Minutes of the FAA, 13 April 1911.

116. Minutes of the FAA, 3 Dec. 1912, in *FAA Minutes, 1 Dec. 1909—9 Feb. 1915* (collection held by the Fifth Avenue Association).

117. For a book-length study of the Municipal Art Society's role in city planning and beautification, see Gregory Gilmartin, *Shaping the City*.

118. Minutes of the FAA, 24 Jan. 1911.

119. Ibid.

120. Fifth Avenue Commission, *Preliminary Report*, p. 2.

121. See Gilmartin, *Shaping the City*, p. 194.

122. In an article on unsightly advertising methods displayed on the Avenue, the FAA showed a photograph of a store with a sign saying "liquidation sale": "Conditions like these destroy the character of a community, injure business and lower property values. They are rare indeed in the Fifth Avenue Section, because destructive influences are promptly detected and corrected by the watchful eye of our Association." *The Avenue,* October 1925, p. 5.

123. Minutes of the FAA, 28 March 1910.

124. Minutes of the FAA, 28 March 1910; 5 April 1910; and 3 May 1910.

125. FAA, *Report for the Year* (1922), pp. 36−39. The Sign Ordinance passed in January of 1922 and also included Madison Avenue between Thirty-fourth and Seventy-second, Thirty-fourth Street between Lexington and Seventh Avenue, and Fifty-seventh Street between Lexington and Broadway. The lawsuit against these restrictions was *Loon Hing v Crowley,* 113 US 703, 708, 709 (1922).

126. Minutes of the FAA, 30 March 1908.

127. Even as the FAA achieved its most fundamental victory, it continued to use more informal, semipublic means to hasten the elimination of the noxious manufacturing enterprises that had settled on the Avenue. Through the Save Your City Committee, the FAA was able to dispatch with manufacturing and eliminate visual "nuisances." See, for example, *RERBG*, 3 January 1920, p. 8.

128. It was McAneny who pushed for the formation, in 1914, of a permanent city-planning committee (instead the standing Committee on the City Plan was created, only to be abolished in 1918 under new Democratic Mayor John Hylan) and initiated a series of important public works projects (including new bridges, street widenings, and subway lines). He was also executive manager of the *New York Times* and director of the Regional Plan Association after 1930.

129. In its 1912 pamphlet advocating height limitations, the FAA's counsel, Bruce Falconer, listed thirteen cities in seven European countries and twenty-five large U.S. cities that enforced some form of height limitations. FAA, *Statement of the Fifth Avenue Association on the Limitation of Building Heights, to the New York City Commission and the Testimony of the Association's Representatives at a Conference, June 19, 1913* (New York, 1913), p. 22.

130. FAA, *Statement*, pp. 2–3.

131. Ibid., p. 19.

132. Ibid., p. 38.

133. See Revell, "Regulating the Landscape," p. 23.

134. The FAA used the tragedy of the Triangle fire to issue the following resolution on 4 April 1911: "Whereas the members of a democratic community are . . . responsible for the conditions existing in the Washington Place building which made it possible for the recent disaster to occur were deplorable and whereas there are many similar buildings in New York City and particularly in the Fifth Avenue district in which it is possible for similar conditions to exist. Resolved: That we offer our co-operation in the various movements now on foot in the community leading towards better legislation for fire prevention and especially endorsing the Bureau of Fire Prevention recommended by the Fire Commissioner." Minutes of the FAA, 4 April 1911.

135. FAA, *Statement*, p. 18.

136. Minutes of the FAA, 15 May 1912.

137. Gilmartin, *Shaping the City*, p. 191.

138. Minutes of the FAA, 23 February 1911.

139. See, for example, Minutes of the FAA, 24 March 1915.

140. Gilmartin, *Shaping the City,* pp. 194–95: "The city's finances were inextricably tangled up with those high assessments. Eight percent of the city's budget flowed from taxes on property or buildings: the whole architecture of the municipal bond market rested on this foundation."

141. See Gilmartin, *Shaping the City,* p. 198; as well as *Housing Betterment* 5, no. 2 (May 1916); and *RERBG,* 3 January 1920. Gilmartin and others have wondered why the FAA never tried to achieve an outright ban on garment factories. This may have been because the FAA was increasingly dominated by members of the garment industry and Jewish businessmen, who may have been more sympathetic to the garment workers' plight, many of whom were Jewish. See Minutes of the FAA, 22 June 1915, for a discussion of the transformation of the FAA leadership.

142. Bruce Falconer, the FAA's counsel, offered an example of the building of a fifty-story skyscraper: "The erection of such a building on one lot would then take the place of four other possible improvements on four other lots. Instead of tearing down five old and antiquated structures, and instead of having five modern buildings of up-to-date requirements and handsome architecture, only one is demolished and one new one erected. Instead of spreading the area of improvements and lessening the congestion of street and living conditions, the improvements tend naturally to confine themselves to a more narrow and prescribed area, and the occupants of buildings to be concentred in a particular district." FAA, *Statement,* p. 15.

143. Henderson, *Loiterer in New York,* p. 237.

144. Reynolds, *History of a Great Thoroughfare.*

CHAPTER THREE

1. Joseph Mitchell, "The Bottom of the Harbor" (1951), in Mitchell, *Up In the Old Hotel* (New York: Vintage, 1993), p. 479.

2. Joel Schwartz, *The New York Approach: Robert Moses, Urban Liberals, and Redevelopment of the Inner City* (Columbus: Ohio State University Press, 1993), p. xv.

3. See, for example, Roy Lubove, *The Progressives and the Slums: Tenement House Reform in New York City, 1890–1917* (Pittsburgh: University of Pittsburgh Press, 1962); Gwendolyn Wright, *Building the Dream: A Social History of Housing in America* (Cambridge: MIT Press, 1981); and Richard Plunz, *A History of Housing in New York City: Dwelling Type and Social Change in the American Metropolis* (New York: Columbia University Press, 1990). Joel Schwartz offers perhaps the most insightful discussion of the roots of urban renewal, at least for New York.

4. Wright, *Building the Dream,* p. 117.

5. Riis himself noted the difference between the legal definition and the "narrower" but more accepted definition in *How the Other Half Lives: Studies Among the Tenements of New York* (1890; reprint, New York: Dover Publications, 1971), pp. 14–15.

6. Plunz, *History of Housing in New York City,* p. 2. Plunz notes several other early-nineteenth-century examples of city-initiated building demolitions.

7. Elizabeth Blackmar, *Manhattan for Rent: 1785–1850* (Ithaca: Cornell University Press, 1989), pp. 172–76.

8. Report of the 1853 Tenement House Committee, quoted in *The Tenement House Problem,* ed. Robert W. De Forest and Lawrence Veiller (New York: Macmillan, 1903), p. 77; and Lawrence Veiller, "Tenement House Reform in New York City, 1834–1900," in *Tenement House Problem,* pp. 83–84.

9. Veiller, "Tenement House Reform," pp. 80, 109.

10. Plunz, *History of Housing in New York City,* p. 52.

11. See Alan Trachtenberg, *Reading American Photographs* (New York: Hill and Wang, 1989), chap. 4, on the relationship of photography and social reform. Recent research into the Riis photographs (and a 1995 exhibit of newly printed images from glass plate negatives at the Museum of the City of New York, the repository of the largest collection of Riis negatives) reveals that Riis was aided by a number of photographers—many of the most famous images attributed to Riis are in fact theirs—and that he was much

less of a self-conscious photographer than previously thought. See Bonnie Yochelson, "What Are the Photographs of Jacob Riis?" *Culturefront* 3 (September 1994): pp. 28–38.

12. Riis, *How the Other Half Lives*, p. 49.

13. Ibid., p. 49.

14. Jacob A. Riis, "The Clearing of Mulberry Bend: The Story of the Rise and Fall of a Typical New York Slum," *American Review of Reviews* 12 (August 1895): p. 174; "crazy old buildings" is a quote of the Society for the Improvement of the Condition of the Poor, in Riis, *How the Other Half Lives*, p. 11. The violence of Mulberry Bend frequently made its way into the literary imagination. See, for example, Edward Townsend's story, "How the Other Half Dies," in Townsend, *Chimmie Fadden Explains, Major Max Expounds* (New York: United States Book Company, 1895), pp. 203–13.

15. Riis, *How the Other Half Lives*, p. 5.

16. Ibid., p. 52.

17. Charles A. Madison, introduction to Riis, *How the Other Half Lives*, p. vi.

18. Riis, *How the Other Half Lives*, p. 214.

19. Josiah Strong, *Our Country: Its Possible Future and Its Present Crisis* (1885; reprint, Cambridge: Harvard University Press, 1963); Joaquin Miller, *The Destruction of Gotham* (New York: Funk and Wagnalls, 1886); and Edward Bellamy, *Looking Backward* (1888; reprint, New York: New American Library, 1960). For a lengthy discussion of the fears of urban America see Paul Boyer, *Urban Masses and Moral Order in America, 1820–1920* (Cambridge: Harvard University Press, 1978), especially pp. 123–33.

20. Ignatius Donnelly, *Caesar's Column: A Story of the Twentieth Century* (London: Ward, Lock and Co., 1890; reprint ed., Cambridge: Belknap Press of Harvard University Press, 1960); James R. McCabe Jr., *Light and Shadows of New York Life* (1872; reprint, New York: Farrar, Straus and Giroux, 1970). A number of other guidebooks established this dichotomy between rich and poor.

21. Riis, *How the Other Half Lives*, p. 229. The belief that social unrest had its roots in bad housing conditions was widespread. For a later example of this view, see Andrew J. Thomas, "Is It Advisable to Remodel Slum Tenements?" *Architectural Record* (November 1920): pp. 417–24.

22. The phrase is from James Bryce, "The Menace of Great Cities," *National Housing Association Publications*, no. 20, June 1913. Bryce was the British Ambassador to the United States.

23. E. R. L. Gould, "The Only Cure for Slums," *The Forum* 19 (1895): pp. 499, 500. These attitudes conform with the emerging picture of adolescent psychology propounded by the likes of G. Stanley Hall. See Joseph F. Kett, *Rites of Passage: Adolescence in America, 1790 to the Present* (New York: Basic Books, 1977).

24. New York State Tenement House Committee, *Report of the Tenement House Committee* (Albany: 1895), p. 41. The fear of adolescent attacks on buildings prevailed throughout this period. See Tenement House Committee of the Charity Organization Society, *Why Abandoned Buildings Should Be Demolished* (New York, 1936); for a later, fictional exploration of youth "house attacks," see Graham Greene's short story, "The Destructors" in Greene, *Collected Stories* (New York: Viking Press, 1973), pp. 327–46.

25. Veiller, "Tenement House Reform," pp. 80, 109.

26. Boyer, *Urban Masses and Moral Order,* chap. 15. Boyer also uses the phrase "negative environmentalists" (p. 190) to describe the "coercive and moralistic approach" of reformers combatting urban ills. I use the phrase here to describe the view that the destruction of certain "bad" places was as important as building better ones.

27. Lubove, *The Progressives and the Slums,* p. 78.

28. The Olmsted legacy was quite direct: Calvert Vaux, Olmsted's partner on Central Park, designed Mulberry Bend Park.

29. Riis, "The Clearing of Mulberry Bend," p. 178.

30. Ibid., p. 177.

31. Ibid.

32. Ibid.

33. Ibid.

34. Note that the subtitle of "The Clearing of Mulberry Bend" article is "The Story of the Rise and Fall of a Typical New York Slum."

35. Riis, *How the Other Half Lives*, p. 5.

36. Ibid., p. 49.

37. Ibid.

38. Charles Dickens, *American Notes*, 2 vols. (London: Chapman and Hall, 1842), quoted in Plunz, *History of Housing in New York City,* p. 51. The Five Points, along with Niagara Falls and the Eastern State Penitentiary in Philadelphia, was one of the primary sites Dickens wanted to visit during his American tour in 1842. About the Five Points, Dickens observed: "What place is this, to which the squalid street conducts us? A kind of square of leprous houses, some of which are attainable only by crazy wooden stairs without. What lies beyond this tottering flight of steps, that creak beneath our tread!" The phrase "battle with the slum" is from Jacob A. Riis, *The Battle with the Slum* (New York: Macmillan, 1902).

39. New York State Tenement House Commission, *Report of the Tenement House Commission* (1884), p. 10.

40. "Condition of Mulberry Bend," *New York Times*, 7 December 1894, p. 2. Seth Low, then the president of Columbia University, was highly critical of the city owning the Mulberry Bend slum. Especially preposterous, at least to reformers, was the claim by some landlords that they be paid not only for the assessed market sale value of the property, but also the rental value. Why, argued reformers, should slumlords be rewarded for packing in over one hundred people in inhuman conditions?

41. "Bought a House for $1.50—Old Buildings in Mulberry Bend Sold at Auction," *New York Times*, 7 June 1895, p. 7.

42. For a good overview of the Mulberry Bend story, see James B. Lane, *Jacob A. Riis and the American City* (Port Washington, N.Y.: Kennikat Press, 1974), pp. 113–15.

43. Riis, *How the Other Half Lives*, p. 223.

44. De Forest and Veiller, *Tenement House Problem*, p. 102.

45. For a discussion of the efforts—and failures—of each of the tenement house commissions, see De Forest and Veiller, *The Tenement House Problem,* which reproduces the entire 1901 Tenement House Commission report.

46. Felix Adler, "Tenement House Reform: What the Government Should Do (The Last of Felix Adler's Lectures)," *New York Daily Tribune*, 10 March 1884, p. 8.

47. For a discussion of the role of the COS, see Plunz, *History of Housing in New York City,* pp. 39–42; and the COS Committee on Housing, *Forty Years of Housing: The Story of the Tenement House Committee of the Charity Organization Society of the City of New York* (New York, 1938).

48. Gould, "The Only Cure for Slums," pp. 495, 500. Robert Moses, Gould's descendant in spirit, used a similar phrase a half century later when he declared that "When you operate in an over-built metropolis, you have to hack your way with a meat ax." Moses, *Public Works: A Dangerous Trade* (New York: McGraw-Hill, 1970), quoted in Marshall Berman, *All That Is Solid Melts into Air: The Experience of Modernity* (New York: Penguin, 1982), pp. 293–94. The architect Le Corbusier used a similar expression in discussing the rebuilding of Paris in the nineteenth century: "I thank Louis XIV, Napoleon, and Haussmann for having cut through the city with some clear and intelligent axes." Le Corbusier, *When the Cathedrals Were White: A Journey to the Country of Timid People* (New York: Reynal and Hitchcock, 1947), p. 47.

49. Gould, "The Only Cure for Slums," p. 498.

50. Ibid.; Tenement House Committee, *Report* (1895), p. 359.

51. De Forest and Veiller, *The Tenement House Problem*, p. 206.

52. *Health Department v Dassori,* 21 App. Div 348, 47 New York, discussed in James Ford, *Slums and Housing,* vol. 2 (Cambridge: Harvard University Press, 1936), 513.

53. *Real Estate Record and Builders' Guide*, 31 March 1900, p. 539.

54. *New York Tribune*, 23 December 1895, quoted in Lane, *Jacob A. Riis,* p. 114.

55. The division between speculators and landlords—admittedly not a simple, permanent division—was exacerbated at the end of the century by the intensity of population growth and the expansion of property ownership to a wider range of people, including more immigrants. The rental business became an important means of upward mobility; these new, immigrant property owners who had little social or cultural connection to speculators or reformers were resistant to demolition efforts that took away what they considered to be legitimate profit-making ventures. Speculators, of course, saw the benefits of public intervention. See Blackmar, *Manhattan for Rent,* p. 173. For a powerful thesis on the "pluralization" of power in turn-of-the-century New York, see David C. Hammack, *Power and Society: Greater New York at the Turn of the Century* (New York: Columbia University Press, 1982). For a discussion of the rise of Italian landownership in the Lower East Side, see Donna Gabbaccia, "Little Italy's Decline: Immigrant Renters and Investors in a Changing City," in *The Landscape of Modernity,* ed. David Ward and Oliver Zunz (New York: Russell Sage Foundation, 1992).

56. New York City Tenement House Department, *Report* (1902–3), p. 513.

57. Ibid., p. 5.

58. Ibid., p. 282.

59. Tenement House Department, *Report* (1914), p. 10.

60. Riis, *How the Other Half Lives,* p. 214.

61. For a discussion of the attack on the Tenement House Law in its first fifteen years, see "Lawrence Veiller," Columbia Oral History Project, Feb. and March 1949, transcript, pp. 44f.

62. Ibid., p. 39.

63. Lawrence Veiller, "A Housing Programme," *National Housing Association Publications*, no. 16, June 1912.

64. For a discussion of how government might aid housing development during the post–World War I housing shortage, see Veiller, "The Housing Situation and the Way Out," *National Housing Association Publications*, no. 55 (December 1920).

65. Lawrence Veiller, "Government Housing in Practice," *Housing* 23, no. 2 (October 1935): p. 168.

66. Lawrence Veiller, "The Housing Problem in the United States," *National Housing Association Publications*, no. 61 (March 1930).

67. *Housing* 23 (June 1935): p. 85.

68. "Veiller," Columbia Oral History Project, p. 55.

69. Ford, *Slums and Housing,* p. 511.

70. Tenement House Department *Reports.* For example, in 1919, only 183 old-law buildings, comprising 1,442 apartments, were demolished. The numbers grew during the 1920s housing boom: in 1924, 356 buildings housing 2,889 were torn down; in 1927, 470 structures housing 4,620 people were demolished. The statistics from 1930, when 7,580 old-law apartments were torn down (due to the slum clearance on Chrystie and Forsyth Streets and in the Lung Block), are the highest for a single year.

YEAR	NO. OF BUILDINGS	NO. OF APARTMENTS
1918	55	493
1919	183	1,442
1925	441	3,733
1929	467	5,191
1930	665	7,580
1931	311	3,355
1934	334	3,934

71. Ford, *Slums and Housing,* p. 511.

72. Ibid.

73. Joel Schwartz calls this view "economic puritanism" (*The New York Approach,* p. 24). In his 1935 work, James Ford discusses the limitations—namely the requirement of market value compensation—of the New York Charter and Building Code, Sections 1299 and 1300.

74. Lawrence Veiller, "How England Is Meeting Its Housing Shortage," *National Housing Association Publications*, no. 56 (September 1920): p. 91.

75. Ford, *Slums and Housing*, p. 513. On the comprehensiveness of the British approach, see Lawrence Veiller, "Government Housing in Practice," *Housing* 23, no. 2 (Oct. 1935); and Ernst Kahn, "Government Housing in the United States, as Seen by a Foreign Observer," *Housing* 23, no. 2 (Oct. 1935).

76. Plunz, *History of Housing in New York City*, pp. 184 ff. The Amalgamated Houses by Springsteen and Goldhammer, on Grand Street near the Williamsburg Bridge, were perhaps the most direct copies of European models of the 1920s. They resemble closely the dramatic design of the Karl Marx Hof in Vienna, designed by Karl Ehn in the late 1920s. See Robert A. M. Stern, Gregory Gilmartin, and John Massengale, *New York 1900: Metropolitan Architecture and Urbanism, 1890–1915* (New York: Rizzoli, 1983), p. 421.

77. Charity Organization Society, *Forty Years of Housing*, pp. 14–15.

78. See Schwartz, *The New York Approach*, p. 23; Roy Lubove, *Community Planning in the 1920s*; and Plunz, *History of Housing in New York City*, pp. 101–2.

79. David Kennedy offers the best overview of the impact of World War I on American life in *Over Here: The First World War and American Society* (New York: Oxford University Press, 1980).

80. New York State Board of Housing, *Report Relative to the Housing Emergency in New York and Buffalo*, table V, cited in Plunz, *History of Housing in New York City*, p. 126.

81. See Edith Elmer Woods, *The Housing of the Unskilled Wage Earner* (New York: Macmillan, 1919), cited in Schwartz, *The New York Approach*, p. 23.

82. Riis, *How the Other Half Lives*, p. 224.

83. Tenement House Department, *Report* (1914), p. 9.

84. See Roy Lubove, "I. N. Phelps Stokes: Tenement Architect, Economist, Planner," *Journal of the Society of Architectural Historians* 23 (May 1964): p. 85; and Lawson Purdy, "Why We Need Excess Condemnation: A Boon to the Property Owner—A Blessing to the Public," *National Municipal Review* (July 1923): pp. 363–68.

85. One of the most startling ideas was offered by Mayor William J. Gaynor in 1910: he suggested cutting a new avenue between Fifth and Sixth in order to ease traffic congestion. See Rebecca Read Shanor, *The City That Never Was* (New York: Penguin, 1988), pp. 11–16.

86. See Stern, Gilmartin, and Massengale, *New York 1900*, p. 443.

87. Simkhovitch quoted in Schwartz, *The New York Approach*, p. 42. Simkhovitch is a fascinating figure: she founded and led Greenwich House (a settlement house) for half a century, in the process becoming one of the leading advocates for city planning, public housing, and the "decongestion" of the city. See the Mary K. Simkhovitch Papers, Schlesinger Library, Radcliffe College.

88. Riis, *How the Other Half Lives*, p. 27.

89. De Forest quoted by Fred F. French (the developer of Knickerbocker Village), in "Housing in Lower Manhattan" (address to the Department of Economics and Social Institutions, Princeton University, 24 April 1934), typescript, p. 3.

90. French, "Housing in Lower Manhattan," p. 8. For the demolition required for Knickerbocker Village, French's company was paid $340,000, mostly funded by the federal government.

91. Schwartz, *The New York Approach*, p. 46.

92. For an excellent discussion of the politics and philosophy of public housing in New York City in the 1920s and 1930s, see Gail Radford, *Modern Housing for America: Policy Struggles in the New Deal Era* (Chicago: University of Chicago Press, 1996).

93. *The WPA Guide to New York City: The Federal Writers' Project Guide to 1930s New York* (1939; reprint, New York: New Press, 1995), p. 18.

94. The Lower East Side still has a number of so-called pre-law tenements—that is, tenements built previous to the first major tenement law, the 1879 "dumbbell" regulations. Even today old-law tenements opposite Columbus Park at the bend in Mulberry Street survive, and throughout the Lower East

Side, hundred-year-old old-law tenements house new generations of Asian and Latino immigrants. Despite New Deal slum clearance, despite Robert Moses's urban renewal projects, the "foul core of New York" persists. The reason is simple: for all the complaints landlords lodged against the city's tenement regulations, the buildings were and continue to be profitable. The work of Jacob Riis and other tenement reformers seemed to mimic the creatively destructive cycle of urban development in the rest of the city. But, ironically, the real estate market had found underdevelopment in the Lower East Side a profitable venture, and successfully slowed the rapid transformation of the landscape.

95. Jane Jacobs, *The Death and Life of Great American Cities* (New York: Vintage, 1961), chap. 16.

96. Ford, *Slums and Housing,* p. 516.

97. "Modernism of the streets" is discussed in Berman, *All That Is Solid Melts into Air,* pp. 314–32.

98. Edward W. Townsend, *A Daughter of the Tenements* (New York: Lovell, Coyell, 1895), pp. 60–61.

99. James Huneker, *The New Cosmopolis: A Book of Images,* quoted in *The Old East Side: An Anthology,* ed. Milton Hindus (Philadelphia: The Jewish Publication Society of America, 1969), p. 293.

100. Riis, "The Clearing of Mulberry Bend," p. 176.

101. John Sloan, for example, noted his explorations of the Bowery, Little Italy, and Chinatown at night, which he found "right interesting," although Chinatown was "a bit too picturesque for my purposes" (10 June 1906 journal entry, quoted in *John Sloan's New York Scene,* ed. Bruce St. John (New York: Harper and Row, 1965), p. 40.

102. James E. Young, *The Texture of Memory: Holocaust Memorials and Meaning* (New Haven: Yale University Press, 1993).

103. Michael Gold, *Jews Without Money* (1930; reprint, New York: Carroll and Graf, 1996), p. 73. Gold, however, also sees something redeeming in destruction. The book ends with its call to revolution—"the true Messiah"—rooted in demolishing the Lower East Side, where the evils that created the poverty of his people were to be seen at their most extreme. "You will destroy the East Side when you come, and build there a garden for the human spirit" (pp. 13, 309).

104. Alfred Kazin, *A Walker in the City* (1946; reprint, New York: Harcourt Brace Jovanovich, 1979), pp. 12–13.

105. Pierre Nora, *Realms of Memory: Rethinking the French Past* (New York: Columbia University Press, 1996). For a discussion of the rise of the Lower East Side as a place of memory for Jews, see Beth S. Wenger, *New York Jews and the Great Depression: Uncertain Promise* (New Haven: Yale University Press, 1996).

106. In this case, the "heritage" of the Lower East Side was troubling and embarrassing. The Chamber found that at least 10 percent of the Lower East Side's realty was owned by these monied estates. See Joseph Platzker, "Who Owns the Lower East Side?" *East Side Chamber News* 2, no. 5 (July 1929).

107. Ibid.

108. Lillian D. Wald, *The House on Henry Street* (1915; reprint, New York: Dover, 1971), p. 81.

109. Typescript of speech by Robert Moses on the occasion of the celebration of the seventieth anniversary of the University Settlement in America at the Commodore Hotel, 14 November 1956, Municipal Reference Library, vertical files, "NYC Slums."

CHAPTER FOUR

1. American Scenic and Historic Preservation Society (hereafter cited as ASHPS), *Annual Report,* 1910, p. 3.

2. William R. Taylor, *In Pursuit of Gotham: Culture and Commerce in New York* (New York: Oxford University Press, 1992), p. xvii. The idea that commerce has ruled New York like some force of nature is common. Gregory Gilmartin, an architectural historian, writes that battling against "progress"—that is, commercial growth and its physical shape—"was like setting oneself against a law of nature or, worst yet, like questioning the American dream." Gregory F. Gilmartin, *Shaping the City: New York and the Municipal Art Society* (New York: Clarkson N. Potter, 1995), p. 342.

3. Henry James, *The American Scene* (New York: Charles Scribner's Sons, 1946), pp. 74–75, quoted in Taylor, *In Pursuit of Gotham,* p. xv.

4. Today, architectural importance remains the dominant criterion for preserving a building in New York; at the turn of the century, it was the building and park's historical import that gave them their value. One of the principal advocates for preservation in the city today observes that the "chief criterion for designating landmarks is architectural integrity; approximately 6 percent have been designated for their historical significance." Barbaralee Diamonstein, *The Landmarks of New York* (New York: Harry N. Abrams, 1988), p. 12. Writings on the history of historic preservation have only recently blossomed. Charles B. Hosmer's classic *Presence of the Past: A History of the Preservation Movement in the United States Before Williamsburg* (New York: G. P. Putnam's Sons, 1965) chronicled the range of local movements. The explosion of social and cultural history in the 1970s and 1980s has made a renewed focus on preservation's history necessary and fruitful. See, for example, Daniel Bluestone, "Preservation and Renewal in Post–World War II Chicago," *Journal of Architectural Education* 47 (May 1994): pp. 210–23; Rudy Koshar, "Against the 'Frightful Leveler': Historic Preservation and German Cities, 1890–1914," *Journal of Urban History* 19 (May 1993): pp. 7–29; Randall Mason, "Shaping New York's Memory: Environmental Reform and Civic Memory, 1898–1925," Ph.D. diss., Columbia University, expected 1999; Michael Holleran, *Boston's "Changeful Times": Origins of Preservation and Planning in America* (Baltimore: Johns Hopkins University Press, 1998); and James M. Lindgren, *Preserving the Old Dominion: Historic Preservation and Virginia Traditionalism* (Charlottesville: University Press of Virginia, 1993), and *Preserving Historic New England: Preservation, Progressivism, and the Remaking of Memory* (New York: Oxford University Press, 1995).

5. In reference to post–World War II preservation battles in Chicago, Daniel Bluestone notes that "The ascendancy of aesthetic preservation over a variety of associational narratives encouraged preservationists in their belief that they could locate the essence of the city and its history in a few representative structures of the Chicago School. The absolute priority given to aesthetic over associational landmarks in the 1950s and beyond further restricted the use that citizens could make of history; their efforts to forge a vital sense of neighborhood and community identity based in part on history could only be frustrated by the limitations of the aesthetic model." Bluestone, "Preservation and Renewal in Post–World War II Chicago," pp. 221–22. See also Mike Wallace, "Reflections on the History of Historic Preservation," in *Presenting the Past: Essays on History and the Public,* ed. Susan Porter Benson, Stephen Brier, and Roy Rosenzweig (Philadelphia: Temple University Press, 1986), p. 173: "In such a culture, the best preservationists could do was declare a few sites to be historic 'reservations'—off limits to developers. The larger culture tolerated these historic battlefields, colonial reconstructions and Indian 'homelands'—partly because there were so few of them, and partly because they were so utterly irrelevant to the onrushing flow of events."

6. Charles Hosmer's long-dominant view was that the "pioneers of the preservation movement prepared the American people to accept the idea of spending money for the seemingly profitless activity of saving a few of the spots that contributed to the study of history or the enjoyment of beauty" (*Presence of the Past*, p. 303).

7. For information on the Roosevelt house, see *Women's Roosevelt Memorial Bulletin* and Roosevelt Memorial Association, *Annual Reports, 1919–1921.* See also Hosmer, *Presence of the Past*, pp. 147–52. See also the indignant lament for the demolition of Roosevelt's home in Helen W. Henderson, *A Loiterer in New York* (New York: George H. Doran Co., 1917), pp. 236–237.

8. See Gilmartin, *Shaping the City,* chap. 5. The issue of women's role in preservation has been the subject of attention in recent years, as preservation has begun to explore its own history. In New York's early preservation movement, women tended to be the "rank and file" members of the preservation movement and were full participants in major preservation efforts—like Fraunces Tavern—when it was mainly about protecting the memory of the Revolution, especially when those memories were held in historic homes. But in cases such as St. John's Chapel, and especially the City Hall fight, when the heart of the city's civic and business district was at stake, men dominated the debate.

9. The notion of historic buildings as "stabilizers" is discussed in Koshar, "Against the 'Frightful Leveler,'" p. 8.

10. There remains no comprehensive, serious biography of Green. John Foord's *The Life and Public Services of Andrew Haswell Green* (Garden City, N.Y.: Doubleday, Page, 1913) is a valuable start.

11. See Kenneth T. Jackson, *Encyclopedia of New York City* (New Haven: Yale University Press), p. 505.

12. City History Club of New York, *Annual Report*, 1898, p. 3.

13. City History Club, *Annual Report*, 1898, p. 1; and 1917–18, p. 13.

14. For a discussion of the founding of the ASHPS, see Hosmer, *Presence of the Past*, pp. 95–101.

15. In 1867, Trinity had sold the park to Cornelius Vanderbilt, on which he built the massive Hudson River Railroad Freight Depot. The destruction of the park and its glorious trees was the subject of many loud laments (see chapter 6).

16. A. W. Halsey, "Trinity as Landlord," *New York Observer*, 24 January 1895, quoted in Trinity Church, *Report as to the Sanitary Conditions of the Tenements of Trinity Church* (New York: Evening Post Job Printing House, 1895), p. 39.

17. Quoted in John P. Peters, "The Tale of Trinity," *The Independent* 16 (18 February 1909): p. 361.

18. Reprinted from the *New York Evening Post* in Ray Stannard Baker, "The Case Against Trinity: The Spiritual Unrest," *The American Magazine* 68 (May 1909): p. 9.

19. Gilmartin, *Shaping the City*, p. 338.

20. Baker, "The Case Against Trinity," pp. 15–16.

21. The Church had spawned numerous smaller churches on its property but remained the holder of their mortgages; some critics urged the wealthy church to nullify the loans and set the smaller churches free. See Peters, "The Tale of Trinity." Trinity also retained very tight control over its direct progeny, such as St. John's.

22. See Baker, "The Case Against Trinity," p. 9.

23. Halsey, "Trinity as Landlord," p. 39.

24. Historian Mike Wallace identifies four groups during 1880–1940 who began to vocally challenge the demolition of the past: New England "Brahmins," descendants of the antebellum planter class in the South, very wealthy industrialists such as Ford and Rockefeller, and members of the "professional and managerial strata" ("Reflections on the History of Historic Preservation," pp. 168–171).

25. Annie Gould wrote that "The acoustics of Saint John's are very good. It would make a capital People's Forum and social center. Our democracy needs such civic temples scattered throughout the town." *New York Times* (hereafter cited as *NYT*), 31 December 1913, p. 8, quoted in Gilmartin, *Shaping the City*, p. 337.

26. Alan Trachtenberg's work on the Brooklyn Bridge is highly suggestive about the ways the bridge, in its symbolic functions, served to link past and future. *Brooklyn Bridge: Fact and Symbol* (Chicago: University of Chicago Press, 1965).

27. The phrase is that of William Taylor. See William R. Taylor (with Thomas Bender), "Culture and Architecture: Aesthetic Tensions in the Shaping of New York," in *In Pursuit of Gotham*, pp. 51–68.

28. The legislature was deeply involved because state courts would be part of the new municipal complex.

29. Georg Simmel's "The Metropolis and Mental Life" (1903)—in which he wrote that money "with its colorlessness and its indifferent quality . . . becomes a frightful leveler—it hollows out the core of things, their specific values and their uniqueness"—is discussed in Koshar, "Against the 'Frightful Leveler,'" p. 7.

30. *NYT*, 11 July 1889, p. 4.

31. See Stern, Gilmartin, and Massengale, *New York 1900,* for a detailed chronology and description of the various plans for City Hall.

32. I am in debt to Viviana Zelizer for her insightful theoretical discussions of the role of cultural values in shaping market values in *Pricing the Priceless Child* (New York: Basic Books, 1985).

33. Walter Benjamin, "The Work of Art in the Age of Mechanical Reproduction," in *Illuminations* (New York: Schocken, 1969). Michael Kammen has also discussed the "American obsession with authenticity" (*Mystic Chords of Memory: The Transformation of Tradition in American Culture* [New York: Vintage, 1991], p. 18).

34. Edward Hagaman Hall, *The Old Martyrs' Prison* (New York: American Scenic and Historic Preservation Society, 1902), p. 5.

35. For a fascinating discussion of the problem of narrative in history, see William Cronon, "A Place for Stories: Nature, History, and Narrative," *Journal of American History* 78 (March 1992): pp. 1347–76.

36. Melusina Fay Peirce, *The Landmark of Fraunces Tavern: A Retrospect* (reprint of speech given to the Women's Auxiliary of the Society for the Preservation of Scenic and Historic Places and Objects, December 1900), p. 30.

37. Andrew Haswell Green, *The Preservation of the Historic City Hall of New York: Letter of Hon. Andrew H. Green to the Commissioners, Appointed to Locate the Site for a New Municipal Building* (New York: New York State Society, Sons of the American Revolution, 1894), p. 7.

38. Ibid., p. 8.

39. "Municipal Opportunity," *Harper's Weekly* 38 (3 March 1894): p. 198.

40. Minutes of the Board of Commissioners for the Erection of a New Municipal Building, 1889, p. 20.

41. Herbert Croly, "New York as the American Metropolis," *Architectural Record* 13 (March 1903): p. 198.

42. Green, *Preservation of the Historic City Hall,* pp. 11–12. Green voiced a common sentiment when he argued that it was self-evident that "no one, however illiterate or however refined, can see the ancient structures of England, Germany, or France, without having his wonder excited or his thinking faculties stimulated."

43. City History Club of New York City, *Annual Report*, 1904, inside cover.

44. Green, *Preservation of the Historic City Hall,* p. 6.

45. ASHPS, *Annual Report*, 1910, p. 15. While calling the park the "refuge of the people," the ASHPS held onto a very narrow notion of how the "people" should act. The ASHPS expressly opposed the notion of encouraging the use of parks for political meetings of all sorts—for example, they protested the proposal to build speakers' platforms in parks throughout the city, much like Speakers' Corner in Hyde Park, London. ASHPS, *Annual Report*, 1910, p. 50.

46. See ASHPS, *Annual Reports*, 1911, 1913.

47. Green, *Preservation of the Historic City Hall,* p. 7.

48. *NYT*, 15 September 1889, p. 4.

49. Green, *Preservation of the Historic City Hall,* p. 10.

50. City Club of New York, *Save the City Hall and the City Hall Park* (pamphlet, New York, 1910), p. 1.

51. One historian anticipated the "recovery and restoration to its pristine appearance" of City Hall Park as the World's Fair approached. Everett A. Peterson, *Thirty Historic Places in Greater New York* (New York: City History Club, 1939), p. 12.

52. Hall, *The Old Martyrs' Prison,* p. 3.

53. *NYT*, 29 January 1893, p. 17.

54. *NYT*, 16 January 1893, p. 4.

55. *NYT*, 29 January 1893, p. 17.

56. *American Architect and Building News* 39 (18 March 1893): p. 161.

57. *NYT*, 7 July 1889, p. 4.

58. Croly, "New York as the American Metropolis," p. 199.

59. *NYT*, 15 September 1889, p. 4. And it was not only the most elite New Yorkers who held City Hall in high esteem. The mayor's correspondence files during these years are sprinkled with

hastily scrawled letters as well as formal declarations of affection for the old City Hall. "I hope you can save our old City Hall—so fine in its external architecture and so intimately associated with our civic pride and growth," wrote Salem W. [illegible] in 1893. In letters to the mayor more "common" citizens expressed their dedication to this "historically sacred ground," as one man said in 1889. Salem W. to Mayor Thomas F. Gilroy, 13 January 1893; Board of Commissioners for the Erection of a New Municipal Building, *Minutes of Meetings: April 4, April 22, Sept. 4, Sept. 18* (New York: Irving Press, 1889).

60. *American Architect and Building News* 39 (18 March 1893): p. 161.

61. *NYT*, 29 March 1893, p. 4.

62. *NYT*, 26 February 1893, p. 4; 13 March 1893, p. 4.

63. *NYT*, 4 September 1893, p. 4. The debate over the Tweed Courthouse would continue for many years, with proposals for its removal made into the 1970s, when it was finally given landmark status.

64. *NYT*, 16 January 1894, p. 1.

65. "A Civic Center for New York," *Municipal Affairs* 6 (1902): p. 478. With the consolidation of the five boroughs, that amount grew to a half million dollars by the end of the century and to a million dollars by 1903. The problem remains an enormous one for New York to this day. See Rebecca Read Shanor, *The City That Never Was* (New York: Penguin, 1988), p. 57.

66. *New York City Globe*, 12 March 1910, quoted in City Club of New York, *Save the City Hall* (pamphlet), p. 13.

67. *NYT*, 21 March 1910, p. 8: "The park site is selected on the erroneous idea that it costs nothing. As a matter of fact it is more valuable than any other land in its neighborhood. The destruction of a park is poor economy from any point of view."

68. *NYT*, 12 March 1910, p. 8; and the *Evening Post*, 16 March 1910, quoted in City Club of New York, *Save the City Hall,* p. 10.

69. Croly, "New York as the American Metropolis," p. 199.

70. Board of Commissioners for the Erection of a New Municipal Building, 18 September 1889.

71. Richard E. Enright, *Police Commissioner Enright's Proposed Civic Center*, pamphlet reprinted from the *NYT*, 25 May 1924.

72. See Thomas Adams, *The Building of the City* (New York: Regional Plan Association, 1931), pp. 348 ff.

73. Adams, *The Building of the City*, p. 382.

74. Berenice Abbott, who photographed many of the disappearing sites of New York (published in her 1939 *Changing New York*), made sure to capture the wedding-cake-like post office building before it was demolished.

75. See Gilmartin, *Shaping the City,* pp. 326–30, for a discussion of the Fort Clinton controversy.

76. Ibid., p. 344.

CHAPTER FIVE

1. I. N. Phelps Stokes, *The Iconography of Manhattan Island*, 5 vols. (New York: Dodd, Mead, 1915–1928), 5:2062 (entry for 30 June 1906).

2. Ibid., 5:2071 (22 November 1908).

3. See William B. Rhoads, "The Colonial Revival and the Americanization of Immigrants," in *The Colonial Revival in America,* ed. Alan Axelrod (New York: W. W. Norton, 1985), pp. 341–362; and Wendy Kaplan, "R. T. H Halsey: An Ideology of Collecting American Decorative Arts," *Winterthur Portfolio* 17 (spring 1982): pp. 43–53.

4. Edward G. Robinson to MCNY Board of Trustees, 26 Jan. 1928. See MCNY Trustees Records, 25 November 1927.

5. "Picturing New York's Past," *Springfield Republican*, 30 April 1929. Newspaper articles about the MCNY can be found in clippings scrapbook, James Speyer papers, New York Public Library.

6. Helen Appleton Read, *Brooklyn Eagle,* 17 January 1932.

7. Anson B. Moran to Robert LeRoy, 12 January 1932, James Speyer Papers, box 1, "Correspondence." LeRoy was the secretary of the MCNY for several years in the late 1920s and early 1930s.

8. "The City Museum," *New York American,* 19 Dec. 1930.

9. The renewed historic preservation movement began with the Municipal Art Society in the 1940s but only gained municipal backing with the establishment of the Landmarks Preservation Commission following the demolition of Penn Station. See Gregory F. Gilmartin, *Shaping the City: New York and the Municipal Art Society* (New York: Clarkson Potter, 1995); and Brooke Barr, "Past Surfaces: History and Theory of Landmark Preservation in New York City, 1945–1989," Ph.D. diss., Yale University, 1996.

10. For a collection of interpretations of the sources and meanings of the colonial revival, see Axelrod, *The Colonial Revival in America.* For a discussion of the status of history museums by the 1930s, see Laurence Vail Coleman, *The Museum in America* (Washington, D.C.: American Association of Museums, 1939), and *Historic House Museums* (Washington, D.C.: American Association of Museums, 1933).

11. For an excellent history of the architectural museum, see Edward N. Kauffman, "A History of the Architectural Museum: From Napoleon through Henry Ford," in *Fragments of Chicago's Past,* ed. Pauline Saliga (Chicago: The Art Institute of Chicago, 1990), pp. 16–31; see also Michael Wallace, "Visiting the Past: History Museums in the United States," in *Presenting the Past: Essays on History and the Public,* ed. Susan Porter Benson, Stephen Brier, and Roy Rosenzweig (Philadelphia: Temple University Press, 1986), pp. 137–64. For a discussion of the first period rooms, see "The Beginnings of the Period Room in American Museums: Charles P. Wilcomb's Colonial Kitchens, 1896, 1906, 1910," in *The Colonial Revival in America,* pp. 217–240. Neil Harris argues that department stores adopted the period room technique for displays and developed it more fully than had museums. Museums, in turn, learned to improve their displays by observing department stores. "Museums, Merchandising, and Popular Taste: The Struggle for Influence," in *Cultural Excursions: Marketing Appetites and Cultural Tastes in Modern America* (Chicago: University of Chicago Press, 1990), pp. 76–77.

12. "Picturing New York's Past," *Springfield Republican,* 30 April 1929.

13. The saying is apocryphal. In the 1940s, the MCNY tried unsuccessfully to verify that Lincoln had actually spoken or written these words. "Lincoln Inscription" folder, Museum of the City of New York Archives (hereafter cited as MCNY Archives), "Miscellaneous Clippings and Booklets" box.

14. R. W. G. Vail, *Knickerbocker Birthday: A Sesqui-Centennial History of the New-York Historical Society, 1804–1954* (New York: NYHS, 1954), pp. 206, 208.

15. *New York Times* (hereafter cited as *NYT*), 2 December, 1920, quoted in Vail, *Knickerbocker Birthday,* p. 209.

16. "Certificate of Incorporation," 21 July 1923, in MCNY, Trustees Records, 1923–27.

17. Henry Collins Brown, ed., *Valentine's Manual of Old New York* (New York: Valentine, 1924), p. 184.

18. Brown had sought the Vanderbilt mansion at Fifty-eighth Street, which was about to be abandoned, for the MCNY's new home. Mike Wallace, "Razor Ribbons, History Museums, and Civic Salvation," *Radical History Review* 57 (1993): p. 223.

19. MCNY, *Annual Report of the Trustees* (1927), p. 18. See also Brown, *Valentine's Manual,* p. 175.

20. Brown, *Valentine's Manual,* p. 176. Brown's *Valentine's Manual* served as the official journal for the museum in its first four years.

21. For photographs and a discussion of the restoration of Gracie Mansion, see MCNY Archives, "Gracie Mansion" box.

22. The problem of "duplication" posed by the existence of both the NYHS and the MCNY has repeatedly resurfaced. In the early 1940s, for example, Robert Moses especially challenged the city's support for two museums doing similar work (he failed to note, however, that the NYHS was privately funded). See Vail, *Knickerbocker Birthday,* p. 259.

23. The Historical Society is trying to refocus itself after virtually going bankrupt in the early 1990s.

In April 1995, the society sold paintings and other artifacts that it had collected over the years but were superfluous to its mission. In June the society attempted, with the "Treasury of the Past" exhibit, to break away from its image as an antiquarian and elitist organization.

24. "Tells Historical Society It Is Dead," *NYT,* 3 January 1917, p. 8, quoted in Robert A. M. Stern, Gregory Gilmartin, and Thomas Mellins, *New York 1930: Architecture and Urbanism Between the Wars* (New York: Rizzoli, 1987), p. 133. The most glaring of these collections was that of Egyptian art, one of the finest in the country. It was ultimately donated to the Brooklyn Museum.

25. Press release presented at 31 May 1928 Board of Trustees meeting, to report on the progress of the building and endowment campaign. MCNY Trustees Records, 31 May 1928.

26. Brown, *Valentine's Manual*, p. 180.

27. Ibid.

28. MCNY Trustees Records, 12 May 1931. See also MCNY, *Annual Report of the Trustees* (1927).

29. MCNY, *The Laying of the Corner Stone of the Museum of the City of New York* (1929), p. 1.

30. Ibid., p. 16.

31. For the discussion of Brown's ousting, see James Speyer to Thomas B. Appleget, Esq. (lawyer to John D. Rockefeller Jr.), 13 February 1926, folder 169, "Cultural Interests: Museum of the City of New York 1923–1929," box 17, Record Group 2 (RG2), Office of Messrs. Rockefeller (OMR), Rockefeller Family Archives, Rockefeller Archives Center (RAC); also see MCNY Trustees Records, 1 and 19 April 1926. While Brown was a favorite of antiquarians like Mrs. Van Rensselaer, he had had little success gaining the respect of some of the city's leading historical authorities. For example, I. N. Phelps Stokes, a leading tenement reformer and chronicler of New York history, met Brown when the latter came to discuss his proposed book of photographs of New York. Stokes noted that Brown was working on a "pictorial history of New York, illustrated largely from old prints, but I believe that many of these have been re-drawn so as to make pretty pictures. . . . I was not very favorably impressed by him or by what he showed me of his book, which I don't think has been put together in a very scholarly way." See Stokes to William Osgood Field, 16 April 1913, box 3, "Personal Letters," Stokes Papers, NYHS.

32. At its height, the firm was involved in some of the major public works projects around the world, including the Mexican railroad system, the Philippine railway, and the London subway. The decline in the value of railroad stocks and the 1920s increase in American investment capital (and hence, less need for the foreign capital handled by Speyer), sent the James Speyer Company spinning into decline. The company was liquidated in 1939. See *Dictionary of American Biography* (hereafter cited as *DAB*), "Speyer," p. 728.

33. In trying to entice John D. Rockefeller to make a second large donation, Speyer noted how he had never given more to a charitable enterprise. Speyer to Rockefeller, 7 March 1927, RG2, OMR, "Cultural Interests," box 17, folder 171, RAC.

34. Speyer was so eager to adopt his wife's heritage that he included her family name in his own in *Who's Who*, while leaving out the names of his own parents! See Stephen Birmingham, *Our Crowd: The Great Jewish Families of New York* (New York: Dell, 1967), p. 406.

35. "Last of His Line," *Fortune*, August 1931, p. 80.

36. See Speyer Papers, NYPL, box 1, "Correspondence," and scrapbook 1, box 5. The decline of Speyer and Co. probably began with the war and the anger it generated from Germany's enemies. The British blacklisted the firm as early as 1916.

37. He also managed to offend some of the most powerful men on Wall Street with his domineering style. Apparently, J. P. Morgan and Edward Harriman refused to serve on corporate boards with him. See *DAB*, supplement III, 1941–45, s.v. "Speyer, James Joseph," by Herman E. Krooss.

38. On efforts to gain a donation from Rockefeller, see Speyer to Appleget, 13 February 1926, and advisory committee [to John D. Rockefeller Jr.] report, 2 March 1926, folder 169, box 17, RG2 OMR, RAC. On the rate of new subscriptions, see MCNY Trustees Records, 23 January 1926.

39. Peter Kihss, "These Other Showmen," *New York World-Telegram,* 10 January 1941.

40. In 1930, Scholle hired Grace Mayer as the prints and photographs curator for the museum, a position she held for decades. She sponsored some of the most innovative exhibits and attracted some of the museum's most valuable collections: the Byron collection of photographs, the Jacob Riis collection, and Berenice Abbott's photographic documentation of New York in the 1930s (which became the basis for her classic work, *Changing New York*, sponsored by the Federal Art Project of the Works Progress Administration).

41. *New York Herald*, 7 November 1926.

42. MCNY Trustees Records, 20 December 1926.

43. The site was between Thompson and West Broadway (now La Guardia Place). See MCNY Trustees Records, 25 November 1927 for an extensive discussion about the site.

44. See Speyer to Appleget, 17 December 1927, in box 17, folder 169, RG2, OMR, Rockefeller Family Archives, RAC.

45. See "Agreement between the City of New York and Museum of the City of New York Inc.," MCNY Trustees Records, December 1927.

46. I cannot agree with Rick Beard that the choice of the Fifth Avenue location was even partly made out of a "positive recognition that a location midway between downtown and uptown [and near Puerto Rican, Greek, and Italian immigrant communities] provided an affirmative nod toward, and acceptance of, New York City's changing face." The board was completely dedicated to the Washington Square site, and only switched because of financial considerations. See Rick Beard, "Life Behind Bars: A Response to Mike Wallace," *Culturefront* 1 (May 1992): p. 33.

47. Freedlander was educated at MIT and the École des Beaux Arts in Paris. He had entered numerous important competitions—including those for the Municipal Building in New York, the master plan for the University of California at Berkeley, and the Missouri State Capitol. His completed projects were largely done in and around New York—residences, the Harlem Hospital, Importers' and Traders' Bank, and proposals for improving Bryant Park and Riverside Park. He also won a much-heralded competition sponsored by the Fifth Avenue Association for the Signal Towers along the Avenue. See Francis S. Swales, "Draftsmanship and Architecture—6, As Exemplified by the Work of Joseph Freedlander," *Pencil Points* 11 (February 1930): pp. 79–90.

48. *Architectural Forum*, February 1932, p. 145; *Brooklyn Eagle*, 17 January 1932; and *New York Herald Tribune*, 14 December 1930.

49. *Architectural Forum*, February 1932, p. 145.

50. *Pencil Points*. For an excellent sketch of the design, see MCNY Archives, "Miscellaneous Clippings" box.

51. More than fifty years later, that expansion will finally take place—if $18 million can be raised to fund the building.

52. Especially jarring was the tragic 1911 fire that destroyed countless documents in the New York State Archives in Albany. See Michael Kammen, "The Rediscovery of New York's History, Phase One," *New York History* 60 (Oct. 1979): p. 379.

53. I. N. Phelps Stokes, a long-time member of the NYHS and trustee of the MCNY, was one of those who strongly urged the NYHS to safeguard its rich collections with a new, fireproof facility. At a ceremony in his honor, he declared there would be "no more fitting memorial" to his work than the new wing. The $1.5 million campaign had begun in 1922, but it was not until 1939 that Walker and Gillette's expansion to the original building by York and Sawyer was completed. See NYHS, *Reception tendered to Mr. Isaac . . . in recognition of his great work, The Iconography of Manhattan Island* (New York, 1926), p. 32; and Vail, *Knickerbocker Birthday,* p. 221.

54. Mary A. Porter, "The Museum of the City of New York," *Stone and Webster Journal* 49, no. 3 (March 1932): p. 177.

55. MCNY Trustees Records, 19 April 1926.

56. Speyer to Edith W. Tiemann (n.d.), in MCNY Archives, "Financial and Membership—1926" folder in "Financial and Membership, Old New York exhibit, etc." box.

57. John Shapley, "The New Museum of the City of New York," *Parnassus* (October 1929): p. 43.

58. Pamphlet on Sunday lecture series in MCNY Archives, "Miscellaneous Clippings, and Booklets, etc." box.

59. "The Wonderful City of the Past," unknown newspaper or date, circa 1931, in James Speyer Papers, NYPL, scrapbook 6, box 5.

60. Ibid.

61. John V. Van Pelt, "Study of Educational Work Proposed for the Museum of the City of New York," *Special Bulletin of the Museum of the City of New York* 1 (February 1932), p. 58.

62. Brown, *Valentine's Manual*, p. 188.

63. Shapley, "The New Museum of the City of New York," p. 43.

64. Speyer to Edith W. Tiemann, Speyer Papers, NYPL, box 1, "Correspondence 1930–32."

65. Mrs. Barclay Parsons to Speyer, 11 January 1932, in Speyer Papers, NYPL, box 1, "Correspondence 1930–32."

66. Some works that discuss the Progressive use of history include Robert Crunden, *Ministers of Reform: The Progressive's Achievement in American Civilization, 1889–1920* (New York: Basic Books, 1982); David Glassberg, *American Historical Pageantry: The Uses of Tradition in the Early Twentieth Century* (Chapel Hill: University of North Carolina Press, 1990); and Michael Kammen, *Mystic Chords of Memory: The Transformation of Tradition in American Culture* (New York: Vintage, 1991).

67. R. T. H. Halsey and Elizabeth Tower, *The Homes of Our Ancestors as Shown in the American Wing of the Metropolitan Museum of Art* (Garden City, N.Y.: Garden City Publishing Co., 1937), pp. xxi–xxii, quoted in Rhoads, "The Colonial Revival," p. 349.

68. Van Pelt, "Study for the MCNY," p. 8.

69. Ibid., p. 2.

70. Ibid., p. 54.

71. Ibid., pp. 46–52. Van Pelt was especially impressed by the branch museum sponsored by Fiske Kimball of the Philadelphia Museum of Art at Sixty-ninth Street in Philadelphia. The MCNY was able to gain some exposure through radio: one program on WNYC called "Voice of the City" took a "verbal visit" to the MCNY in 1937. Barron Collier Jr., "Voice of the City" radio program, WHN radio station, 19 December 1937, transcript in MCNY Archives, box "Miscellaneous Clippings, and Booklets, etc." box.

72. Van Pelt, "Study for the MCNY," p. 58.

73. "City Museum Nears Completion" (unknown newspaper or date), circa September 1930, in Speyer Papers, NYPL, scrapbook 6, box 5.

74. Brown, *Valentine's Manual*, p. 181.

75. "New York City Museum to Open Next Month," unknown newspaper, 13 December 1931 in Speyer Papers, NYPL, scrapbook 6, Box 5.

76. MCNY, *The Laying of the Corner Stone*, p. 4.

77. Members of the American History Faculty of Columbia University, *Report on the Survey of New York Museums* (New York, 1948), pp. 30–37.

78. *Report on the Survey of New York Museums*, p. 30.

79. "City Museum Nears Completion."

80. *Time*, 25 January 1932; Holland trip discussed in MCNY Trustees Records, March 11, 1930. Scholle requested that $1,000 be allotted to send staff members to Holland for research in relation to the model of New Amsterdam.

81. *New York Times Magazine,* 21 December 1930, p. 14.

82. In the effort to travel "authentically" to another place and time, the MCNY's use of dioramas

and models is similar to another institution, just across Central Park: the American Museum of Natural History. The AMNH, founded in 1869, was one of the pioneers in the use of dioramas and models. As at the MCNY, the dioramas at the AMNH were utilized to bring "exotic" places and peoples to life. For example, one guide to the AMNH boasted that "a visit to the African Hall will resemble as nearly as is possible in a museum a visit to Africa itself." Henry Fairfield Osborn, *The American Museum of Natural History: Its Origin, Its History, the Growth of Its Departments,* 2d ed. (New York: Irving Press, 1911), p. 137. Osborn offers an excellent overview of the museum's organization.

83. *New York Times Magazine,* 21 December 1930, p. 14.

84. "A City Restored," no date or newspaper, circa December 1931, in Speyer Papers, NYPL, scrapbook 6, box 5.

85. "The Wonderful City of the Past." The models inspired some to propose even more extensive efforts to preserve the aura of the past. Robert Littel urged the museum to preserve sounds of contemporary New York, asserting that when the museum opened, it would be a "historic feast for the eye. But not for the ear. Sights, yes, but no sounds." The MCNY needed a "sound gallery." Littel was also deeply nostalgic: Along with "those urban sounds, visitors to the museum should be made to hear a less urban record of the noises that New York can never have that some of its inhabitants never hear all their life long—sleighbells and sheep on a lonely pasture and the brushing of branches against the window and the noise made by small-town children running and rattling a stick against a picket fence." Robert Littel, "Blindfold," *New York World,* 19 December 1930.

86. See a 1931 flyer included in MCNY Trustees Records, 14 April 1931.

87. "City Museum Nears Completion." Governor Al Smith, speaking of the cornerstone laying, stated the "hope that the work will progress to the end that we ourselves may be able to learn something about New York which we have been unable to learn from books because of a lack of time." MCNY, *The Laying of the Corner Stone,* p. 4.

88. MCNY, *The Museum of the City of New York: Its Collections and Activities* (New York, 1935), p. 68.

89. "The Wonderful City of the Past."

90. Speyer to Robert LeRoy (secretary of the MCNY), 24 December 1931, Speyer Papers, NYPL, scrapbook 6, box 5.

91. MCNY Trustees Records, September 1930; in another major gift, the Altman Foundation donated $100,000 for a room on the history of Fifth Avenue.

92. William C. Garner, "A Fortune in Old New York Pictures," *Little Old New York* 4 (June 1929): p. 23.

93. See MCNY Trustees Records, February 1929, for the agreement with Davies and the discussion surrounding the donation. The board also offered to hire Davies' personal curator, J. H. Jordan, as an added incentive for Davies to make the donation.

94. *Who's Who in New York* (1929), s.v. "Davies, J. Clarence."

95. Garner, "A Fortune in Old New York Pictures," p. 23.

96. *New York Herald Tribune,* 2 March 1929.

97. MCNY Trustees Records, 15 June 1926.

98. Beginning in 1935, Rockeller discussed the possibility of donating several complete rooms from the home of John D. Rockefeller Sr. Finally, even as the building was being demolished to make way for Rockefeller Center, James Speyer and architect and trustee John Van Pelt visited the old home at 4 West Fifty-fourth Street and discussed how the period rooms could be brought to the MCNY. They are installed today in the top floor of the museum. See the extensive correspondence and newspaper clippings in box 145, folder 1453, "Homes, 4 West 54th Street, 1935–1953, Gift of Rooms to Museums of the City of New York," RG2, OMR, Rockefeller Family Archives, RAC.

99. For a discussion of the meaning and impact of J. P. Morgan's collecting see Neil Harris, "Collective Possession: J. Pierpont Morgan and the American Imagination," in Harris, *Cultural Excursions.*

100. MCNY, *Annual Report of the Trustees,* 1948.

101. MCNY, *Annual Reports*. See Mike Wallace, "Razor Ribbons," p. 222, for a discussion of the museum's later history.

102. Federal Writer's Project, *The WPA Guide to New York City: Federal Writers' Project Guide to 1930s New York* (1939; reprint, New York: Pantheon, 1982), p. 377.

103. MCNY, *Laying of the Corner Stone*, p. 5.

104. Jews alone (most of the first generation) made up close to a third of New York City's population by 1930.

105. Rick Beard makes a similar argument in "Life Behind Bars," p. 33.

106. Mike Wallace, "History Museums and the Prison of the Past," *Culturefront* 1 (May 1992): p. 26.

107. "New York's Memory," *NYT*, editorial, 9 January 1932. Ironically, the NYHS now frequently calls itself the "collective memory of New York."

108. MCNY Archives, "Miscellaneous Clippings" box.

109. William Faulkner, *Collected Stories of William Faulkner* (New York: Random House, 1950), p. 110.

110. Ibid., p. 114.

111. Dwight Franklin, the curator of models and dioramas, went to the top of the Empire State Building to be sure his models depicting the construction were true to life. In a wonderful irony, all the models and dioramas could be symbolically "purchased" with a sizeable donation. See *New York Times Magazine*, 21 December 1930, p. 14.

112. This theme was also the basis for the organization of the American Museum of Natural History. Its massive building on Central Park West (it would eventually encompass four full blocks) was arranged to provide visitors with two different "sequences": the geographic and the "evolutionary." In the latter, the "sequence of development" led from "primitive races" to the "more civilized." The visitor "follows the progress of eolithic, palaeolithic, and neolithic man . . . traces the evolution step by step into the higher organism of the earth and of the air." The arrangement moved from the fourth floor and its exhibits on the "Past History of the Earth" and the collections of Africa, Polynesia, China, Japan, and "Siberian Tribes" down to the first floor where American anthropology, especially that of North America, resided. The apex of civilization was symbolized by a memorial room dedicated to the trustees of the museum, members of the scientific staff, and "men distinguished in the history of American science." Osborn, *The American Museum of Natural History*, pp. 132–34.

CHAPTER SIX

1. E. Idell Zeisloft, *The New Metropolis: Memorable Events of Three Centuries, from the Island of Mana-Hat-Ta to Greater New York at the Close of the Nineteenth Century* (New York: D. Appleton, 1899), p. 218.

2. Luc Sante, *Low Life: Lures and Snares of Old New York* (New York: Vintage, 1991), p. 5.

3. "Even the Grand Canyon, a spectacular example of the erosive power of running water, cannot compete with New York's complex tale of past crises and upheavals, an account documented in stone and spanning more than one billion years of the earth's history." Christopher J. Schuberth, *The Geology of New York City and Environs* (Garden City, N.Y.: Natural History Press for the American Museum of Natural History, 1968), p. ix. For a recent book of New York City nature photographs, see Jean Gardner, *Urban Wilderness: Nature in New York City* (New York: Earth Environmental Group, 1988).

4. In describing the destruction of one element of the natural environment, I intend to evade the trap of two simplistic arguments about nature in the city. One attempts to impose a current political argument onto the past by nostalgically decrying industrial cities as "a bad mutation" of "an older way of building a city" (Sam Bass Warner, *To Dwell Is to Garden: A History of Boston's Community Gardens* [Boston: Northeastern University Press, 1987] p. xii). The second, on the opposite end of the spectrum, offers a dim illustration of the false truism that nature cannot flourish in cities. I accept neither of these arguments, for they are neither historically accurate nor intellectually illuminating. We cannot speak of a disregard for nature in the turn–of–the–century city when vast new parklands were being

set aside and citizens of all classes filled them with increasing fervor. And recent literature has argued against the sharp distinction between city and nature (which mimics the rhetoric of the turn of the century), showing how nature remains a powerful force in cities and is not inherently at odds with the dictates of urban life. William Cronon discusses the problems and possibilities of urban environmental history in "Modes of Prophecy and Production: Placing Nature in History," *Journal of American History* 76 (March 1990): p. 1131. Anne Spirn offers an extended argument against this view that "nature" and "city" are antonyms in *The Granite Garden: Urban Nature and Human Design* (New York: Basic Books, 1984), p. 174.

5. Elizabeth Blackmar and Roy Rosenzweig, *The Park and the People: A History of Central Park* (Ithaca: Cornell University Press, 1992).

6. The phrase "second nature" is discussed in William Cronon, *Nature's Metropolis: Chicago and the Great West* (New York: W. W. Norton, 1991), p. xvii.

7. Ernest H. Gruening, "New York: The City—Work of Man," *The Nation* (29 Nov. 1922): pp. 571, 574–75.

8. Elizabeth Barlow, *The Forests and Wetlands of New York City* (Boston: Little, Brown, 1971), p. 16.

9. Schuberth, *The Geology of New York City,* pp. 213–14.

10. Barlow, *The Forests and Wetlands of New York City,* pp. 10–11.

11. Described as such by Van Der Donck, a Dutch chronicler, in Barlow, *The Forests and Wetlands of New York City,* p. 33.

12. Today, coffee-table books celebrate the odd corners of the city from which the "frontier" New York can be experienced, or where one can momentarily see no evidence of the modern city. Remnants of the diverse colonial forest lie in obscure sections of Inwood Park and in a recreated "living art" exhibit in Greenwich Village, beneath the cement towers of New York University. See John Staller, *Frontier New York* (New York: Hudson Hills Press; distributed by Rizzoli, 1988).

13. Tree Planting Association of New York City (hereafter cited as TPA), *Annual Report,* 1897, p. 10.

14. Barlow, *The Forests and Wetlands of New York City,* p. xviii.

15. Henry James, *The American Scene* (1907; reprint, Bloomington: Indiana University Press, 1968), p. 111.

16. William Beebe, *Unseen Life of New York as a Naturalist Sees It* (New York: Duell, Sloane, and Pearce, 1953), p. 4.

17. Frederick Law Olmsted and J. B. Harrison, *Observations on the Treatment of Public Plantations, More Especially Relating to the Use of the Axe* (Boston: T. R. Marvin and Son, Printers, 1889), reprinted in *Forty Years of Landscape Architecture,* ed. Theodora Kimball and Frederick Law Olmsted Jr. (1928; reprint, Cambridge: MIT Press, 1973), p. 363.

18. Indeed, Olmsted had been the focus of attacks by defenders of trees in the park a decade earlier. He noted, in a letter to Gifford Pinchot in early 1895, that "the Park Board of New York passed an order forbidding me to have a single tree felled without a special order of the Board for that particular tree. There were at the time many thousands of poor, cheap rapid-growing trees scattered over the Park that had been planted to serve as nurses, and which were then, because of previous neglect when I was absent, over-growing, crowding and making wholly unfit for their purpose the trees which had been planted with a view to ultimate landscape effect." Kimball and Olmsted, *Forty Years of Landscape Architecture,* p. 166.

19. Olmsted and Harrison, *Observations on the Treatment of Public Plantations,* p. 375.

20. Thinning refers to the cutting down of trees within a group of trees to prevent depletion of nutrients and sunlight. Pruning concerns the cutting of branches on individual trees.

21. See *New York Times* (hereafter cited as *NYT*), 3 March, 14 March, and 30 May 1889.

22. Kimball, and Olmsted, *Forty Years of Landscape Architecture,* p. 166.

23. For example, see the letters of E. A. Hammond to the mayor in April 1887 and May 1889 (when

Hammond had become an alderman), New York City Municipal Archives (hereafter cited as NYCMA), Mayor's Papers, 87-HAS-23. Hammond began his correspondence about two months before; only his letters of April 1887 and May 1889 are extant.

24. Samuel Parsons to M. G. Borden (president of the Department of Public Parks), 31 March 1887 (in reference to earlier letter from E. A. Hammond), NYCMA, Mayor's Papers, 87-HAS-23.

25. More than a hundred years after the tree battle in Central Park, another New Yorker went a little crazy in defense of the city's trees. This time, however, it was the city's parks commissioner, Henry Stern, who led a campaign to identify and publicly humiliate those who had torn down trees without the consent of the Parks Department, the guardian of all the city's trees. Stern especially singled out a Brooklyn man, Peter Dworan, in March 1995 for his removal of several trees in Sunset Park, Brooklyn. Stern called Dworan "the Ted Bundy of arbor-cide": "He's a serial tree killer." For the lost trees, Stern offered a moving funeral service, complete with burial and eulogy. Stern's crusade, odd as it may have seemed, struck a chord with citizens around the city. Indeed, the lamentation for a fallen tree, or a mistaken removal of one, has continued to provoke a strikingly large response from park advocates and the general public. See *Newsday*, 29 March 1995, p. A25; and *NYT*, 26 March 1994, p. B23.

26. David Schuyler, *The New Urban Landscape: The Redefinition of City Form in Nineteenth-Century America* (Baltimore: Johns Hopkins University Press, 1986), p. 64, quoting Henry P. Tappan.

27. Rosenzweig and Blackmar, *The Park and the People*, p. 80.

28. The notion of sacralization is used in Viviana Zelizer, *Pricing the Priceless Child: The Changing Social Value of Children* (New York: Basic Books, 1985).

29. Rosenzweig and Blackmar, *The Park and the People*, pp. 162, 150, 82.

30. *NYT*, 21 February 1859, quoted in Rosenzweig and Blackmar, *The Park and the People*, p. 240.

31. Frederick Law Olmsted, "Report to the Commissioners" (1857), in Kimball and Olmsted, *Forty Years of Landscape Architecture*, p. 58.

32. It is remarkable how, from the start, many citizens rejected the ideology of the naturalistic park. "If every project proposed for Central Park in New York City had been built, the park would now consist of little but buildings surrounded by landscaped bits. Proposals for churches alone would have nearly obliterated the park by 1918, had their construction been permitted." Spirn, *The Granite Garden*, p. 174.

33. Ibid., p. 26; and Rosenzweig and Blackmar, *The Park and the People*, pp. 269–273, 288–297.

34. Olmsted and Harrison, *Observations on the Treatment of Public Plantations*, p. 369.

35. "The Spoils of the Park" (February 1882), reprinted in Kimball and Olmsted, *Forty Years of Landscape Architecture*, pp. 117–55. Quote is from Rosenzweig and Blackmar, *The Park and the People*, p. 288.

36. Samuel Parsons, "Central Park and Its Destroyers," *Harper's Weekly* 55 (27 May 1911): p. 17. Hugh Findlay made the same connection between overuse by rowdy crowds and the decline of the physical state of the park. "Our Central Park has been the butt of ridicule because many of the trees are dying. Some are dying of old age which is natural, some from drought because the water table has been lowered by subways, cellars, etc. Others are dying because of the continued packing of the soil about them. Thousands of people pass over the ground in a single day and the root system, being near the surface soil, is injured." Hugh Findlay, "The Practical Care of Trees," in Horticultural Society of New York, *Year Book* (1926–27), p. 38.

37. For "The Spirits of the Trees," De Long Rice, while recalling with sweet nostalgia the memorial value of trees, understood the necessary use of the axe. For his book he provided the clever subtitle "Trimmed by the Silent Scissors of God."

38. Frederick Franklin Moon and Harold Cahill Belyea, "Forestry for the Private Owner," *Bulletin of the New York State College of Forestry* 25, no. 7A (June 1925): pp. 20, 60. The exploration of the struggle for existence in the natural world was quite popular in this period. I would like to explore further the application of Social Darwinist ideas to city development. James Rodway's account of his study in Guiana is particularly eloquent:

Guiana, is above everything else, famous for its varied and rampant forms of vegetable life. It is a country of magnificent timber trees, elegant palms and wonderful creeping, climbing, and scrambling vines, enormous arums, and stately grasses. All of these seem conscious that they have to struggle for existence and that the fittest only will survive. Here we have no forest of one species—in which there appears to be something like combination, but every plant is an individual, and as such strives with all its might to get ahead of its neighbor, no matter how. Its whole aim and end is to obtain a share of the bright sunlight which is so plenteously bestowed, but nevertheless is so hard to get at. As long as the individual succeeds it does not care what becomes of the others; "everyone for himself and the sunlight for him who outstrips the others" appears to be their motto.

James Rodway, "The Struggle for Life in the Forest," Smithsonian Institution, *Annual Report*, 1893, p. 337.

39. The phrase "uptown utopia" is from David Moisseiff Scobey, "Empire City: Politics, Culture, and Urbanism in Gilded-Age New York," Ph.D. diss., Yale University, 1989.

40. Kimball and Olmsted, *Forty Years of Landscape Architecture*, p. 46.

41. TPA, "Report on the Condition of the Street Trees of the City of New York, with Suggestions for an Organized System of Scientific Culture and Conservation of Trees for the Greater City," *Bulletin of the College of Forestry at Syracuse* 15, no. 1c (December 1914): p. 27.

42. Laurie Davidson Cox, "A Street Tree System for New York City, Borough of Manhattan," *Bulletin of the College of Forestry at Syracuse University* 16, no. 8 (1916): p. 75.

43. TPA, *Annual Report,* 1914, p. 6.

44. TPA (1914), pp. 17–18.

45. Carl Bannwart, "The Movement for City Street Trees—A Survey," *National Municipal Review* 4 (1915): p. 239.

46. The life span of the average tree in Manhattan is difficult to estimate. R. E. Loeb has argued that in 1921, the average life span was twenty-five years. More recently, parks officials suggest that enormous numbers of new trees die within their first decade. Interview with Peter Eckert, New York City Parks Department, March 1994. See also R. E. Loeb, "Will a Tree Grow in Brooklyn? Developmental Trends of the New York City Street Tree Forest," *Journal of Forestry* 90, no. 2 (January 1992).

47. Gruening, "New York: The City—Work of Man," p. 574.

48. N. H. Egleston, *Arbor Day: Its History and Observance* (Washington, D.C.: U.S. Department of Agriculture, 1896), p. 80.

49. Ibid., p. 18.

50. Harlan Hoyt Horner, *Arbor Day Annual for Friday, May 7, 1909* (New York: State of New York Education Department, 1909).

51. TPA, *Annual Report*, 1897, p. 6.

52. Ibid., p. 7.

53. Carl Bannwart, "The Movement for City Street Trees," p. 242.

54. See for example TPA, *Informational Bulletin*, 1910.

55. Statistics complied by R. E. Loeb, "Will a Tree Grow in Brooklyn?" p. 20.

56. City of New York Department of Parks and Recreation, *Great Tree Walk Guide: The Great Trees of New York City* (1990), no pagination.

57. New York specified that elms had to be planted. William F. Fox, *Tree Planting on Streets and Highways* (Albany, J.B. Lyon, 1903), pp. 4–5.

58. See Albert D. Taylor, *Street Trees: Their Care and Preservation*, Cornell University Agricultural Experiment Station Bulletin 256 (1908).

59. Stephen Smith, "Vegetation a Remedy for the Summer Heat of Cities: A Plea for the Cultivation of Trees, Shrubs, Plants, Vines and Grasses in the Streets of New York for the Improvement of the

Public Health, for the Comfort of Summer Residents, and for Ornamentation," *Appleton's Popular Science Monthly* 54 (February 1899): p. 449.

60. "Street Trees: Planting and Policy," *New York City Department of Parks, 1902–1955,* New York City Parks Department.

61. TPA, *Annual Report,* 1912, p. 17. See also TPA, *Informational Bulletin,* 1910, p. 8. Chapter 453 of laws of the State of New York decrees that "no tree may be lawfully planted in any of the boroughs of the city without a previously obtained permit issued for the purpose by the Department of Parks."

62. J. H. Prost, "What Chicago Is Doing for Its Trees," *Garden Magazine* 12 (1910): pp. 18–20.

63. Like the bricks and windows and boilers of Mulberry Bend that were sold at auction when the tenements were razed, dead trees or those cut down to make way for train lines or even Riverside Park were sold. See the Parks Department Minutes, 16 Aug. 1882, p. 153.

64. Parsons, "Central Park and Its Destroyers," p. 17.

65. Kimball and Olmsted, *Forty Years of Landscape Architecture*, p. 166.

66. In New York several forestry schools—including Cornell, Syracuse, and the New York State College of Forestry—were founded at the beginning of the century. Although they were more concerned with rural forests and the perpetuation of trees as a marketable resource, these schools provided extensive studies of New York's street trees, which were used by the Tree Association and others to bolster their efforts to replant the streets. These schools spawned an increasingly sophisticated literature on "tree culture." For example, the Davey Tree Expert Company of Akron, Ohio, published several volumes that covered every aspect of tree planting, maintenance, and "surgery." Their guides, reprinted numerous times, brought the latest techniques of tree care to the general public. Though aimed at the general reader, these books heightened the expectations and implicitly and explicitly called for the use of experts in the care for trees. Olmsted and Parsons, as well as researchers at the forestry schools, all called for the use of professional "tree men" to plant, maintain, and repair street trees. The respect for professional park and tree experts was probably heightened in New York City, where landscape architecture had truly gotten its start, and which had served as the testing ground of the most important of America's landscape architects—not only Olmsted, but also Calvert Vaux, Egbert Viele, and Ignaz Pilat.

67. Carl Bannwart, "Greatest Enemy of the Shade Tree," p. 620.

68. Indeed, many of the values espoused were repeated by advocates from the early twentieth century forward; today's Central Park Conservancy or Parks Council would offer very similar justifications for "greening" the city. See, for example, Herbert Muschamp, "From Stereotypes of Urban Decay to Signs of Life," *NYT*, 3 April 1994, p. H32.

69. See Peter Schmitt, *Back to Nature: The Arcadian Myth in Urban America* (Baltimore: Johns Hopkins University Press, 1969), on efforts to bring poor children to the country.

70. Smith, "Vegetation a Remedy," p. 434.

71. TPA, *Annual Report,* 1914, p. 17.

72. Cox, "A Street Tree System for New York City," p. 75. As part of an obsession with counting the number of trees extant and newly planted, Cox urged the creation of a regular "tree census."

73. TPA, *Annual Report,* 1914, p. 5.

74. Ibid., p. 18.

75. *NYT,* 8 March 1903, p. 24. See also TPA, *Bulletin*, 1914, p. 6.

76. See *NYT ,* 1 March 1903, p. 8; 2 July 1903, p. 8; 12 November 1904, p. 8; and 2 May 1905, p. 10.

77. Cox, "A Street Tree System for New York City," map accompanying article. In the very first report of the Tree Planting Association, Cornelius Mitchell acknowledged that "A large portion of the City south of Twenty-third street is destined to be encroached upon by the resistless advance of business enterprise, and it is only in special instances such as Fifth avenue, which has already been referred to, and the more spacious avenues and streets on the east and west sides and upon the barren open spaces, enlarged intersections of streets . . . to which our recommendations would apply." TPA, *Annual Report*, 1897, p. 26.

78. TPA, *Annual Report*, 1897, p. 9.

79. The issue of "sham" architecture, as critiqued by Montgomery Schuyler, the preeminent architectural critic of the time, is discussed in Michael Millender, "Montgomery Schuyler and the Building of Beaux-Arts New York," unpublished manuscript, 1991.

80. Cox, "A Street Tree System for New York City," p. 24.

81. Carl Bannwart, "Greatest Enemy of the Shade Tree," p. 621. Bannwart looked and found in history proof for his beliefs. For example, he argued that Baron Haussman's work in Paris was successful largely because of the "stately avenues of trees which form the most conspicuous and charming feature of Paris' civic landscape."

82. Bannwart, "The Movement for Street Trees," p. 238.

83. Cox, "A Street Tree System for New York City," p. 17.

84. A debate on this issue raged for several days in the *New York Times* in April 1901.

85. Cox, "A Street Tree System," p. 20.

86. Bannwart, "Greatest Enemy of the Shade Tree," p. 619.

87. Elbert Peets, "Street Trees in the Built-up Districts of Large Cities," *Landscape Architecture* 6 (October 1915): p. 16.

88. R. E. Loeb, "Will a Tree Grow in Brooklyn?" p. 21.

89. Peets, "Street Trees in Large Cities," p. 30.

90. Ibid., pp. 29, 30.

91. Loeb, "Will a Tree Grow in Brooklyn?" p. 22.

92. Practical tree manuals often opened with an illustration of an ideal street. See, for example, Albert D. Taylor, *Street Trees: Their Care and Preservation*.

93. Oliver Allen, "A Tree Grows in America," *American Heritage* 35, no. 3 (1984).

94. Allen estimates that some "half a million renegade ailanthuses flourish, independent and unauthorized in crevices, deserted lots, air shafts, and backyard." Ibid., p. 46.

95. Peets, "Street Trees in Large Cities," p. 15.

96. For an extended study of the influence of trees and other elements of the natural landscape on Western thought and culture, see Simon Schama, *Landscape and Memory* (New York: Alfred A. Knopf, 1995).

97. In December 1908, the last of the thirteen trees that Alexander Hamilton allegedly planted to symbolize the thirteen original states were cut down. American Scenic and Historic Preservation Society, *Annual Report*, 1909, pp. 81–82. Currently, there are plans to move the Grange for a second time and replant the trees next to the house.

98. Katherine Stanley Nicholson, *Historic American Trees* (New York: Frye, 1922), p. 5.

99. Charles E. Randall and D. Priscilla Edgerton, *Famous Trees* (Washington, D.C.: U.S. Department of Agriculture, June 1938), p. 1.

100. American Scenic and Historic Preservation Society, *Annual Report*, 1913, pp. 192, 196, 197.

101. The NYHS apparently continued its tree preservation work. A cartoon in the *New York World* portrayed a stalwart Historical Society employee standing guard over "The Last Tree in Central Park" as tourists pass by. *New York World*, 22 May 1925, reproduced in R. W. G. Vail, *Knickerbocker Birthday: A Sequi-Centennial History of the New-York Historical Society, 1804–1954* (New York: New-York Historical Society, 1954), p. 223.

102. Robert Haven Schauffler, *Arbor Day* (New York: Dodd, Mead, 1909), p. 3.

103. For a discussion of trees as memorials, see the 6 September 1938 Parks Department press release, which notes that "there was a pronounced wave of tree dedications in memory of those who had lost their lives in the World War." "Trees" file, New York City Parks Department, Historian's Office.

104. John Flavel Mines, *A Tour Around New York and My Summer Acre* (New York: Harper and Brothers, 1893), pp. 16–17, quoted by Judith A. Gilbert in letter to the *NYT*, 7 May 1990, p. 14.

105. Mines, *A Tour Around New York*, p. 16.

106. Robert W. De Forest and Lawrence Veiller, eds. *The Tenement House Problem*, 2 vols. (New York: The Macmillan Company, 1903), 1:395.

107. Horner, *Arbor Day Annual,* p. 23. The height of this anthropomorphizing of trees was perhaps reached the same year, across in the river in Newark, where the trees of Newark "petitioned" the city to protect them from various enemies:

> We, the street trees of Newark, descendants of the great Forest, humbly petition the people of Newark. . . . We are Americans just as you are. Some of us, like some of you, are to the manor born, and some of us are from beyond the sea. But most of us have lived here a long time; and our forefathers welcomed yours when they came here years ago. Our forbears have done all they could for you since the founding of your city—yea, since the beginning of time.
>
> Now we have a sad story to tell. Bad people, and thoughtless people too, make it hard for many of us. They sin against us both by what they do and by what they leave undone. They allow horses to bite us, linemen to cut us, builders to maul us, vandals to hack us, and borers to tunnel us. They neglect to keep the soil about us loosened, so that our roots languish for needed air and water; and we are left to choke and strangle for these elements of life. They leave us exposed to the bites of horses for lack of a tree guard. . . .
>
> We humbly pray you, to whom these presents come, to put a stop to this and save us from the fate which threatens us.

Newark Shade Tree Commission, "The Trees of Newark Make Petition," broadside, 9 April 1909 (New York Public Library).

108. Gruening, "New York: The City—Work of Man," p. 574.

109. Barbara Novak, *Nature and Culture: American Landscape and Painting, 1825–1875* (New York: Oxford University Press, 1980, 1995), p. 160–61. Simon Schama explores the cultural meaning of trees, forests, and wood itself, focusing on European traditions, in *Landscape and Memory* (New York: Knopf, 1995), especially chaps. 1–4.

110. Quoted in Novak, *Nature and Culture,* p. 165.

111. Betty Smith, *A Tree Grows in Brooklyn* (New York: Harper and Brothers, 1943).

112. E. B. White, "New York Soil," *New Yorker,* 9 September 1950, reprinted in *E. B. White: Writings from The New Yorker, 1927–1976,* ed. Rebecca M. Dale (New York: HarperCollins, 1990), p. 202.

113. William R. Taylor, *In Pursuit of Gotham: Culture and Commerce in New York* (New York: Oxford University Press, 1992). The phrase "stories people told themselves about social change" is Timothy Breen's, borrowed from anthropology literature and discussed in *Imagining the Past: East Hampton Histories* (New York: Addison-Wesley, 1989).

CHAPTER SEVEN

1. I. N. Phelps Stokes, *Random Recollections of a Happy Life* (privately printed, 1932; revised 1941), pp. 170–71.

2. *Pro Urbis Amore* was the motto of the Society of Iconophiles, a small club to which Stokes belonged, dedicated to printing engravings and lithographs of primarily old buildings still standing in New York. See Richard Hoe Lawrence, Harris D. Colt, and I. N. Phelps Stokes, eds., *History of the Society of Iconophiles* (New York: Society of Iconophiles, 1930), p. 19.

3. R. W. G. Vail, "Isaac Newton Phelps Stokes, 1867–1944," *New-York Historical Society Quarterly Bulletin* 29 (January 1945): p. 42. For example, Grace Mayer, the influential prints and photographs curator of the Museum of the City of New York, educated herself about New York history when she began her position at the MCNY by reading the *Iconography* from cover to cover.

4. I am indebted to Deborah Gardner for her insights into I. N. Phelps Stokes, about whom she is completing a book-length study. See also Francis Morrone, "The Ghost of Monsieur Stokes, *City Journal* 7, no. 4 (autumn 1997).

5. Michael Kammen, *Mystic Chords of Memory: The Transformation of Tradition in American Culture* (New York: Vintage, 1991), p. 300.

6. See Deborah S. Gardner, "Practical Philanthropy: The Phelps-Stokes Fund and Housing," *Prospects: An Annual of American Cultural Studies* 15 (1990): pp. 361, 363.

7. Ibid., p. 370.

8. Ibid., pp. 370–71, 396–97.

9. Among other activities related to its history, the Stokeses recorded family events in a newsletter. See *Random Recollections*.

10. *Dictionary of American Biography*, supplement III, s.v. "Stokes, Isaac Newton Phelps," by Marvin E. Gettleman, pp. 743–44.

11. James Speyer, one of the founders and primary benefactors of the Museum of the City of New York, was also instrumental in establishing the University Settlement.

12. See Gardner, "Practical Philanthropy," note 25. For information about the work of the firm, see *Random Recollections*, pp. 119–35; and the Howell and Stokes Collection at the Avery Architectural Library, Columbia University.

13. Some of the firm's better-known buildings included the Royal Insurance Building (William Street and Maiden Lane); the Title Guarantee and Trust Building (176 Broadway); and the Commercial Cable Annex Building (New Street and Exchange Place). Stokes considered his proposal submitted for the Municipal Building competition in 1907 as having "had as far-reaching an influence on 'Sky-scraper' architecture as that of any building of the period." Stokes, *Random Recollections*, p. 216; for a general discussion of the firm, see pp. 119–135.

14. Stokes complained to his friend Robert De Forest that the law was "so complicated that few Architects are able to cope satisfactorily with its intricacies." Stokes to Robert De Forest, 6 November 1912, Stokes Papers, New-York Historical Society (hereafter NYHS), personal letters, box 3 (1912–13), arranged alphabetically.

15. Roy Lubove, "I. N. Phelps Stokes: Tenement Architect, Economist, Planner," *Journal of the Society of Architectural Historians* 23 (May 1964): p. 81. See also Stokes to Mayor Fiorello H. La Guardia, 28 December 1933, Stokes Papers, NYHS, letterbooks vol. 25, in which he wrote "I, of course, agree with you that slum clearance and rehousing should be undertaken on a large scale."

16. I discuss excess condemnation—the "excess" taking of private property for public purposes—in chapter 3.

17. Lubove, "I. N. Phelps Stokes," p. 86.

18. The park was named after Franklin Delano Roosevelt's mother, Sara Delano Roosevelt, in part because the Roosevelt family had owned land near there in the Dutch era of the city. She in fact urged the Board of Aldermen to name the park after former Parks Commissioner Charles Stover, but they denied her request. See Carol von Pressentin Wright, *Blue Guide: New York* (New York: W. W. Norton and Co., 1991), p. 181.

19. See I. N. Phelps Stokes, *The Iconography of Manhattan Island, 1498–1909*, 5 vols. (1915–28; reprint, New York: Arno Press, 1967), 5:2056.

20. See plate opposite p. 124 in *Random Recollections*. Stokes noted that the Madison Square Apartment Hotel running from Twenty-fifth to Twenty-sixth Streets was "covering the site of Grandfather Stokes's house." Interestingly, Stokes had more than a decade earlier discussed with his aunt Olivia the possibility of building a "tenement of the best type" in honor of his recently deceased aunt Carrie, on the "same block where Great Grandfather Phelps lived and brought up his children." See Stokes to Aunt Olivia, 6 January 1910, Stokes Papers, NYHS, letterbooks (1910–12).

21. Stokes, *Random Recollections*, p. 134.

22. Stokes's quiet, technical expertise in urban planning prevented him from becoming a major figure in the history of social reform or even low-income housing in New York or the nation. His importance lay in his work behind the scenes. Rather than speaking publicly on housing, he drafted the 1901

Tenement House Law, promoted numerous low-income housing competitions, and sponsored (through the Phelps-Stokes Fund) James Ford's seminal work, *Slums and Housing* (1937).

23. Numerous competitions for designing "model" tenements were held in the nineteenth century, beginning with the notorious 1875 competition that led to the "dumbbell" form—a plague to reformers in the Progressive Era.

24. Lubove, "I. N. Phelps Stokes," p. 84.

25. Stokes, *Random Recollections*, pp. 149–50.

26. See "One Solution of the Court House Problem Showing a Civic Center North of City Hall Park," carbon copy of letter to various newspapers, 17 March 1910, Stokes Papers, NYHS, letterbooks (1910–12). Stokes also wrote a lengthy, unpublished article on the history of City Hall. See "An Enlarged City Hall or a New One?" typescript in Stokes Papers, New York Public Library (hereafter NYPL), box 35.

27. Stokes, *Random Recollections*, p. 216. This approach was not unlike that taken by James Gamble Rodgers, whose designs for the Yale University campus included the Harkness Tower, built entirely of masonry without steel support. Stokes's preservation and beautification efforts took more concrete and public form in his work on the city's Art Commission. As a member from 1911 to 1938 and chairman after 1929, he oversaw all significant municipal and private designs. Although the commission had only an advisory role, it was influential with the city's building agencies.

28. See *Random Recollections*, p. 150; and the February 1924 issue of *The Architect* magazine, in which Stokes discussed the house and its history. In reassembling and adding onto the house, Stokes went to extraordinary lengths to use authentic construction techniques. He "followed as closely as possible the spirit of the best English practice of the 16th Century" by using oakpins to hold timber together and bronze bolts for the roof rafters and purlins. See Stokes to A. Holland Forbes (editor of *The Architect*), 4 January 1924, Stokes Papers, NYHS, letterbooks, vol. 19, p. 151.

29. Vail, "Isaac Newton Phelps Stokes, 1867–1944," p. 42.

30. Stokes's primary assistant on the project was Victor Hugo Paltsits. Stokes had worked closely with Paltsits in salvaging what remained of the state archives after the disastrous fire of 1911. Losing his position as state historian to political infighting, Paltsits was hired to head the staff for the *Iconography*. Later Stokes, as a trustee of the New York Public Library, promoted Paltsits's appointment as chief of the American History Division of the library. See Stokes, *Random Recollections*, p. 141; and Michael Kammen, "The Rediscovery of New York's History, Phase One," *New York History* 60 (October 1979): pp. 395–401.

31. Stokes, *Iconography* 1:x.

32. NYHS, *Reception Tendered to Mr. Isaac Newton Phelps Stokes in Recognition of his Great Work, The Iconography of Manhattan Island* (New York, 1926), p. 30.

33. Some of the most important works included Albert Ulmann, *A Landmark History of New York* (1901); Thomas A. Janvier, *The Dutch Founding of New York* (1903); Charles Hemstreet, *Literary New York: Its Landmarks and Associations* (1903); and John W. Leonard, *History of the City of New York, 1609–1909* (1910). For a more comprehensive list, see Kammen, "The Rediscovery of New York's History."

34. Thomas Adams, *The Building of the City*, vol. 2 of *Regional Plan of New York and Its Environs* (New York: Regional Plan Association, 1931), reprinted by Arno Press (1974).

35. *The WPA Guide to New York City* (1939; reprint, New York: New Press, 1992).

36. WPA Federal Writers' Project—NYC Unit; Housing Handbook, microfilm 21112, roll 113, series 30, reel 113.

37. Stokes, *Iconography*, 4:ix.

38. I. N. Phelps Stokes and Daniel C. Haskell. *American Historical Prints, Early Views of American Cities, Etc. from the Phelps Stokes and Other Collections* (New York: New York Public Library, 1933), p. x.

39. Stokes to Robert W. De Forest (president of the Metropolitan Museum of Art), 12 November 1909, Stokes Papers, NYHS, letterbooks (1909–10).

40. Stokes, *Iconography*, 1:xxv. Stokes aided the museum in the preparation of its first exhibit in 1926.

41. The society produced no more than one hundred copies of each print, sixty of which were purchased by its members. Stokes himself was roundly criticized by one reviewer because the "paltry few hundred copies . . . will never be generally known to his countrymen, and what should have been the common property of all New Yorkers is doomed to be the choice possession of only the few." See "History Making in Its Practical Side: Work of Sparks, Bancroft, Stokes," in *Valentine's Manual of Old New York*, ed. Henry Collins Brown (1917–18), p. 367.

42. Stokes and Haskell, *American Historical Prints,* pp. ix–x.

43. Ibid., p. x.

44. Stokes, *Iconography*, 1:xxiv.

45. Ibid.

46. In an attempt to accurately and completely recapture the past, Stokes sought out only "original" views for the *Iconography*. A leitmotiv in his letters to collectors and museums and other institutions in search of old views of the city was the pursuit of "original sources" and "original investigations." Stokes, *Iconography*, 1:xiv. Walter Benjamin emphasizes the importance of the "original" in a time when "authenticity" was called into question by new technologies of reproduction: "The presence of the original is the prerequisite to the concept of authenticity." "The Work of Art in the Age of Mechanical Reproduction," *Illuminations* (New York: Schocken, 1969), p. 220. For a discussion of the American obsession with "imitation and authenticity" in this era, see Miles Orvell, *The Real Thing: Imitation and Authenticity in American Culture* (Philadelphia: Temple University Press, 1986).

47. Stokes, *Random Recollections*, p. 140; also discussed in Stokes, *Iconography*, 1:xii.

48. Stokes and Haskell, *American Historical Prints*, p. ix.

49. Stokes, *Iconography*, 1:vii–x, xxi.

50. Ibid., 1:5.

51. In characteristic fashion, Stokes began his research by consulting the New York Public Library's catalog under the heading "New York City." He found ten thousand titles. Stokes, *Iconography*, 1:xiii.

52. Stokes, *Iconography*, 5:805.

53. Stokes balked at the notion that his work on the *Iconography* made him an expert on New York history. When asked to lecture about his work at the John Carter Brown Library in Providence in 1913, for example, Stokes panicked: "I must confess I do not quite see how I could contribute my share toward making such an occasion really interesting," he wrote to George Parker Winship. "I could, of course, spend an hour in handing around photographs of important New York views and in pointing out a few points of historical or of collector's interest in connection with each . . . but I do not believe that what I should have to say would be of particular interest, except to New Yorkers." See Stokes to George Parker Winship, John Carter Brown Library, 8 December 1913, Stokes Papers, NYHS, box 3 (1912–13).

54. Stokes, *Iconography*, 4:ix.

55. Ibid.

56. Ibid., 1:425. The print, incidentally, was owned by Amos Eno, the proprietor of the famous Delmonico's restaurant.

57. Ibid., 1:xxv.

58. Ibid.

59. Stokes and Haskell, *American Historical Prints,* p. xv.

60. Ironically, the *Iconography* was dependent on photography and new photographic processes, which would make the plates truly collectors' items rather than the grainy reprints that were so common. Much of the work of the Stokes "history manufactory" involved locating and photographing prints from the collections of institutions and private collectors around the country and world. Stokes was very concerned about using the latest processes, and worked very closely with the publisher to reproduce the prints.

61. Stokes, *Random Recollections*, pp. 22, 55.

62. Richard Hoe Lawrence, whose father was a founder of the Grolier Club, was himself an assistant to Jacob Riis, and the author of several images that were long believed to have been taken by Riis. See Bonnie Yochelson, "What Are the Photographs of Jacob Riis?" *Culturefront* 3 (September 1994): pp. 28–38.

63. See, for example, the work of Wanda Corn, Alan Trachtenberg, and William Sharpe.

64. Richard Hoe Lawrence, *History of the Society of Iconophiles* (from meeting of 5 February 1910), p. 12.

65. Society of Iconophiles Archives, Grolier Club, Box 4, "Correspondence." Andrews gave this speech on 13 January 1913.

66. Ibid., p. 14.

67. Ibid., p. 6 (from speech of 28 January 1901).

68. Ibid., p. 6 (from speech of 18 January 1901).

69. William Loring Andrews, *The Journey of the Iconophiles around New York in Search of the Historical and Picturesque* (New York: Gillis Press, 1897), p. 13.

70. Ibid.

71. Ibid.

72. See *New York Times Saturday Review*, 1 May 1909.

73. Lawrence, *History of the Society of Iconophiles,* p. 13 (from meeting of 27 January 1912).

74. Andrews, *Journey of the Iconophiles*, quoted in Lawrence, *History of the Society of Iconophiles,* p. 19.

75. Ibid., p. 18.

76. Andrews quoted in *New York Times Saturday Review,* 1 May 1909.

77. Stokes, *Random Recollections*, pp. 139–140; also told in Stokes, *Iconography*, 1:x–xii.

78. Stokes, *Random Recollections*, pp. 140–141.

79. Stokes, *Iconography*, 1:xi.

80. Stokes, *Random Recollections*, p. 162.

81. Ibid., p. 143.

82. See Stokes Papers, NYPL, box 1, "Correspondence, 1909–1911." The *Iconography*, it should be noted, was in no way the product of a Causabon, the character in George Eliot's *Middlemarch* who squirreled himself away to pursue a lonesome scholarly journey. The *Iconography* was the collaborative effort of not only a group of researchers, but also an international network of collectors, libraries, scholars, and museum officials. Stokes was a master at traveling through the social networks his family had established, in search of elusive prints or scholarly advice. Stokes relied heavily on the collections of the New-York Historical Society and the New York Public Library (where he had an office during his years of work on the *Iconography*). The NYPL was, in turn, the recipient of Stokes's collection, which now makes up the core of its virtually unrivaled collection of city views.

83. Stokes, *Iconography*, 1:xiv.

84. Ibid., 1:xix.

85. Ibid., 1:xxii.

86. William Leach, *Land of Desire: Merchants, Power, and the Rise of a New American Culture* (New York: Pantheon Books, 1993.

87. Stokes and Haskell, *American Historical Prints*, p. xx.

88. Stokes, *Iconography*, 1:xxii.

89. Ibid., 1:xxiii.

90. Stokes, *Random Recollections*, pp. 143–45.

91. Stokes and Haskell, *American Historical Prints*, p. xx.

92. From the early 1920s onward, Stokes regularly had his collection appraised. See, for example, Stokes to Robert Fridenberg, 20 October 1923, Stokes Papers, NYHS, letterbooks, vol. 19 (1923–24). For a discussion of why Stokes chose to donate his collection to the New York Public Library, see *Ran-*

dom Recollections, p. 162. The NYPL Stokes Papers include extensive correspondence concerning Stokes's efforts to sell his collection.

93. See John D. Crimmins to Stokes, 12 September 1908, Stokes Papers, NYPL, box 1, "Correspondence, 1909–1911."

94. See my discussion of Davies in chapter 6. For a discussion of some of the most important print collections in New York, see Stokes and Haskell, *American Historical Prints*, pp. xiv–xvii.

95. Michael Kammen has most fully synthesized recent work on the place of history and tradition in Progressive and 1920s culture. See Kammen, *Mystic Chords of Memory: The Transformation of Tradition in American Culture* (New York: Vintage, 1991), chaps. 9–11.

96. For an overview of that renewed interested, see Kammen, "The Rediscovery of New York's History."

97. John Elsner and Roger Cardinal, eds., *The Cultures of Collecting* (London: Reaktion Books, 1994), pp. 4–5. Elsner and Cardinal argue that the history of collecting should be removed from its ghettoization in the "history of taste" and be treated as an important tool for understanding important cultural dilemmas.

98. Isaiah Berlin, *The Hedgehog and the Fox* (1953; reprint, Chicago: Ivan Dee, 1993), p. 3.

99. The phrase is from Betsy Blackmar, "Re-walking the 'Walking City': Housing and Property Relations in New York City, 1780–1840," *Radical History Review* 21 (1980).

100. Stokes, *Random Recollections*, p. 143.

101. Ibid., p. 182.

102. For a brilliant discussion of the changing sense of time, see Stephen Kern, *The Culture of Time and Space, 1880–1918* (Cambridge: Harvard University Press, 1983), p. 58.

103. Walter Benjamin, "Unpacking My Library: A Talk About Book Collecting," in *The Art of the Personal Essay,* ed. Phillip Lopate (New York: Doubleday, 1991, essay orig. pub. 1955), p. 364.

104. Elsner and Cardinal, *The Cultures of Collecting,* p. 5. "In the myth of Noah as ur-collector resonate all the themes of collecting itself: desire and nostalgia, saving and loss, the urge to erect a permanent and complete system against the destructiveness of time."

105. Benjamin, "Unpacking My Library," p. 363.

CHAPTER EIGHT

1. Maurice Halbwachs, *On Collective Memory*, ed. Lewis A. Coser (Chicago: University of Chicago Press, 1992), p. 231.

2. An early volume published by the *Journal of American History* of new scholarship on memory included no essays dealing directly with memory and landscape. Some recent works that have developed this aspect of collective memory include David Lowenthal, *The Past Is a Foreign Country* (Cambridge: Cambridge University Press, 1985); Christine Boyer, *The City of Collective Memory: Its Historical Imagery and Architectural Entertainments* (Cambridge: MIT Press, 1994); and Simon Schama, *Landscape and Memory* (New York: Knopf, 1995). For a model of recent work on the history of historic preservation see Daniel Bluestone, "Preservation and Renewal in Post–World War II Chicago," *Journal of Architectural Education* 47 (May 1994): pp. 210–23; see also *Buildings, Landscapes and Memory: Theories of Historic Preservation in America* (New Haven: Yale University Press, forthcoming).

3. The term "lifeworlds" is from Ewa Morawska, *For Bread with Butter, Life-Worlds of East Central Europeans in Johnstown, Pennsylvania, 1890–1940* (Cambridge: Cambridge University Press, 1986). Some of the key theoretical works in the growing literature of place include Yi-Fu Tuan, *Space and Place: The Perspective of Experience* (Minneapolis: University of Minnesota Press, 1977); Edward Relph, *Place and Placelessness* (London: Pion, 1976); and E. V. Walter, *Placeways: A Theory of the Human Environment* (Chapel Hill: University of North Carolina Press, 1988). Reflecting a renewed concern for the visual homogenization of America's cities, there has been a recent spate of popular books on the subject as well. See Tony Hiss, *The Experience of Place* (New York: Vintage Books, 1990); Winifred Gallagher, *The Power of Place:*

How Our Surroundings Shape Our Thoughts, Emotions, and Actions (New York: HarperCollins, 1993); and James Howard Kunstler, *The Geography of Nowhere: The Rise and Decline of America's Man-Made Landscapes* (New York: Simon and Schuster, 1993).

4. Daniel T. Rodgers, "In Search of Progressivism," *Reviews in American History* (December 1982): p. 124.

5. My guide in charting how cultural values affect and are shaped by the "cash nexus" is Viviana Zelizer, *Pricing the Priceless Child* (New York: Basic Books, 1985). Elizabeth Blackmar has also made that an important theme of her work. See, for example, Betsy Blackmar, "Uptown Real Estate and the Creation of Times Square," in *Inventing Times Square: Commerce and Culture at the Crossroads of the World, 1880–1939,* ed. William R. Taylor (New York: Russell Sage Foundation, 1991), pp. 51–65.

6. See especially Robert Crunden, *Ministers of Reform: The Progressive's Achievement in American Civilization, 1889–1920* (New York: Basic Books, 1982), on the "innovative nostalgia" of the Progressives; as well as David Glassberg, *American Historical Pageantry: The Uses of Tradition in the Early Twentieth Century* (Chapel Hill: University of North Carolina Press, 1990).

7. William R. Taylor, "Launching a Comercial Culture: Newspaper, Magazine, and Popular Novel as Urban Baedekers," chap. 5 in William R. Taylor, *In Pursuit of Gotham: Culture and Commerce in New York* (New York: Oxford University Press, 1992).

8. Virginia Lee Burton, *The Little House* (Boston: Houghton Mifflin, 1942). All subsequent references are cited by page number in the text.

9. William Cronon has suggested that practitioners of environmental history, and historians more generally, tell not only their own new and ever more inventive stories about the past but also "stories about stories" of environmental change. William Cronon, "A Place for Stories: Nature, History, and Narrative," *Journal of American History* 78 (March 1992): p. 1375.

INDEX